ANTHROPOLOGICAL PAPERS OF
THE UNIVERSITY OF ARIZONA
NUMBER 29

COCOPA ETHNOGRAPHY

WILLIAM H. KELLY

THE UNIVERSITY OF ARIZONA PRESS
TUCSON, ARIZONA 1977

About the Author . . .

WILLIAM H. KELLY's chief interest throughout his teaching and administrative career has been in the history of North American Indians, particularly the tribes of the Southwest, and in the social and psychological problems encountered by Indians in adjusting to the American way of life. In pursuit of these interests Kelly has served with many organizations concerned with Indian affairs, and from 1961 to 1966 he was the U.S. State Department representative on the Board of Governors of the Interamerican Indian Institute. He received his B.A. in anthropology at the University of Arizona in 1936 and his Ph.D. at Harvard University in 1944. After teaching at Harvard, McGill University, and the University of Minnesota, he joined the faculty of the University of Arizona in 1952 to establish and direct the Bureau of Ethnic Research. He retired in 1973.

THE UNIVERSITY OF ARIZONA PRESS

Copyright © 1977
The Arizona Board of Regents
All Rights Reserved
Manufactured in the U.S.A.

L. C. No. 76-18469

Library of Congress Cataloging in Publication Data

Kelly, William Henderson, 1902-
    Cocopa ethnography.
    (Anthropological papers of the University of Arizona; no. 29)
    Bibliography: p.
    Includes index.
    1. Cocopa Indians. I. Title. II. Series: Arizona. University. Anthropological papers; no. 29.
E99.C842K44 301.45′19′709 76-18469

CONTENTS

FIGURES

TABLES

PREFACE

Information on the Cocopa was gathered during about ten months of fieldwork in five different visits from 1940 to 1952. The two most extended visits were made in the spring of 1940, when my wife and I spent three months in the field in Baja California, Mexico; and in the spring of 1947, when we spent five months in the Yuma Valley near Somerton, Arizona. Most of the information contained in this ethnography was secured in interviews with an interpreter and an informant. This technique is highly productive under certain circumstances and when accompanied by observational controls, but has definite shortcomings when used to secure the bulk of the data. In the present instance, our work was slowed materially by the narrow range and unreliability of Cocopa generalizations with respect to their own culture. An inability to generalize about what people do, rather than what they should do, is more or less true of any group, but the Cocopa possessed a minimum range of such awareness. This lack of consciousness of patterns of behavior undoubtedly correlates with their general lack of formal organization and their tendency in actual behavior toward directness and attention to surrounding circumstances. They had little feeling for form, and only in rare instances did they exhibit an interest in the execution of form as an end in itself. The inability of Cocopa informants to give us extensive generalizations increased our volume of concrete data, but simultaneously decreased the scope of our inquiry.

Another difficulty that was encountered in the interview technique is perhaps universal. When an informant and an interpreter are in a mood for talking on some particular subject, few questions are necessary, and invaluable material is volunteered in long, connected statements. Such times were not frequent in our experience with the Cocopa, so one-third to one-half of our interview material follows the train of thought of the investigator and not the informant. At its worst, this situation degenerates into "yes" and "no" answers that are hardly worth recording.

Wherever possible without unduly burdening the material, I have indicated the extent and reliability of the data upon which generalizations are based. I have attempted to follow the general rule of reporting the most concrete data and providing verbatim statements from our field notes where my knowledge is weakest or the information inadequate. Occasionally I have reported material that does not make complete sense, for it sometimes happens that information of this kind turns out to be invaluable to another investigator.

We used 9 principal informants, 7 of whom were men. Interviews of varying length were held with 22 others, 15 of whom were men. (All these informants, and other individuals to whom they referred in their statements, have been given fictitious names in this ethnography.) Following are rough estimates of the time spent in formal interviews with the 9 most important informants: Sam Spa, 16 weeks; Jim Short, 6 weeks; Mike Alvarez, 2 weeks; Alice Olds, 9 days; Sam Woods, 8 days; Jane Olds, 5 days; Tom Juarez, 5 days; Jay Bell, 5 days. Our principal interpreter, Frank Gomez, also acted as an informant in odd hours and occasionally for whole days, perhaps a total of a week.

Our most important informant was Sam Spa. At the time of his death in 1951, he was about 77 years old. His youth and early manhood were lived during the years when Cocopa culture had changed little from aboriginal days. He had information on a wide variety of subjects and was endowed with a lively curiosity and an alert mind. He was by far the most interested in talking about his life and experiences, and with due allowance for any man's memory, I place great faith in the reliability of his information. His sincerity and honesty were never questioned. He was born into the Kwakwarsh group of Cocopa and lived with them for the first 12 to 14 years of his life. As was the case with so many of that group, he was of mixed Diegueño-Paipai-Cocopa descent. In using so much information from him, this report is weighed in favor of Mountain Cocopa culture rather than in favor of River Cocopa culture, as would have been the case had my principal informant been from the Hwanyak group. The chief difference was in subsistence activities, and for this reason, we took extensive notes from Jim Short, a Hwanyak Cocopa, on this subject.

Frank Gomez, a Wi Ahwir Cocopa, was our interpreter in 90 percent of our interviews. He was born in 1895 and lived with the Wi Ahwir Cocopa until he was a young man, when he went to the Pacific Coast for about 20 years. After returning to the Colorado River Valley, he spent the remainder of his life working on ranches around Calexico, Yuma, and Somerton; he died in 1970. His knowledge of English was not good, so it was frequently necessary to question and rephrase his statements before they could be recorded. Besides introducing another screen between the informant and the interviewer, this difficulty materially slowed our work. However, we continued to use Gomez, in spite of the availability of interpreters with better English, because he did not edit the material given us and he was not conscious of, or concerned with, the possible effect of his statements on some future readers of a book. He was unusually accurate, and on numerous occasions took the trouble to make inquiries on his own account to correct statements he had previously made, either as informant or as interpreter. He was also a reliable workman and a pleasant companion.

ACKNOWLEDGMENTS

My first and greatest debt is to my former wife, Dorothea S. Kelly. She and I are the "we" throughout this report. She conducted a great many of the interviews, typed our field notes, kept records of material to be covered or checked in interviews, did a large share of our library research, maintained our several camps in the field, did all of the cooking, and made friends with informants and neighbors who found my let's-get-the-job-done attitude sometimes irritating and abrasive.

I am also indebted to the Cocopa people and to my informants and interpreters who helped us and made us welcome in the field. Cocopa culture contains polished prescriptions for the conduct of interpersonal relations, with the result that the typical Cocopa, once a stage of shyness and silence is passed, is friendly, generous, trusting, and cooperative.

I am aware that members of the Cocopa tribe will read this report. For this reason, I regret that the time period it covers begins only toward the end of the last century. Earlier in the 19th century, the Cocopa were a powerful and much more numerous people, with their institutions and cultural goals fully intact; it is a shame that the story of those days cannot be recovered. Present-day members of the tribe will detect many of my misinterpretations and omissions. This is not a complete report on the Cocopa; it is no more than a sample — and a weird sample, at that, as though someone had taken a book ten times this size and torn from it whole chapters and pages at random. This effect partly stems from the ethnographer's biases when, forced to a choice by limited time, he tends to follow his own interests and often the lines of least resistance. It also partly stems from limitations imposed by his field methods, and from sheer ignorance or the failure to follow leads that might have disclosed unknown areas of cultural activities.

The encouragement to do a study of the Cocopa came from Clyde Kluckhohn and Leslie Spier while I was a graduate student at Harvard University, and the results of early work among the Cocopa were used in my Ph.D. dissertation in 1944. The outstanding professional attainment of these men was well known, but what was not so generally known was their willingness to devote an unconscionable amount of time to their students. I was fortunate to have known and worked under them. Southwestern ethnographies prior to 1940 were written in the tradition of history; one of the primary interests was to recover an account of the pre-European cultures before the memory of an earlier way of life was lost. Since this was my interest, I chose to write a monograph in a style reminiscent of those written by Alfred Kroeber, E. W. Gifford, Grenville Goodwin, and Leslie Spier.

My fieldwork was sponsored, and given some financial support, by Peabody Museum, Harvard University. I am especially grateful to its late director, Donald Scott, for this and other assistance.

A very large number of the sentences and paragraphs in this volume have been smoothed, polished, and made understandable through the patient effort of editorial assistants attached to the Department of Anthropology, University of Arizona. I wish especially to thank Gail Hershberger, who insisted that no reader should be forced to guess at what an author is trying to say.

William H. Kelly

NOTE ON ORTHOGRAPHY

Phonetic characters used in writing native words in this volume are taken from the Simpler System found in "Phonetic Transcription of Indian Languages" (American Anthropological Association 1916), and revised partially in accordance with the recommendations made by Herzog and others (1934). This phonetic system is neither complete nor very accurate, but it does aid in recording native words.

Discrepancies noted in the spelling of Cocopa words are due to variations in recording that cannot now be reconciled or, frequently, to the operation of grammatical rules — for example, singular and plural nouns are spelled differently.

Accents and Pauses
Accent is on final vowel
’ short, forceful sound; appears at end of words accompanied by aspiration
· extra long pause

Vowels
a   as in *father*
ε   as in *met*
e   as in *fate*
ι   as in *pin*
i   as in *feet*
o   as in *note*
u   as in *boot*
ə   as in *but*

Semiconsonants[1]
y   as in *youth*
w   as in *water*

Stops[2]
k   as in *kid*
p   as in *poor*
t   as in *take*
ʔ   glottal stop

Nasals
m   as in *man*
n   as in *name*

Spirants
l   as in *let*
ł   surd fortis
s   as in *sum*[3]
š   as in *shoot*
h   as in *hat*
x   German *ch*

Trills
r   as in *red*
R   as Spanish *r* in *señor*

Affricatives
č   as in *charge*

If my Cocopa readers will look at the following list of English words, then think of the Cocopa words for the same things, they will quickly catch on to the manner in which I have arrived at the transcriptions given in the second column.

English Word	Cocopa Word
good or O.K.	*phwe*
good or real	*ahan*
mesquite tree	*anał*
man	*apa'*
flower	*arιn*
Indian	*čapai*
to cry	*čιkap*
twins	*hawðk*
river	*ha·wιł*
screwbean	*ιš*
crow	*ka·k*
south	*kðwak*
fish	*siʔιł*
bow guard	*šas waʔap*
clan or family	*šιmuł*
one	*šιt*
pine nut	*εhwi*
black-eyed beans	*hεm·ma'*

---

[1]Sometimes the characters for these semiconsonants are raised to indicate labialized or palatalized consonants; sometimes they are written as separate sounds. It seemed best to record the word as it was heard at the time, rather than to maintain complete consistency without known accuracy.

[2]There is no doubt that these *k, p,* and *t* stops are somewhat intermediate between voiced and voiceless.

[3]There are at least three sounds in this class that appear consistently in certain words. They do not, however, seem to be distinguishing.

1. HISTORY

The Cocopa Indians of today are the scattered descendants of a once powerful people who, from earliest known times, occupied the southernmost section of the rich delta country of the Colorado River in what is now Sonora and Baja California, Mexico. They exhibit elements both of the fully developed River Yuman culture area and of the somewhat simpler Western Yuman culture area of the mountain tribes. Their language is a Yuman dialect most closely related to the dialects of their former delta neighbors, the Kahwan and Halyikwamai, and of the Southern Diegueño of the Baja California mountains.

The material to be presented in the chapters following this historical survey is mostly from two time periods. The first is the period from about 1880 to 1900; the second is the period during which my fieldwork was conducted — 1940 to 1952. These and other time periods will be clearly indicated.

In the latter part of the 19th century, the Cocopa numbered about 1,500, scattered through the Mexican section of the delta. Their society was viable at that time and, compared with other Western tribes, was influenced but little by European contact. They had acquired some items of material culture and adopted European dress, but they had not substantially altered their subsistence activities or their political, social, and religious patterns.

The remarkable aspect of the culture of the Cocopa is that although they lived in a land well-suited to agriculture and knew and practiced the art of agriculture, they failed to become an agricultural tribe either in their dependence on farm crops, in their attitude toward this mode of subsistence, or in the development of religious and social patterns usually associated with agricultural peoples. Their culture was remarkably simple. They had no central political leadership but were organized into four politically independent bands. The band leaders had little authority, and there was no mechanism for enforcing their decisions. There was no intervening organization between the band and the family. The clan was without political or religious function, and there were no villages or associations. The family was of the conjugal type, composed of a man, his wife, and their children. In actual practice, however, the functional unit frequently included one or more other individuals — older dependents, siblings of the married pair, spouses and children of sons and daughters. Each family,

without exception, was responsible for its own subsistence and the maintenance of its own camp, so that there was no division of labor at the group level except for the part-time activities of specialists such as shamans, band or local leaders, funeral orators, and the like. Role placement was exclusively by age, sex, kinship, residence, and ability or magical power. Such criteria as wealth, class, profession, and association membership were absent.

ETHNOGRAPHIC POSITION

When written records are lacking, anthropologists turn to other sources of information in order to reconstruct the history of a group and its relationship with surrounding people through time. The following material on archaeology, linguistics, anthropometry, and ethnology is presented for this purpose.

Archaeology

The archaeology of the Colorado River Valley is little known because of the lack of archaeological sites with depth. Pottery and stone tools are scattered widely over the surface, but in no case has trash accumulated to a sufficient depth to permit stratigraphic analysis (Rogers 1945: 167-98). This lack of trash depth, however, is of some significance in itself. It would seem to indicate, although negatively, that former modes of habitation were of the same order as at present — with people living in scattered single dwellings of pole-and-brush construction, frequently abandoning them, and rebuilding at a new site. This practice is in sharp contrast to the custom of both the Anasazi and the Hohokam, who built house groups over the foundations of former ones.

Archaeological comparisons indicate, in fact, that the order of difference that in pre-European days set apart the advanced cultures of Arizona and New Mexico from the Colorado Yumans is one that goes back at least to the early agriculture and pottery horizons. There are some resemblances, of course, but none that would indicate any great influence of the more elaborate southwestern or Mexican cultures in the lives of Yuman-speaking peoples.

According to Rogers (1945: 181-2), locally manufactured pottery (and with it, no doubt, a knowledge of agriculture) first appeared in the Colorado River Valley about A.D. 800. The pottery identified with this horizon has been termed Yuman I because, although changes occur, there appears to be a generic relationship with historic Yuman wares. This pottery was a new type in the Southwest and cannot be traced to any single source, but, since various cultures to the east and southeast had previously developed highly sophisticated agricultural societies, the general source of the knowledge of agriculture and pottery presents no great problem.

Rogers (1945: 196) is inclined to the opinion that, although Yuman-speaking people may go back to Yuman I times, they first came into the lower Colorado Valley about A.D. 1000, at the beginning of the Yuman II period. This conclusion is tentative, but in view of Rogers' long and intimate acquaintance with the archaeology of this area, it cannot be brushed aside. Whether Yuman (Hokan)-speaking tribes occupied the valley of the Colorado before or after A.D. 1000, the important conclusion to be drawn is that the relative uniqueness of the culture of this area is of long standing, and that the present River Yuman culture is the end product of a cultural-geographical adjustment process that has been going on for at least a thousand years.

While the evidence points fairly clearly to the occupation of the Colorado River Valley by the linguistic, cultural, and racial ancestors of the modern Yuman tribes by about A.D. 1000, there is no surety that the Cocopa are descended from one of the river valley groups. The Cocopa cannot with certainty be placed in their delta habitat, or even on the Colorado River, before about A.D. 1450. For approximately 400 years before that date, the Colorado River emptied into Blake Sea, a now extinct fresh-water lake located to the northwest of the present delta. In all probability, the country south of the present city of Yuma was essentially uninhabitable at that time. Kniffen (1932: 188) summarizes the geological situation as follows:

[Five hundred to 1,000 years ago] the Colorado entered the gulf at a point near Yuma and extended its delta across the gulf toward Cerro Prieto. As the delta advanced westward and became higher (assisted perhaps by general uplift) the deflection of the Colorado to the northward caused the water enclosed by the extreme head of the gulf to become fresh, or at least brackish. Along the western margin of the delta the tide maintained an opening along the line marked by the Hardy, Volcano Lake, and New River depression. The embayment to the north was subject to tidal fluctuations and through the opening the excess waters passed to the gulf.

The lake thus formed, about 100 miles long and from 10 to 35 miles wide, covered approximately 2,000 square miles. Yuman camp sites and Yuman II pottery are found scattered around the shore line of the lake and have been assigned by Rogers (1942: personal communication) to the period A.D. 1000 to 1450. The modern Diegueño and Imperial Valley Kamia, he is certain, were formerly located on the western shores of Blake Sea. It is possible, too, that the Kahwan, Halyikwamai, and Cocopa, historically located in the delta and speaking very similar dialects, had their former homes on the shores of this ancient lake:

The beginning of the Yuman III period is marked by several population shifts, some of which must have been of considerable magnitude and rather abrupt in nature. Apparently, the extinction of the Blake Sea and the lakes in the Mohave Sink, as well as the passing of favorable living conditions in general throughout much of the California desert area, were all closely related in time. Of necessity the Colorado valley, from Black Canyon south to the delta, had to provide the major haven for these migrating desert groups and its ecology the additional strain of the sudden increase in population. It is even possible that the historic arrangement of the two well-marked speech groups, designated as River and Delta by Kroeber, took location as early as this, but not without a certain amount of subsequent shifting of boundaries and positional jockeying about of the members within a group. [Rogers 1945: 192-3]

Linguistics

There is nothing in the linguistic evidence that runs contrary to the theory of a long occupancy of this region by ancestors of the modern Yuman tribes. Yuman languages are clearly related to the larger Hokan linguistic family, which, as evidenced by its spread through California, Oregon, and Baja California, is probably one of the ancient languages of the Pacific Coast region (Dixon and Kroeber 1919: 47-118; Sapir 1929: 138-41). The closest Hokan relatives of the Yuman speakers are the Chumash of south central California. In Spanish days and for an unknown period prior to that time, the Chumash and Yuman-speaking tribes were separated from each other by a belt of Shoshonean speakers who occupied all of southern California, with the exception of the area in extreme southern California where the Yuman-speaking Diegueño lived. It is probable that the Shoshonean tribes moved into this area and thus separated a formerly solid and ancient block of Hokan speakers.

Anthropometry

In physical characteristics, the Colorado River Yumans are difficult to place in relation to surrounding tribes. They are distinguished from their neighbors and from Californian and Southwestern peoples, generally, by being tall, round-headed, broad-nosed, and long-faced. (Anthropometric information on this area is contained in ten Kate 1892: 119-44; Hrdlička 1935; Gifford 1926: 217-390; Gabel 1949; Seltzer 1936.)

Height is the distinguishing characteristic of the River Yumans but is perhaps attributable to local intensification of a condition that is only less pronounced among their immediate neighbors; slightly shorter people are found both to the east and to the west. The characteristic is notable only in contrast with the very short Zuni and the even shorter Yuki of northwestern California (20 Yuki men averaged 157 cm. [Gifford 1926: 225]).

The Yumans are also extremely brachycephalic, but the figures may simply reflect a greater degree of artificial deformation. All the surrounding peoples are notably brachycephalic, with this characteristic diminishing to the south in Mexico, where some groups are dolichocephalic (Gabel 1949: 90-1). The brachycephalic characteristic diminishes again to the northwest, where the Yuki and the Western Mono are relatively long-headed (Gifford 1926: 225). It appears that the Yuman peoples, like some northern California tribes, have a rather wide nose, but they differ in this respect from the Pueblo tribes on the northeast and the Papago on the east. In length of face, the River Yuman tribes are in an intermediate position (Yuma, 83.41; Maricopa, 83.22; Mohave, 80.15) between the relatively short-faced Apache and Navajo and the very long-faced Papago (Gabel 1949: 34-6).

Thus Gifford (1926) is probably justified in placing the tribes of the Colorado River in his broad "California Type," which he sets up on the basis of long faces and broad heads. Within this larger category, he has classified the Colorado tribes in a special subclass because of their high stature and wide noses. While their stature does set them apart, their extreme nasal breadth is perhaps more significant in tracing genetic affiliation. Other broad-nosed people are found in north central and northwestern California, while people with significantly narrower noses are found to the east and south. The break with the Papago is especially interesting (Gabel 1949: 40-1):

Tribe	Number of Individuals	Nasal Index
Papago	219	65.90
Zuni	346	67.74
Navaho	75	72.93
Yaqui	100	77.38
Hopi	278	79.58
Yuma	29	80.60
Mohave	85	81.10
Maricopa	40	81.60

No measurements were taken on the Cocopa. The attempt was made but was almost immediately abandoned when I discovered that even my informants would not submit to measurement without ill will. However, notes were taken on individuals without the use of instruments, and it was apparent that the descendants of those individuals who were known to have migrated into the valley from the Baja California mountains were markedly different in size and in face and head morphology from the more

common Mohave-Yuma physical type. This "Baja California" type is shorter in stature and more gracile in bone build. Their faces are long, but many have rather prominent cheekbones. Head form and nose form appeared quite variable. These evaluations are subjective, but they do indicate a physical difference between the recent Indian population of northern Baja California and that of the Colorado Valley.

Ethnology

The most ambitious attempt to reconstruct the history of southwestern and California groups upon the basis of ethnographic data was presented by Strong in 1927 (1-61). Strong's thesis is that the southwestern United States and southern California once formed a single culture area with the following set of uniform culture patterns: social and religious organization with moiety, perhaps lineage descent, elaboration of an institutionalized priesthood, the use of a fetish bundle, and a ceremonial chamber. Other associated traits included ground painting, secret societies and initiation, and impersonation of spirits. This areal uniformity, he says, was later broken by the intrusion of Shoshonean, Yuman, and Athapascan peoples.

The theoretical approach and historical conclusions of this study have been questioned by a number of authors, but Strong has shown quite clearly that there are important socioreligious differences between the southern California culture and the River Yuman. Whether or not the Pueblo, California, and Pima-Papago patterns are comparable involves another consideration. Strong (1927: 52) describes his theory of the "intrusion" of Yuman peoples:

> Since the Yuman peoples of the Colorado River show comparatively few similarities to the Pueblos, it seems probable that their incursion into their present range, as well as the southwestward movement of the Shoshoneans, presumably from the Great Basin, severed whatever connections formerly existed between the southern coast of California and the early Pueblo culture.

The theory is ingenious, but it does not explain the archaeological and linguistic evidence. I suggest that a modified version of Strong's conclusion would be the more nearly correct one. That is, there need not have been a solid-block contact between the southern California, Pueblo, and Pima-Papago cultures, but this contact might well have been through a restricted area. This theory indicates, simply, that only minor migrational shifts are required to fit the facts: the Shoshonean tribes, at least the Southern Paiute, Tübatulabal, Kawaiisu, and Koso, could have expanded southwestward from Nevada, and the Yuman tribes could have expanded northward from the lower valley of the Colorado River. This has some backing from archaeological evidence, since Rogers (1945: 184) places

Yuman I cultures only as far north as Parker, on the Colorado.

The California-Pueblo contact, if one is granted, could well have been through the vicinity of Parker and Needles, and a theory of major population shifts is unnecessary. I have treated the question more fully elsewhere (Kelly 1944), and additional information may be found in Parsons (1939: 987-98); Haeberlin (1916); Rogers (1929: 12-3); and Kroeber (1925; 1928: 380, 382).

PERIOD OF EXPLORATION

All of our written records, beginning with Alarcón in 1540, make it quite clear that the lower Colorado River Valley, from the Grand Canyon to the Gulf of California, was predominantly in the possession of Yuman-speaking tribes. The following groups seem to have been the most prominent: Mohave, Halchidhoma, Yuma, Kahwan, Halyikwamai, and Cocopa (Kroeber's [1943: 21-40] anglicized spelling of tribal names; see Table 1).

TABLE 1
Colorado River Tribes Seen by Early Explorers

Tribe	Alarcón 1540	Oñate 1605	Kino 1701	Garcés 1776
Mohave		Amacavas		Jamajab
Halchidhoma		Halchedoma	Alchedomas	Jalchedun
Yuma			Yuma	Yuma
Kahwan	Coana	Cohuana		Cajuenche
Halyikwamai	Quicama	Tlalliquamallas	Quiquimas	Jalliquamay
Cocopa		Cocapa		Cucapá

Tribes in the area, at least those in the delta, were loosely organized, and, although we have the long-standing identity of names, there is every reason to suppose that there were tribal splits, regroupings, and shifts of various kinds of which we have no record. To think of these tribes as "nations" with continuity, solid identity, and territorial identification throughout the period of our early records would probably be misleading. One known case warns of caution: the "Maricopa" of the 19th-century American explorers (referred to as Cocomaricopa and Opa in Spanish accounts) are now known, thanks to the work of Spier (1933: 1-41), to have been composed of the original Maricopa plus the Halchidhoma, Halyikwamai, Kahwan, and Kaveltcadom.

Fernando de Alarcón (1904: 279-318), the first European to visit the Colorado River country, gave an excellent account of native life in the delta country. He was on the river during August and September of 1540, sent by Mendoza, viceroy of New Spain, to explore the country and to make the attempt to carry supplies by water to Coronado's expedition. It is quite difficult to judge how far up the river he went: he says he traveled 85 leagues by boat. This distance would be something over 200 miles by early Spanish values, and even allowing for the winding river channel, it would have placed him somewhere in the vicinity of the modern town of Parker. It is probable, however, that he did not go far beyond Yuma, which is about the distance he could have traveled in the two and a half days he reported spending on his return trip. It is also significant that he mentions passing only one mountain-bordered channel, which was probably the narrow pass at Yuma.

Alarcón presents the picture of a rather heavily populated river valley occupied by a series of tribes of agricultural people. He gives no estimate of the total population of the delta; however, he mentions seeing a thousand armed men at one point and five or six thousand more at another, and he makes frequent mention of hundreds. He does not identify the first group he met but names the next two as the Quicama and Coana. He lists a third tribe, farther up the river, as the Cumana, but he did not reach their territory.

On the whole, his report of the river culture seems plausible to the modern ethnographer, and it would probably be safe to assume that, except for differences incident to a denser population and perhaps a more elaborate material culture, life on the river did not change materially between 1540 and 1850. Alarcón found the people scattered in summer houses through the delta:

> I asked . . . whether every people were living in one towne together; and he answered me, No: but that they had many houses standing scattered in the fieldes. . . . Then I asked him whether the people which dwelt on the rivers side, dwelt always there, or els sometime went to dwell in some other place; he answered mee, that in the summer season they aboade there, and sowed there; and after they had gathered in their croppe they went their way, and dwelt in other houses which they had at the foote of the mountaine farre from the river. . . . The houses were of wood compassed with earth without. [Alarcón 1904: 296-7]

War between the tribes was frequently mentioned. The war parties were under the command of a leader with considerable authority, but the question of political leadership is difficult to determine. Alarcón refers to lords and chiefs, and even kings, but was probably in no position to judge their authority. The following report of one encounter with a leading man no doubt requires some discounting:

> But to returne to my journey, I arrived at Quicama, where the Indians came forth with great joy and gladnes to receive me, advertizing me that their Lord waited for my comming; to whom when I was come I found that he had with him five or sixe thousand men without weapons, from whom he went aparte with some two

hundred onely, all which brought victuals with them, and so he came towards me, going before the rest with great authoritie, and before him and on each side of him were certaine which made the people stande aside, making him way to passe. [Alarcón 1904: 313]

Shamans were mentioned and are described as conducting their cures by "charmes and blowing which they make." There was a belief in an afterworld, and the dead were cremated. Berdaches, dressed in women's clothes, were observed in several camps, and Alarcón understood his informant to say that the unmarried men of the tribe had access to them. Clothing and body adornment seem to have been much more elaborate than in later times. Face and body painting was quite common. The men wore a deerskin headdress (like a helmet) decorated with feathers, shell and bone necklaces, and ear and nose pendants. Around their waist they wore a varicolored girdle (with breechclout?) with a round bunch of feathers hanging below the waist at the back. One man is described as wearing a skirt of fish skins in front and back, held together with buttons. Women wore "glued and painted" feather skirts. War equipment included bows and arrows, war banners, and maces. Household equipment consisted of bags, earthen pots, and grindstones; there was no mention of basketry. Specific crops mentioned were maize, another "corne like unto Mill," gourds, and cotton.

The following account of social practices could be reasonably accurate, allowing for the European bias:

I asked him whether their women were common or no; he tolde me no, and that hee which was married, was to have but one wife only. I desired to know what order they kept in marying; and he told me, that if any man had a daughter to marry, he went where the people kept, and said, I have a daughter to marry: is there any man here that wil have her? And if there were any that would have her, he answered that he would have her: and so the mariage was made. And that the father of him which would have her, brought some thing to give the yong woman; and from that houre forward the mariage was taken to be finished, and that they sang & danced; and that when night came, the parents tooke them, and left them together in a place where no body might see them. And I learned that brethren, and sisters, and kinsfolks married not together; and that maydes before they were married conversed not with men, nor talked not with them, but kept at home at their houses and in their possessions, and wrought; and that if by chance any one had company with men before she were maried, her husband forsooke her, and went away into other Countreyes; and that those women which fell into this fault, were accompted naughty packs. And that if after they were maried, any man were taken in adultery with another woman, they put him to death; and that no man might have more than one wife, but very secretly. They tolde mee that they burned those which dyed: and such as remayned widowes, stayed halfe a yeere, or a whole yeere before they married. [Alarcón 1904: 297]

Sixty-five years elapsed before another Spaniard, Oñate, visited the river valley. The account of his journey in 1605, from the Hopi villages to the delta of the Colorado River and back, was written by Zárate Salmerón (1916) in 1626. In the Mohave valley, Oñate found the Amacavas or Amacabos (Mohave); below the Mohave were the Bahacechas. No one has identified the Bahacechas with any known Yuman tribe, but since they spoke a language similar to that of the Mohave and to that spoken below the mouth of the Gila, it seems reasonable to believe that they were Yumas (Quechans), perennial allies of the Mohave, and grouped with the Mohave, Maricopa, Halchidhoma, and Kaveltcadom in speech (Kroeber 1943). (One wonders whether "Bahacecha" could stand for "Baja Quecha," simply the Spanish for "Lower Quecha.")

At the mouth of the Gila River, Oñate found a tribe of "difficult" language and different manners and appearance. He calls them Ozaras, or Osera. The presence of this group has proved a mystery to historians of the region. The tribes, in order south of the Ozaras at the Gila, are given by Oñate as follows: Halchedoma (Halchidhoma), Cohuana (Kahwan), Haglli (?), Tlalliquamallas (Halyikwamai), and Cocapa (see Fig. 1). It is of particular interest not only that he reports the Cocopa according to the native pronunciation (*koapa'*), but that he found them in their traditional

Fig. 1. Approximate location of delta tribes seen by Oñate in 1605.

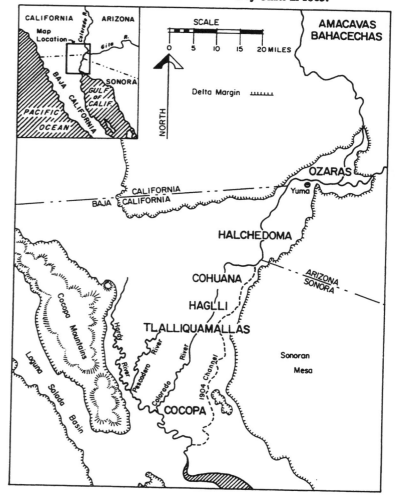

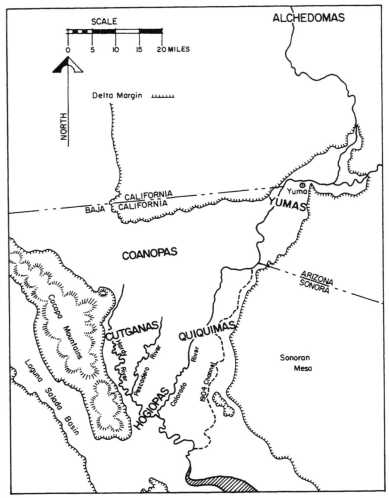

Fig. 2. Location of delta tribes in 1701, as reconstructed by Bolton (1919) from Kino's account.

Yuma and occupied a considerable territory, since Kino entered their first "pueblo" 18 leagues south and west of the mouth of the Gila, and, on a later trip the following spring, reported them as being the first tribe on the east side of the Colorado above the Gulf (Bolton 1919: 344-5). These observations would indicate that the Halyikwamai occupied the whole of the east bank of the river in what is now Mexican territory, plus some land on the west bank, since he crossed the Colorado to visit one of their pueblos. In regard to their agriculture, Kino reported in his diary on November 21, 1701 (Bolton 1919: 317):

> All the road was full of small but very continuous rancherias. . . . All this road was through . . . most fertile lands, of most beautiful corn fields very well cultivated with abundant crops of maize, beans, and pumpkins, and with very large drying-places for the drying of pumpkins, for this kind lasts them afterwards all the year.

Father Garcés, one of the most famous of the Spanish explorers of the 18th century, made three extended trips into the Colorado area, California, and northern Arizona between 1771 and 1776. His data on the tribes of the delta region are as complete as any given prior to the time of modern ethnographic investigations. He not only took a census of the Colorado tribes, but also provided some information on the location of the neighboring groups.

At the close of his diary for 1776 (Coues 1900: Vol. 2, 443), Garcés lists the following tribes of the region (see Fig. 3):

Papaga: 3,000, in their present position
Pima: 2,500, in their present position
Cocomaricopa (Spier's Kaveltcadom): 2,500, between the Maricopa and the Yuma on the Gila River
Cucapá: 3,000, near the mouth of the Colorado, mostly on the west side
Jalliquamay (Halyikwamai): 2,000, north of the Cocopa
Cajuenche (Kahwan): 3,000, north of the Halyikwamai
Yuma: 3,000, at the mouth of the Gila
Jalchedun (Halchidhoma): 2,500, north of the Yuma
Jamajab (Mohave): 3,000, in their present position

Garcés speaks of the Yuma as being the most powerful tribe on the Colorado River, but (and this comes as a surprise to most of us who speak of the "peaceful, gentle Pima") he rates the Pima near the confluence of the Gila and Salt rivers as being the most dominant and warlike of all (Coues 1900: Vol. 2, 446). It would appear that the Halyikwamai had already started on the road to final extinction, and that the Cocopa were lying low, as usual.

Although Garcés had wandered half lost through the southern part of the delta in 1771, his first real contact with the southern tribes came in 1775 when he left Anza and his group of immigrants who were on their way to the

location at the mouth of the river. Little was said concerning the life of the people that he visited, but it is clear that they were practicing agriculture and that the population was fairly densely settled along the banks of the river. He estimated the delta population at 20,000, which is, no doubt, too high.

It is unfortunate that the missionary Father Kino was unable to give us as complete a record when he visited the river 100 years later. Only two of these historic tribes were positively accounted for by him: the Alchedomas (Halchidhoma), noted by Kino as then being north of the Gila River, and the Quiquimas (Halyikwamai) (Bolton 1919: 252). The Yuma were mentioned by that name for the first time in Kino's account, and during his visit (1701) were in their established position near the mouth of the Gila (see Fig. 2). The Cocopa were not mentioned, although he listed two tribes in the delta that have never been identified: the Coanopa or Hoabonoma and the Hogiopa; one or both of these groups were probably the Cocopa. No mention was made of the Kahwan.

The most important tribe in the delta in Kino's time, according to his estimate, was the Halyikwamai. They seem to have lived on more favorable farming land than the

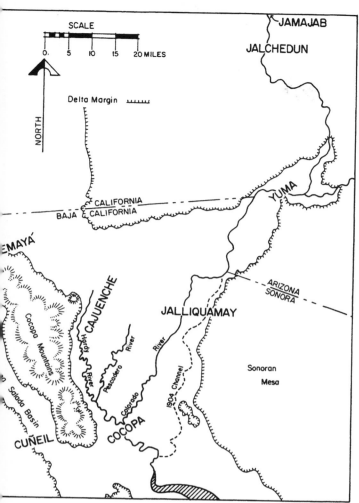

Fig. 3. Approximate location of delta tribes seen by Garcés in 1771-76.

[Map labels: SCALE, 0 5 10 15 20 MILES, NORTH, Delta Margin, JAMAJAB, JALCHEDUN, CALIFORNIA, BAJA CALIFORNIA, YUMA, ARIZONA SONORA, EMAYÁ, CAJUENCHE, JALLIQUAMAY, Sonoran Mesa, Cocopa Mountains, Hardy River, Pescadero River, Colorado River, 1904 Channel, COCOPA, Salada Basin, CUÑEIL]

visit, the Cocopa had occupied all of the southern third of the delta to a point above Colonia Lerdo, but that they had since been pushed west.

After five days of further traveling and visiting among the Kahwan and Halyikwamai, Garcés started south to visit the Cocopa camps in that direction. On December 16 (or 17?), his Kahwan guides took him across the Laguna de San Mateo and left him to go on alone, since the Cocopa were their enemies. Four leagues to the south, he found an abandoned rancheria where, he was told, the Yuma, Kahwan, and Halyikwamai had fought with the Cocopa. On December 18 and 19 he continued south, visiting in Cocopa camps but recording no information on their numbers or condition. He mentions, however, that some of the camps were occupied by "people of the lowlands and ... mountaineers (*de la tierra y Serranos*)" (Coues 1900: Vol. 1, 186-7). Garcés reached the limit of fresh water on the 19th, and then returned to the last Cocopa camp, where he remained several days. His diary says:

Dec. 22. . . . During my stay in this place arrived many mountain Indians to eat of the fruits which those of these rancherias gather, and they asked me if I was going to visit the padres of California Baxa, or those of San Diego. . . .

Dec. 23. We departed for the east, and passing by a laguna, having gone half a league there was a rancheria of about 200 souls, and another which would appear to be of mountain Indians. I made them some presents, and having gone about 4 leagues northwest [this almost certainly should read northeast] and north approached the river opposite (*enfrente de*) some high hills which were on the other side of the river, to which in the diary of the year of 1771 I gave the name of Buenavista. . . . [Coues 1900: Vol. 1, 196-8]

The "high hills" on the other side of the river are probably Mesa Andrade. It was in the vicinity of this mesa that the Hwanyak Cocopa were concentrated during the last part of the 19th century, and, strangely enough, a River Paipai settlement of at least three generations' standing was located by my informants in the very neighborhood where Garcés placed the "Serranos" (see Fig. 6, page 12).

The first English-speaking explorer to give an account of the native tribes of the delta was Lieutenant Hardy (1829: 312-84), who made a trip by boat up the Gulf of California and into the lower channel of the Colorado in the late summer of 1826. Hardy refers to the natives as the "Axua" because one of the Indians who spoke Spanish and acted as interpreter said he was a chief of the Axua Indian nation. It is to be assumed that he was a River Paipai (since Hardy took this for granted), and it is tempting to suggest that he gave Hardy the name of his clan, which could have been the *xwa·t* clan of the River Paipai.

founding of San Francisco. Garcés traveled south from Santa Olaya (difficult to locate with certainty, but probably 40 or 50 miles west southwest of Yuma), with the intention of surveying sites for future mission stations.

On December 11, 1775, Garcés was camped in a Kahwan settlement south of Santa Olaya, and there he interviewed his first Cocopa. This man told him that his tribe occupied "a wide area from the Laguna de San Matheo to the sierra and the desemboguement of the Rio Colorado" (this is no doubt the country between the Hardy River and the southern half of the Cocopa Mountains). The Cocopa, he was told, were hostile to the Jalliquamay or Quiquima (Halyikwamai), to the Quemayá (probably Southern Diegueño) who lived in the Sierra (see Fig. 3), and to the Cajuenche (Kahwan) (Coues 1900: Vol. 1, 177).

A few days later Garcés visited a Halyikwamai camp to the east. There were 200 Indians in the rancheria where he spent the night, and he reported them as being both friendly and generous, with plenty of provisions. From there he wanted to continue east to visit the Cocopa, but he learned that "the enemy" had driven all these people to the west side of the river. This, plus other information that he gives, would indicate that in 1771, at the time of his former

Hardy made no effort to explore the country and reported only what he saw from his boat, which was grounded on a sandbar for several days, and on a three- or four-mile trip up the Hardy River. His report indicated a close intercommunication between the river Indians and the Baja California Indians, and the usual and continuous fighting among the river tribes. In one of the camps that he visited, he found some old men and women eating "mesquite pods," and in the camp he saw a fishnet made of grass (?) and burnt earthen jars. The jars were two feet in diameter, very thin, light, and well-formed. The Indians, he said, lived upon fish, fruits, vegetables, and the seeds of grass, "and many of them are dreadfully scorbutic." It is to be remembered that he was on the river in late summer, before the crops had matured. That the population near the mouth of the river was fairly dense is indicated by the fact that one day 5,000 to 6,000 Indians assembled along the banks near his boat.

Much better information on the location of tribes during this period is given by Pattie (1905: 131-7, 181-220), who was with a party of beaver trappers on the Colorado River above its confluence with the Gila during February and March of 1827, and on a subsequent trip below the confluence during the last part of 1827 and the first two months of 1828.

On his second journey, Pattie encountered "Umeas" on the west bank of the Colorado at the mouth of the Gila. At a camp 16 miles below the Gila, the Indians stole all the horses belonging to the party. After this disaster, the trappers built some canoes and continued their journey down the Colorado. Eleven days later (they were trapping the river as they went), at a point estimated by Pattie (1905: 194-5) to be 60 or 70 miles below the camp where the horses had been stolen, Pattie reported:

We saw ten Indians on a sand bar, who fled into the woods at the sight of us. We knew them to be different people from those who had stolen our horses, both by their size and their different manner of wearing their hair. The heads of these were shaved close, except a tuft, which they wore on the top of their head, and which they raised erect, as straight as an arrow. The Umeas are of gigantic stature from six to seven feet high. These only average five feet and a half. They go perfectly naked, and have dark complexions, which I imagine is caused by the burning heat of the sun.

The party entered an Indian village three days later, and, taking the inhabitants by surprise, were able to make friends. These were later identified as Cocopa, and it would appear that the territory between the Yuma and the Cocopa, previously occupied by the Kahwan and Halyik-wamai, was then empty of inhabitants. (The Kahwan and Halyikwamai moved up the river, north of the Yuma villages, sometime after 1776 and then joined the Maricopa on the Gila early in the 19th century [Spier 1933: 16-7]).

Pattie and his party remained with the Cocopa in this and another village for three or four days, and they were royally entertained by the "chief" after it was learned that they had with them two scalps of Yuma Indians that they had taken a few days after the horses had been stolen.

Three days later, Pattie says, "we once more received a shower of arrows from about fifty Indians of a tribe called Pipi, of whom we were cautioned to beware by the friendly Indians we had last left" (1905: 200). The editor, in a note, suggests that these Indians were from a settlement of "Pimi" then living on the Colorado. There is little doubt, however, that these are the "Serranos" reported by Garcés in 1776 and the same River Paipai who my informants told me were permanently located on the river with their own settlement, chief, and farm lands.

In the winter of 1850-51, Lieutenant George H. Derby was sent by the United States War Department to explore the Gulf of California and the lower reaches of the Colorado River, to discover whether or not river boats could be used in taking supplies to the newly established military camp at Fort Yuma. This was the first European settlement on the river since the destruction of the Spanish missions near Yuma in 1781.

Derby sailed from San Francisco to the head of the Gulf, and he camped near the mouth of the Colorado in January, 1851, in order to assemble his boat. He gives the following information about the natives:

On [our] arriving at the beach they [a group of Indians] laid aside their bows and arrows and made signs to us to approach, and addressed us in Spanish. We took six of them, including their chief, on board. They were very much like all other Indians, with coarse black hair, like a horse's mane, cropped straight across their eyes, and with no clothing except the inevitable dirty rag worn apron fashion about their loins: they were, however, a little nastier than any Indians I had ever before seen, being beplastered from head to foot with mud, with which some of them had filled their hair.... I ascertained from the chief that they were acquainted with Major Heintzleman [commander of the post at Fort Yuma] and would carry a letter....
They call themselves the Co-co-pas, and live in a little village of from twenty to fifty inhabitants, dispersed about near the bank of the river; the men are very tall and strongly made as a general thing, and the women are modest, well behaved, and rather good-looking; their huts are precisely like those of the California Indians, made of sticks in a spherical or oven shape, and covered with dirt. They live on fish, small game, and bread made of grass seeds, and raise pumpkins, watermelons, etc. on little patches of ground which they cultivate; we found them very friendly, quiet, and inoffensive; they brought fish to sell to us nearly every day, and though continually on board the vessel, we never missed even the most trifling article. Their arrows are made of reed with a pointed end of hardwood, and their bows are of willow, so that if they were disposed to be as hostile as had been falsely represented to us, they would be incapable of doing

much damage. . . . The villages higher up the river own many horses, and the chiefs always rode when coming to visit us. I suppose the whole tribe may number 1000, including men, women, and children. The men frequently wear beads, rings, etc. in their noses, and paint their faces black and red with charcoal and ochre. [Derby 1852: 16-7]

(At the time of Derby's expedition the river was running along the east side of the delta, so it is reasonable to suppose that his population figures refer to the eastern Cocopa — the Hwanyak and Mat Skrui. There would have been no opportunity for him to estimate the total population in the delta.)

In June of that year, Fort Yuma was abandoned because of trouble with the Yuma Indians, but it was reoccupied with a stronger force in February, 1852, under the command of Major Heintzelman. Heintzelman (1856-57) made a number of trips into the delta country and was well acquainted with the Cocopa and Yuma. In his account of the Yuma, he says that crops were planted in July or when the flood subsided, except for wheat, which was planted in December or January. Summer crops were watermelons, muskmelons, pumpkins, corn, and beans. A spot that was subject to overflow was cleared, and then after the water receded, an inch or two of soil that might cake was removed, and holes were dug with a stick. Heintzelman added: "They also grow grass seed for food [but] the great dependence of the Indian for food is upon the mesquite and his fields."

Heintzelman reported that in the summer of 1851 there was no overflow of the river at Yuma and only a partial one below, and that as a consequence the natives were short of food. The lower river (just below Yuma), he stated, was more subject to flooding and more valuable for planting. Heintzelman (1856-57: 36) referred to the Yuma Indians as "Cu-cha-no," giving them the name by which they refer to themselves. They lived, he said, in an area extending from about 60 miles above the Gila to about 40 or 50 miles below it. Along the sloughs and in the desert to the west were the "Yum" (Kamia) Indians, and below the Yuma on the Colorado were the "Co-co-pa," who extended to the mouth of the river on both sides, but principally on the right, and into the mountains of Baja California (Heintzelman 1856-57: 42). This last reference to a mountain habitat is difficult to interpret. Since the mountains immediately to the west of the river valley are uninhabitable except for short periods, he no doubt had reference to Cocopa camps above high water along the base of the Cocopa Mountains and into Laguna Salada Basin.

Heintzelman reported that the Cocopa informed him that they formerly could muster 5,000 warriors (surely an exaggeration), but this number, according to his own estimate, was now reduced to 300. He knew of three separate groups of Cocopa, under the leaders Chi-pi-ti,

Colorado, and José. The Cocopa were in an alliance at that time with Jacum (Southern Diegueño) Indians and others in Baja California, and were at war with the "Yum" and "Cuchano." Heintzelman's 300 warriors may be roughly translated into a population of something over 2,000. This would check with Derby's estimate of 1,000 on the east side of the delta.

The establishment of a permanent American army post at Fort Yuma in 1852 marked the effective end of aboriginal life for the Indians of the Colorado and Gila rivers. First, it put an end to tribal warfare, and second, it brought the Cocopa for the first time into face-to-face relations with Europeans. The American army was brought into the area to assure safe passage for immigrants to California and to protect a proposed river steamboat system for bringing freight from California into western Arizona. Having its location at Fort Yuma, the American army formed an effective wedge between the Mohave and the Yuma, who were at war with the Pima, Maricopa, and Cocopa.

Americans were well acquainted with the Cocopa during the next 25 years, when river boats made regular and frequent trips from the mouth of the Colorado to the Gila, carrying supplies for the army camp at Fort Yuma. However, none of the boatmen, engineers, or army officers of that time bothered to leave an account of the native inhabitants of the region, even though they used a number of Cocopa men to help run their boats and barges (see Fig. 4) and employed Indian families to cut wood and stack it along the river banks. Even greater obscurity descended upon the delta country after 1877, when river traffic came

Bureau of American Ethnology
Fig. 4. Indian men on board Admiral Dewey's hydrographic survey ship at the mouth of the Colorado River in 1874.

to an end with the building of the Southern Pacific railroad into Yuma from the Pacific Coast. Sykes (1937: 37) sums up the conditions in the lower delta for the decade ending in 1890 as follows:

By the beginning of the last decade of the nineteenth century the delta south of the international boundary had once more become almost a *terra incognita*. River traffic had ceased entirely, and a few semi-nomadic family groups of Cocopa Indians, who ranged from the *bajadas* of the Cocopa Mountains to the banks of the Colorado, were practically the only inhabitants of the region.

The shipyard which had been developed and maintained by the Colorado Steam Navigation Company at Shipyard Slough on the Sonoran shore had been abandoned, the stores and equipment removed to Yuma, and the crews withdrawn. The two remaining river steamers rarely made trips down stream, and then only for the purpose of obtaining soft-wood fuel for their boilers from the abundant willow and cottonwood thickets. Knowledge of the lower river and of the extensive regions subject to tidal influences and overflow was rapidly slipping away, and channel changes in both the river and estuary were generally unnoticed and unrecorded.

Several small ranches were operated, principally upon the more stable Sonoran side of the river, and a few hundred head of stock — cattle and horses — were run upon the more accessible parts of the bottom lands; but agriculture generally, and also such development schemes as had originated during the steamboat days, had been allowed to lapse. The Colonia Lerdo which had been planned near the southwesternmost projection of the Sonoran mesa as one of the more ambitious of such schemes was occupied by a family of Mexicans engaged in stock raising, and the tule lands about the head of tidewater were overrun by numbers of hogs, the wild descendants of some domesticated swine that had been brought into the region years before as a commercial enterprise; and these were hunted at times by parties from north of the border.

POPULATION HISTORY

Cipriano Dominguez, a resident of Colonia Lerdo, told Lumholtz (1912: 250-2) that he took a census in 1900 and estimated the tribe at 1,200. Lumholtz was given the following Cocopa population figures in 1911: Pescador, 15 families; Pozo Vicente, 100 families; Yuma Valley, 30 families. He goes on to say that "the usual diseases acquired through contact with 'civilization' are found in the tribe, and many die from syphilis."

Chittenden (1901: 196-204), who visited the western part of the delta about 1900, calculated the population at not less than 450. This number refers to the Wi Ahwir (Lumholtz's Pozo Vicente) Cocopa. Since Chittenden had no knowledge of the other Cocopa groups, the computation

by Dominguez, a resident of the delta, is certainly more reliable for the tribe as a whole.

My own information tallies with that given by Dominguez. Jim Short (one of my informants) estimated that there were about 600 Cocopa (Hwanyak and Mat Skrui) on the east side of the delta in 1900, and Mike Alvarez reckoned a similar number for the Wi Ahwir group on the west side around 1905. Neither of these figures includes the few Kwakwarsh families living in the extreme southwestern section of the delta or some scattered families out in the center. My best guess is that there were about 1,500 Cocopa living in the delta in 1905.

The population of the delta area of the Colorado was considerably reduced between 1776 and 1900: 8,000 as against 1,500 (the latter almost all Cocopa). But in terms of Cocopa population, set by Garcés at 3,000, the reduction has not been unusual. Garcés, it will be recalled, found three Yuman tribes south of the Yuma: the Kahwan, Halyikwamai, and Cocopa. Some time after his visit and before 1825, the Kahwan and Halyikwamai joined forces and moved out of the delta to a new home on the Colorado between the Mohave and the Yuma. Within a very few years, no doubt as the result of continued warfare, they left the Colorado and took up residence among the Maricopa on the Gila (Spier 1933: 14-8). It is assumed that not all the Kahwan and Halyikwamai families made this move and that some remained in the delta (or returned to the delta) to become absorbed by the Cocopa. These three tribes speak very similar dialects, and the Kahwan-Halyikwamai, at least after their move to the Gila, were allies and friends of the Cocopa.

The only population figure that seems out of line is the one given by Oñate in 1605 (Zárate Salmerón 1916: 277). He said that there were 20,000 people on the eastern side of the delta from the confluence of the Gila and the Colorado to the Gulf. It is difficult to believe that Oñate was in a position to make any more than a guess at the number of inhabitants of the river valley, but his figures must certainly mean that there was a dense population on the river.

COCOPA NEIGHBORS

During the 17th and 18th centuries the Colorado River delta was occupied by the Yuma (Quechan), Halchidhoma, Kahwan, Halyikwamai, and Cocopa. Most of the Halchidhoma, Kahwan, and Halyikwamai, perhaps as a consequence of wars with the Yuma and Mohave, had moved out of the delta by about 1800 and eventually became a part of the Maricopa community on the Gila River (Spier 1933: 1-41). Some members of the Kahwan and Halyikwamai (whose language was similar to Cocopa and who were the last to leave the delta) either did not move from the delta or returned to the delta from the Maricopa villages. Gifford reported a Halyikwamai settlement in Hwanyak territory as late as 1848 (Gifford 1933: 260), and during the lifetime of my informants, some Halyikwamai and Kahwan were members of the Hwanyak band of Cocopa. The Yuma have occupied the northern part of the delta and the region north and south of the confluence of the Gila and Colorado rivers from at least the beginning of the 18th century. Immediately west of the Yuma, in what is now the Imperial Valley of California, were the Kamia (Gifford 1931). Other Yuman-speaking neighbors to the north and east were the Mohave, Walapai, Havasupai, and Yavapai (Fig. 5). However, the neighbors with whom the Cocopa were in most intimate contact during the latter part of the 19th century were the Yuman-speaking mountain groups of Baja California. These tribes, from the international border south, are referred to in the literature as the Southern Diegueño or Tipai, the Paipai or Akwa'ala, and the Kiliwa. My Cocopa informants knew these groups, in the same order, as *kamya'* (Kamia, or Southern Diegueño), *kw?aɬ* (Kwatl, a branch of the Southern Diegueño), *kw?aɬwa* (Kwatlwa, a branch of the Paipai), *paipai* (Paipai), and *yɪkwele'o* (Kiliwa) (see Table 2). The Kwatl and the

Fig. 5. Distribution of Yuman-speaking tribes in the late 19th century.

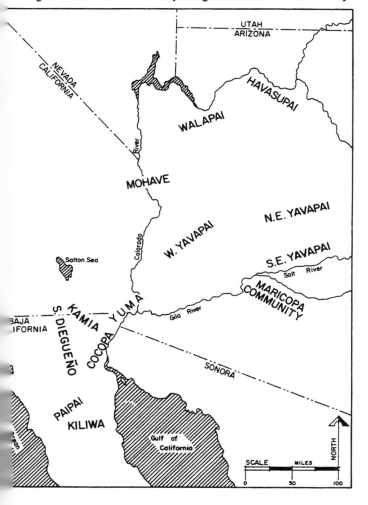

TABLE 2
Identification of Tribal Groups of Baja California
(North to South)

Cocopa Term	Anglicized Cocopa	Terms Used in the Literature
kamya' kw?aɬ mɪtsha	Kamia Kwatl Mitsa	Imperial Valley Kamia
kamya'	Kamia	Southern Diegueño or Tipai
kw?aɬ	Kwatl	Southern Diegueño or Tipai
kw?aɬwa	Kwatlwa	Paipai or Akwa'ala
paipai	Paipai	Paipai
yɪkwele'o	Yikweleo	Kiliwa

Kwatlwa are localized lineages of the Diegueño and Paipai, respectively, but had come to be thought of by the Cocopa as independent groups. There were at least a dozen such lineages among the Paipai and an even greater number among the Southern Diegueño (Kelly 1942), but only these two were singled out by the Cocopa and given band status in their thinking. However, the Cocopa did distinguish the southernmost Diegueño lineages from the Diegueño living near the international border; they referred to the southern groups as Kamia, but I failed to record their designation for the northernmost groups. A final note: Gifford's Kamia, the groups occupying the Imperial Valley and the northwestern corner of the delta proper, must not be confused with the people referred to as Kamia by the Cocopa; the latter, as noted above, occupied the mountains west of Cocopa territory during the 19th century. Gifford's Kamia are referred to by the Cocopa as *kamya' kw?aɬ mɪtsha.*

The association of the Baja California tribesmen with the Cocopa has been of long standing and, without question, has influenced their history and culture. Spanish and American explorers, as we have seen, made frequent mention of mountain tribes living and visiting in the delta, and this fact is frequently mentioned in my field notes. Informants stated that some Paipai had always lived in the delta as well as in the mountains, and that the delta group had its own section of land and its own band organization. Diegueño and Kiliwa also lived in or near Cocopa camps, mostly in the southern and western section of the delta. The Wi Ahwir community, located at the foot of the Cocopa Mountains (see Fig. 6), was always referred to by my informants as a mixed Cocopa-Diegueño population. The Kwakwarsh community, just south of the Wi Ahwir and on the trail that led into the mountains through the southern entrance to the Laguna Salada Basin, was made up of Cocopa, Kiliwa, Paipai, and Diegueño families. Some of these "foreigners" made their permanent home in the valley; others came there only seasonally. Although most of

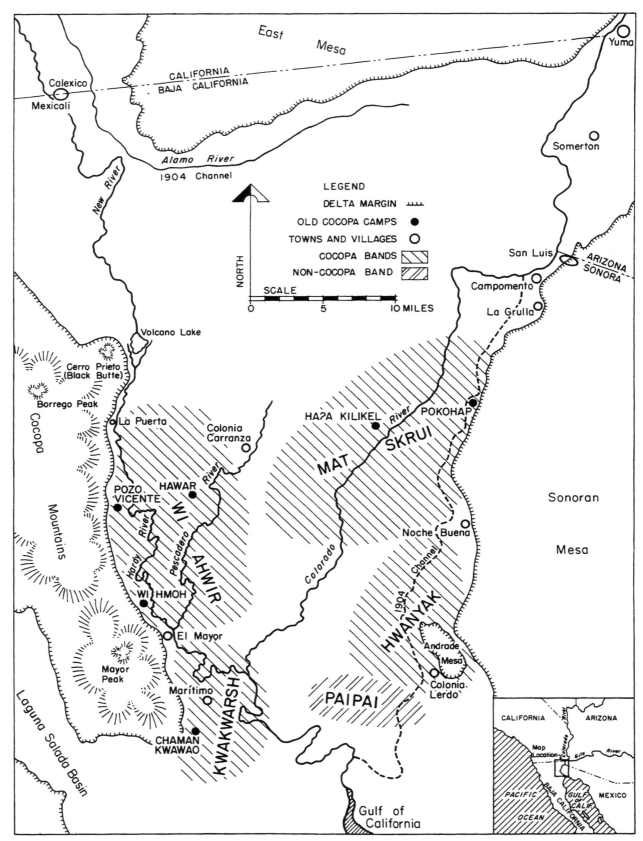

Fig. 6.   19th-century Cocopa band territories and 20th-century Mexican towns.

the contact between the Cocopa and the mountain Indians took place in the delta, the Cocopa, principally from the Wi Ahwir and Kwakwarsh groups, made regular trips into the mountains to visit or to gather wild food products, especially pine nuts. Some married into mountain families and went there to live.

The Hwanyak community was made up almost entirely of Cocopa, but it was in their territory that the above-mentioned Paipai band lived in the late 19th century. The Mat Skrui community was also almost entirely Cocopa. It is interesting to note that the Mat Skrui were known, both among themselves and among the Cocopa, as the "real Cocopa" (*koapa' ahan*). Descendants of the Hwanyak and Mat Skrui Cocopa now look down on Wi Ahwir and Kwakwarsh Cocopa, call them "mountain" as opposed to "river" people, and are of the opinion that they are troublemakers and witches. The Cocopa (especially those living on the western side of the delta) have intermarried with the Paipai, with the Diegueño, and, to a lesser extent, with the Kiliwa.

Cocopa contacts to the north and east with the Yuma, Mohave, Maricopa, Pima, and Papago were neither so frequent nor so intimate. Before the tribal wars were ended in the 1850s, the Cocopa were allies of the Maricopa and the Pima, and frequently joined them on the Gila in defense of their villages or on expeditions against the Yuma and Mohave. Groups of Cocopa continued to visit in the Maricopa villages after this time, and I have record of at least two semiformal return visits by Maricopa and Pima leaders about 1880. Contact with the Papago was apparently very slight, although some Sand Papago must have traveled up the eastern shore of the Gulf of California to visit in Cocopa camps, since their territory extended to the Gulf.

RECENT HISTORY

Between 1890 and 1900 there were four Cocopa bands. The Wi Ahwir occupied the sand hills and neighboring delta for a distance of 15 to 20 miles north of Mayor; the Kwakwarsh lived below Mayor to the limit of fresh water; the Mat Skrui inhabited the center of the delta and the eastern edge north of the Hwanyak; and the Hwanyak band was located along the east side of the delta from about 20 miles below San Luis to the limit of fresh water (Fig. 6). The River Paipai, a segment of the Mountain Paipai tribe, had their home at that time about seven miles southwest of Colonia Lerdo.

Between 1900 and 1910, most of the Wi Ahwir Cocopa moved into the neighborhood of Mexicali and along the Inter-California railroad just south of the border. The Mat Skrui Cocopa were also spread along the Baja California border; some families moved into Arizona around Somerton, and others settled a little to the south of San Luis, Sonora. Most of the Hwanyak settled around Somerton,

Arizona, but some stayed in Sonora where they mixed with the Mat Skrui families near San Luis. In the years between 1907 (when the river was turned back into the delta after having broken through into the Imperial Valley) and 1936, there was a constant shifting of families and groups back and forth across the border, and between Sonora and Baja California. In 1917, some of the Cocopa who were permanently settled near Somerton received recognition as United States Indians and were given two small reservations under the Yuma Indian Agency jurisdiction. (The enrolled Indians numbered about 50 in 1952, but little attention was paid to enrolled status for purposes of tribal identification or residence on reservation land.)

During the years between 1935 and 1950, when Mexicans and the Mexican government came into possession of some of the land formerly worked by American interests, and when new delta land was being developed under the *ejido* system of cooperative farms owned by the Mexican government, the Mexican Cocopa found it increasingly difficult to obtain regular employment. In earlier years they had been employed in construction work and as farm laborers by American companies. After the loss of their jobs, Mexican Cocopa moved to Arizona, again as agricultural laborers, or to unoccupied land in the southern part of the delta, where they made a living as best they could by chopping wood, picking cotton, and raising a few head of cattle.

In 1936 many of the families in Baja California were gathered together to form an *ejido* that was intended as an all-Cocopa enterprise. Poor direction of the project on the part of the Mexican authorities, together with lack of ability and interest on the part of the Cocopa, forced the inclusion of Mexican families and the appointment of a Mexican manager and storekeeper. After 1940 the Cocopa gradually left to make a living as laborers and woodcutters again, and their place was taken by additional Mexican families. Most of the families from the *ejido* had settled in Sonora by 1943.

In the late 1930s free movement into the United States was ended by the United States Immigration Service, acting in response to county boards of supervisors who found Indians a welfare burden during the depression. This sudden closing of the border, almost without warning so far as the Cocopa were concerned, brought about the arbitrary separation of some Cocopa kinsmen into Mexican and American groups.

In the 1940s the tribe included about 600 people, divided nearly equally into two groups located north and south of the international border. The American group was scattered through the Yuma Valley south of Yuma, but mostly on or near two small reservations on the outskirts of Somerton, Arizona. A few families also lived just east of Yuma in the Gila Valley. The Mexican group was largely concentrated just south of San Luis, Sonora, with scattered families in Baja California, mostly along the southwestern edge of the delta. For a number of years prior to 1940 the Cocopa in Sonora held a few acres of land along the canal between San Luis and La Grulla (see Fig. 6). In 1947, a dozen or more families occupied an undeveloped tract south of La Grulla that had been set aside for them when a new irrigation system was laid out in 1940. At least as late as 1952 Mexican Cocopa could make short visits to the United States on temporary permits but could not legally take jobs. American Cocopa born in the United States could go back and forth at will, but American Cocopa born in Mexico did not dare visit in Mexico for fear of being excluded from the United States when they tried to return.

At the time of my fieldwork, the Arizona Cocopa as a whole had maintained their tribal solidarity and preserved the old ways in a much more complete form than those in Mexico. There were no mixed marriages in Arizona so far as we knew, while many of the younger Cocopa girls in Baja California and Sonora were living with Mexican men. Our records, taken for another purpose, show 15 adults, in a sample of 112, who were children of such unions, and my guess is that a good third of the Cocopa children in Mexico in 1950 were of mixed descent.

Although most young and middle-aged Cocopa were bilingual (either in Spanish or English), only Cocopa was spoken in the camps we visited in the United States and Mexico. Cocopa children in the United States did not learn English until they entered school, and the children in Mexico probably did not learn Spanish until they started working for Mexican farmers.

Anita Alvarez de Williams has published a good account of the many changes and improvements that have been introduced since 1960 by the Cocopa tribal council, private foundations, and governmental agencies (Williams 1974: 78-99).

2. HABITAT

The aboriginal home of the Cocopa Indians was the delta of the Colorado River. Climatically, the region is a severe, hot desert, made habitable in former times by the annual floods and perennial waters of the Colorado River, which produced a sharply defined tract of rich vegetation and varied animal life. The region resembles in many particulars the delta of the Nile River in Egypt (see Fig. 7), and so the historian and the ethnographer must wonder why no advanced culture developed here. No satisfactory answer has been suggested, but much of the data in this and

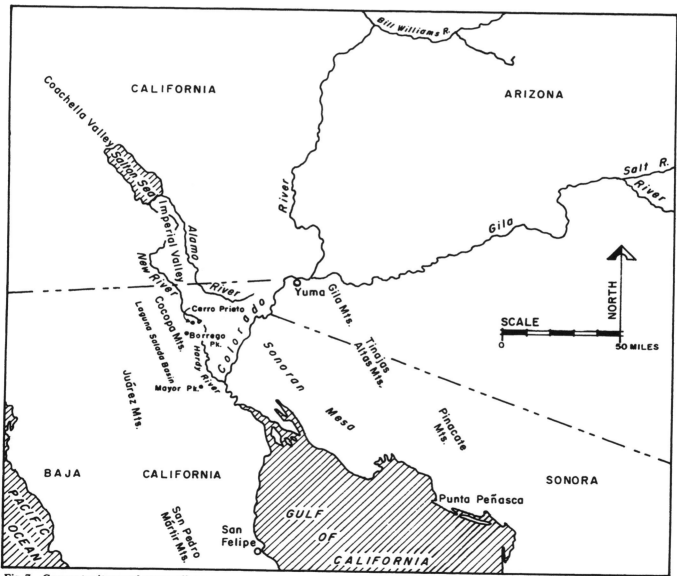

Fig. 7. Cocopa territory and surrounding areas.

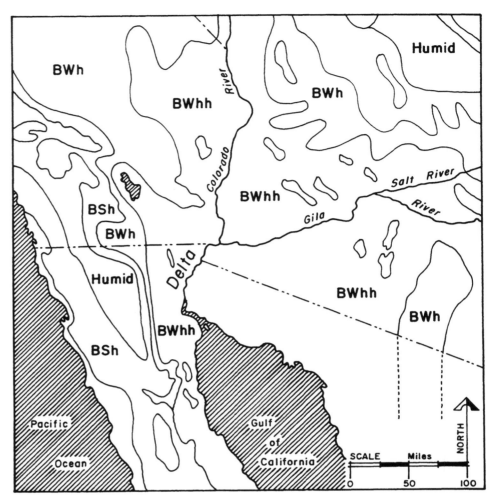

Fig. 8. Climates of the lower Colorado River area. BWhh, the low desert, surrounds the delta on all sides. Beyond are the areas of high desert (BWh and BSh), and, on the west, the pine-covered mountains in a humid climate.

subsequent chapters will be given in greater than ordinary detail so that the reader might test for himself a possible physical environmental, diffusionist, racial, historical, or other hypothesis.

So far as physical environment is concerned, the outstanding fact is that the Cocopa, living in the Colorado River delta, were at the center of four radiating zones, each in its own way dictating subsistence resources, travel, and trade. For convenience I have designated the four zones as follows: (1) delta (or river valley), (2) low desert, (3) high desert, and (4) pine forest. Each will be discussed in turn, following the classification of climatic zones.

CLIMATE

In the Southwest, climatic lines follow geographical contours in large measure. Russell (1931: 40-1) has made a study of the southwestern area, and the climatic zones he delimits correlate well with the work of botanists who have investigated much of the same territory. This is because temperature and precipitation, which influence plant and animal life, are in turn a response to elevation as shown in geographical contours. As one travels away from the Colorado River delta, a change in elevation of a few thousand feet makes the difference between hot desert and cool pine forest. Russell, following Köppen, sets up a basic distinction between dry and humid climates, designating a dry climate (B) as one in which centimeters of precipitation equals mean annual temperature (centigrade) plus 22 in areas with wet winters, to plus 44 in areas with wet summers. Areas with greater precipitation or lower temperatures, or both, are classified as humid (C and D). Russell (1926: 75) says: "... under the winter rainfall régime prevalent in California, the boundary between Dry and Humid areas lies along the isohyet [rainfall line] of 14 inches when the mean annual temperature approximates 55 °F. When the evaporation rate is increased with higher temperatures higher rainfall values are demanded." In other words, the dry climate areas are those in which the temperature is the same as at the Humid-Dry border and the rainfall is lower; or where the rainfall is the same as at the Humid-Dry border and the temperature is higher; or where there is both higher temperature and lower rainfall.

Dry climates (B) are subdivided into Desert (BW) and Steppe (BS). The Steppe, being more humid, borders the Humid (C and D) areas. The transformation to Desert occurs at a line where precipitation values in centimeters equals mean annual temperature (centigrade) plus 11 (areas with wet winters) to 22 (areas with wet summers). There is thus a reduction in precipitation of from 11 to 22 centimeters (given a constant temperature) between the line separating the Humid area from the Steppe area and the line separating the Steppe area from the Desert area. For our purposes, two sub-areas within the Desert (BW) area are of interest: the hot desert (BWh) and the very hot desert (BWhh). The hot desert has mean January temperatures above 32 °F (this criterion also applies to the Steppe area, BSh). The very hot desert has mean January temperatures above 32 °F and mean maximum temperatures of three months above 100 °F. These climatic zones are mapped in Figure 8. In Arizona, California, and the adjoining states of Mexico it so happens that the amount of annual precipitation drops with increases in mean annual temperature. In the center of the BWhh climatic zone at Yuma, Arizona, for example, the average annual precipitation is 3.83 inches (Smith 1956: 65).

The correlation between climatic zones and the four botanical zones may now be summarized as follows:

Delta: BWhh climate; mesquite, screwbean, willow, poplar, arrowweed, quelite, cane, cattail
Low desert: BWhh climate; creosote bush, desert saltbush
High desert: BWh and BSh climates; agave, yucca, prickly pear, cholla, sahuaro, manzanita, sumac, oak, walnut
Pine forest: Humid climate; piñon, yellow pine

THE DELTA

The most important, as well as the most sharply defined, alteration of the landscape in this southern desert country is found along the water courses that make up the Colorado River drainage system. Within the floodplains of the Colorado, Bill Williams, Gila, Salt, San Pedro, and Santa Cruz rivers (see Fig. 7), high temperatures, rich soil, and floodwater irrigation combined to produce both dense thickets of native plants and land suitable for agriculture. The river environment not only permitted fixed habitations, but also, in certain favored districts, permitted populations of considerable density.

During the period immediately preceding Spanish intrusion, agricultural lands were confined to the lower floodplains. In prehistoric times, in the vicinity of the confluence of the Salt and Gila rivers in Arizona, extensive canals were constructed for the purpose of carrying water to thousands of acres of land lying above the floodplain. This area was occupied by the Hohokam, who developed the only complex civilization within the area under discussion (see Haury 1976).

South of the point where the Colorado River passes through the final range of hills near Yuma, some 300,000 acres of delta land were subject to summer flooding. Within the territory reached by these floods, what would otherwise

have been a complete desert was transformed into a region of dense and fruitful vegetation. Rainfall is less than 4 inches a year, but there was no dependence, of either animals, plants, or man, upon this source of water — the life of the region was wholly sustained by the river, ground moisture, and overflow irrigation.

In terms of Russell's classification of climates, the delta is in the climatic center of the BWhh zone. This is the climate of the northern gulf coast of Baja California, the Colorado Desert, the Sonoran Desert of northwestern Mexico and western Arizona, and southeastern Nevada. This BWhh desert is surrounded by what Russell calls the Mohave type (BWh), except where it borders the Gulf of California (see Fig. 8). So far as the delta is concerned, this classification gives an adequate picture of climatic conditions, but it does not give any indication of the length and intensity of the growing season. Average January temperature for a BWhh climate must be above 32 °F; in the Colorado delta it is 54.6 °F (12.6 °C) (Smith 1930: 374). The southern latitude and a low elevation (141 feet at Yuma) combine to produce this relatively high temperature with a consequently long growing season (see Fig. 9). A 23-year record at Yuma (Smith 1956: 51) shows the following data on killing frosts: average date of killing frost in spring, February 20; average date of killing frost in autumn, November 26; average length of the growing season, 280 days.

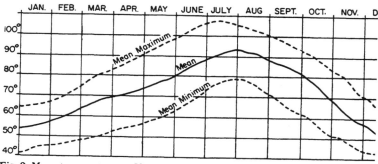

Fig. 9. Mean temperatures at Yuma, Arizona. (Adapted from Smith 1956: 15.)

It is impossible now to estimate either the probable acreage of land suitable for agriculture under aboriginal conditions or the actual number of acres cultivated by the native inhabitants prior to 1905. Kniffen (1931: 51) estimates that 300,000 acres could have been brought under cultivation, but this is the total area of fertile soil reached at one time or another by floodwaters. Without flood control and in view of the year-to-year changes of land contour, this estimate should be drastically cut. Given the native technology and knowledge of agricultural methods, probably no more than 50,000 acres could have been available. How many acres actually were utilized is another matter. The Cocopa of the late 19th century probably never farmed more than three or four thousand acres, so an overwhelming portion of the delta must have maintained its primitive vegetational aspect.

The native plants of the region and their distribution have been fully described by MacDougal (1906: 10-1):

> The soil, climate, moisture, and temperature of the entire delta are fairly uniform, and also differ but little in elevation and exposure — a condition which tends to promote the multiplication of the number of individuals of a few species of plants and these species are also able to maintain themselves in pure culture of some extent. . . . Canes (*Phragmites*), cattails (*Typha*), willows (*Salix*), poplars (*Populus*), arrow-weed (*Pluchea sericea*), quelite (*Amaranthus Palmeri*), wild hemp (*Sesbania*), each occupy extensive areas, to the almost total exclusion of other seed plants, although there are many places in which several of these will be found contending for the mastery. . . .
>
> Nearer the Gulf are found great sloughs, in which are extensive fields of the "wild rice" (*Uniola Palmeri*), while the land subject to the action of the overflow of the tides supports a carpet of salt-grass (*Distichlis*) and *Cressa*. Throughout the entire delta the mesquite (*Prosopis velutinea*)* and the screwbean (*Prosopis pubescens*) dot the landscape, and furnish examples of one of the few components of the vegetation, the individuals of which grow separately and apart. The salt-bush (*Atriplex*) also grows singly in great globular bunches overtopping the head of a man, on the lower stretches of saline soil.

(MacDougal's observation regarding the nature of mesquite and screwbean growth, made in 1906, does not conform to my own observations in 1939-40. His statement that the willows, poplars, arrowweed, and other plants occupy extensive areas is one I should also apply to the mesquite and screwbean. Thousands of acres of one species or another of these plants were found along the western margin of the delta mixed with little other than grass. I suspect that an important change in the nature of the flora has taken place since 1906, and the situation presents a warning against attributing to aboriginal times the natural resources found here, or in other areas, at the present time.)

MacDougal's botanical list for the delta is surprisingly short; he lists only 25 species, 20 of which grow in nonbrackish water or nonsaline soils.

The geographic, and particularly the hydrographic, nature of the delta was of the utmost importance to primitive life. The delta cone is, in fact, a double cone, since an original central elevation running west-southwest from Yuma was created when the Colorado River began forming its first delta in the gulf trough. A second cone, starting from the same point but running more to the

south, was created when the river swung south and its floods were hemmed in on the west by the first elevation and on the east by the Sonoran mesa. The true delta is a great plain, the surface of which is minutely broken by characteristically deltaic features: meandering channels, lakes, natural levees, and the somewhat specialized network of channels in secondary deltas. However, work begun in 1940 has now converted most of the delta into level cotton fields.

The main channel of the Colorado River was on the extreme eastern side of the delta before 1905 — often a few miles west of the mesa, occasionally touching it (see Fig. 6). Ten or 12 miles southwest of Yuma, at this same time, was the channel of the Alamo, which carried excess flood waters to the Imperial Valley through the old delta crest. Southwest of this point at the southern extremity of the crest of the cone, which formed the barrier to the Imperial Valley, Volcano Lake was fed by a network of sloughs during periods of high water. This lake emptied into two streams: New River, flowing north through another gap in the barrier to Imperial Valley, and the Hardy, flowing south and rejoining the Colorado near the estuary. The Hardy River, Volcano Lake, and New River, all on the west side of the delta, are believed to represent the remnants of the old tidal channel that connected the Gulf with Blake Sea (an extinct lake, whose beach line is now 26 feet above the Imperial Valley floor, at the international line).

Other landscape forms in the delta include Mesa Andrade, a former part of the Sonoran mesa, in the extreme southeastern corner of the delta; it is about thirty square miles in extent. Near Cerro Prieto (Black Butte) are a series of mud volcanoes. To the north in former times, a number of sand dunes that had originated in materials eroded from the western hills traveled eastward across an area of the delta seldom reached by the Colorado waters. (For a complete description of the geology and geography of the delta, see Kniffen 1932.)

The most important natural phenomenon affecting aboriginal culture in the delta was, of course, the Colorado River itself. A great deal depended upon the direction and amount of flow from year to year, and even from season to season. All European explorers found that the river was emptying into the Gulf, but very little is known concerning its course through the delta prior to 1851.

Sykes (1937: 169-70) says that the river shifted from one side of the delta to the other during the period of exploration. He sees some evidence in early accounts for stating that it was probably on the west side when visited by Consag in 1746, Hardy in 1826, and Pattie in 1827; and on the east side when visited by Alarcón in 1540, Díaz in 1540, and Kino in 1701. The first definite knowledge of the exact location of the river in the southern delta is provided by Lieutenant Derby's report (1852), the result of a joint reconnaissance with Major Heintzelman in 1851. At

---

*Bell and Castetter (1937: 9-10) classify *velutinea* as a variety of *Prosopis chilensis*.

that time, the Colorado River flowed along the eastern margin of the delta; the river remained in that position without a serious break until 1905. From approximately 1851 to 1905, fresh water derived from Colorado River floods was being backed up the channel of the Hardy, and perhaps was reaching the Hardy through sloughs from the east and northeast as well. One such slough, connecting the Colorado and Hardy and running west from the vicinity of Colonia Lerdo, was traversed by Sykes (1937: 44) in 1892, and informants indicated other such connecting channels to the north during this general period. In periods of flood, surplus water entered the Hardy and other western channels from the vicinity of Volcano Lake, and at intermediate points between there and the mouth of the Hardy near the estuary. Some water also escaped through the Alamo and New rivers into the Imperial Valley (Sykes 1937: 99-100). From 1909 to the present, the main channel of the Colorado has been directed westward, and has reached the Hardy at various points along a stretch from 20 to 25 miles long north of the former confluence (Sykes 1937: 80-4).

Although the low-water channel of the Colorado remained quite stable during the known period between 1851 and 1905, there was no comparable stability in the direction of overflow during periods of high water. Channel breaks, sloughs, and areas of extensive sheet flooding occurred in ever-shifting positions on both sides of the river from Yuma to the Gulf. Innumerable small openings allowed excess water to pass through the higher elevations west of the main channel of the Colorado, and this water was then collected and discharged by the Hardy. The position of these gaps, as well as the volume of water that passed through, varied from year to year. During the latter part of the 19th century, however, much of the generalized flooding took place west of the main channel between Yuma and San Luis, following southwest until it entered Volcano Lake; from there the water usually drained south through the Hardy or, in cases of very high water, drained north into the Imperial Valley of California (Sykes 1937: 37-42). (Since 1936 river runoff has been controlled by the Hoover Dam and other structures upriver.)

Generally speaking, low water was expected from September through March, when an average monthly volume of 614,000 acre feet passed the gauging station at Yuma (Table 3). The river then began to rise, usually in a series of separate floods, reaching the average maximum during the last week in June. No discharge records were kept prior to 1902, but gauge readings were made by the Southern Pacific Railroad Company between 1878 and 1909 (Table 4). What the records indicate is a runoff pattern that was highly unpredictable both in amount and in time of occurrence — a situation quite different from that found in the Nile Valley. Two major climatic zones, neither of which is subject to the same conditions that operate in Africa, are included within the watershed of the

TABLE 3
Average Monthly Runoff on the Colorado River at Yuma, Arizona, 1903–1934

Month	Acre Feet
January	508,900
February	641,200
March	876,300
April	1,241,800
May	2,489,200
June	3,986,000
July	2,243,300
August	1,041,400
September	685,700
October	622,500
November	482,900
December	479,000

SOURCE: Official records, Yuma office of the U.S. Reclamation Service.

Colorado River: the plateau and Rocky Mountain regions of Utah, Wyoming, and Colorado, where heavy winter snows cause the late spring and early summer floods; and the warmer desert and mountain area of Nevada, Arizona, and New Mexico, where "flash" floods originate at all times of year, but more typically in late summer and late winter. These flash floods, generally from the Gila, can be of considerable magnitude; one in February, 1891, raised the Yuma gauge of the Colorado River to the unprecedented height of 33.2 feet (Table 4), and another in February, 1920, brought the Yuma discharge up to 164,000 cfs, only 22,000 cfs less than the greatest recorded flood produced by the Colorado alone (official records, Yuma office of the U.S. Reclamation Service).

Much more important to the life of the aboriginal inhabitants, however, was the unpredictability of the number and magnitude of flood crests in the summer. Very frequently the annual summer flood occurred not in one peak, but perhaps in two, three, or four maxima; these sometimes came at monthly intervals, as they did in 1926, the first on April 12, and the fourth on July 19 (Kniffen 1932: 163). The destructive threat to aboriginal farms dependent upon sheet flood irrigation is obvious.

THE LOW DESERT

Surrounding the delta is the low desert, characterized by low elevation, a long, hot summer season, and low precipitation; it is coterminous with Russell's BWhh zone

(see Fig. 8). The predominant vegetation consists of creosote bush (*Larrea tridentata*) and desert saltbush (*Atriplex
polycarpa*); in the foothill washes and other favorable spots,
there is a thin distribution of palo verde, palo fiero,
catclaw, and ocotillo (Nichol 1937: 183).

In such an environment, permanent habitation is impossible, and the BWhh desert would have been without human
occupants had it not been for the occasional higher ridges
with their plant cover more typical of the BWh zone.
Certain local and seasonal food plants occurred, but these
harvests were relatively unimportant when considering the
region as a whole.

Shreve (1936: 15-7) summarizes the climate and flora as
follows:

> The most arid part of the desert lies on the eastern or
> lee side of the great mountain ranges of northern Baja
> California and southern California. . . . The plains and
> mountains which border the lower course of the
> Colorado River and the head of the Gulf of California
> have the smallest flora and the most scanty vegetation
> of any part of the North American Desert.

East and southeast of the delta, this uninhabitable area
continues for 100 miles, broken only by the comparatively
unimportant high desert (BWh zone) near the summits of
the Gila, Tinajas Altas, and Pinacate mountains (see Fig. 7).
In this 8,000-square-mile desert, no more than 150 Papago
were able to maintain life, migrating back and forth
between mountain water tanks (*tinajas*) and the clam beds
of the Gulf (Castetter and Bell 1942: 6-7). This part of the
low desert was probably never visited by the Cocopa,
except when they traveled through it to reach the Maricopa
villages on the middle Gila.

Southward along both shores of the Gulf there stretched
the salt-charged tidal flats of the gulf plain. Although of no
economic importance, this region was a phenomenon with
which the Cocopa were forced to cope. It intervened
between their delta habitat and the gulf shore, and it had to
be crossed by any parties traveling south or southwest into
the Baja California mountains. In land contour, it is almost
indistinguishable from the delta, but an increased salt
content in the soil brings about changes in vegetation that
make it distinctive. Brackish water in the vicinity of the
estuary supports some plant life, but outside this section,
notably along the gulf shore north from San Felipe and up
to the Cocopa Mountains, the gulf plain presents a great
reach of salt flats almost devoid of plant life, stretching for
about 60 miles north to south and 4 to 12 miles east to
west. Not even the most arid parts of the surrounding
desert present such an extreme of utter lifelessness, and
nothing could be so outstanding as its contrast with the
lush vegetation of the nearby delta. It was in this desolate
area that the Cocopa believed their departed ancestors lived
in a spiritual world of plenty.

TABLE 4

**Annual Maximum and Minimum Gauge Heights on the
Colorado River at Yuma, Arizona, 1878–1909**

Year	Maximum		Minimum	
	Feet	Date	Feet	Date
1878	23	6-24	14.7	12-31
1879	20	5-12	13.2	10-14
1880	24	5-31	14.9	12-8
1881	23.5	6-14	15	1-25
1882	22.6	6-18	15.5	12-20
1883	24.5	7-13	14	12-14
1884	28.5	6-17	14.2	12-5
1885	24.7	6-13	13.7	2-8
1886	26.8	6-6	14.4	1-19
1887	23.5	6-10	14.9	1-26
1888	21.8	6-15	14.8	1-4
1889	22.4	6-7	15.4	9-27
1890	25.5	6-5	16.4	1-29
1891	33.2	2-26	16.4	9-22
1892	25.5	7-3	15.5	12-31
1893	25.2	7-28	15.5	1-2
1894	23.7	6-14	15.9	1-23
1895	28.2	1-20	16.8	2-13
1896	24.5	9-30	17.4	12-17
1897	26.1	6-9	17.9	12-21
1898	23.6	6-27	17.5	1-8
1899	27	7-1	17	10-17
1900	25	6-10	16.4	9-10
1901	27.2	5-31	16.2	1-14
1902	24.5	5-26	16.6	9-28
1903	27.7	6-26	16.8	1-13
1904	26.3	6-5	18.3	12-27
1905	31.3	11-30	17.8	12-31
1906	28.8	6-3	17.4	1-19
1907	29.2	6-20	18	12-31
1908	26.3	12-19	18	1-1
1909	30.8	6-24	14.6	12-31

SOURCE: Official records, Yuma office of the U.S. Reclamation
Service.

From the standpoint of human habitation, there is little or no difference between what is technically the river delta and the bordering mesa and foothill desert if neither area is reached by river water. The irrigated section of the delta, where the Cocopa had their homes, was thus surrounded by a low desert (BWhh climate) that was made up of dry mesa land to the east, salt flats to the south, a combination of salt flats, delta, and foothills to the west, and a combination of delta and mesa land to the north (see Figs. 7 and 8).

As an uninhabitable desert, the Laguna Salada (Macuata) Basin equals the gulf plain in its desolation. Where one ends and the other begins is, in fact, indistinguishable to the ordinary traveler. There are three reliable, and three or four sporadic, water holes in the region, which, under aboriginal conditions, perhaps provided temporary camping places (Kniffen 1931: 49). Nevertheless, during those years when the conditions of flood and tide forced fresh water from the Hardy into this basin, certain sections along the main slough could be farmed. Some western Cocopa planted crops there, but there were no permanent habitations.

Northwest of the delta was the great basin of the Imperial and Coachella valleys. Conditions there were quite similar to those found in the Laguna Salada Basin, except that the system of sloughs was apparently more extensive and inundation more frequent, permitting semipermanent occupation (Gifford 1931: 3-9). Along these sloughs and in areas with a high underground water table in the Coachella Valley, mesquite and screwbean trees occurred, providing a source of food more typical of the nearby delta proper (Gifford 1931: 23; Barrows 1900: 55-6). Along either side of the Colorado River as far north as the Grand Canyon, the low desert stretched to the west and to the east, forming an effective barrier that for the most part kept permanent settlements of desert Indians well back from the Colorado River Valley.

THE HIGH DESERT

Within the low desert at points of increased elevation and surrounding it on all sides are areas with slightly modified summer temperatures and increased rainfall; here, with few exceptions, the whole range of desert plants is found. These areas, which I have called high desert, include both the BWh and BSh climatic zones, in which differences in vegetation are mainly quantitative.

Human occupation of this desert depended upon both the presence of wild foods and access to ground water. In any detailed study these two variables would have to be mapped carefully, but for present purposes it is sufficient to note that, in general, food and water under aboriginal conditions were most plentiful at the higher elevations and least plentiful in the lower areas near the low desert. Life in this region was so dependent upon the time and amount of precipitation that it is possible to make the general statement that plant, animal, and human life gradually thinned from its border with the humid zone to its border with the BWhh zone.

Typical food plants of the high desert were prickly pear, cholla, sahuaro, agave, yucca, manzanita, oak, walnut, and sumac (Nichol 1937: 183; Castetter, Bell, and Grove 1938: 15; Bell and Castetter 1941: 15, 22). Of these, by far the most important was the agave, of which, in the wider area under consideration, the most important species were *Agave utahensis* Engelm, *A. deserti*, *A. Toumeyi*, *A. Couesii*, *A. Nelsoni Trel*, *A. Goldmaniana*, and *A. Shawii Trel* (Castetter, Bell, and Grove 1938).

Botanical maps show the occurrence of agave, notably *A. deserti*, within the low desert as well. However, this is a reflection of the difficulties of mapping on a small scale. For purposes of botanical mapping, the sporadic and thin occurrence of the plant at higher elevations within the BWhh zone must be shown, but as an item in human diet, the agave, along with associated plants, may be considered absent in the low desert, as the following summary indicates:

> Of the Yuman tribes of the Colorado and Gila rivers, the Mohave and Yuma used agave very little as it did not grow in their immediate vicinity. . . . The Cocopa, particularly those south of the present international boundary, did pit-bake *A. deserti* to some extent; however, the Maricopa made little use of mescal since it did not grow in their locality, but did sometimes secure the baked product from the Papago. The Kamia of Imperial Valley, a people marginal to the Southwest, secured mescal by trade, but never baked it; it was, however, baked by the Southern Diegueño. . . .
> As regards the utilization of agave for food in the Southwest, we may say in brief that the only peoples who did not use mescal rather extensively for food were the Pueblos, Navajo, Pima, Papago, Mohave, Yuma, Maricopa, and some of the Cocopa, and this because of its scarcity or absence in their territory. [Castetter, Bell, and Grove 1938: 80-2]

Other important food plants of general distribution in the high desert were various species of cactus, mesquite, and yucca.

In the west, the most commonly occurring cacti used by the natives were species of prickly pear, cardon (*Pachycereus Pringlei* S. Wats.) (Castetter and Bell 1937: 35-7), cholla, and certain barrel-shaped cacti, such as *Echinocactus cylindricis* (Barrows 1900: 67-8).

The full range of southwestern cacti was found to the east, among the more notable being the sahuaro, *Carnegiea gigantea*. The fruit of the yucca was also available throughout the high desert. It was not merely a food plant, but was also an important source of fiber and of saponaceous ingredients for use as a detergent. In the opinion of Bell and Castetter (1941: 64-5), yucca has ranked "foremost among the wild plants utilized by the inhabitants of the Southwest. It holds this place because of the great variety of uses to which it could be put and to the wide accessibility of the genus within the southwest."

Although these were perhaps the most important desert plants, the list of all the vegetable foods found in the high desert and used by the natives in former times would, no doubt, number several hundred. Barrows (1900: 55), in his study of the Desert Cahuilla alone, discovered 60 distinct products used for food and 28 used for narcotics, stimulants, or medicines.

The Cocopa Mountains are the only food-producing desert area, either high or low, within Cocopa territory. This long, narrow range of hills rises almost immediately out of the western border of the delta bottom and extends southward from the Mexican border for about 50 miles. It is a rugged range having many steep rocky slopes that are entirely devoid of vegetation. The highest point is 3,480 feet in elevation; most of the ridges are between 2,000 and 3,000 feet high. This elevation is not sufficient to attract much increase in precipitation, but, according to Kniffen (1932: 217-8), it is sufficient to bring something of a reduction in temperature, as is indicated by an occasional snow cover on the higher peaks. The elevation means a reduced evaporation rate, with consequent significance for plant life. Kniffen further reports that there is only one permanent spring in these mountains; it is located high up on Borrego (Pescadores) Peak in the Cocopas and supports a grove of native palms (*Neowashingtonia*). Rock tanks, or *tinajas*, are fairly common; some of them retain water throughout the dry period, and in past years they made it possible for the region to support wild sheep and other mammals.

The Cocopa Mountains could never have provided the entire subsistence for a permanently settled human group. Cactus, agave, and palo fiero (*Olneya tesota*) (MacDougal 1908: 41) are the only food plants of any consequence; the cactus and palo fiero occur as thinly scattered single growths, and the agave is confined to the highest elevations. Kniffen, who explored the upper ridges of the Cocopas, tentatively identified the agave as *Agave consociata* and has the following to say in regard to its occurrence:

> Just why this maguey is so restricted in distribution is not clear. It is highly valued by the natives, both as being edible and as furnishing the base for a distilled liquor [for modern commerce]. Its absence from the lower slopes may represent a removal by man of the individuals growing there. It does not, however, appear on the Peninsular Range until elevations of around 2500 feet have been reached; possibly its habitat is restricted by climatic conditions. The small but distinct difference in temperature existing between the base and summit of the Cucopas might, therefore, be sufficient as a determining factor in its range. [Kniffen 1932: 218]

Not within the territory of the Cocopa, but frequently visited by them (especially the western and southern

groups), was the high desert (BWh and BSh zones) of Baja California (see Fig. 8). A narrow strip of this desert extends along the sharply rising eastern slopes of the Juarez Mountains. South of the Juarez Mountains in Paipai and Kiliwa territory, elevation was considerably reduced, and the high desert type of vegetation spread over many hundreds of square miles. This region was separated from the Colorado delta by the Laguna Salada Basin and the gulf plain, and then by the low valleys referred to by the mountain Indians as "El Desierto" (Meigs 1939: 6), a total distance of about 65 miles (see Fig. 7). Products of this territory were brought into the river valley by mountain Indians, who traded them for agricultural products.

THE PINE FOREST

Piñon and juniper woodlands occurred throughout the lower elevations of the Humid climatic zone, both in Arizona and in California. Except for the Papago, all of the desert tribes — the Kiliwa, Paipai, Diegueño, and Yavapai — had access to a piñon harvest. The annual migration to the higher mountains to secure this product formed an important aspect of their subsistence activities.

The Cocopa, perhaps alone among the river tribes, made annual trips to the Baja California mountains to gather pine nuts; these expeditions were eagerly discussed by my informants. Pine forests occurred in both the Juarez and the San Pedro Mártir mountains (to the southwest), as well as on some of the higher ground in the intervening region:

> The principal source of pine nuts for the [Kiliwa] Indians was south of the permanently occupied Kiliwa territory: the Parry piñon forests of the north slopes of the San Pedro Mártir Plateau. Similarly, acorns were brought in from the outside, either from the live-oak groves fringing the San Pedro Martir Plateau or from the groves in the cañons west of the Arroyo Léon Upland. [Meigs 1939: 8]

Meigs's observations about the country south of the Kiliwa apply similarly to the Juarez Mountains to the north.

Pinus monophylla (*P. cembroides* var. *monophylla*) also grew in extreme southern California and northern Baja California. The nuts mature in late August and early September. Acorn-bearing oaks extending south into Baja California include *Quercus agrifolia* and *Quercus Kelloggii*, the acorns of which ripen in October and November (Herbert L. Mason 1946: personal communication).

To reach the Juarez Mountains, the Cocopa were forced to climb through or go around the Cocopa Mountains, travel across Laguna Salada Basin, and scale the eastern face of the escarpment, which rose more than 4,000 feet in about six miles. The Indians followed up the narrow canyons that cut this eastern face. Once out of the valley floor, although the climb was steep and difficult, they were able to find plenty of water and food, including dates from native palms that grew at the lower levels.

3. SUBSISTENCE

No other Indians in the Southwest, not even the other River Yuman tribes, possessed the quantity, diversity, and seasonal spread of wild food resources available to the Cocopa. The Cocopa also understood and practiced agriculture in a land well suited to the growing of the native Indian crops of corn, beans, and squash. From the point of view of their natural environment and their technology, the Cocopa of the 19th century should have been well fed and prosperous, but they were not. The facts on subsistence reveal chronic short rations during the late spring and early summer, and near-famine conditions in some years when the summer floods failed.

An increase in time devoted to subsistence activities, especially farming, and tighter organization would have solved this problem for a society with interests in that direction, but the Cocopa were living in a cultural system that did not encourage them to think of subsistence as a "problem" to be solved. Not that they enjoyed going hungry, but they could not envision, and would never have sought, the social and cultural changes that would have made possible a more reliable food supply. So far as I could discover, there was no anxiety, either conscious or unconscious, with respect to food. There was no magic in the food quest, no myth surrounding it, and, most interesting of all for an agricultural people, neither prayers nor rites associated with the planting, growing, or harvesting of their crops. Old men and old women were ardent and constant food gatherers, but this activity seemed to be more a matter of what was expected of them than a response to the immediate food situation or a sign of anxiety. Also typical of the Cocopa was a marked generosity with food, but food was never a symbol of wealth or an avenue to social prestige.

The food situation, as it will be described in this chapter, was consistent with the economic system as a whole. There was no wealth, no public works, no building of monuments. The Cocopa, individually and collectively, were as economically poor as it seems possible to be. In most cases of this kind around the world today, we seek the cause in some situation over which the victims of poverty have no control: lack of capital, absentee landlords, technological ignorance, excessive taxes, high interest rates, and so on. None of these hold for the Cocopa. The situation over which the individual Cocopa had no control was his own culture, which gave him no knowledge of any other way of life and no incentive for the attainment of security, personal comfort, wealth display, or economic progress. The Cocopa represent a special case for economics, a case in which, in a rich physical environment, the absence — not the presence — of kings, priests, warlords, landlords, and tax collectors correlates with poverty. These statements, of course, are from the point of view of an outsider. It is the outsider's frame of reference that produces "poverty" in the midst of "plenty." We shall probably never know how the Cocopa viewed their own way of life in pre-European days. All of my informants had long since been caught up in systems of thinking generated by their contact with Mexicans and Americans.

THE YEARLY ROUND OF ACTIVITIES

The Cocopa possessed no calendar in the usual sense. Some activities during the year fell at no set period, others were tied to the flow of the river and the seasonal demands of the farms and the natural environment.

The fact that some neighboring tribes divided the year into twin sections of six lunar periods each was known to my informants, but none could repeat the terms or their meanings. An attempt was made to discover whether the Cocopa used some substitute system, such as seasonal terms, but great variations in the list from one informant to another soon convinced me that there was no pattern in this matter. What I obtained was, of course, the designations for certain outstanding events: rising water, flood, retreating water, first frost, cold season, hot season, appearance of mesquite and cottonwood leaves, appearance of mesquite flowers, planting season, weeding season, harvest season, and the like.

Table 5 presents a summary of the yearly subsistence round, together with monthly runoff rates and temperatures, which are important determinants of the resources available and thus of the subsistence activities. Selecting a "new year's day" for descriptive purposes, however, is an arbitrary thing. I have chosen the planting season because it marked the beginning of new activities for everyone, and it was the annual period of promise for better times ahead.

Planting started after the river began to fall, usually toward the middle of July. It continued for two to three weeks, sometimes for as much as a month, and coincided

TABLE 5
Annual Round of Subsistence Activities

Month	Colorado River Runoff at Yuma (acre feet)[1]	Mean Temperature (Fahrenheit)	Agriculture	Gathering	Hunting	Fishing
Jan.	508,900	54.6		In poor years this was the period of greatest want. Few wild products were available. Hungry families gathered tule and some went to Baja California mountains for agave and cactus fruit.	Some rabbits and rats. Ducks and other birds fairly plentiful.	Fishing important but supply diminishes until river begins to rise.
Feb.	641,200	58.9				
Mar.	876,300	64.2			Game becoming scarce.	
Apr.	1,241,800	70.1	Clearing			
May	2,489,200	76.8		Wild rice harvest.		
June	3,986,000	84.7				Fish plentiful in river, sloughs, and lakes.
July	2,243,300	91.3	Planting	Bird's eggs, mesquite, and quelite greens.	Rabbits.	
Aug.	1,041,400	90.5	Weeding			
Sept.	685,700	84.8		Screwbeans. Some families to mountains for agave, dates. Pine nuts in late September.	Rabbits, birds, and other small game become important in late summer through early winter.	Fish diminishing.
Oct.	622,500	73.2	Harvest	Great quantities of grass and weed seeds gathered.		
Nov.	482,900	62.4	Storage			
Dec.	479,000	55.5		Some gathering.		

[1]Average for the years 1903–1934.

with the gathering of ripe mesquite pods from the trees and the early period of the harvest of dry mesquite pods from the ground. This was also the best season for catching the Colorado "salmon." There were few years — perhaps one in four — when any of the harvest of the year before remained on hand in July, and there was consequently a problem of balancing the distribution of time between seeking daily food, getting in the mesquite harvest, and planting. All informants agreed — and collateral evidence supports their statements — that this planting month was their time of greatest and most sustained labor. This labor was made especially onerous by the intensity of the heat, swarms of biting flies, and half-empty stomachs.

The daily round for men and older boys at this time of year was most commonly divided into a morning of hunting and fishing and an afternoon of planting. The women and older girls spent the morning, and frequently the whole day, gathering mesquite beans and some other less important products such as birds' eggs and quelite greens. When not otherwise occupied, the women helped on the farm. Formal division of labor beyond this was at a minimum. Men frequently cooked the midday meal while the women were still out gathering mesquite beans, and women often worked on the farms alone while the men were fishing. Both men and women performed the camp chores as circumstances dictated.

Through the summer and early fall, while their crops were maturing, the Cocopa lived by hunting, fishing, and gathering. As the season progressed, more and more wild plant foods became available, and the women were busy every day gathering food for daily needs and laying in the harvest of mesquite and screwbeans. Within a few weeks after their crops were planted, the whole family took some time off from all other tasks and pleasures to hoe and pull the countless weeds. No other work was so repugnant to the Cocopa, who limited their attention to those weeds that threatened to choke or steal moisture from the crops. With the first weeding out of the way, work on the farm was pretty much a matter of individual enterprise and convenience. Most families, however, did some weeding through the entire growing season. With the exception of the times weeding had to be done, the late summer and early fall months were easy and pleasant for the men. Fish were plentiful and easily caught, and with this supply of food on hand the men could spend many days and hours in visiting and gambling.

After the first weeding, many Wi Ahwir and Kwakwarsh families and individuals abandoned the delta for a trip into the Baja California mountains to gather agave, cactus fruits, dates, honey, and pine nuts. Perhaps half the families in the western part of the delta made such trips; some went every year, others went every two or three years. It was not uncommon for these people to remain in the mountains for two months or more, and to return, accompanied by visiting mountain friends and kinsmen, just in time to harvest their crops.

The harvest season was an especially busy time for the women. Besides helping with the farm, it was their exclusive responsibility to gather, prepare, and store the many varieties of wild grass and weed seeds. If the farm was small, or if the season was bad for crops, the gathering of wild seeds became doubly important. This work persisted throughout the fall and early winter, and thus the older women continued their labors through the time when the men, older girls, and younger married women were spending their days and nights in visiting and in attending the round of harvest fiestas and mourning ceremonies.

From January to mid-May, life in a Cocopa camp varied from year to year in relation to the quantity of food stored at harvest time. In good years this was a period of comparative leisure for everyone. The men hunted and fished to supplement the vegetable diet, but there was no great urgency to do so if the hunting or fishing area was far away or if the days were especially cold. At this time also, men, women, and children spent odd hours gathering arrowhead tubers, which were considered something of a delicacy. Some individuals, especially the older women, were constantly occupied in the food quest no matter what their stored resources might be. They tended bird traps, searched out rat nests, and harvested what remained of the weed and grass seeds.

If the year had been a bad one, all of the food-procuring activities were stepped up and the Cocopa, with their stored food consumed, lived from day to day on the products of the natural environment. There was no real hardship, since wild food remained fairly plentiful through the winter. Gathering food was a time-consuming business for everyone, however, and never pleasant. The Cocopa did not dress for cold weather and suffered real hardship, at least in their own eyes, if the food quest was started before the morning sun could warm them or when hunger forced the men into cold water to net fish.

In favorable years, perhaps one in five, when winter rains were heavy or when there was a January or February flood, some families attempted an early crop of corn. However, the size of any such crop would be too small to be of economic importance.

The regular farming activity for the spring months was the clearing of fields in late March or April, before the river began to rise. This was mostly man's work, and was confined to those families that planned to work new land. When a favorable location had been selected, the men cut and piled the brush and smaller trees and then burned them. Larger trees were killed by ringing or burning.

The worst period of the year, and the time of famine if it was to strike, came just before the wild rice harvest in mid-May. In bad years, anything and everything was eaten in late spring, and most families left their homes to wander over the delta in search of whatever food they could find. At this time every animal, with the exception of the coyote and the snake, was eaten, and many wild plant products that were never consumed when other food was available were gathered and eaten. The chief of these, and the food all Cocopa fell back on when everything else was gone, was tule roots. Some families, living where the tule was abundant, ate little else for a month or more in the most difficult years.

Early in May, most Cocopa families started their annual trip to the wild rice fields in the estuary. Men, women, and children, in single families or in groups of families, made the journey in easy stages, gathering, fishing, and hunting as they traveled. Frequent stops of several days were made in favored gathering, fishing, or hunting areas, so that it was not uncommon for a group to spend two weeks on the trip. Everyone looked forward with the greatest pleasure to the weeks spent in the rice harvest. They loved this food, and it was relatively easily gathered in great quantities. The rice harvest was a time when large numbers of people came together in a single area with ample leisure for visiting, dancing, singing, gambling, and courting. Again, as during the fall harvest, it was the older women who assumed the chief responsibility for gathering and preparing the food, while the men and younger women could take much more time to enjoy themselves.

The return from the wild rice fields, towards the middle of June, usually coincided with the time of highest flood water. For the trip to many parts of the delta, it was most convenient for the men to load their families and stores of wild rice on rafts, and to pull or pole their way for part of the distance. It was on this trip that many stops were made to pick the first few ripe mesquite pods and to gather eggs.

There was little for anyone to do while the water remained high and planting could not yet be started. The older boys and girls formed parties to go after birds' eggs, and the men fished. The women could commence their harvest of mesquite beans, but for the first few weeks the beans were more a delicacy than a food; the still moist pods were chewed for the sweet juice they contained.

There were a good many exceptions to this subsistence round. Perhaps the principal difference was between those families who chose to devote most of their time and energy to farming and those who farmed not at all or very little (see below, *Group Differences*). The non-farmers — mostly western Cocopa — spent proportionately more time than the farmers in gathering activities, particularly in making trips to the mountains for agave and cactus products and for the pine nut harvest in September.

The majority of Cocopa families had farms, however, and the crucial point for them was the planting season. The very late floods on the Colorado demanded rapid, uninterrupted planting if a large crop was desired. Yet at this time the families were forced to spend considerable time

gathering wild foods, and in some cases actual hunger prevented the expenditure of time and energy needed for the planting of an adequate crop.

AGRICULTURE

The Cocopa depended entirely upon the flood waters of the Colorado River for the moisture to mature their crops. But Colorado River floods, unlike those of the Nile, are highly variable in both time and volume, producing a concomitant uncertainty in the success of both planting and harvesting. The three variables that operated were: amount of river discharge, time of peak flood or floods, and direction of flood overflow. The highly unpredictable nature of the first two factors can be judged from the river runoff records given in Chapter 2 (Tables 3-4). The variability in the direction of overflow within the delta was not studied by Europeans before 1907 (Sykes 1937: 37-64), and so my information is from data supplied by the Cocopa.

If the flood was of such minor proportions that it did not reach a prepared plot, or if a shift in delta contour left a farm high and dry, a substitute plot was found whenever possible. If a second rise in flood water returned to a planted area and washed out the seed, or if the ground remained wet so long as to damage the seed, the plot had to be replanted, provided the season had not progressed too far. A high flood of any duration after the crops were well up was, of course, ruinous. Sam Spa remembers only one such case: "Once we had the fields well along and then a flood from the Gila covered everything with water and the plants died. This was early in September when the watermelons were fairly large."

One result of the variable nature of river floods was the constant shifting of families and groups. Most frequent, of course, was the shifting of family farm plots and homes within the relatively stable farming territory of a group. On occasion, however, major changes in delta contour forced a shift by the whole group.

River instability, for the period of this report, was perhaps most critical for the Wi Ahwir. From about 1885 to 1895, and for an unknown period prior to 1885, these people were concentrated along the west side of the delta just north of Mayor and in the vicinity of Hawar, about 10 miles northeast of Mayor in the delta (see Fig. 6). The following statement by Mike Alvarez on the movement of families was confirmed many times, but the exact hydrographic picture that caused these movements always remained obscure and contradictory:

At that time [when Alvarez was a small boy, probably in the early 1880s] most of the Wi Ahwir people were living out in the delta, where they had their homes above the reach of floods, or along the sand hills on the western edge of the delta. No one then lived as far north on the Hardy as Pozo Vicente because the floods didn't go that way.

When I was a little older [about 1890] my family moved from *wi hmoh* to *manyu kamip*, a few miles to the north. The floods were better there. People still lived out in the delta and were on ground high enough to be dry the year around.

When I was about seventeen [voice had changed and nose had been pierced] a big flood came one June and all the people had to move out of the delta. Some families from Hawar had to put their possessions on long rafts to escape the flood. No one ever moved back to live in the delta after that. Pozo Vicente became the center of our group and most of the people lived on the edge of the sand hills near there. About ten years later the Colorado River broke through at Yuma and flooded the Imperial Valley.

In some instances, families were forced to live far out in the delta during the summer and fall while working their fields, and then to move to the delta edge until the late spring floods of the following year had subsided. This practice was not, however, as constant as it probably had been in earlier times, since it no doubt depended upon shifts in the position of the river and its main drainage tributaries in the delta. Alarcón (1904: 296) found people scattered in summer houses out in the delta, and was told that after the harvests were in they moved to the mesa edge to escape late winter and spring floods.

The only major shift in the contour of the delta that resulted in the dispersal of an entire group came when my oldest informant, Sam Spa, was a small boy. From his story of the group's history and from incidents in his own life, I have reconstructed the following sequence of events. From about 1860 (and no doubt for a considerable period before that) until 1880, the Kwakwarsh Cocopa occupied good farm land all along the foothills of the Cocopa Mountains from Mayor south to the entrance of Laguna Salada Basin. By about 1880, floods were reaching this area with decreasing frequency and many families had started to move east and north. By 1885 this movement had reached such proportions that the Kwakwarsh Cocopa had ceased to exist as a distinct and localized political group.

Water Control Systems

Some protection against the variability of floods was afforded by the building of systems of dams, levees, and ditches (Castetter and Bell 1951). When I first saw the remains of artificially constructed earth banks, used in recent years as levees, I immediately dismissed them as being inspired by Cocopa experience while working for European farmers. A later and more complete check, however, convinced me that, whatever the source of systems of water control, they were sufficiently old to have been integrated into the social and economic system of the late 19th century. In any event, these systems of water

control bear no close technical resemblance to European irrigation systems. Ditches, dams, and levees had been used when my oldest informants were growing up in the delta, and it was the opinion of both Sam Spa and Jim Short that the Cocopa had "always" used them. These techniques were used most in Mat Skrui territory. The Hwanyak attempted to control the water only on infrequent occasions, and, according to my informants, no such devices were used by the Wi Ahwir group until about 1920 to 1930, when the dams and levees that I saw were built.

The simplest of such structures, used in years when floods were inadequate, consisted of a ditch dug through the naturally high land immediately bordering the major sloughs. On either side of the sloughs the land was usually much lower, and by cutting through the bank, the farmers could flood-irrigate the surrounding fields. According to Sam Spa, the older boys and men of several families cooperated in the work of digging these ditches. During his lifetime they used European shovels for such work, but even so, on one particular job it took ten or eleven men three days and two nights to cut through a slough bank.

The irrigation system most common among the Hwanyak, according to Jim Short, was to build a dam near the source of a major slough in order to direct water onto adjacent land. Along smaller sloughs the water was spread out over the land by building a series of earth dams across the slough. When the rising water had backed up behind the first dam and had spread over the land, this dam was cut and the water permitted to reach the second dam, to spread again from that point.

As a protection against late floods, or to take advantage of the earliest floods without having their fields endangered by later high water, the Cocopa, on rare occasions and in certain favorably located sites, lined the river or slough sides of their fields with high earth levees. Openings in these levees permitted the first flood waters to reach the fields. When the water had stood long enough to saturate the ground, the openings were closed and the fields permitted to dry out. If later floods reached the area, the same levees that previously trapped the water were then utilized to keep the water out. Levees put up for this purpose were visible in 1940 near the extreme western edge of the delta, extending south for about two and one-half miles from a point five miles south of Pozo Vicente (see Fig. 6); one of them enclosed a plot of about 20 acres and was still five feet high. The most recent use of these levees was about 1930, when a number of Wi Ahwir families were farming in the area. The work of building the levees was done during the years when floods were flowing directly against the sand hills on the west side of the delta. The farm was surrounded on three sides by sand hills, and protected from the flood on the other side by the levee.

The most energetic use of artificial irrigation structures during the latter part of the 19th century was undoubtedly

Fig. 10. Abandoned Cocopa farm, located between sand hills on the west side of the delta; note use of dikes to hold Colorado River floodwater.

in the vicinity of a major slough near Pokohap. During the 1890s, the leader of the Mat Skrui Cocopa used the system of diversion from sloughs to ensure a crop for his harvest celebrations. The ditches were called *ha ɫaokwa'k*, the levees *mats ma·in*, and the dams across the sloughs *ha čupit*. Jim Short drew my attention to the fact that the use of Cocopa words was evidence for the ancient use of these devices.

Group Differences

Not all areas of the delta were equally suited to agriculture. During the latter part of the 19th century the Hwanyak had the best farm lands, in terms of both soil and regularity of floods. This land was along both banks of the main stream just above the area influenced by tidal action (see Fig. 6). The next best farming territory, just north of the Hwanyak, was held by the Mat Skrui group. These people also lived along both banks of the main stream and along sloughs running toward the west; flood waters reached their lands with fair regularity. The Wi Ahwir farms were difficult to work, both because of the "heavy" soil so subject to cracking, and because a good deal of grass covered the region and was difficult to control. The least favorable farming area (after 1880) was in Kwakwarsh territory. Farms there were inferior for the above reasons and also because of the high concentration of salt in the soil.

The most favorable spots for planting were on relatively high ground, along the sides of streams and major sloughs. The poorest farm land was in areas where the flood waters tended to stand or move very slowly. The fine silts deposited in such a place formed heavy soil, frequently

subject to cracking. The following summary is from Sam Spa:

> Along the river the water ran fast, caved the banks, and deposited sand. This was good farm land. Watch for a place where the water has been running more than a foot or two high, then when it goes down push a single arrowweed stem into the ground. If the stick goes in easily when the ground is wet that will be a good place to plant. The ground should be a little sandy, but that is not always necessary. Stay away from low, spreading weeds and grass and look for a place where quelite, arrowweed, or willow seedlings come up thick. Sometimes we planted just a little here and there and then we came back and planted more where the corn shoots looked the best.

In non-farming activities, the most important variations occurred in the west, where families were most apt to go into the mountains for agave, pine nuts, and other non-delta products, and in the south, where they were most apt to go into the estuary for wild rice and to the Gulf for clams and salt water fish.

The difference in emphasis on farming appears to have been related directly to the natural conditions, with the best farm land and the most reliable flooding conditions existing along the main stream of the Colorado. It is very probable, however, that there was also a cultural element involved so that, even allowing for the poorer conditions in the west, farming was not pursued by the western Cocopa with the interest and energy found among the eastern Cocopa. It is no doubt significant in this connection that traditionally non-farming Indians from the Baja California mountains were influential in determining the form of subsistence activities in the western sections of the delta.

Land Use

Since land was never leveled for planting, and unfavorable spots and obstructions were avoided, the Cocopa fields were hit-and-miss affairs of all possible shapes. In addition, there were no rows or order in planting. The farmer simply started from any arbitrary spot in a favorable area and continued his planting in all directions until poor land or other interference turned him back. It was more common than not for a farmer to have a series of disconnected fields rather than a single field.

In some instances a rough boundary line existed where two families occupied a favorable area. The lines in such cases were marked by leaving a path between the fields, by piling up brush, or by planting contrasting crops along the dividing line. None of my informants had heard of disputes over boundaries, and arguments over land, as such, made no sense to them. There were certainly no formalized patterns for adjusting such disputes, as are reported for other Yuman tribes.

De Lancey Gill, Bureau of American Ethnology

Fig. 11. Old Cocopa cornfield near Colonia Lerdo in 1900, showing excavations where corn had been planted. The shape of the field has been determined by natural land contours and quality of soil.

It was all but impossible to secure an estimate of the average amount of ground farmed by a family each year. Size varied uniformly with the number of children and adults available for farm work, and it varied from one section of the delta to another and from one year to the next in accordance with existing conditions. There was also, of course, considerable individual variation in initiative and interest in farming. The total land area used by a family with two adults and two or three children of working age probably rarely exceeded three or four acres of ground actually planted. The family average for good years in the areas best suited to farming was probably two acres for all crops. A fairly typical general statement on this was made by Jim Short:

> Some farms were little and grew white beans. Others had watermelons. It depends on the soil and other things. Farms were scattered around; some places where the river went high, there was a big clearing. If the river didn't come up high enough, go plant some other place. If there were a lot of people they cleared and planted a big place. A little family just planted a little spot.

There is some evidence that lack of seed was a limiting factor in the size of farms in some years, but for some reason, although I went back to the subject frequently, I could never formulate a statement that satisfied me. The following is one among four or five similar statements in my notes: "Some people had big farms, some small, because not enough seed." Invariably, however, when the subject of seed supplies was pursued, it was made perfectly

clear that seed was readily shared by friends and kinsmen and that, in a pinch, a man could get enough seed for planting even if he had to make an extended trip, getting a little here and a little there until he had enough. It is more than possible that lack of seed was a favorite rationalization for growing a small crop.

One thing, however, seems fairly certain: there was no great variability between families within any one of the Cocopa groups in per capita land use from year to year; there were no families with small farms and other families farming great tracts of land. The ultimate leveling factor was the Cocopa tradition that no man could command or hire the labor of another man outside his family. No matter how free or plentiful good farming land might be, farm size in the end was controlled by family size.

Crops

The Cocopa of the late 19th century were growing corn, beans, cowpeas, pumpkins, watermelons, and muskmelons almost exclusively. If they had previously grown more than an occasional small crop of wheat or barley, they had given up this practice by the time my informants were living. I made no separate check of these products, relying upon the work of Gifford (1933: 263-7) and of Castetter and Bell (1942, 1951) for identification. The following list and much of the information on each crop is taken from Castetter and Bell.

Corn
1. Flour corn (*hača·s ðhan*). Grown in five colors (yellow, white, blue, red, speckled blue and white). Green corn ripens in about 60 days and the corn matures in 80 to 95 days. Pre-Spanish.
2. Flint corn (*hača·s wɪr*). Only yellow reported. Slower to mature, larger (nine feet), and more resistant to drought. Pre-Spanish.

Tepary Bean (*Phaseolus acutifolius*)
Only one variety (*merik*). Grown in four colors (white, yellow, brown, black), plus various speckled, spotted, and mottled varieties. White and brown most common. Pre-Spanish.

Pumpkins (*Cucurbita moschata*)
1. Common cheese pumpkin (*kwɪra'*). Buff to reddish buff and occasionally dark green. Late maturing. Pre-Spanish.
2. Cushaw (*hamča'*). Large and pear-shaped. Dark green through yellow to striped or netted and mottled green on a cream background. Pre-Spanish.

Pumpkins (*Cucurbita pepo*)
My field notes contain no reference to any other pumpkins than *kwɪra'* and *hamča'*. There are several references to pumpkins being scorched in the flames for peeling, and in one instance I recorded the pumpkin in question as *kwɪra'*. This is the only evidence I have for the presence of *C. pepo* if, as Castetter and Bell say, *C. pepo* was the only pumpkin treated in this way. Either Castetter and Bell may not have known that the

cheese pumpkin was scorched, or the Cocopa did not distinguish linguistically between the cheese pumpkin and *C. pepo*.

Gourds (*Lagenaria siceraria*)
Gourds (*halma*) were grown occasionally and in very small quantities. They were used exclusively for containers and rattles. Pre-Spanish.

Watermelons (*Citrullus vulgaris*)
Watermelons (*kwi·yup*) were grown in several varieties. Post-Spanish.

Muskmelons
Muskmelons were grown in at least two varieties: one quite small and smooth with black seeds, the other larger, about 12 inches in diameter, with lengthwise grooves on a smooth surface. Post-Spanish.

Cowpeas (*Vigna sinensis*)
Cowpeas, or black-eyed beans, were grown in two sizes (*hema patai*, large, and *hema ramas*, small), the smaller averaging about 4 mm in length and the larger about 6 mm. Post-Spanish.

Clearing, Planting, and Harvesting

Preparations for the summer planting started in late April and early May, when the families most interested in farming, and those who would not leave home to gather wild rice, began clearing the fields. On previously planted plots, the trash and weeds were piled and burned or carried away. On a new field the work would be much heavier because of the presence of thicker shrubbery and sometimes growing trees. The usual procedure was to pile the brush for burning; where trees were present, the brush was piled around the green trees to kill them. Some trees, especially mesquite and screwbean, were chopped down, since the Cocopa, after 1850, were well supplied with axes.

Summer was the time for planting, but occasionally high water during the winter months would permit some families to plant a little corn after the middle of January. There was ordinarily not enough moisture to mature these crops, so that they frequently failed unless, as sometimes was the case, an older woman took the trouble to carry water to save some part of the crop. As much as a spring crop was appreciated by these people, my notes indicate that no more than one family in fifteen or twenty ever bothered with this planting even in favorable years.

High water on the Colorado River normally came during the month of June. It was not unusual, however, for the river to rise again in early July; therefore, planting was delayed until about the middle of July, after which (in most years) there would be no new flood crest to wash out the newly planted seed. As soon as the water was low enough, or when the men judged that the chance for a major rise in the river had passed, prepared fields were cleared of flood trash and planting was started. Additional new fields might be cleared at this point, and the planting of these fields was therefore delayed somewhat.

All informants agreed that flour corn was planted first in the higher ground. There was probably no established order for the rest of the planting. Jim Short gave the following order: corn, watermelons, pumpkins, large cowpeas, white teparies, small cowpeas, yellow teparies. Sam Spa gave the following order: corn, teparies, cowpeas, watermelons, cheese pumpkins, muskmelons, cushaw pumpkins. Castetter and Bell (1951: 149–50), referring to the Colorado tribes in general, state that tepary beans were the first crop planted, followed by maize and watermelons.

Men were the farmers, and it was primarily their responsibility to direct the work and to take the lead in the actual labor of clearing, planting, and weeding. No one was exempt from farm work, however, and allowing for the interruptions of other necessary duties, women and older boys and girls spent much of their time helping the men in the fields. Here, as elsewhere, individual interest and surrounding circumstances dictated a great deal of the behavior in actual cases. The most usual pattern during the planting season was for the man to spend a third to a half of his time in hunting and fishing, usually in the morning, and the balance of the time in clearing and planting. The women spent almost every morning and frequently full days gathering mesquite pods. The remainder of their time was divided between cooking, caring for the camp, and helping with the farm work. Older boys could assume the responsibility for hunting and fishing, thus giving the older men more time for planting. Older girls tended to work with their mothers.

Alice Olds: Both the man and his wife work on the farm. The man digs the hole and the woman puts in the seed and covers them. Sometimes there is someone else in camp to go after mesquite beans and go fishing. If the man and his wife have to get their own food they do this in the morning, then they eat, and then they plant together in the afternoon.

Jay Bell: Corn was planted first. . . . During planting time men worked nearly every day, women helped when they could. Younger girls, when full grown, started helping with this work but they don't know how, they don't cover the seed properly. Girls worked in the mornings, sometimes in the evening. Very often the work is held up because the water goes down so slowly. Full-grown boys also help with the planting.

Sam Spa: That whole family worked at planting. When the water went down they found a good place to plant. The husband told them what to do, to work no matter how hot it gets, no matter how bad the flies.

This man had a reputation as a good farmer. He knew how to find good places to plant and he did not have dry spots in his farm the way some people had. Everything was even and the seed came up and matured.

This was a big camp. There were three men and about nine women and older girls. The men were busy farming, hunting, and fishing, and they had the help of the women in farming. When there are so many women this way they do much of the work ordinarily handled by men.

The land was free and a man could plant as much as he wanted to take care of. The chief would tell the people to get their farms ready and to plant lots of corn, beans, and everything. Some years the floods were small so we had to move maybe two, three miles to find a place to plant.

Mike Alvarez: Digging up the ground for planting is man's work, but some women helped, and if a woman had no man she did this work herself. When the man dug up the ground the women and older children followed and put the seed in the ground.

The lack of Cocopa formality and the importance of circumstances and enthusiasms is best shown by the following:

Sam Spa: Sometimes a boy's friends hang around his new camp when he gets married. They eat everything around there. Then when the father-in-law gets ready to plant he calls all these boys to help him and they work four or five days. You can get a big place planted in a hurry this way. The boy's wife stays home to cook and to work around camp while they are planting. If a boy takes a girl to his own home he might not work so hard. Some boys don't work so hard for their own father.

When I started a farm of my own I had three big fields and I worked hard there every day. I never stopped to swat flies or to fight mosquitoes because I knew I would have a good farm. When I was dreaming I walked through a place where people had been defecating. I stepped on some of this and got it on my feet. This was a good sign; it meant that I would have so many watermelons and pumpkins that I would have to leave them in the fields to rot.

In planting, the top crust of ground was broken with a digging stick and then earth scooped out with the fingers. Four to eight kernels of corn (probably depending upon the seed supply) were placed in each hole. Sam Spa described the corn as being planted a pace and a half apart. Jim Short said that corn and beans were planted about two and a half feet apart, and pumpkins and watermelons six feet apart. All seed was planted from four to five inches deep. Beans and pumpkins were kept in separate fields; corn and watermelons could be planted together. Jim Short explained that when the corn ripened, the stalks were removed, and then the watermelons ripened rapidly in the sun.

Underground moisture, remaining in the ground after the flood subsided, matured the crops; no dependence was placed upon rainfall, although some rain might be expected in August and September. If the areas planted were not thoroughly saturated so that a high water table persisted, there would not be enough moisture to make a crop. This latter possibility did not occur to me until it was too late to

make a thorough check; thus it is quite possible that the frequent statements of "no flood that year" or "not enough flood" referred to an inadequate soaking period rather than to an actual failure of the water to reach the fields.

The Cocopa were careful to select good seed for future planting, and they exercised considerable care in the protection of the seed in storage. Special ollas, storage baskets, and gourds were used for different kinds of seed, and these were ordinarily kept inside the house. Sam Spa told me that if the family left their home for an extended trip, such as to gather wild rice, they put the seed in big ollas, covered the top with a tight seal of mixed mud and straw, and placed the ollas in a crevice or shelter in the rocks of the nearby foothills or buried them in a sand hill. This precaution was taken to prevent anyone from eating the seed. Some families, he said, regularly hid their seed in this way rather than keep it in their homes. Jim Short said that other families may have done this, but his family always kept their seed in the house, whether they went away or not. It was believed that if a person ate any of the seed during the winter, the balance of the seed would be stolen by birds and mice *after* it had been planted.

Seed was stored only from one year to the next, except on those occasions when the flood failed and little or no planting was accomplished. In this event, seed was held over for use during the following year. Informants stated that farmers along the main stream yearly stored twice as much seed as would be required so that in the event of a second flood the fields could be replanted. (This is a corollary of the frequently volunteered statement that late floods would sometimes ruin a planted field. No informants ever volunteered that they saved double quantities of seed, and the practice was denied until its necessity was pointed out. Such contradictions place a cloud upon much of the information gained by the interpreter-informant method, and they serve to warn the reader that even the most careful investigator cannot iron out all the doubts and contradictions that accumulate in his field notes.)

Farms were occasionally cultivated, but no hills were formed around growing corn. Men usually took charge of the weeding but were helped by the older children. In most cases, weeds were pulled by hand, although a weeding-hoe was used by those families who could not secure a European hoe. The weeding-hoe differed from the digging stick only in having a widened end; it was frequently short so that the farmers worked in a sitting position. The work was haphazard; only the weeds that were closest to the crops were pulled, and there was no set time or organized responsibility for the work. There was nothing in my informants' manner or words to indicate that a family would take pride in the appearance of its fields or in any elaboration of tools or organization beyond the barest requirements for the securing of a crop. This does not imply that they did not understand and work with the natural laws of agriculture for this region, but simply that they kept their agricultural interests at the instrumental level.

Animals and insects were a constant threat to the crop. Sam Spa and Jim Short agreed that the menace of birds and other animals was constant from the time the seed was put in the ground until the crop was harvested. When the plants first came up they were attacked by birds. Both men and boys went into the fields early in the morning to keep the birds and rabbits out, but ordinarily this was a job for the smaller boys, who shot at them with a bow and arrow. It was almost impossible to keep rabbits out of the fields because they usually came at night. To reduce the threat as much as possible, the men and boys hunted the rabbits near the farm and frequently spread rabbit entrails over the fields in the belief that this would keep other rabbits away.

Coyotes and raccoons also stole from the fields. As the harvest matured, crows were perhaps the most troublesome of all. Boys were sent out with bows and arrows to keep them away. Crops were especially well guarded after the harvest began because, as one informant said, "when the crows saw the people picking the corn they would know it was ripe and would come in flocks." The only scarecrow reported to me was a stuffed hawk hanging on a string from a high pole.

Caterpillars were a nuisance, and these were checked by burning them with arrowweed firebrands. A small green, odorous bug (*kwιsčakιl*) climbed over the plants and ruined the crop unless controlled. In order to restrain this bug, a menstruating woman chewed some of them and spit the chewed bugs over the plants. The chewing made them smell bad and this kept other bugs away. If there were no menstruating women in the farmer's camp at the time, he would call on some neighboring women for help.

Another bug (*nyεhar* [*nohal?*]), no doubt a species of aphid that secreted a sweet substance, injured the watermelons and other plants. Nothing could be done about this bug. Some insect almost wiped out the watermelon crop for four or five consecutive years and then disappeared. There were no stories of the destruction of crops by grasshoppers or locusts.

The first crop to ripen, sometimes as early as the first part of October, was green corn. Green corn was, of course, a great delicacy and was eaten in large quantities, so that it was not unusual for a small crop to be entirely consumed at this stage. Within a month or so after the green corn harvest, the ripe corn was ready. From then on, everyone was busy with the harvest for several weeks. Visitors, especially boys and girls from other camps, according to Sam Spa, were welcome at this time. The older women cooked big meals for them while they worked. Women and girls picked and husked the corn, and the boys and men carried it to camp. During the late summer, the men,

sometimes helped by the women, made or repaired the big bird's-nest storage baskets needed to store the crop.

Harvest time was the season for "tremendous eating," according to Sam Spa. Ordinarily only two meals a day were served in camp, but during harvest season three or four were prepared and people "ate all the time." Sometimes during the harvest season the boys awakened hungry during the night and got up and ate something. When there were plenty of watermelons, Spa said, boys took them to bed and would eat them if they woke up in the night. (Frank Gomez said that Sam Spa did this at the very time I was interviewing him in early August of 1943.)

GATHERING

In order of their importance, the major wild plants harvested for food in the delta were the following:

1. Mesquite and screwbean
2. Wild rice
3. Quelite, or pigweed
4. Panic grass
5. Crowfoot grass
6. Arrowhead
7. Tule, or cattail

Mesquite and Screwbean

The importance of the food gained from the ripened pod of the mesquite tree (*Prosopis juliflora* [Schwartz] D.C.) cannot be overemphasized, especially when it is considered together with the pod of the related screwbean tree (*Prosopis odorata* Torr. & Frem.) (Castetter and Bell 1951: 181). Both plants attained maximum size in this environment, and they occurred in great groves of trees within the overflow plain.

No other plant approached the mesquite in the number of uses made of it by the natives. Branches and roots provided material for a wide variety of manufactured products. The bud was valued as a sweet tidbit in the early spring, and the black sap was used in treating hair, as a paint for pottery and other articles, and as a medicine. The pulp underlying the skin of the mesquite pods (never the bean or seed) provided a juicy food as early as the first week in June, but the main harvest commenced only a few weeks later after the pods had dried out. Screwbean pods matured some weeks later than mesquite. However, mesquite and screwbean pods were not a never-failing food source. One particular time when the mesquite crop was unusually poor stood out in Sam Spa's mind. One spring the mesquite and screwbean trees had just begun to leaf out and flower when high winds and cold weather injured the blossoms, greatly reducing the harvest. That same year the usual flood failed to appear, and it was one of the hardest years that he could remember.

On June 2, 1940, some of the children in a camp on the Hardy River spent several hours scouring the mesquite thickets nearby for ripened mesquite pods. The pods are juicy and sweet when ripe, and the children had no doubt been waiting patiently for them to ripen. They found not more than three double handsful, which they brought back to camp and shared with the adults. In 1935 or 1936 the people at this same camp had gathered a quantity to be stored for winter use. Between 1936 and 1943, so far as I know, none were gathered for this purpose. In 1943, however, because of lack of employment and higher prices for staple foods, a number of families in Sonora were gathering mesquite beans and making mesquite cakes.

Gathering mesquite pods from the trees as soon as they were fully ripe was an important enterprise for women and older girls, since this was the most plentiful food during the planting season. None of the trees were owned, and since they bore great quantities of pods at this time, the women exercised some care in finding the trees with the sweetest and fullest pods. This was determined by breaking the pod and tasting. When harvesting directly from the trees, the women used a long hooked pole to pull down the higher branches. Only enough mesquite was harvested in this way to supply immediate wants, since the crop ripened at a time when all available help was needed for planting.

In late July and August, when the men had finished planting and were busy weeding, the women gathered the main harvest of mesquite for winter storage. By this time most of the pods had dried and fallen to the ground and were fairly easy to secure, but the women took the same care to select pods from the best trees. After the pods were selected and piled for transport, the men frequently helped the women carry them to camp, using blankets or carrying nets. Mesquite gathered in this way could frequently be stored in the bird's-nest baskets immediately, without further drying out. The harvesting of dry pods could continue into early fall, except in those rare years when heavy rains might spoil them.

All informants spoke of robbing rats' nests for mesquite and screwbeans. I cannot be sure from the information at hand, but this was probably done most frequently in bad years and in areas where mesquite and screwbean trees were not so plentiful.

Storage for winter and spring use was always in large bird's-nest baskets, usually on a specially built platform five or six feet above the ground. Only beans that were thoroughly dry were put in storage. The pods were packed as tightly as possible and broken into small pieces in the process, since people would stand in the baskets and tramp with their feet. The tight packing was supposed to help keep the bugs out.

Since screwbeans ripen later than mesquite, they were never harvested until August, when the planting season was well over. Although gathered in great quantities where the trees grew thickly, screwbeans were not so popular as mesquite pods because they were not so sweet, and they also required special preparation before they could be eaten. Harvest methods were the same as for mesquite, except that screwbeans were almost always harvested from the ground because by that time plenty of mesquite pods were available. A special ripening process was required to bring out their full sweetness. Most commonly a large pit was dug, usually about five feet wide and four feet deep, lined with arrowweed. The screwbeans were packed into this hole and the top was covered with branches, arrowweed, and then dirt. Within six weeks or a little more the pods, originally yellow, would begin to turn dark brown and were then ready to dry and store. Usually, however, the family simply used the pit for storage and would not take the pods out until spring when the food was needed. The ripening process could be hastened by building a fire in the bottom of the hole to heat it before lining it with arrowweed. As the beans were being packed, they were frequently sprinkled with water, then covered with brush and earth, and a fire built on top. Just how much this practice hastened the process is not clear in my notes, but the time was probably about three weeks.

To extract mesquite pulp (the seed was never used), the pods were ground in a mortar. Some of the heavy fiber and seeds were removed while grinding and the remainder by shaking the ground meal in a basket so as to separate the larger pieces. Grinding the pods of both mesquite and screwbean was usually women's work, but, as must always be said, the men frequently helped. After grinding, the fine meal could be made into a drink by mixing with water, eaten in meal form and washed down with water, or formed into a cake for storage.

Mesquite and screwbean meal was never cooked, but sometimes a few mesquite pods were placed in a pot of cooking squash in order to add flavor. Sam Spa said that it was a Maricopa practice, adopted by some Cocopa, to cook corn meal in mesquite-sweetened water.

To make the mesquite meal into a cake it was built, handful by handful, while being sprinkled with water. The whole was then shaped in the hands and covered with dry meal to keep it moist overnight. A modern method is to place the meal in a cloth and shape it by tying the cloth, which also acts to retain the moisture. In either case the cake is allowed to dry if it is intended for storage. A mesquite cake collected in the field was made in this modern way and was 20 cm in diameter, 10 cm thick, and weighed just under 3 pounds when thoroughly dry. My information on mesquite cake size is from a single informant, who told me that in former times the cakes were about twice the size of the one I collected. The cake is at Peabody Museum, Cambridge, and I warn against eating it since I frequently sprayed it with Flit to protect it from insects.

The mesquite meal cakes were prepared for convenience in storage and for transportation, and pieces were then broken off and used the same as loose meal. According to Sam Spa, cake meal was sweeter than freshly ground pods. Cakes were made only four or five at a time, except in preparation for an extended trip, when as many as ten were made.

Screwbean meal was never made into cakes. The pulp behaved differently in grinding so that it did not "stick together" as did the mesquite pulp. This peculiarity, however, saved winnowing and preparation time since the pods, when ground, could be placed in a pan of water and the strings and seeds dipped out when they floated to the surface.

Mesquite and screwbeans were frequently the only food supplies stored through the winter by non-farming families. According to Sam Spa:

> When we had no farm we would leave stores of mesquite and screwbeans in big baskets on platforms in camp and then spend the rest of the winter moving around the delta gathering, hunting, and fishing. At these times we would carry quelite and other wild seeds with us and two or three families would travel together. When the leaves came out all the wild plants would be gone and fishing would be very poor, then we moved back to camp and lived off our mesquite and screwbean stores until time to leave for the wild rice fields.

Mesquite meal was not a favorite food, but neither was it disliked, and during certain periods of the year it provided the only bulky food available. When other foods were short and the major dependence was upon mesquite and screwbean, members of the camp would drink the sweetened liquid and eat the meal all through the day, whenever they felt hungry. Question asked Alice Olds: "Do you get hungry eating nothing but mesquite?" Answer: "No, you feel filled as though you had eaten a lot of stuff. Eat the pulp [meal] too, to fill the stomach. Do this all day long to keep your stomach full." Question: "How many days did you eat mesquite beans and nothing else?" Answer: "For a month, with a little fish. This is in the month when they start planting." With due allowance for a European stomach, my experience with mesquite meal would class it with marshmallows as a steady diet.

The mesquite flower was also used as food, mostly as a sweet tidbit, but often as a welcome addition to the food supply in the perennially hungry weeks of April and May. Women and girls would sample flowers for their sweetness and throw the acceptable ones into a pan or bowl of water. The flowers would then be mashed gently and the sweetened liquid consumed. After two or three such baths, the smashed flowers would be sucked directly to remove the last bit of sweet. (For more detailed information on the use of mesquite and screwbean, see Bell and Castetter 1937, and Castetter and Bell 1951: 179–86.)

Although some Mexican Cocopa still eat mesquite and screwbeans, their greatest importance in recent years has consisted in their use as animal food. A few head of cattle owned by Indians north of Mayor in 1940 lived almost exclusively upon mesquite beans and mesquite leaves. Riding horses in all camps were staked out in the mesquite groves. The head of a camp in Sonora was harvesting mesquite beans in August, 1941, to feed two hogs.

Wild Rice (*Uniola palmeri* Vasey)

The wild rice (*nyιpa*) harvest required an annual expedition to the mouth of the river; this usually consumed five weeks' time, from about the end of April to the first part of June, not counting the trip to and from the field. The importance of wild rice to the Cocopa cannot be overemphasized. The grain makes a good food and it was much enjoyed, but more important, it was the first sizable wild food crop, coming much earlier than mesquite, and was obtainable in sufficient quantities to help tide the families over the most critical food period of the year. In addition, the nature of the harvest was such as to bring large groups of families together with ample food and time for visiting, dancing, and courting.

Palmer, who visited the area in 1870, 1885, and 1889 (when the type specimens were collected), supplied the most complete information on the plant from the European point of view. His information was contained in a letter which, together with botanical information, was published by George Vasey (1889; referred to in Castetter and Bell 1951):

> In 1885 Dr. Edward Palmer collected, near the mouth of the Colorado River, some specimens of a grass from which he said the Cocopa Indians obtained the seeds in large quantities and used them as food. At the time he was there the grass was out of flower; he found only a few disconnected spikelets, and the botanical characters could not well be determined. In April of the present year Dr. Palmer, being employed by the Department of Agriculture to make botanical investigations, made another visit to the locality and obtained in that region specimens in good condition, enabling me to locate the plant botanically. As the genus Uniola is defined by Bentham and Hooker, our grass must be considered as of that genus. Its general appearance and habit is that of Distichlis, from which it differs in having four of the lower glumes (instead of two only) in each spikelet empty, i.e. without palet or flower, and in the disarticulation of the rhachis between the spikelets of both sexes — that is, the spikelets break apart between the several flowers when mature. This disarticulation occurs also to some extent in the fertile spikes of Distichlis, but not in the male or infertile ones. On the other hand it differs from Uniola in its dioecious character and here agrees with Distichlis. It seems, in fact, to connect these two genera, but so long as the two are kept distinct it must stand as Uniola. Specifically it is new, and I have given it the name of *U. Palmeri*.

The following notes I collect from Dr. Palmer's letter:

The specimens were collected at the Horseshoe Bend of the Colorado River 35 miles south of Lerdo by the river, and twelve to fifteen miles from its mouth. This is the most extensive locality of the grass, thence extending down to the mouth of the river. It covers a space of from one to twenty miles wide, and occurs on both sides of the river. It is estimated that there are from forty to fifty thousand acres covered with this grass. It grows from two to four feet high, from strong, deep root-stocks, frequently many culms from the same root. The stems are covered to the top with the sharp, stiff leaves. The sterile plant grows more or less mixed with the other, but at times in masses entirely by itself. Dr. Palmer noticed several forms. One of these is more slender, with the leaves shorter, more numerous and more finely pointed. This, he says, grows on land that has but little overflow. Where, by changes in the river, any patches are left above tide-water, they soon die.

The Indians come together here at the proper season, in April, and gather this, to them, important food. As its quantity depends upon the overflow of the tides, and the tides are sure to occur, they have an assured crop without any other labor than gathering and caring for the grain. The gatherers enter the fields as soon as the tides have entirely run off, where the soil is an adhesive clay so soft that the Indians often sink nearly to their knees in gathering the grass, and as soon as the tide begins to flow they return with the result of their labor to their camps. It is quite difficult to pull up the plant by the roots, as these are often two to four feet long, but the stems are brittle and easily break off above the root. The Indians in harvesting use any old knife, or, if they have none they take a flat piece of wood and form an edge on each side and with this they sever the stems, the left hand grasping the tops, which are then thrown into a basket. The rigid spiny-pointed leaves make the process a painful one. The grain has to be cut when a little green, because of the easy separation of the spikelets. In order to dry the heads as quickly as possible, large fires are made, and the heads are piled around so that the flames penetrate between them. When they have been sufficiently exposed to the fire a stick is used to thrash the heads, which breaks up the spikelets, but does not separate the chaff or glumes from the grain. The dried and dissevered spikelets are then taken to a piece of ground prepared for the purpose and the Indians tread upon and rub the grain between their feet until the seeds are shelled out.

This process is more easily accomplished after the grain has been exposed a while to the sun, but in any case it is pretty trying to the feet because of the sharp, stiff points of the chaff. The action of the tide knocks off and carries away considerable of the grain, but this is left in rows at the edge of the contiguous dry land, and the Indians gather much of it and rub it out. They have to be expeditious in their harvest, as wind storms are liable to arise and destroy or injure the product of their labors.

Dr. Palmer was accompanied on his trip by two gentlemen connected with the United States Fish Commission, who took photographs of the grain-field, and of the thrashing and treading out of the seed from the chaff.

It is not yet ascertained how far up the river this grass extends, but probably to the limit of tide-water, and in this case it will yet be found within our boundaries. The related *Distichlis maritima* grows not only on the sea coast, but in nearly all saline and alkaline grounds in the interior of the country, but we cannot infer from that fact that this species might be cultivated outside of the reach of the tides.

According to my informants, women did all the harvesting and winnowing of the grain, while men did the burning and thrashing. Sam Spa described the burning and thrashing as "hard, hot, and dirty." No mention was made of the pain suffered in cutting the grass stems and no one mentioned the treading operation to remove the chaff. Grain removed from the green stems involved a great deal of labor, but it provided a harvest at least two weeks earlier than otherwise, and the "green" grains were also said to have been sweeter. Eight to ten days were spent in harvesting, thrashing, and winnowing the green crop. During the next two weeks or so, no grain was harvested; the people waited until the grain matured sufficiently to be knocked directly from the spikelets in the field. The two-week period was spent in games, dancing, songs, and idleness, interrupted only by occasional hunting and fishing expeditions by the men who desired some meat to supplement the grain diet.

The next harvest period lasted about seven to ten days, during which time the women went out each morning to knock the dried seeds into a basket with a seed beater (the seeds would not fall later in the day when the plants dried out). The harvest gained in this way was brought into camp, spread out to dry, and thrashed with sticks. In the meantime, much grain had fallen into the water from the plants and been washed to shore. The final period of harvesting was devoted to gathering this grain in great quantities — not a difficult task, for some of the naturally formed piles were as much as a foot or more high, according to Sam Spa. This water-washed grain was not considered to be so good but was nevertheless taken because it supplied by far the larger quantity to be transported home.

During the time of the harvest, families lived on nearby sand hills in rudely constructed houses made entirely from driftwood. Water was available twice each day when the tides backed fresh water up the sloughs. Men and older boys carried the water, which was frequently as much as two miles from camp, and did much of the cooking. This division of labor was probably a carry-over from the day when camps were subject to attack by enemies and the men always stayed on the exposed side of the gathering areas.

In most years the return home was into a country much changed by the onset of the summer flood. During the lifetime of my informants, the rice harvest was packed in cloth sacks and blankets, and then transported part way by land, the men making multiple trips to carry the great quantities of grain, and part way — wherever feasible — by water, on rafts that were poled or pulled by willow bark ropes. By this time, the mesquite beans had begun to ripen, and it was the height of the season for birds' eggs, so many stops were made to gather these products. Families living near the northern limit of Cocopa territory frequently consumed two weeks on this trip, arriving home just before time to plant.

Wild rice was cooked and used in much the same fashion as other wild seeds. Unparched grains were ground on the metate and then made into a mush, frequently with tule pollen added for sweetening. The grains were also mixed with fish or other meat to make a sort of stew. Flour was made into cakes and cooked over hot coals. Meal from parched seeds was used in this same way or eaten with no further preparation.

Quelite (Pigweed)

In terms of quantity of harvest, quelite (*koa·p*) was perhaps the next most important wild food plant after wild rice, and may even have been harvested in greater quantities. Quelite (*Ameranthus palmeri*, S. Wats., *A. caudatus* L.) (I. J. Johnson: personal communication) is a fast-growing annual weed that springs up in great fields immediately after the floodwaters have subsided. When it is 8 to 12 inches high, the Cocopa, as in former years, gather it and cook it as greens. This is called *hǝpši*. When the plant reaches its full growth and turns brown, the branches are covered with small thorn pods containing black seeds. The importance of quelite as a food plant is indicated by its constant mention by my informants. Whenever they were asked about any phase of wild food gathering, they would almost always mention this plant and the arrowhead tuber, *čeł*.

There always seems to have been an adequate supply of quelite, even during years of poor floods. However, it must be noted that this plant was as dependent upon flood irrigation as were the domesticated plants. When floods failed, the supply was cut down in total quantity, though this might not have made a difference to the reduced population of the late 19th century.

The following material on quelite gathering will provide a good description of seed-gathering activities in general, since my notes on quelite (obtained from five informants) are the most complete. Quelite matured at about the same time as the domesticated plants but usually was not harvested until after the corn and bean crops were taken care of. The work was done by women who went in groups, carrying their babies with them, but leaving younger children at home in the charge of older girls or some elderly relative. Occasionally whole families would move to a good harvesting area and camp for a week while the harvest was in progress. Two methods were used in harvesting. Either

the seed heads were broken off and carried in a basket or in the crook of one arm to a collecting and threshing area, or the plant was pulled down over a basket and the seed pods rubbed off the branch between the hands. In either case some threshing, or at least cleaning of sticks and debris, was done in the field.

On being brought into camp, the harvest was piled against the outside house wall and, if in sufficient quantities for storing, was covered with arrowweed or willow branches. Sam Spa described a big harvest of unthreshed quelite as being a pile about five feet high. Threshed and winnowed quelite seeds were stored in fired or mud-and-straw ollas in the house, but these were rarely filled since the piles of unthreshed seed would keep very well and families worked the seed out of these piles as needed.

Quelite pods were usually threshed first by being beaten with a stick and then threshed again in a mortar and pestle (any one of the three types of Cocopa mortars being used); sometimes the pods were given only the latter threshing. After the seeds had been separated in this way, they were winnowed by being poured onto a blanket from a pottery pan or shallow basket or, on occasion, by being shaken and blown in a pottery pan. All this was women's work.

Preparation of seed for eating was always just prior to the meal in question and, according to Sam Spa, if it was eaten three times a day it would be prepared three times a day. Seed was ground with a metate and mano either in its natural state or after having been parched in a pottery pan. The parched flour could be eaten without further preparation. Mush made from parched seed was not usually mixed with other grains. Raw quelite flour was made into a mush by pouring it, little by little, into an olla of boiling water while constantly stirring to prevent it from lumping. Only salt was added. A similar mush was often made of a mixture of corn, bean, and quelite flour. The mush was done, and sufficiently thick, when it came off the stirring sticks in a certain way. A fish and quelite stew was made by first cooking the fish, removing the head and bones, and then pouring in quelite flour in the above fashion. Raw quelite flour was also mixed with water, formed into a cake, and baked in hot ashes. Such cakes were one to two inches thick and seven to ten inches in diameter. Quelite flour was never made into tortillas. (As when speaking of other dishes, informants seldom failed to add that when the mush or fish stew was ready, small pans of the food were sent to near neighbors.)

Quelite greens were ready to eat during planting time and so formed an important addition to the diet during this period of short food supplies. The gathering and preparation was work for older girls, one of their few consistent subsistence responsibilities, and an enterprise to be conducted in groups. Plants from 8 to 12 inches high were preferred and were cooked in two different ways. The most common method was to lay a thick mat of quelite leaves over a bed of hot coals, smash the leaves down, and pack them with the feet. The leaves were covered with green quelite plants, then with dry weeds and branches that were set on fire. After an hour or so (one informant said two or three hours), the cake was removed from the coals, the burned parts and ashes were removed, and the cake was cut into chunks for division among the girls and their families. The other method was to boil the leaves in water. After being boiled for about 30 minutes, the whole was poured into a basket to drain off the water. The leaves were then eaten with no further preparation except the addition of salt, if desired. Surplus greens cooked in this way were squeezed into round balls and stored for eating at a later meal, but the balls were not good to eat if they dried out.

Cultivated Grass Seeds

During the lifetime of my informants the Cocopa planted and harvested two wild grass seeds. The more important of these in terms of quantity was shimcha (šɪmča), a panic grass, and the other was kacha (kəča), crowfoot grass. The fact that Colorado River Indians cultivated wild grass seeds had been known to investigators in this area since at least 1870, but botanical identification had not been satisfactorily resolved. My own efforts in this direction follow.

The United States National Museum provided me with samples of a number of types of wild grass seeds that had been collected by W J McGee during his field trip to the Cocopa country in 1901. One of these (National Museum No. 209,823) was readily identified by all eight informants to whom it was shown as kacha. I later sent some of my kacha seeds to Edward F. Castetter of the University of New Mexico, who published his findings as follows:

> kəča. One of our Cocopa informants, Jim Barley, on several occasions described a plant under this name, formerly semicultivated by his people, but we were never able to locate any specimen among the Cocopa. Fortunately, Kelly secured . . . a specimen. Paul Russell, of the Bureau of Plant Exploration and Introduction, U.S.D.A., has identified this specimen as crowfoot grass (*Dactyloctenium aegypticum* (L). Richt.), and this identification was later confirmed by Richard W. Pohl and Dale West. In this connection it is interesting to note that there is in the Iowa State College herbarium a specimen of this grass collected by Dr. Edward Palmer at Yuma, Arizona, in 1881, showing that this tropical weed, introduced from the Old World, was already on the lower Colorado by that date. This is a decumbent, spreading annual grass, growing about a foot tall and bearing reddish-brown seeds. [Castetter and Bell 1951: 171-2]

The identification of kacha, an Old World plant, is thus resolved.

The identification of the National Museum specimen No. 209,822, which was recognized by all my informants as

shimcha, has not been so easy. It was identified by the Bureau of Plant Industry, Washington, D.C., as probably Panic grass, *Panicum stramineum* Hitchc. & Chase (letter from E. F. Castetter, May 24, 1947). It was later identified by Miss Lute of the Colorado Agricultural College as *Panicum mileaceum* (letter from E. F. Castetter, October 8, 1948); still later it was identified by Richard W. Pohl and Dale West of the Herbarium and Seed Laboratory, Iowa State College, and by J. R. Swallen of the Division of Plant Exploration and Introduction, U.S.D.A., as probably *Panicum hirticaule* Presl, with *Panicum stramineum* Hitchc. & Chase as a remote possibility (Castetter and Bell 1951: 169). All are New World plants excepting *P. mileaceum*.

A sample of semicultivated seed collected by Castetter and Bell from their Yuma informant, who gave it the Yuma name *aksam*, was identified by the same experts and in the same way as my National Museum specimen of shimcha. It is significant that when my informants identified the National Museum seeds as shimcha, they told me that the Yuma called it kšəm.

The seed identified by my informants as shimcha is certainly a New World panic grass. Castetter and Bell (1951: 170) sum up the evidence as follows:

> *P. hirticaule* Presl and *P. stramineum* Hitchc. and Chase are closely related. Both are native to the New World, and to the lower Colorado Valley. The first species is reported as growing on rocky or sandy soil in dry open ground or waste places in the Southwest, the second on rich bottom lands and moist sandy plains of southern Arizona and northwest Mexico.
>
> While there is an element of uncertainty in the identification of this grass which was semicultivated by the Cocopa and Yuma, it appears clear that we are very near to an exact determination in view of the close similarity in habit of growth and in seed structure of *P. hirticaule* and *P. stramineum*. It would seem that *P. stramineum* could be eliminated as a possibility in view of the agreement of two seed laboratories on the high probability of both seed specimens mentioned above being *P. hirticaule* and the tentative identification of one of the specimens as *P. stramineum* by the third laboratory. In any event, the species utilized is native to the lower Colorado Valley.

In the field there was no reason to suspect that my Cocopa informants might also have identified *Panicum sonorum* Beal as shimcha had I shown them specimens of this latter grass. Yet this remains a possibility in light of investigations of Castetter and Bell. They have the following to say:

> Evidently a second species semicultivated by the Cocopa, at least, was *P. sonorum* Beal. On a herbarium specimen of *P. sonorum* in the U.S. National Museum, collected by Palmer in 1885, there is a note which reads: "Seeds largely used as food by the Cocopas."

Panicum sonorum is also possibly the species which Palmer identified in 1870, and which he reported as sometimes planted, also as gathered wild by the Indians on the Colorado. He observed that when the water had laid bare the river banks in June, they scattered the seed of panic grass over the moist ground by blowing it from their mouths. The Indians harvested the seed with much care, winnowed and stored it for winter use; when utilized it was ground, mixed with water, and the mass kneaded into hard cakes which, when dried in the sun, were ready to eat. Gruel and mush were also made of the flour. These statements are probably the basis of the reference by Hitchcock and Chase: "Palmer states that it is used by the Cocopa Indians, the seed being sown in spring on wet ground". Swallen informs us also that on a more recent specimen of *P. sonorum* collected by Howard Scott Gentry in Chihuahua, there is the following note: "Cultivated by the Warihios for its seed which they grind into a pinole for eating." Moreover, Gentry himself has described this species as occurring in barrancas and foothills in Sonora and Chihuahua. He points out that this is one of the indigenous plants cultivated by the Warihio Indians, who planted it among their maize. The seeds were ground into flour. Seasoned with a little salt and sugar, they made an excellent pinole; mixed with milk, a palatable, nourishing drink. [Castetter and Bell 1951: 170-1]

Panic grass was planted by the Cocopa in the sandy mud flats along the main channel where the flood had caved the river banks and carried away all vegetation. One such area was described by Sam Spa as being five miles long and up to 500 yards wide, planted in five plots by five different men. Every effort was made to plant the seed as soon as the water stopped running; the planters always waded in deep mud and water, and frequently carried a pole under one arm for support in bad spots. Seed was carried in a gourd hung with a strap around the neck and planting was done by blowing the seed from the mouth, preferably on a windy day. Spa described some fields as being so large as to require six days for one man to plant; the work, of course, was very slow in the deep mud. Once a field was planted, no further attention was given it until harvest time. No grasses were planted in the delta beyond the main channel, and Spa estimated that only one family in five living near the river bothered with this crop.

Panic grass could be planted in any suitable spot, and the river frequently created these areas naturally, but to insure the creation of a good field the Cocopa believed that magic could be employed to force the flood to cave the river banks. This was the only use of magic reported for any planting activity. It involved the use of badger (*nyɩmhwa*) claws, which were buried near the river bank in the belief that the stream would copy the digging action of the animal. Both Sam Spa and Jim Short denied that magic was used to ensure a good crop, as was reported by Gifford (1933: 267).

Few men knew how to use the badger claws, and this reason was offered to explain why so few families bothered to plant this wild grass. To become ritually pure for the task of killing a badger and planting its claws, a man fasted and abstained from sexual intercourse for four days. During this period the man also bathed and washed his hair each morning and then spent the balance of the day sitting quietly in camp, avoiding any women that might be menstruating.

On the evening of the fourth day, having already located a badger hole, he would go out to secure its claws. The badger was dug out of its hole or chased on foot and killed with a club; no other weapon was used. Two claws from one front foot (Sam Spa did not know which one) and one claw from the other were cut away, and the badger was then discarded. The next morning the three claws were deposited in a hole in the river bank on the side that was expected to cave. With the onset of the flood and once this bank started caving, the claws were moved farther and farther away as needed. According to Sam Spa, it was not necessary to be a shaman or to dream for the power. (This was one of the rare explicit denials of the necessity of dreaming to acquire ability or power.) Only knowledge was required, and this was gained from an older relative, usually a father.

Arrowhead (Wild "Onion")

The wild "onion," known to the Cocopa as *čeɬ*, was identified as *Sagittaria latifolia* Willd. by Edward Castetter (personal communication), from a specimen I sent to him. The plant is a bulbous-rooted, not very tasty food that apparently grew in large quantities through the delta. It matured in midsummer and served as a "famine" food during the period when weed and grass seeds and agricultural products were maturing. The plant was dug with a stick, and this was considered hard work, so most of it was harvested by men. It was baked in coals, the skin rubbed off, and eaten whole or mashed. It could not be stored, according to Sam Spa, and so was never gathered in large quantities.

Strangely enough, the wild "onion" was the only food ever mentioned as being put up for stakes in a gambling game. One day I was asking Sam Spa about fights that might have taken place between men. One of his answers follows: "Near where we went to get *čeɬ* there lived a lot of people. One man lost some *čeɬ* in a gambling game and they got mad over it and fought." *Question*: "What was the game?" *Answer*: "The hoop and pole game." *Q.*: "What other food was used in gambling?" *A.*: "Nothing else." *Q.*: "You never gambled for corn, or watermelons, or pine nuts?" *A.*: "No, nothing else but *čeɬ*."

This is difficult to explain. It may be that since *čeɬ* was plentiful in season and could not be stored, the stakes did not involve family food supplies but merely the labor involved in digging the plant. Stored food wouldn't have made sense as a stake in gambling, since patterns for sharing food would have made a large supply won in gambling pointless.

Tule (Cattail)

The last of the important wild plant foods was tule, or cattail (*Typha latifolia* L., *T. angustifolia* L.) (Castetter and Bell 1951: 207). The roots of this plant supplied a never-failing, though relatively unpopular, source of food. The root, especially when it grew in dry ground, was gathered, dried in the sun, and worked on a metate to get out the dry powdery pulp. It was then boiled in water to make a mush, which was described as tasting like flour. (It is possible that my informant is hefe referring to cane, *Phragmites*, and not tule, *Typha*). Young plants growing in water were pulled and the root was eaten raw "like green onion." The pollen heads were harvested in large quantities and brought back to camp to dry before the yellow pollen powder was extracted. Both Jim Short and Sam Spa agreed that gathering and extracting the pollen was a tedious job, considering the amount secured. Short said that after the pollen heads were dry, they were held over a pottery dish; the pollen was knocked into the dish by striking the head against the rim. Spa said that the pollen was knocked into the container by striking it with a stick. Pollen thus extracted was highly prized and was used to add a sweet flavor to many dishes, most commonly mixed with corn in making mush. Pollen was also placed in a hollow pumpkin stem and baked for about ten minutes in coals. The result was described as being "just like candy."

Pollen was still gathered in large quantities during our fieldwork, especially around Somerton, but was no longer used as a food. It was considered a particularly potent medicine and was used in a curing ceremony sponsored by a Yavapai religious leader who made frequent visits to the Cocopa community. Pinches of pollen were placed in the patient's mouth and rubbed on the body. Its use as a medicine in former times, however, was denied by Sam Spa.

Other Delta Food Plants

In addition to those already mentioned, there was an extensive variety of less important seeds and wild plants gathered and used. Among the wild grass seeds used during the 19th century were some that have been identified as having been introduced from the Old World. Following is a list of some of these plants, with their Cocopa names. The plants were gathered from uncultivated fields and along irrigation ditches between Somerton, Arizona, and the present Colorado River channel, and they were identified by I. J. Johnston, Gray Herbarium, Harvard University:

nyɪkɪɫ: *Echinochloa colonum* (L) Link.
nyɪkašri: *Echinochloa crusgalli* (L) Beauv.
koarš: *Echinochloa cursgalli* Var. Mitis Peterman.
kwarao: *Cyperus esculentus* L.
kɪš: *Rumex crispus* L.

pa?ai: *Atriplex lentiform* Wats.
kwakoɫ: *Erichloa aristata* Vasey.
košom: *Eragrostis Mexicana* Link.

Rumex (*kɪš*) was perhaps next in importance to wild rice as an early spring source of food. The seed matured during the early part of May, and the plant was fairly common in the delta. To prepare it for eating, the seed was pounded in a mortar to remove the skin and then placed in a bag. Water was poured through the bag three or four times to remove the bitter taste, and the mass was then wet-ground on a metate and made into tortillas or boiled into a mush.

Seeds of *pa?ai* were available even earlier in the season, but the Cocopa did not care too much for *pa?ai* as a food. The seeds were beaten off the plant into a basket with a stick and were then winnowed. To prepare these seeds for eating, a small hole was dug and lined with hot coals. The seeds were poured on top of these coals and covered with another bed of coals, and then everything was covered with dirt and allowed to cook for about three hours. When removed, the seeds were ground on a metate and eaten dry, or boiled in water to make a mush.

Erichloa (*kwakoɫ*) and a wide variety of other wild seeds were gathered in small quantities. They were usually parched before grinding, and the flour was eaten either dry or cooked into a mush.

A plant identified as sandroot (*Ammobroma sonorae* Torr.) by Castetter and Bell was never mentioned by my informants.

[Castetter and Bell's] Cocopa informants described a plant known to them as *oyðt* which grew in the sandhills. The roots ranged in size from the thickness of a finger to that of the wrist. They were baked in hot ashes and eaten after stripping off the thin bark. Also, the baked roots sometimes were dried, then later boiled and eaten. If our guess that this is the parasitic sandroot be correct, it was the long succulent underground stems, rather than the roots, which were eaten. This plant is found in southeastern Arizona, northwestern Sonora, and in southwestern Arizona, being common in southern Yuma County along the Mexican border. It is interesting to note that Havard, in 1895, wrote that the Cocopa and Yuma eagerly sought the sandroot as a source of food. [Castetter and Bell 1951: 208-9]

Desert and Mountain Food Plants

The desert to the east, within Cocopa range, is barren of food plants. It is too dry even for the prickly pear and the cholla cactus, and well below the elevation for agave. A few palo verde and palo fiero trees are found, but not enough to be of any importance. To the west, however, in the washes coming down from the Cocopa Mountains, these latter two trees are fairly common, and their pods were gathered in considerable quantity by the western Cocopa. Only the seeds of these plants were used (not the pod itself, as in the case of mesquite). The seeds were roasted with coals in a pottery tray, ground on a metate, and made into mush.

Cactus fruit and agave were gathered in the foothills of the Juarez Mountains and may also have been gathered from the higher slopes of the Cocopa Mountains.

I have no information on the use of cactus plants as food, although these plants were unquestionably important to the western Cocopa, who made occasional food-gathering and visiting trips into Baja California. All informants considered the agave the most important desert plant food. Sam Spa said that some Cocopa who "knew how" would gather and cook the agave plant on their way to the Juarez Mountains to gather pine nuts. However, most of these foods that were eaten by the Cocopa were brought to the valley by Paipai and Diegueño men to trade for agricultural products. Sam Spa had seen agave prepared in a large pit on a number of occasions. Hot stones were put around and above the central stalk, the whole was covered with dirt, and a fire was built over the top. If the plants were large, they were left in the pit for three days. For trading purposes or for storage, the large stalks were pounded in a mortar and made into a cake much like mesquite cake. The young plants could be shaped without pounding.

The annual trip for the pine nut harvest seems to have been an established routine for the western Cocopa and their River Paipai neighbors. Jim Short and other Hwanyak informants said that the Cocopa from the eastern side of the delta never went on these trips. Both Mike Alvarez and Sam Spa went to the Juarez Mountains several times when they were boys to gather pine nuts, and my information is taken from them. According to Alvarez, the trip required three days or more of travel with women and older children along, but it was sometimes extended by camping for a number of days at a place called *wi puk* in the Juarez foothills. Here the party gathered agave, wild dates, and wild honey for a big feast. These same foods would also be sought on gathering trips made at other times of the year when food was scarce in the valley. Frequently, too, a man alone or with some members of his family would take the trip into the mountains for a visit or to secure help and supplies for a mourning ceremony: horses, eagle feathers, tobacco, medicines, and minerals for paint.

To go to the mountains from Wi Ahwir territory, Alvarez said, the party traveled through the Cocopa Mountains at a pass called *yamečus wanya*, crossed the Laguna Salada Basin (*ha wi mɘk* — water on the other side of the mountain), and passed through the sand hills to a water hole called *haspai hamɘoł*. From there, the trail led into the foothills to *wi puk* and then on up the face of the escarpment to the pine country. This place was called *wi kwɪs ček kwɪska'rɘ* (place where two high rock peaks cast two shadows). The area was uninhabited, but it was also visited by Diegueño Indians who lived in the vicinity. They

were friends of the Cocopa and were reported as being glad to visit and trade with the river people. No tribe or group was considered to be the owner of the groves, and anyone was free to take part in the gathering. People of the two tribes who carried the same lineage names were apt to seek each other out and camp together. The Cocopa stayed in the mountains and ate pine nuts until they were tired of them, and then started home carrying as much as they could in bags woven from the broad leaf of a mountain plant. These bags were usually hung in trees about a day's march from home, and the people went back for them later.

The Cocopa who lived below Mayor, according to Alvarez, made the mountain trip in company with River Paipai. They took a more southerly route and reached the mountains in Paipai territory (see Fig. 5).

MacDougal (1907; quoted by Kniffen 1931: 53), who investigated these mountain trails, reports that the more northerly trail mentioned above descended the western slope of the Cocopa Mountains to a perennial spring, Agua de las Mujeres. It then struck across the plain to the mouth of Palomar Canyon, at the base of the Juarez Mountains. Another trail, he says, led around the southern point of the Cocopa Mountains. From Pozo Coyote (at the entrance to Laguna Salada Basin) the trail forked, one branch going to Pozo Cenizo (due west on the other side of Laguna Salada Basin), another to the south through Tres Pozos and Arroyo Grande to the mountains. Water holes on these trails are surrounded by broken pottery, charred wood, and other artifacts.

The difficulty of this journey is witnessed by the experience of the Pattie party, which crossed from the Colorado River to the mission at Santa Catarina in 1828. They traveled with Indian guides from one of the water holes near Laguna Salada Basin (sometimes called Pattie Basin, as a result of his account) and did not reach water again until they came to the foothills of the Sierra Juarez at the end of the second day. Pattie's father and one other man became so exhausted from traveling through the sand, and from thirst, that they were left behind and were only able to resume the trip when Pattie and another man returned to them with water (Pattie 1905: 210-20).

Kniffen's (1931: 53-4) informant told him that the Indians did not carry water with them for this trip, but trusted to a quick passage. He also states that when a small group was leaving, friends accompanied them to Pozo Coyote and remained there until signal smoke informed them of the party's safe arrival at the next water. (Alvarez agreed that this latter precaution was necessary, but I am none too sure that he understood my question.)

The hazards of the journey are also revealed in the following incident told by Sam Spa. His sister had gone to the mountains with her Paipai husband, his father, an old woman relative of her husband's, and her two-year-old baby. Her husband was sick and was being taken to a Kiliwa doctor for treatment. The party stayed in the mountains for about two months and then, the husband having died, they set out on the return trip. This was in late June, and if they had not had a horse to carry water and other supplies, they probably would never have undertaken the trip. Coming down one of the canyons into Laguna Salada Basin, the horse rolled with his pack and in so doing smashed and spilled their water ollas. The nearest spring was some 15 miles away and the girl started out to secure water (riding the horse?) while the others made camp. She was gone all that day and part of the night, and when she arrived back in camp the old lady and the baby were dead. (The facts of time and distance are probably correct. Death probably came so soon on account of the travelers' near exhaustion from a long trip at the time the water was lost.) After reviving the old man, Spa's sister put him on the horse and they finally reached a Paipai camp in the Laguna Salada Basin.

Although the trip to the mountains was a long and difficult one, Sam Spa said that no one hesitated to go on that account. Many Wi Ahwir and Kwakwarsh families looked forward to the trip and the opportunity it gave them for visiting with mountain friends, not to mention the prospect of such a welcome change of diet.

Sam Spa spoke of the trips he made as a small boy from *hose kwakus*, below Mayor. He said that whole families made the trip, leaving about the middle of September (it was the time of year when the Mexicans celebrated Diez y Seis de Septiembre). They went to the vicinity of Mayor the first afternoon and camped there all night. The next morning they got up early and traveled to a water hole in a pass through the Cocopa Mountains, and across Laguna Salada Basin. They marched most of the night, made a dry camp, and then started out again in the morning, journeying all day to reach the first water hole in the Juarez foothills. From there it was a trip of about a day and a half to the pine forests. The whole expedition thus took from five to six days. The group carried both food and water, the water in large ollas that were later used in the mountains to bring water to camp.

The traveling party, according to Spa, usually comprised four or five men, two or three women, young people, children, and even babies. In the pine forest, each camp consisted of eight to ten families, including both visiting Cocopa and mountain Diegueños. To a large extent, however, the gathering and preparation of the pine nuts were conducted by family groups.

To maintain these camps it was necessary to travel long distances for water. The men and the older boys carried ollas strapped to their backs, and to keep the water from splashing out they covered the tops with long strips of cane bound down with cords tied around the necks of the vessels. The men also spent considerable time in deer

hunting and wood gathering. As a result, much of the work of harvesting and preparing the pine nuts fell to the women. If the party reached the mountains in mid-September, the nuts would not yet be ripe and it would be necessary to climb the trees and knock down the cones; this job was done by young women and girls. The green cones were then roasted in a large brush fire. As the cones broke open, men and women working with long poles drew them from the fire. They removed the nuts from the cone by pounding them with a stick and shaking them by hand, and then cleaned them by winnowing.

The nuts were transported to the river in large deerskin bags, according to Sam Spa. I neglected to check with him on the use of woven bags, as reported by Alvarez, but it must be presumed that these were alternative methods depending upon convenience and opportunity. Some families gathered a supply of pine nuts and returned to the river as soon as possible, perhaps not staying in the mountains more than two weeks. Others stayed much longer. On the return trip, according to Spa, the men worked in relays, going ahead of their families one day with a load and returning the next to pick up a second load and their families. This extended the time of the return trip, which might be prolonged even more by making long stops at watering places in order to gather and prepare agave.

The pine nuts were eaten by breaking the shell between the teeth. If a large quantity were to be prepared, a woman cracked the shells by grinding them lightly in a mortar and then extracted most of the broken shells by hand. The meat, with some unextracted shell, was made into a cake. Paste from this cake was sometimes boiled for a short time in a pot of water before being eaten.

Sam Spa volunteered a number of remarks on deer hunting in the mountains, and I gained the impression that deer hunting was not just a matter of supplying food for the pine nut camps but that it was one of the reasons for making the trip. The deer were hunted with bows and arrows, but the actual capture was made by surrounding them and running them down. A number of men took part in the chase, and after they closed in on a wounded animal, they first cut the leg tendon and then cut the animal's throat.

STORAGE

The ideal pattern was for each family to store enough agricultural and wild plant foods to last through the winter. The sum of my evidence indicates that this ideal was attained perhaps half the time. Some years the stored food lasted into the succeeding harvest, but in other years supplies were exhausted within a few weeks after harvest time. Usually stored food was consumed by March or early April, and families were on short rations until May, when some seeds matured and wild rice could be harvested. Failure to store a full year's supply of agricultural products, under the system as it existed, is traceable to four factors: (1) generosity, waste, and "feasts" at harvest time; (2) failure to plant and care for large enough farm plots; (3) the related failure to efficiently organize food production, storage, and consumption in a year-round and year-to-year system; and (4) failure of adequate flood waters to reach the land. It is possible that pests were more destructive in some years than in others, but I have no evidence on this point.

Storage techniques were apparently quite adequate. For corn, dried pumpkin strips, beans, mesquite beans, wild seeds, and such products, care was taken to keep the food up off the ground in well-covered containers. Watermelons and sometimes pumpkins were stored in dry pits or sheds.

Both pottery ollas and woven baskets were used as storage receptacles (see descriptions in Chapter 4). Some of these were placed on the roofs of houses, but the main storage place was a specially built platform near the entrance to the house. This unusual food-storage arrangement has been remarked upon by a number of writers. Chittenden, who visited the delta in 1901, reported (1901: 203):

> As one approaches their habitation, the most conspicuous structure is the raised platform about six feet in height upon which, in great baskets coarsely made from willow and tule, secure from flood, storms and wild animals, were stored their most important vegetable foods, especially mesquite beans, corn, and beans.

Obviously, a reliable statement of the amount of food stored over a period of years could have been obtained only by an observer on the spot. Quantity in measured units

meant nothing to the Cocopa, and my attempt to secure general statements about earlier times from informants was a most frustrating experience. The following information, however, is not without value in giving the reader a picture of the approximate nature of their storage habits. The estimates that follow are for an "average" year for a family of five or six.

Corn

Sam Spa: Two large bird's-nest baskets (corn stored on the cob).

Jim Short: Two or three large bird's-nest baskets (on the cob). In answer to the same question a year later, he said one basket, sometimes two.

Alice Olds: One large bird's-nest basket (on the cob), plus one small basket of shelled corn.

Tepary Beans

Sam Spa: Three to three-and-a-half small baskets.

Jim Short: Several small baskets. Enough to fill two or three 100-pound seed bags.

Alice Olds: Several small baskets. Enough to fill two five-gallon oil cans.

Cowpeas

(These are harvest figures. According to Jim Short, cowpeas could not be stored for very long because of bugs. The seeds were kept in an olla that was periodically inspected and cleaned.)

Sam Spa: One large bird's-nest basket.

Jim Short: Several small baskets.

Alice Olds: Several small baskets. Enough to fill one five-gallon oil can.

Pumpkins

Sam Spa: Five or six piles, breast high.

Jim Short: 50 to 100. When dried in strips, enough to fill one large bird's-nest basket. Sometimes more.

Alice Olds: When dried in strips, one large bird's-nest basket.

Watermelons

Sam Spa: Five or six piles, breast high.

Jim Short: 50 to 100.

Pumpkin Seeds

Sam Spa: One small basket.

Jim Short: One small basket.

Mesquite Beans

Sam Spa: Two large bird's-nest baskets. In answer to the same question a year later: Two to three large bird's-nest baskets.

Jim Short: Two to three large bird's-nest baskets.

Alice Olds: One to two large bird's-nest baskets.

Screwbeans

Sam Spa: Two or more large bird's-nest baskets.

Jim Short: Two to three large bird's-nest baskets.

Sherman Foundation

Fig. 12. Cocopa storage platform with earth-covered bird's-nest baskets.

Quelite Seeds
   Sam Spa: One small bird's-nest basket.
   Jim Short: Several small baskets. Enough to fill two or three 25-pound flour sacks.
   Alice Olds: Enough to fill one or two 25-pound flour sacks.

Cultivated Grass Seeds
   Sam Spa: One small bird's-nest basket.
   Jim Short: A big harvest would fill six or more small baskets.
   Alice Olds: Enough to fill three to five 25-pound flour sacks.

The dry climate and absence of danger from freezing made food storage comparatively easy. It was only necessary to keep the food off the ground, covered enough to keep out the occasional rains, and in containers tight enough to protect the food from small animals. There was no protection against insects unless the food was kept in ollas and carefully watched. Bugs were in everything, of course, especially in the mesquite beans. Corn was always husked for storage. Sometimes the kernels were shelled off the cob, but only in small amounts. Tepary beans and cowpeas were threshed to remove the stems and pods.

Pumpkins could be kept for a period of a month or two by storing them in dry underground pits, or in a shallow trench covered with a shed of branches and earth. Usually, however, the pumpkin was cut into strips and dried for storage. A large pile of pumpkins was put into an outdoor fire and cooked long enough to soften the skins, which were scraped off; the flesh was then cut into strips. The strips were hung on poles to dry, then stored in bundles on top of the house or ramada. If enough were dried to last through the winter, a quantity was broken up and stored in baskets.

Watermelons, which were not much larger than canteloupes, were regularly stored for winter. Some families dug a pit large enough to hold their harvest. After lining it with arrowweed or tule, they filled it with watermelons and covered the top with branches and dirt. The storage pit was inspected regularly and melons with bad spots were eaten. Other families dug a shallow pit and stored the watermelons inside a shed built over the pit. Melons stored in this way lasted for three or more months.

The Cocopa were, and still are, liberal with their food supplies. Mike Alvarez told me that any group of Cocopa would help any other group that was short of supplies. He said that between 1895 and 1905 the farms around Pozo Vicente were particularly bountiful while the other areas of the delta were suffering. People from these other groups came regularly to Pozo Vicente for help, and it was given to them without thought of exchange or payment. Jim Short told me that people were expected to help each other, particularly relatives, whether by blood or marriage. The result, he said, was that when any one family had plenty of food, everyone had plenty, and that when one was short, all were short.

Sam Spa's statements were of the same order. Visitors were always welcome and always fed. Frequently they were given food to take home. There was some exchange, however, since there is frequent mention of families from one section of the delta taking eggs or some other form of supplies to trade with families in another section. Of course, Cocopa families regularly traded farm products with mountain Indians for pine nuts, acorn meal, agave, dates, honey, buckskins, and other products. Nothing was measured, however, and according to both Sam Spa and Mike Alvarez, mountain people who visited the delta during harvest time could go into the fields belonging to their hosts and take all the food they needed to supply their camp.

My own observations indicated that the usual Western ranching custom of feeding all visitors prevailed. When a meal had been prepared in any of the camps where we were visiting, everyone who happened to be present helped themselves without being asked, so far as I could tell. During the summer of 1943, economic conditions in Mexico were such as to bring a certain amount of hardship to Indian families living in Baja California and Sonora. Many of these families traveled to Somerton to visit with relatives, and were willingly taken care of by their relatives and friends. Here again there was a pattern, of course, but there was no verbalization of what should be done and nothing so formal or regular in the behavior itself as to permit my informants to frame a generalization.

As in all such cases, however, there were sanctions operating to discourage laziness and indifference. My informants described a "good" man as one who worked hard, took care of his family, was willing to cooperate with others, and was generous. It must be assumed that some sorts of informal sanctions were operating to punish behavior contrary to this ideal.

When food supplies were seriously short, there was a tendency to tighten family units as the sharing group; this meant short rations for those members of the household, mostly old people, who were not closely related to the family and who could not shift for themselves. However, while malnutrition was no doubt a contributing factor in fatalities, and starvation was given as the reason for some deaths, it is doubtful whether anyone ever actually starved to death in this area of at least periodic plenty. Jim Short had the following to say: "In the spring wild products were scarce, fishing was poor, and not enough game could be taken by the men to feed everyone in camp. Old people who had no close relatives to care for them would sometimes die of hunger during this time. Other people had just barely enough for themselves, and couldn't take care of these old people."

Most societies faced with these conditions create patterns related to the supernatural that function to offset the disappointments at poor harvests and to reduce the anxieties connected with an irregular and unpredictable food supply. Attempts to control the supernatural as a response to this situation were, however, almost certainly absent among the Cocopa. During the latter part of my fieldwork I missed few opportunities to suggest to my informants the use of religion in agriculture, but nothing, not even the simplest of magical devices, was ever reported in association with this department of their life.

Ceremonies were generally absent in Cocopa culture, but in the few that did exist, such as the boy's initiation, the mourning ceremony, and the scalp dance, there was nothing that was concerned directly with fertility of crops. In the mourning ceremony, for example, food was destroyed, used in offerings, and given away, but the idea behind this had nothing to do with agriculture as such. Mythology accounts for the river but does not give it a god or put it in control of any god or spirit. It was "alive," as trees and clouds were "alive," but it obeyed natural laws, coming into flood when the accidents of snow and rain brought this about. Harvest festivals, which will be discussed in Chapter 7, were, in my opinion, religious in nature; yet their function, explicit and implicit, was in connection with group life and social organization, and they were neither related to the harvest as such nor a mechanism aimed at increasing effort or diligence in farming.

FISHING AND HUNTING

In the 19th century, fish unquestionably provided an important source of food — almost surely more important, in terms of quantity, than game animals and birds. Sam Spa said that men and boys were occupied with fishing a great deal of the time, but that when fish were needed most, to make up for a shortage in stored food during the early spring, the river was too low to make fishing worth while. Fish were most plentiful in late spring and early fall, when the river was rising or falling from the June-July flood.

Early travelers always spoke of the great quantities of fish seen in Cocopa and other River Yuman camps. The following is from Chittenden (1901: 201), who visited the delta in March. Fish were supposed to be scarce at that time of year:

> I asked [two young hunters] for fish. They hastened to a net which they had woven from wild hemp and set across a lagoon near us, and in a few minutes brought me a large mullet. . . . Before evening they returned, bringing five more members of their tribe. . . . Two Mexicans having arrived, it was decided to celebrate the occasion with a feast of fish served in Indian style. Accordingly, after a great fire had been built, the young men, taking long poles, sprang naked into the narrow

lagoon, and began to beat the water vigorously as they advanced toward the net, which was buoyed on the surface with wild cane. They were so successful that by the time the bed of hot coals was in readiness a pile of fish of several varieties, including carp and mullet, were floundering alongside. After being cut open and cleaned they were filled with, laid upon, and covered with, red hot coals; and in less than twenty minutes were so thoroughly roasted that skin, scales and fins peeled off, leaving the flesh as clean and palatable as if cooked by the most skillful modern caterer.

During the time of our fieldwork, however, perhaps because of changed conditions on the river, fish was not an important source of food. Every Cocopa family in Mexico possessed fishing nets but used them only rarely. Only two of the poorest families, both living near water, usually had fish in camp when we visited them.

According to Sam Spa, when a man or boy fished alone, he ordinarily used a hook and line. Alternative methods were bow and arrow and a crossed-pole fishing net (see description in Chapter 4). Spa referred to the use of European steel hooks, and these have no doubt been available to the Cocopa since the middle of the 19th century. When groups of men went fishing together, they used a long net supported by poles at regular intervals. Men walked or swam out into the lake or slough, taking the net with them. Fish caught in the net were taken out by hand, run through the gills with a sharp stick, and strung on a willow-bark strand.

Among Hwanyak Cocopa, parties of men frequently went to the Gulf to fish. They watched the sea birds to discover where a school of fish was located. When the fish came near the shore, the men ran out into the water and drove the fish further in by beating the water with sticks. When the fish entered shallow water, they were picked up and thrown ashore. These ocean fish were dried before being carried home. The men simply stamped on them to break them open and then spread them out to dry.

In the estuary, a certain species of fish (šunyah) could be captured by digging them out of soft mud. These fish were quite small and resembled catfish. They were located by looking for an opening in the mud. None of my Cocopa informants had ever dug for clams or heard of them.

Hunting was confined mostly to small game: rabbit, quail, duck, and other small animals and birds. This type of food was quite valuable in early spring when fishing was bad and other supplies were exhausted or getting low, but the best time for rabbit drives was in the fall. Sam Spa told me that rabbit drives were quite common when he was a boy. The only weapon was a bow and arrow; the Cocopa did not use a club or throwing stick, nor did they use a rabbit net. Occasionally men went deer hunting in the river bottoms, but this source of meat was not important.

Next to rabbit, the most important game, especially in winter, was duck. Great flocks of these birds migrated to the area during the winter, and in earlier times they might well have been more important in the Cocopa diet than rabbit.

Only one informant admitted to eating rats in the early days: "When we were awfully hungry we would eat the rats' stores. We got the mesquite beans he had stored and also the rat." The eating of domestic dogs was reported in 1828 by Pattie (1905: 180-220), and the eating of rats was reported by Chittenden (1901).

All of my informants made frequent mention of eggs as an important source of food. Sam Spa mentioned several times that Kwakwarsh families who had no farms brought eggs to the east side of the delta to trade for farm products. Men, women, and children, he said, were constantly on the lookout for eggs, and during the season when mesquite was being harvested they almost always brought home a supply of eggs that they had found while gathering mesquite beans.

Little information on trapping was obtained, although Gifford (1933: 269) reports a simple snare for taking quail. The only game animal that was not eaten was the dove. This was one of the totem animals (while quail, rabbit,

deer, duck, fish, and other small food animals were not), but the taboo against eating doves extended to the entire tribe and may not be a simple totem taboo.

Sam Spa and Jim Short both volunteered the taboo that prevented a boy or young man from eating any of the fish he caught or any of the game he killed. The taboo on eating his catch was extended to members of his own immediate family. Spa said that if his mother had eaten any of the fish or meat he brought home, this would have "spoiled his eyes." If he had eaten any of his own catch, it would have "spoiled his hair, his form, and his eyes." There was no regular procedure, however, for disposing of the game. Spa gave his to the family with whom he was living, but said that boys would give their catch to anyone who needed it — that it need not be given to any special relative. Spa also told me that at one period in his childhood his family lived at some distance from their nearest neighbors, so when he killed a rabbit or some other animal with his bow and arrow he would simply throw it away. I do not have any statement on the specific age when this taboo ended.

4. HOUSES, TOOLS, AND EQUIPMENT

The Cocopa of the 19th century had little interest in arts or crafts and minimal interest in tools and manufacturing processes. Their pottery was well made but with an eye to utility rather than aesthetics. The same was true for baskets, houses, clothing, musical instruments, hunting and fishing equipment, and the rest. Art forms and aesthetic expression appeared only in face painting and in body ornaments such as nose pendants, necklaces, bracelets, armbands, and, in historic times, women's beaded yokes.

SHELTER AND STORAGE

Permanent Houses

The old-style Cocopa house (*wa čawip*) was a rectangular or square earth-covered structure with rounded corners, a flat roof, and an excavated floor (Fig. 13). Mike Alvarez said that the family house was about 15 feet square and 6 feet high, with a ramada or shade projecting out from the front, which always faced east. The depth of the excavation for the floor averaged about 2 to 2½ feet. Larger houses were built by local leaders and by band captains, the latter having structures in which 40 to 50 people could gather and with attached ramadas that could accommodate as many as 100 people. Taking the average family house with four upright posts as a module, the larger houses were constructed by adding modules. The same construction principle applied to ramadas.

Although a detailed description of the construction of a Cocopa house appears complicated, the structure was in fact quite simple: upright posts supported roof beams, across which were laid smaller poles or rafters, then a thick layer of branches, and finally a foot or more of dirt. The

Fig. 13. Late 19th century Cocopa house, showing buttress poles used to support earth covering. Entrance structure is lacking.

De Lancey Gill, Bureau of American Ethnology

sloping walls of the house were similarly constructed, using poles leaned against the central roof frame, covered by bundles of arrowweed and dirt. The finished structure gave the appearance of a high mound of earth and could easily have been mistaken for one, but for the almost universal presence of a projecting ramada.

The following is a step-by-step description of the construction process as recalled by Mike Alvarez. Four upright posts were first set in the four corners inside the excavation. These posts were forked at the top and positioned so as to support two logs laid horizontally and parallel with each other in an east-west line (the two south posts supported one beam and the two north posts the other). The forks were padded with branches because, as Alvarez said, "in the old days we had no axes and couldn't smooth the forks so we needed a pad to keep the beams level and firm." An average of about 9 rafters or cross-poles (running north and south and projecting a foot or so beyond the beams), were placed on the two beams inside the corner posts, and an additional cross-pole was placed at each end outside the corner posts. Small branches were then placed in a thick layer in an east-west direction, and to complete the construction, these were covered with dirt.

The side walls and door frame called for slightly more ingenuity. A series of substantial posts, interspersed with smaller posts (about 40 all together) were leaned against the roof structure with their butts resting on ground level 18 inches or so outside the excavated house floor. These posts surrounded the house in a circular fashion except for a space of 2½ feet or more on the east side that would be used as a door. Small bundles of arrowweeds were laid horizontally against the leaning posts from bottom to top and these, in turn, were covered with arrowweed bundles placed vertically (see Fig. 14). A layer of dirt, 3 to 4 feet

thick at the bottom and partially supported by upright wooden posts driven into the ground, was piled against the lower third of the slanting arrowweed wall. More vertical posts were then driven into this dirt with their tops extending 4 to 5 feet above ground level. Between these posts and the arrowweed wall a thick layer of arrowweed was laid horizontally, and finally, on top of this arrowweed and on top of the original bank of earth, more dirt was applied, continuing up over the projections of the leaning side posts and across the top of the house to a thickness of 12 inches or more.

The entrance projected about two feet beyond the eastern wall and was constructed on a frame of four upright posts, two against the house and two at the outer end of the doorway. These were covered with branches, arrowweed, and earth in the same fashion as the rest of the house (with earth again covering the roof of the entrance). The entrance was typically so low that it was necessary for adults to stoop to enter. The smoke hole was placed near the center of the roof, but no cooking took place inside the house and a live fire was seldom used. For warmth in winter live coals were produced in an outside fire and then placed in a depression in the center of the house floor. Willow bark, worked until it was soft, was woven to serve as a curtain or door at the outer opening of the entrance, or a rabbit-skin blanket could be used for the same purpose (see the description under *Clothing*, below).

Ramadas (or shades), open on all sides and placed against but not attached to the house, were all but universal and have been retained in their same form in conjunction with the modern Mexican-style home. In structure and materials the ramadas merely duplicated the roof section of the Cocopa house.

Summer Houses and Temporary Shelters

The most elaborate type of summer house was a six-pole round or oval structure with a slightly excavated floor. The butt ends of the poles were buried in the ground, and the pointed ends were pulled together and tied at the top center. With this as a frame, the open spaces were filled with smaller uprights and bundles of willow branches or arrowweed. The entrance was no more than a space between uprights left open on the east side.

Driftwood houses were occasionally constructed near the wild rice fields at the mouth of the river, where no trees were available. The house was a four-post shade covered with tule. Three walls of the structure consisted of a series of posts supporting a "fence" of horizontal branches or tules, which was not attached to the roof. Where ample supplies of driftwood permitted, the wall was made of tightly spaced upright poles leaning against the roof. These houses, used only in May and June, had no eastern wall.

The Cocopa, especially those on the western side of the delta, were also familiar with a temporary house built by

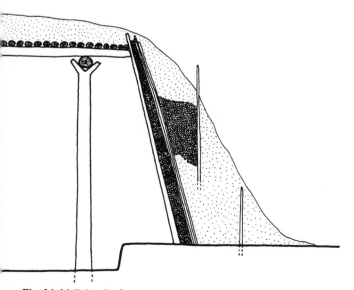

Fig. 14. Wall detail of earth-covered Cocopa house.

Fig. 15. A view of a single woman's summer shelter, showing pottery jars, dishes, pumpkins, and storage platform in the background; near Colonia Lerdo, 1900.

visitors from the Baja California mountains. This shelter, which had no excavation, was oblong. Slanting posts along the sides were joined where they met at the top, and horizontal poles were attached to these uprights. The whole was covered with a thatch of overlapping bundles of arrowweed laid vertically and fastened down by outside horizontal poles.

In addition to the above, many temporary shelters were used in conjunction with the main Cocopa house. Small brush shelters were built outside and apart from the main house and used as sleeping quarters for those who were not immediate members of the family (see Fig. 15). One informant said that when she and her grandmother lived with another family, they had a small shelter south of the main house. Sam Spa and his mother slept in a shelter with walls and no roof; when the weather became rainy or extremely cold they slept in a nearby kinsman's home. This custom was still practiced during the time of our fieldwork. In 1940, an old blind man living with relatives near San Luis, Mexico, had a small separate brush shelter; an old woman at Marítimo, also in Mexico, had a hut with three walls and a roof. An ancient blind woman at another camp had a shelter built in one corner of the family ramada. Mike Alvarez had a temporary shelter near the home of his stepdaughter and her Mexican husband.

Storage Structures

One of the outstanding features of a Cocopa camp during the 19th and early 20th centuries was the storage platform (see Fig. 12). Most families had one or more, and all families probably used the roofs of their houses and ramadas as storage platforms. Foreign visitors always remarked on this method for keeping food away from moisture, children, dogs, and large animals. The structure itself was similar to the house described in the preceding

section. In this case, a house "roof," complete with the exception of the layer of dirt, was built as an elevated platform about 5 feet high. Here baskets and pots of beans, corn, mesquite, and other food products could be kept. Access to the platform was by way of a notched-log ladder. The floor of the platform, being composed of tightly packed willow branches or arrowweed, served as the bottom for the large "bird's-nest" baskets (sokwin), which were, actually, no more than gigantic circular walls of woven willow stems (some were more than 4 feet in diameter) (see below, Figs. 18-19). For this type of basket a specially constructed cover was required. This consisted of the usual cross-poles, covered at right angles with stems of willow or arrowweed, the whole covered with a thick layer of dirt.

In addition to the platform storage structure, the Cocopa also had subterranean structures. These were used to store watermelons and to cure screwbeans. The excavation for this purpose was several feet deep, lined with brush or arrowweed, and covered with a thick layer of earth supported by cross-poles and willow matting (see also Chapter 3, under *Storage*).

HOUSEHOLD EQUIPMENT

Clay utensils and baskets were the all-purpose items in every Cocopa home, although during the childhood of my older informants these were already beginning to be replaced by tin cans, enamelware, gunnysacks, and boxes. By the time our fieldwork started in 1940 none of the women, either in Mexico or in the United States, were making pottery or baskets. Some still knew how, and made samples for us, but the skill of an earlier day was gone.

Pottery

Our information on pottery was secured from informants, from a study of items of pottery still retained by some Cocopa families, and from one potter, Maria. Water jars, cooking pots, dishes, parching pans, cups, and ladles were manufactured. In addition, there were the large storage ollas, and the serving pots 2½ feet in diameter that were made to hold food at fiestas and mourning ceremonies, according to Sam Spa. Large containers were also used to transport food and to carry small children in flooded areas.

Handles were placed on trays, bowls, and pitchers; a small olla had two vertical handles. A collar of clay was constructed just below the rim of ollas to strengthen them and to form a better grasping surface. Large canteens (sło patai), jars with lugs (skwin nyawi niłosawa, cup-put-anything-in), and frog figurines (hanya) were also made.

The following Cocopa shapes are described by Rogers (1936: Plate 9, illustrations 3, 7, 8, 12, 13, 16, 19, 20, 23): water jar (olla), sło ha niłarši·s (these were painted); bowl, skwin hayar (cup with big, round mouth); plate (pan), ska;

deep bowl with ears, *skwin kwiši mal*; jar, *skwin*; small cooking pot, *sɬo mɘs ilčes*; canteen (pot wrapped with carrying cord), *sɬo hopap*; cup, *ska heyel* (*ska*, plate; *heyel*, small); cooking pot (olla), *sɬo mɘs*.

Cocopa pottery manufacture corresponds quite closely to the method used by the Diegueño and Maricopa (Rogers 1936: 5–15; Spier 1933: 106–10), but with these important differences: our potter, Maria (with Sam Spa offering supplementary advice and information), did not start her pot over the base of an old one; and the undecorated pot was fired, cooled, then decorated and gently baked again (the standard practice is to decorate the pot before firing). Ochre (*kwa'R*) was formerly used both as a wash for pottery and for the designs. It was applied before firing. Black paint (*anye sa-ɬuɬ*) was made from mesquite sap reduced by boiling it with water, and it was applied after firing (the method Maria used).

Maria had never been a potter but had learned some skill in pottery making as a young girl. For the first collection of pottery that she made, she used river-bottom dirt (*mat hwit*) gathered near her camp, and tempered it with ground sherds. The attempt was a total loss, as not a single pot survived firing.

The second time, Maria used red clay (*mat hwat*), which she excavated with our help from an area just west of Cerro Prieto known to former Cocopa potters (Fig. 16). To this she added a little river-bottom soil after the clay had been ground and sifted and the water added. She kneaded, patted, and hit the damp clay with her hands until it was a little firmer than puff paste. A metate and mano were used for grinding the clay, a piece of window screen served as a sieve, and a large open-mouthed olla held the powdered clay.

Anvils were of two types: both were saucer-shaped with smooth, rounded bottoms and a central elevation. On one (*lohai kilᵃhwe*), the raised portion was hollow and large

enough to accommodate the insertion of the first three fingers; the other (*lohai kilyᵃalk*) had a solid, somewhat tapering knob. (For illustrations of these two types, see Rogers 1936: Pl. 4 *g* and *h*.) Paddles were both large and small (*skoka patai*, large; *skoka ilčes*, small). The general type is illustrated by Spier (1933: Pl. VII *e*), but the larger Cocopa paddle had a slightly rounded working surface.

Maria dipped her anvil into dry river bottom dirt, placed a lump of clay on its bottom, and patted and smoothed it into place with her hands. She removed the clay from the anvil, and, using the paddle (also dipped in the dirt), worked the base until it measured about 6 inches across, with walls 2½ inches high. It was well smoothed, and the rim was pinched to receive the coil (see Fig. 17, depicting various stages in making the pot).

A coil was formed by rolling clay between the palms until it was about ¾ inch in diameter and 5 inches long; it was added counterclockwise to the rim. This coil was

Fig. 17. Various stages in the manufacture and decoration of Cocopa pottery, 1940. The potter had not used her skills for many years, and these may be the last pieces of Cocopa pottery made in the pre-European tradition.

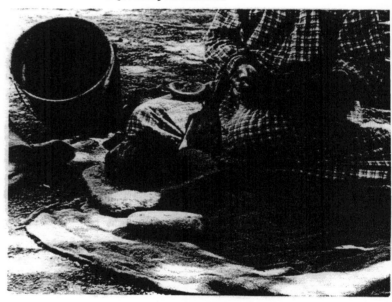

Fig. 16. Gathering pottery clay at the edge of the highway west of Cerro Prieto (Black Butte), 1940.

Fig. 17 (continued).

paddled smooth, and another placed on it. Both interior and exterior were smoothed with the paddle, while bits of clay and a small amount of water were added as necessary. Finally, the rim was flattened by paddling, with the edges left slightly rounded; the pot was left overnight to dry.

For firing, a trough was dug 1½ feet deep, 4 feet long, and 2½ feet wide. It was filled with fuel (mesquite chips and dry arrowweed), and the pots were placed around the edge. During firing, the breakage rate was very high. After the fire had burned for half an hour, it was raked to one side of the trough, and the pots were placed upon the coals. A little later, dried arrowweed was placed between and over the pots, followed by more arrowweed and green mesquite branches. Two hours later horse and cow dung were added inside, between, and over the pots. The pots were left for 10 to 12 hours.

For decorating the pottery, a small mesquite fire was built and a pot of boiled mesquite sap set upon the coals. The pot to be painted was heated and then decorated while still upon the coals. A stick wrapped in cotton cloth was dipped into the paint; the pot was revolved with the aid of

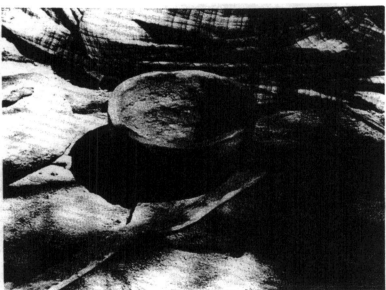

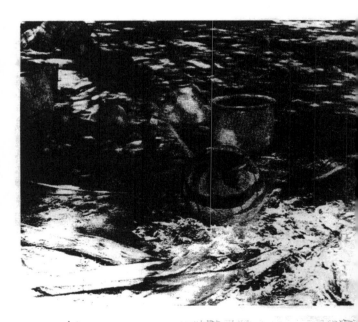

two plain sticks, and no attempt was made to keep the newly painted area away from the coals and ashes as the pot was turned. When the decoration was completed, the pot was left in the coals for about 10 minutes, then removed, wiped, and rubbed with a piece of blue denim to remove the surplus paint. The wiping reduced the sharpness of the black design.

Baskets

No special study of basket making was undertaken. None of our informants had ever made anything other than storage baskets, and no examples of Cocopa household basketry could be found. In fact, the only Cocopa basket we saw, other than those specially made for us, was the remnant of a "bird's-nest" basket found in a Cocopa trash heap near Mayor in 1940 (Figs. 18-19). The large "bird's-nest" granary, mentioned in the discussion of storage platforms (Chapter 3), was identical with the Maricopa basket described by Spier (1933: 90). Arrowweed twigs and

small branches, leaves and all, were worked into a "rope" or coil sometimes 2 or more inches thick. As one such coil was added to another they were tied to each other by sewing with twigs or willow bark. The large "bird's-nest" basket was 4 feet high and 4 feet in diameter, and the small one was half that size.

There were two other kinds of storage baskets, both olla-shaped. The first, a willow basket called *sawa'* (Gifford 1933: Pl. 35), was usually made by men. It had a bottom, and the lid was of wet mud mixed with grass. The second, called *matsuw\i l*, was of woven grass covered with mud, and was made by women. This type of basket was so fragile that, once filled, it was never moved (Fig. 20).

Food Preparation

For crushing and grinding food the Cocopa made extensive use of both the metate and mano and the mortar and pestle. Metates were formed from natural boulders with a minimum of pecking to shape a crude grinding surface. Mortars were made of short pieces of mesquite logs and were from 10 to 14 inches in diameter (a split in one mortar I saw was halted by wedging the mortar into a tin water bucket). The log or stump was shaped by alternate burning and chipping of the wood. A pestle to be used while sitting was made from a hard stone about 15 inches long and 3 or 4 inches in diameter at the base. A pestle to be used while standing was made from a mesquite branch about 4 feet long and 6 inches in diameter at the base.

Baskets and pottery in a wide variety of shapes and sizes were, of course, standard household items in the late 19th century before the Cocopa had access to manufactured containers. For cooking and eating the most common

Fig. 18. Discarded bird's-nest storage basket found near a Cocopa camp in Baja California, 1940.

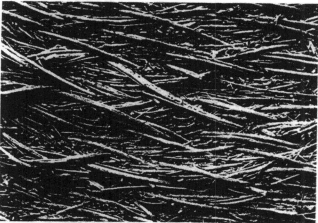

Fig. 19. Detail of bird's-nest basket, showing the long diagonal sewing elements in coil construction.

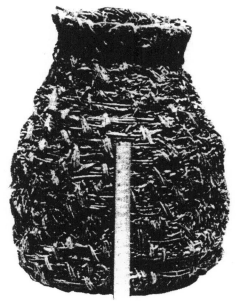

Fig. 20. Olla-shaped storage basket made by informant in 1940, to demonstrate construction method and shape.

forms of pottery were ollas and shallow bowls or plates. Women used ollas for almost all cooking over the campfire; they were sometimes supported on rocks but probably more often on rounded lumps of baked clay. Ollas were used for serving as well as cooking. The process was described as follows: "Everybody ate with their fingers and would gather around a pot and eat until they were full and then make room for someone else." Or, for the more fastidious: "When the family eats they pour food out of the pot into a pan; two or three people can eat out of a pan. If there are more in the family they use more pans." Where many people were being served: "We would keep big pots [circle of arms indicated 2 feet in diameter] over the fire and these were kept full of food. People would come up and dip their hands into the pot to eat. The big pot was replenished from other pots being used for cooking."

Fish and ducks, when cooked by a man, were placed upon the coals, and burning sticks were stuck in the ground at an angle over the food so that it would cook on top as well as on the bottom. If the fish was large it was not removed whole from the fire, but when it was done the coals were pulled back and everyone reached in to take a piece. Women baked fish in an olla.

Wild seeds were roasted in a pottery pan and were sometimes mixed with live coals to speed the process. When roasted in this fashion they were then ground and the flour was made into cakes or used in a mush.

SUBSISTENCE IMPLEMENTS

Hunting

Hunting implements among the Cocopa were restricted to the bow (*ıčim*), arrow (*ıpa*), and traps. Throwing sticks, rabbit nets, and other such devices were not used. Tradition has it that the Cocopa got the bow and arrow and two kinds of fish nets from the creator; the Diegueño, but *not* the Cocopa, received the small rabbit net (*sana'm*) used as a trap, and the throwing stick (*č'perowi*). Sam Spa said that a bow could be shaped by putting hot coals on wet ground and steaming the barkless willow branch over it, shaping it as it softened. The bow had a three-ply plant fiber string.

Arrows usually had a hard wood point made from brush growing in the salt flats below *čaman kwowao* (near the head of the Gulf). The point was hardened by fire and made very sharp; it was brittle and would break off in the wound. For war points, the Cocopa used *mešwip* — a bush growing in the mountains and said to be so poisonous that if the arrow penetrated deeply, the victim would be dead in an hour or two after being shot. Sam Spa said that sometimes, especially in war, a few men used stone arrow points. These were rather small triangular points with two side notches. Reed for the shaft was called *h'ča'*. Gall-bladder fluid (*čulum*) from the rattlesnake (not poison from the sac) was put on both stone and wooden points.

Deer were killed in the mountains with the bow and arrow, but very few were found in the valley. Rabbit drives, comprising around 15 men and boys, were conducted by firing the brush, and the rabbits were shot with the bow and arrow. If a rabbit ran into a hole or hollow log it was dug out with a barbed stick, which was twisted until it caught in the rabbit's skin. No club was used. Boys customarily carried a small bow and arrow, and used a sling for small game hunting and for scaring birds. One informant said that women made "box traps" for catching birds; these were very similar to one illustrated by Spier (1933: 72, Fig. 5). Men, however, made a bent stick trap with a string loop. Bird traps were used during the entire year. Three informants in Baja California and Sonora used bows and arrows in 1940 for killing rabbits and fish; one bow had bailing wire for the string and long fishing arrows.

Fishing

A cross-pole net (*lewao*), a rectangular net attached to stakes (*čawıs*), bow and arrow, and hook and line were used to take fish from the river and sloughs. A cross-pole net was made for us by Mike Alvarez (Fig. 21). He used cotton string from the store and a wooden needle 3 inches long, less than 1/8 inch thick, and with an eye less than ½ inch long. Alvarez sat on the ground with his feet extended; beyond his feet, in a midline between them, he had driven a stake into the ground. A shirring cord that held the end of the net was looped around the stake. Work progressed from left to right, and when the end of a row was reached, the net was turned over and work continued. Mesh was measured by pulling the loops toward the worker; when they were the right size, the junction place was held between the thumb and forefinger of the left hand — the right hand held the needle. The knot was made by running the needle under the loop above, measuring for size, and pulling the cord tight; then inserting the threaded needle under and up through the junction through the loop, and pulling it tight. All stitches were made by inserting the needle from top right under the material to top right again, and down underneath. Thread was held in the needle by tying it in a knot just below the needle. After the completion of each row, the entire net was stretched toward the worker. This type of net, and the one described below, are illustrated by Forde (1931: 119, Figs. 3*a*, *b*).

Cordage for nets, called *war čawıs okwaš*, was made from a dry plant (*kw·š*) that was gathered when it was a little green. It was macerated or gently broken, and the fibers were peeled off. Fibers were twisted by hand on the thigh to make either two- or three-ply cord. Strings from black-eyed bean plants (cowpeas) were also used for cordage. As the cord was twisted, it was wound in a figure 8 on a stick. When nets were being made, the stick became the bobbin.

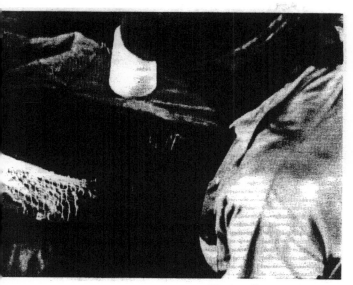 

Fig. 21. Cocopa informant making a cross-pole fishing net.

Gathering

Implements used in gathering were, in most cases, used only for that activity. Standard equipment for women — who did most of the gathering — was a digging stick and a carrying net. The net or bag was large, square, and flat, with a drawstring that held up the corners and sides when full and that was attached to a tumpline when the bag was carried on the back. Sam Spa said that the Cocopa knew of the double-U-shaped carrying frame and net cover used by other Indians, but never had it.

The Cocopa bag was an all-purpose affair but was used most for transporting mesquite beans and screw beans. Mike Alvarez said that he carried pine nuts from the mountains in bags woven from the broad leaves of a mountain plant, but Sam Spa stated that his parties carried them in deerskins worked by men who had learned from the mountain Indians.

Agriculture

In the years between 1850 and 1877 the Cocopa were employed by steamboat companies to cut firewood for the boats traveling between the mouth of the river and Yuma. For this purpose the Indians were supplied with steel axes and sledgehammers, and no doubt they bought with their earnings, or were given, steel knives, hoes, shovels, fish hooks, and other items. However, having little or no cash after the river boats stopped running, the Cocopa of the late 19th century reverted to their native farming tools. Such tools were limited indeed: a long mesquite digging stick for planting and a similar pole, flattened at one end, for weeding.

TRANSPORTATION

Rafts

For water transportation the Cocopa used both rush or tule boats (Freeman 1923) and log rafts. My informants were acquainted only with the raft. Sam Spa, who built a model for us, described it as being from 9 to 10 feet long, 6 to 7 feet wide, and 3 feet high when resting on the ground. First a frame was made of 5 willow logs, 2 long logs on the bottom and 3 shorter logs laid across them. The logs were attached to each other at the corners and center with willow bark strips. Two floors of tule bundles were laid upon the cross-logs — one lengthwise, the other crosswise. The bundles were of dry tule and measured 12 to 18 inches in diameter, depending upon the size of the raft. A clay floor at one end for a fire completed the raft.

Rafts were used in gathering wild rice, in transporting the rice (and members of the family) from the rice harvest area to the family's permanent delta home, and later, while the river was still in flood, in gathering mesquite beans and other food such as bird's eggs. Rafts were poled, paddled, or pulled from the shore with a willow bark rope.

Baby Cradles

Baby cradles were not made in advance of birth, according to Mike Alvarez. People waited four or five days to see if the baby would live before making the first cradle. A person who gathered the material for the cradle had to be old, preferably the grandfather of the husband or wife. "If the man who gathered the material knew how to make a cradle, he did it; if he did not know, then a woman, who should be the wife's mother, made it, and she needed no

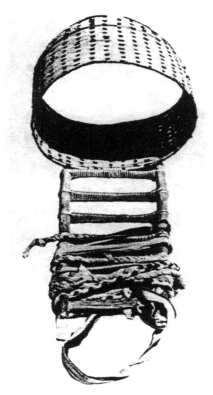

Fig. 22. Modern (1940) Cocopa baby cradle.

help from a man." Alvarez went on to say that the baby was put in the cradle "when it could see" — when it was about ten days old. A second, larger cradle was made when the baby was about a month old. Sam Spa said that a baby was left in the cradle a long time, and its legs were kept straight. When the baby didn't totter and could walk a few steps, the cradle was no longer used.

Baby cradles were equipped with a bark mattress, a pillow consisting of a wrapped ring of bark bound in the middle, and a binding band of woven or plaited plant fiber (other than cotton) wound around the cradle. Cradles were carried horizontally or crosswise upon the head, horizontally on the hip, or in the arms (Drucker 1941: 111).

Although the hood decoration on a Cocopa cradle was essentially the same as that of the Maricopa (Spier 1933: 316-7), one informant said that people used to tie egret feathers on a boy's cradle. In the old days, an adult twin put a toy bow and arrow on a boy twin's cradle, and white feathers in his hair. Beads were put on a girl twin's cradle and on her neck and wrist, according to Sam Spa.

Litters

According to Sam Spa, there were two ways of carrying a sick person to a doctor. First, the sick man was laid upon a blanket with knots tied at the corners. Long poles were run through the knots, and six men carried him in relays. The other method was to make a litter of poles and cross-poles to be carried by two men. To carry old people to a new camp, they put the person upon the carrier's back, with the arms around his neck, and the legs clasping the carrier's body. The oldster was supported by the carrier's hands behind.

The wooden carrying frame for the dead was made by "a person who knew how," preferably a relative of the deceased. The frame, according to Tom Juarez, consisted of poles and cross sticks, like a baby cradle, and was called *i-yo*. The dead person was covered, rolled in blankets, and tied to the frame. This frame, which later served as the funeral bier, was used to transport the corpse from the home to the crematory site, usually near the camp of the group leader.

According to Jim Short, men traveling from one section of the delta to another made rattles and tied them on themselves at night so that they would not get lost from one another or "follow a ghost." Short also stated that the Cocopa did not carry torches for heat when on expeditions in cold weather, but women carried a glowing log for future fire. Sam Spa confirmed the absence of torches for heat.

CLOTHING AND PERSONAL ADORNMENT

Reminiscence, early photographs, and mythology supply the basis for our knowledge of the appearance of former best-dressed Cocopa men and women. The myths were related by Sam Spa.

In one tale, two little frog girls were talking about getting married, so they put on their willow-bark skirts, necklaces, and bracelets, and combed their nice long hair. They painted their faces by blackening their eyelids and their tattoo marks, and added a vertical line on each cheek and a line under the eyes in red. They also put red paint across their breasts and on their arms. They met Coyote (who fancied himself quite a dandy), with his hair fixed, and two eagle feathers stuck in the back. He, too, wanted to get married. He was painted, had beads around his neck, and wore a rawhide wrist band decorated with fringe and painted white circles. Another myth describes a man dressed to go visiting: he wore a necklace, feathers in his hair, a bowguard, and a belt around his waist.

Jim Short said that in the old days, when a boy was looking for a wife, he wore egret feathers in his hair and a necklace around his neck, and painted his face. Girls dressed up, painted their faces, and wore necklaces. This was especially true for large gatherings. He added that Cocopa girls didn't put color on their hair, the way Yuma and Mohave girls did.

Sam Spa said that when he went visiting in his youth, he wore a feather in his scalp lock, face paint, a necklace, and a belt made from unraveled black cloth. A shaman described by Spa adorned himself for curing by painting one eye black, the other red, and the area around his mouth white. He wore an eagle feather in his hair, a necklace, and a belt. In addition, he had four pendants made of pieces of mirror hanging around his neck.

Clothing

A man's breechclout was called *am·kohap*, and in the last 40 to 50 years was always made of cloth. A long strip was fastened in front by a belt and passed under the crotch and over the belt in the back. The end was left long behind, reaching to the knees, and when a man was running it would fly out like a tail; however, it could also be brought back under the crotch and fastened into the belt in front. When Sam Spa was in his teens, he wore only a breechclout made of a piece of dress goods about 8 inches wide and 3 feet long. He said that one would last a year.

Apparently a blanket was part of the standard equipment for the young man of courting age, because Sam Spa reported that one of his wives tricked him into sleeping with her by taking his blanket away from him. Another girl took his blanket just before he got in bed with her. He didn't tell me how he wore the blanket (or carried it around) when it was not in use.

Sam Spa described the way he made his belt: he unraveled American cloth (in this case, a black coat) and plied several long strands together by rolling. Then the "rope" was passed under his extended foot several times to loop the strands, which were finally sewn together and worn as a belt.

Sandals described to us fit Gifford's description (1933: 276-7; Fig. 3). In 1940, both Sam Spa and Jay Bell were wearing identical footgear made out of cowhide.

A wrist guard used for decoration was worn by men. It covered most of the lower left arm, and was made of hide with buckskin fringe hanging from the underside to a length of 6 to 8 inches. The strands of the fringe were painted different colors, and beads were sewn on top "to make it shine." Sam Spa made one for himself of saddle leather, but it wasn't nearly as elaborate as one he described as being worn by a captain. The captain's wrist guard was made of red and white deerskin with a fringe; as a crowning glory

De Lancey Gill, Bureau of American Ethnology

Fig. 23. A young Cocopa man with Professor W J McGee near Colonia Lerdo in 1900. Note tip of long wooden pestle and part of wooden mortar at extreme left (and in Fig. 25).

De Lancey Gill, Bureau of American Ethnology

Fig. 24. Cocopa woman wearing willow bark skirt, near Colonia Lerdo in 1900.

De Lancey Gill, Bureau of American Ethnology

Fig. 25. Cocopa girls model new and old style garments near Colonia Lerdo in 1900 (see also Fig. 26). These girls, with painted faces, elected to wear cotton skirts but are holding their willow bark skirts.

De Lancey Gill, Bureau of American Ethnology

Fig. 26. Girls wearing "modern" dress, near Colonia Lerdo in 1900. Seated girl models the glass bead yoke that soon went out of style.

there were silver conchas from a saddle fastened on top. Spa said that some people would point with the right (uncovered) arm, and then with the other, to show the wrist guard.

Further indication of the more elaborate dress sometimes worn by captains in the past was provided by Frank Gomez, who had been told of an incident that occurred in 1870. His description of the captain is particularly interesting. The captain had been called to assist in settling a marital dispute, and he arrived wearing a derby hat, shirt, and frock coat, but no trousers. Under the tails of the frock coat he wore the usual loincloth. His face and legs were painted and his hair was done up in a tight knot under the derby hat. In his hand he carried a European cane.

Two of Spa's wives wore willow bark skirts and white cotton mantles over their heads and shoulders in the daytime; in bed they covered themselves with the mantles and rolled up their willow bark skirts for pillows.

Before she began to menstruate, Alice Olds wore a "white cloth around her under her armpits and another around her hips." Another of Spa's wives wore an old willow skirt when she was menstruating, and a new one when she was not. He said that she pushed the old one down between her legs in bed. Some women wore a rag between their legs, Spa said, but "now they wear long dresses, and I can't see what they do."

Women used to wear basketry hats when they ground corn, according to Alice Olds; their hair hung down in the way, so they put it up and wore the hat on top. Sam Spa said that when he was a boy he saw many Cocopa women wearing these hats, especially with the tumpline. The Cocopa from the river went to a canyon in the mountains called *wi yal* to get the small center fan-palm leaves with which to make these hats. The mountain people wore them, but Spa never saw or heard of a Yuma woman wearing one (see Williams 1975: 98).

Although Jim Short denied the use of rabbit-skin blankets in his time, Drucker (1941: 112, 180) says that they were made by both sexes. One-ply strips of rabbit skin were twisted upon themselves with no foundation. They were used on beds and also worn:

The circular blanket reported by Akwa'ala [Paipai] and Cocopa was made by coiling a long warp of rabbitskin "string" in a spiral (on the ground) and fastening the turns together with wefts of mescal-fiber string, or occasionally a short length of rabbitskin string (Akwa) or willow-bark string (Coc.). The wefting was not in a twine, but in a wrap stitch, the single weft elements making a turn about each warp in passing over it.

In addition, Drucker says that men and women made robes of willow bark for wearing apparel; the warps were suspended on a half-loom and the weft was twined (Drucker 1941: 112).

Mike Alvarez was our Beau Brummell. In him was epitomized all the paint, feathers, nose pendants, belts, and necklaces of the old-time Cocopa, transferred to a love for modern clothes and gewgaws. When he worked on neighboring farms, or helped build our ramada, he wore faded blue jeans and a blue shirt; his feet were bare and his long hair was covered by an ordinary red bandana. Acting in the capacity of informant, he changed his shirt and added an old pair of army shoes and a battered, bandless felt hat. When he went visiting, however, he wore his Sunday best: shoes, black wool trousers, a white shirt, a purple bandana tied ascot fashion around his neck, a black silk scarf over his hair, and the hat. He had made a pair of sleeve garters out of a red inner tube, but these were soon replaced by a red silk elastic pair. His son-in-law had given him a discarded brass watch chain, which he fastened, quite properly, to his plain black belt, with the other end dangling empty in the watch pocket. After we added a dollar Ingersoll watch, he would pull it out and examine it whenever he had an audience. He also had a pair of dark blue glasses. No matter how glaring the sun, they never served any utilitarian purpose — their value was entirely aesthetic; Alvarez donned them only when entering another camp to pay a call, and as soon as the amenities were over, he removed them.

Sam Spa, on the other hand, was a gay, happy-go-lucky man who sang to himself while riding along in the car or when he was idle in camp. His lively curiosity and excellent memory, together with his sense of the dramatic, made him an invaluable informant and a good companion. His appearance, however, was pretty terrible in comparison with that of most Cocopa. His clothes were torn and dirty, and his blanket ragged and soiled. He almost always went barefoot, and never cut his long, curling toenails, although on a very few occasions he wore cowhide sandals made in the old style. His hair never looked neat; sometimes it just hung and other times he parted it down the middle with his forefinger and wound the two sides around his head, tucking in the ends. It was so badly matted that I am sure he rarely, if ever, combed it. Nevertheless — and this was true of all Cocopa with whom we came into close contact — he kept his body clean, and he always washed his face and hands and rinsed out his mouth before eating.

Mutilation

A boy's nose was pierced and a girl's chin tattooed in connection with mourning ceremonies (the ceremonies and the methods of piercing and tattooing are described in Chapter 7). Spa, Alvarez, and Tom Juarez had apertures nearly large enough to accommodate a lead pencil, but none wore any ornament in his nose. Cocopa men formerly wore a shell pendant suspended by a cord through the puncture in the septum, according to Alvarez, and never wore a stick as the Mohave did.

Girls were tattooed (tattoo, *nia kwis*) on the chin as soon as the proper occasion for the ceremony presented itself. The custom obviously prevailed well into the 1900s, since nearly all of the older women and many of the young girls in both Mexico and the United States had tattoo marks.

Drucker (1941: 116-7) says that males were tattooed on the chin, forehead, arms, legs, shoulder, and chest; and females in all but the latter two places. Nearly all the men we saw had their foreheads tattooed; a few were also tattooed on the chin.

Ear piercing was practiced as well. Mike Alvarez and Sam Spa agreed that it was done on the third or fourth day after birth. Alvarez said that it was done by the wife's mother, or by the same woman who had attended her at the birth. Ears (lobe and helix) of both boys and girls were punctured.

Another custom was that of artificial occipital flattening. Sam Spa stated that after birth, a pillow was made by filling a cloth with warm earth. This pillow was attached to the cradleboard, and the baby's head was fastened to the pillow. (Spa also said that the process lasted only four nights, but this is surely a misunderstanding.) In 1940, in Frank Gomez's camp, a seven- to eight-month-old baby with an extremely flat head was kept in the cradle at night with a sand pad behind its head.

Face and Body Painting

Painting of the face and body was a custom common for all special occasions and at all ages. Little boys and girls, too young to paint themselves, were painted by their mothers. Four colors were used: red, black, white, and yellow. The paint was washed off in the morning since it smeared during sleep.

Paint made of red powder was called *kwa'R* (Gifford's *akwura*, identified as red hematite; 1933: 277); it was from a rock gathered in a mountain pass beyond *wi sła* (in the Cocopa Mountains west of Pozo Vicente). This rock was dug out of the ground in big chunks, brought to camp, burned in a fire, ground on a metate, and mixed with water. As it was stirred, heavy pieces settled to the bottom; the fine particles stayed in suspension and were poured off. This process was repeated two or three times to remove the "sour" material. The wet mass was patted into cakes and placed on the ground to dry. After a day it was ready for use, or was put away for sale or trade.

Maria and Sam Spa said that the necessary amount of powder was scratched off the cake and put into the palm of the left hand. Grease or lard was added, and the face was painted with the right second finger. Alvarez said that the powder was mixed with pumpkin seed oil to make it stick to the body. *kwa'R* was used alone, with other colors, or mixed with black to make dark brown. Red and white pigments were put into water and sprinkled on the body. The body and legs of a small child were also painted red. Girls, men, and women used *kwa'R* for face and body paint; men used it in their hair.

The black pigment, *kunyił*, was identified by Gifford (1933: 277 — his *kwinyiL*) as black manganese dioxide. It was found at the top of the Juarez Mountains, which were reached by traveling through the Cocopa Mountains and crossing Laguna Salada Basin. Gomez wasn't sure, but he thought that it was mined from a drift that had been dug in the hill by Indians. This was in Diegueño territory. Gomez and Spa agreed that *kunyił* was used to put on babies' eyelids "to keep the eyes clean and white." It was applied by dipping a small dry stick into the powder and rubbing the powder above and below the roots of the lashes. On special occasions, women put *kunyił* over their tattoo lines for emphasis; those who were not tattooed applied it in place of the tattoo. Frank Gomez went on to say that men applied it as a face paint, drawing horizontal lines under and over the eyes or a vertical line extending from the forehead along the nose to the point of the chin.

Another black paint, Spa said, was made by reducing pumpkin juice over the fire until it was black. It was often used to spread on a baby's body.

mat hapa (talc?) was the white pigment commonly used by young men to paint their eyebrows, make a complete circle around their eyes, or daub in spots on their hair. Both young men and girls used the white pigment as a body paint. It was also used by girls to make rows of white dots down the cheeks from forehead to chin, just outside the edge of the eyebrows. Some painted white spots on their eyelids, while others streaked their faces vertically. It was most commonly used by men and women as face decoration over solid areas of *kwa'R*. Burned and pulverized fish bones also made a white paint.

Gomez said that yellow paint, called *metskwƏs*, was now bought in the store. He didn't know what other native product was formerly utilized in addition to tule pollen.

There was a difference in painted designs for men and women: men generally used horizontal lines, and women vertical. If a man had side horizontal lines, he could run a red, black, or white line down his forehead and nose to his chin. Women, too, used the latter line, but did not paint it black. Combinations of red, white, and black could be used "to make people laugh," according to Gomez. This was done mostly by men, who might paint the right half of the face red, the left half white; or the upper face red, and the lower lip and chin area black.

Hair

Head hair seems to have been a true crowning glory to the Cocopa. References to "fine, long hair" occur in diverse contexts, from myths to accounts of scalping; regard for hair is apparent in the care it was given and in its central position in ritual purity.

A coloring lotion was made by scraping sap off a mesquite tree with a knife and boiling the sap with water. This produced a black dye to be applied to the hair. Mesquite sap was also added to wet mud and plastered on the head if an all-night cake on the hair was desired.

Sam Spa said that they put mud and mesquite juice on their hair because if they left it alone, it would get dusty and greasy. In addition, the mesquite juice kept the hair dark; otherwise it would turn red (sunburned). It "also killed lice." This decoction was used both as an ordinary shampoo and for special purposes — for example, as a part of the purification rites after scalping; following nose-piercing; and for the husband and wife in a first marriage, subsequent to each of the wife's first four menstruations. At certain times, arrowweed juice was substituted for mesquite sap.

In the old days, according to Sam Spa, little boys' hair was cut with bangs, side locks, and a scalp lock. It was then allowed to grow after age ten so that it was long at the time of nose-piercing. Little girls' hair was cut short on top, and the sides and back were cut below the ears. At about eight years, it was allowed to grow.

Women wore their hair plain and hanging, except for bangs. Sam Spa said that men dressed their hair in from 5 to 60 braids, and for running these braids were tied at the back of the neck. Before the end of the 19th century men did not roll their hair on top of their heads and cover it with a cloth as they did after that time and as late as the period of our fieldwork. The Cocopa used a cylindrical fiber hair brush, doubled and wrapped (Drucker 1941: 116).

MUSICAL INSTRUMENTS

Flutes and rattles were the principal musical instruments known to the Cocopa. Both were very similar to those used by the Yuma (Forde 1931: 130-1):

[The flute was] made from a length of cane . . . from 18 inches to 2 feet long. This included two or three notches which were bored through inside and smoothed without. The flute was . . . blown obliquely at the upper end. There were four stops in the middle section. [They were painted in bands of color, usually red.]

The gourd rattle is the usual accompaniment to songs and dances. Globular gourds are opened at the junction of the stalk, cleaned out, and dried. A handful of small pebbles are inserted and a wooden handle, about six inches long, fixed in the hole with arrowweed or mesquite gum. Rows of holes are punched in the surface of the gourd, forming patterns and increasing the resonance.

The Cocopa also used the Diegueño deer's-hoof rattle, but only to accompany the songs in the kerauk mourning ceremony. Thirty or more deers' hooves were pierced at the apex and threaded on individual cords. The cords were then assembled and bound to form the handle of the rattle (Fig. 27). Forde (1931: 130) reports a slightly different form: "[the hoofs are] threaded in pairs, one at each end, on lengths of cord. The cords are then looped up and bound together to form a handle."

Fig. 27. Diegueño deer's-hoof rattle used by the Cocopa in their kerauk mourning ceremony. The usual rattle would have many more deer's hooves.

5. FAMILY LIFE

Few people in the world have equaled the Cocopa in loading the institution of the family with so many of society's important tasks. The reader has already learned that the Cocopa family, in aboriginal times, was the central unit in subsistence activities, and in the production of the tools and equipment for feeding, clothing, sheltering, and protecting its members. The present chapter will extend this theme to show that the family was also the unit responsible for education, recreation, social order, ritual purity, and the care of the sick. Another way of saying this is that there were no educational, recreational, police, religious, or medical institutions to which an individual could turn.

Cocopa life revolved around the family and, to a much lesser extent, the band or local group. Other groupings were unstable cooperating units of individuals whose membership, outside the activity of the moment, was never defined. Hunting, fishing, and gathering expeditions, neighborhood children at play, harvesting parties, and similar activities are examples of such groupings.

But before describing the family organization in relation to its contribution to the maintenance of Cocopa society, it is necessary to describe how a Cocopa family was formed and how it was dissolved. Considering the family's great importance to the society, it might be expected that strict attention would be paid to courtship and weddings and that both would be elaborate and formal activities. Quite the contrary: courtship and marriage were preliminaries to the formation of a "trial family." Cocopa society thus contained two types of families, which selected personnel in the same manner but differed in function and in structural meaning. The first type of family served to satisfy the sexual needs of the younger people, and to define a place for the offspring in the kinship system. Obligations and loyalties between the married pair were as yet weakly developed, and the individuals maintained strong ties with their natal families, as evidenced by their alternating residence. Such a family broke up easily, and no pressure was exerted to keep the spouses from separating. The second type of family developed from the first. It functioned, as does the American family, as a continuing arrangement for sexual satisfaction and as the responsible unit in the production, care, and training of children. In addition, it was this second type of family, and particularly its adult members, who took on most of the burdens of the society's work. The existence of these differing family types must be kept in mind, particularly in connection with the division of labor and the distribution of rights, duties, and responsibilities according to age.

COURTSHIP

There were no formal patterns of courtship and only a slightly developed sense of a need for preliminary activities between the families of the couple concerned. Courtship was not a device for adjusting one or both parties to a radical, and generally permanent, change in personal relationships; what courting did take place served only as a preliminary to sexual intercourse.

All my male informants, when they were older boys and before they were married, made frequent visits to surrounding camps where there were young girls. There they did what they could to attract the attention and win the favor of the very "shy" young ladies hiding "behind their mothers' skirts." As such courtship proceeded, and a couple became paired off, a more direct pattern of behavior was permitted. Jim Short and Tom Juarez walked and talked with the girls they later married. Sam Spa probably did the same, at least with some of his wives, but I have no record of it. Short had known his first wife "a long time," and in the months preceding his marriage he used to visit her camp, talk to her when they were alone, and frequently made love to her: "When no one was looking I used to put my arm around her, but I never slept with her until after we were married."

Tom Juarez had much the same experience with his first wife. According to his statement, they had known each other since they were small children, and neither of them had had previous sexual experience. When they grew older and realized that they were attracted to each other, Juarez visited her and had ample opportunity to talk to her alone. He said, however, that he never "made love" to her before they were married.

Some marriages took place at group gatherings when widely scattered families came together for a mourning ceremony, initiation, or celebration. For these affairs, the marriageable boys and girls who were so inclined wore special insignia to indicate their intentions. Jim Short said that the boy wore egret feathers in his hair, painted his face with a special pattern, and wore all his finery of earrings, necklaces, and decorated armbands. The girls painted their faces and wore necklaces. Yuma and Mohave girls, he said, put color in their hair for such occasions, but not the Cocopa.

The method of courtship was violent and direct. The boys (probably on some sign of approval) chased the girls they wanted back and forth through the dancing area and camps, and finally into the bushes where they could make love. (One of Sam Spa's most vivid early memories was of having his cradle knocked off a pile of blankets and being stepped upon by a boy chasing a girl in this way at a mourning ceremony.) If a marriage was intended, the couple stayed in the bushes until the ceremony or fiesta came to an end. Of my various informants, only Alice Olds was married in this way: "Most girls have fathers and mothers to take care of them and keep boys out of their beds. I wasn't like that. I didn't have a father and mother so when I got married I slept out and then came home. I met the boy at a meeting and he played with me and took me out in the bushes."

Premarital sexual activity was frowned upon, but there were Cocopa girls available to the boys for an occasional sexual act. Some girls were referred to as "crazy hearts," and all my informants, with the exception of Tom Juarez and Mike Alvarez, admitted having had affairs with them. There was no direct payment, and I know of no gifts, but I think it likely that some gifts were made. Girls living at home with their fathers and mothers were expected to be virgins when they first married; however, girls who had lost their mothers and who lived with other relatives, and thus had no one to "protect" them, were apt to be "crazy hearts." Premarital sexual experience was probably infrequent and certainly made little sense in this society, with its trial marriage customs. (The sexual life of the Cocopa was not a subject we pursued in our field work, although we did receive unconfirmed reports of incest, homosexuality, and the rape of children. There is no reason to believe that the Cocopa differed in any significant way from the Mohave, whose sexual attitudes and practices have been fully reported by Devereux [1935; 1937a; 1937b; 1939b; 1940].)

MARRIAGE

The Cocopa were forbidden to marry anyone belonging to their mother's or father's lineage, any first cousin, and certain individuals who were apt to live in the same camp, such as a wife's daughter (or mother's husband), or a father's wife (or husband's son). The incest rule did not apply to a wife's sister (or sister's husband), or to a brother's wife (or husband's brother), however, and such marriages were encouraged, but not demanded, under certain circumstances.

Girls preferred tall, well-built men with pleasant dispositions and the energy to keep a camp well provisioned. Boys preferred heavy girls with round arms and wide hips.

The wedding ceremony consisted in the simple act of a boy going to bed openly with a girl — that is, with her and her family's consent, and, preferably, in her parents' house or camp. First marriages came at a relatively young age: 16 to 18 for boys, and soon after first menstruation for a girl. Informants agreed that some girls were married before they menstruated, but only Sam Spa claims to have married a girl so young. The only two first marriages that came to our attention in the field involved girls who had just commenced to menstruate. So far as I know, there were no unmarried girls older than 20 at the time of our visits, but there were a number of boys up to 25 years of age or more who had never married. The marriage of Cocopa girls to non-Indians probably accounted for this.

After a couple had been married for a time (from a month or so, to as much as a year), the marriage was usually broken, and in the following few years the boy and girl married a succession of partners, perhaps three or four on the average. It was, in fact, a matter of cultural expectation that this should happen; the partners in a first marriage, or even in the first few marriages, felt that they were not required to form a permanent union. Eventually, one of these trial marriages became permanent; two or three children were born, and the pair set up their own camp, establishing a family of their own. Tom Juarez was the only mature adult who I knew had been married only once, although there were of course others, since my information on this point comes from only 15 adults. Jim Short was married six times, Sam Spa seven, Alice Olds twice, and other informants from two to four times. Some of these remarriages followed the death of a spouse, but most followed a divorce, which was no more than a couple's mutual decision to stop living together.

If the girl was reputed a virgin, and also, perhaps, if she exhibited qualities that made her desirable as a wife, the ideal pattern for her first marriage was for a somewhat formalized approach to be made to her family, by either the prospective groom or his father. (My information on this subject comes from Sam Spa; three other informants agreed with his statements, although they had had no personal experience with the practice.)

The boy or his father was expected to visit the girl's father with a horse, some money, wearing apparel, or a combination of these gifts. He would present the gift, making a verbal request for the girl, and return home. After he had gone, the family was expected to discuss the matter and consult with the girl, who would hang her head, act bashful, and say nothing. Her father usually led in this talk, although an older brother would take part, and perhaps the mother (I have a record of one such instance, in the case of Sam Spa's fourth marriage). After some time, often a matter of days, the girl was supposed to agree to the marriage. Word of her agreement was transmitted to the prospective groom by the girl's brother or by some other male relative.

When marriage was not arranged by gift, the two young people talked it over between themselves and made their own arrangements. This type of marriage was called *nyιmpa pum*. Overt negotiations were instituted by the boy, but the girl's mother (or someone else from the household) often talked around camp in such a fashion as to indicate which boy would be welcome in her daughter's bed. How often the girl herself took an active part in these affairs, I do not know. The boy was supposed to take the lead, and there is no doubt that this was the behavioral pattern, but I recorded at least one case in which the girl was the aggressive one (that of Sam Spa and his first wife).

Except for the couples who consummated their courtship at group gatherings, most young couples started sleeping together in one of two places: either in the girl's house or in a house adjoining hers in the same camp. Whether arrangements had previously been made between the two families, or whether the two young people themselves had come to an agreement, the boy came to the girl's bed after she was supposedly asleep, and he expected to be welcome. Sometimes the boy returned three nights in succession, and then was given a final acceptance on the fourth night (I have no specific example of this, since my informants claimed that they themselves were never rejected). Acceptance consisted in permission to remain and did not necessarily involve coitus. The account of a boy's being rejected at first and finally accepted is perhaps true; however, the pattern of three trials, with success on the fourth trial, occurs in other contexts, and it need not be taken literally.

Boys undertaking this enterprise for the first time were bashful. Sam Spa said they stood outside a girl's house for a long time before working up their courage to enter, and that their "hearts would beat fast" with nervousness and excitement. Quite frequently, a boy asked a cousin or a close friend to go along with him; for instance, Spa was urged by a boy's mother to accompany her son on his wedding night. In such cases, the boys entered together, and the second boy slept nearby.

Sexual intercourse was not expected, and rarely occurred, on the first night of marriage. Quite commonly, it was a week or so before the girl permitted the boy to have access to her. Both Jim Short and Sam Spa volunteered the information that a girl was quite carefully instructed in these matters by her mother. She was told to welcome the young man, permit his embraces, not to cry out, and not to pull his hands away from her body. She was told that she must become accustomed to having him hold her and fondle her, and that in a few nights, when he attempted coitus, she was to remain quiet, and not embarrass him by trying to fight him off.

Jim Short's statements in regard to his first marriage are typical of the expected behavior; they were verified in detail by Sam Spa, Tom Juarez, and Alice Olds. Short went to his wife's bed in the night and lay down beside her. They talked for a while and he just made love to her, felt her breasts, and held her in his arms. He went home next morning and returned to sleep with her for several consecutive nights, confining himself each time to lovemaking. In reply to my questions about intercourse he made the simple statement: "It takes time." More than a week went by before he had access to her, and when this fact came out in the interview, my interpreter interposed with the remark: "This was a good girl." With slight variation, this routine was repeated in Short's other marriages when the wife had not been married before. Women who had had sexual experience were not expected to be so "shy" in their wedding beds. Sam Spa's sixth wife had previously been married three times and was a woman "young enough to have two or three more children." When it developed that he had had sexual intercourse with her the first night they were together, he explained: "Young girls take time, they are like wild horses and have to be gentled for three or four days. Old people are not like that."

My information on postmarital sexual behavior varies, both because of individual dissimilarities and because of differences in my informants' readiness to give an uncensored report. Sam Spa was apparently guided almost entirely by the response of the particular girl; with certain wives, he practiced coitus every night at first, and with one he not only had coitus the first night but repeated it seven times each night for three nights running. (This statement has some meaning since he made no similar statement in speaking of his other wives.) Jim Short said that he had had sexual intercourse every night with certain of his wives. There was no mention of frigid wives, and the probabilities are that most Cocopa girls were uninhibited in this respect. (Once when Mike Alvarez's Mexican son-in-law had been ill for several days and went to Calexico for treatment, I met him on the street there; he told me that the doctor could do nothing for him, and he then asked me, quite seriously, if his trouble might not be the excessive passion of his Cocopa wife.)

After having spent the night with a girl, the boy was expected to leave the house at dawn, but he often stayed around camp for the next day. He might go hunting, or fishing, or gather wood. Sam Spa always did this, but Jim Short returned to his own camp every day for the first week or so.

After the boy had been in his wife's camp for three days, his mother was expected to arrive for the purpose of taking her new daughter-in-law to her camp. She would first speak to the girl's mother, telling her that she had "heard" that her son was there, and that now she wanted the girl to come live with her, since she needed someone to help grind corn and carry water. The girl usually went along with her mother-in-law but, sometimes, if she was very bashful, she refused and delayed the change of residence for a week or two. When the girl left with the mother-in-law, a crowd would gather and the boys would shout at the girl, make jokes about her, and put their hands to their mouths and cry "hoo-hoo-hoo."

There was general agreement among my informants that residence should be patrilocal (with the husband's family), but this was not insisted upon. In all the cases I have recorded, however, the early years of marriage were either matrilocal (with the wife's family) or alternated between matrilocal and patrilocal. Although my sample is small, I am inclined to believe that my case material reflects the actual pattern, and that my informants were thinking of the later years of marriage, rather than the first few years, when they reported patrilocality. I was told that in ideal cases residence was alternating during the first few years, and patrilocal or in the vicinity of the groom's father's camp after that. Whenever the boy's family was dissolved or whenever the girl's family was in real need of help, residence was matrilocal.

During residence at the boy's camp, the son still worked for his father and the girl took the place of a daughter. In the girl's camp, the bride resumed her former habits and her husband became a "son" to his father-in-law. The couple was not expected to assume any responsibilities, and, since it was highly probable that the marriage would not endure, no very permanent personal relationships were entered into. The young couple ate their meals with the other members of the family, and they had no possessions of their own other than what they had had before. If the marriage continued in force, the couple gradually accumulated their own household equipment and built a house of their own; then, as children came along, they cleared their own fields and became quite independent of the parents. This was the ideal pattern, and my record of actual cases indicates a high degree of conformity of the actual to the ideal behavior.

Sam Spa's Marital Experiences

While the following biographical material is divergent because of Sam Spa's loss of his father and his residence in the camp of a distant kinsman, it nevertheless gives an intimate view of the Cocopa attitude toward marriage and family behavior.

Sam Spa was married seven times. His first wife, hearing that a married girl was planning to leave her husband in order to marry Spa, sent a male relative to bring him to her camp. The boy told Spa that he was going to sleep with one of the girls and that Spa should come along and get a girl for himself. When they arrived in the girl's camp, she snatched Spa's blanket from under his arm and refused to return it to him. After some scuffling, the girl finally asked Spa whether he chose to sleep with her or to return home without his blanket. Spa decided to stay, and the two were married. This incident is unusual in two respects: first, because the girl was the aggressor; second, because the boy in such cases would usually slip into the bed of a

supposedly sleeping girl, but here the two very brazenly retired together.

After the girl had induced Spa to stay the night with her, they went to one side of the house and prepared for bed. The girl removed her willow bark skirt, rolled it up to make a pillow, and covered her legs and hips with a large cotton cloth that she used in the daytime as a mantle. Spa removed his pants and shoes but left his shirt on. They rolled up in Spa's blanket, and he began to make love to her. He held her in his arms and felt her breasts, legs, and thighs. He was "too ashamed" to do anything more than this, and did not try.

It came out later in the interview that the girl was menstruating at the time. Whether Spa knew this in advance or whether he discovered it the next morning, I do not know. In any event, the girl's mother put them both under menstrual taboo the next morning, and she pursued the daily rites of bathing, hair washing, and food taboos for twelve instead of the usual four days. Spa continued to sleep with the girl but did not attempt coitus until the sixth night after the end of the twelve-day period. They had been sleeping in the same house with the girl's mother and a younger sister during this eighteen-day period, but on the night that Spa first attempted sexual intercourse, they moved to a nearby house occupied only by some children. This was at the suggestion of the girl.

Spa had dreamt some years earlier that if he stayed away from girls, he would become a great runner, and that if he had intercourse with a girl, it would make him sick. This very clearly was on his mind, and he was worried for fear that the effects of the dream had not "run out." In any event, according to his story, he attempted coitus the first four nights without success, and when he did succeed, on the fifth day, he became violently ill. His legs became heavy, his stomach bothered him, and he could hardly see. He went home that day to his mother's camp; the girl went along and stayed with him for two days, and then returned to her own camp. Sam Spa was ill for "about a year," but was finally cured when he coughed up some "dried blood" and decided that the effect of his dream had finally come to an end. He returned to live with his first wife, but they were separated soon afterward. (I could never get Spa to say that his illness resulted from marrying a menstruating girl. The twelve-day purification rite and this reference to "dried blood" may indicate that it was not only his dream that was actually in his mind as a rationalization of the illness.)

Spa's second wife was the younger sister of the first, and at the time that Spa married her she had never menstruated. Her mother had died a short time previously and she was living with some relatives in a camp near Spa's house. Arrangements for visiting her were made directly with the girl by Spa himself. He came to her early in the evening after the people in the house had gone to bed, but before they were asleep. Spa knew where the girl's bed was and went to it without being told. This girl was also using her bark skirt for a pillow and was covered from the waist down with a mantle.

After they had made love for a short while, the girl wanted Spa to have intercourse with her. He replied that he would be ashamed to do that (on the first night) because the other people in the house were probably still awake. She told him not to mind them: "This belongs to me, it doesn't belong to them, and we can do what we please." After a while, Spa did what she wanted. During coitus the girl pulled his hair and bit him on the cheek and neck.

Spa stayed with the girl for three nights, and had intercourse with her seven times each night. He then left for Yuma to find work. He was gone a full year, working around Yuma and traveling as far as Phoenix, working with a section gang on the railroad. When he returned, he started living with the girl again and learned that she had menstruated for the first time during his absence. (This story, told long after the event, is probably not unrelated to Spa's experience with his first wife.)

Two of Spa's seven wives were acquired by making a present to their fathers. The first time was on the occasion of his third marriage, when he arranged with a friend to take the girl's father a horse. Spa's father had died when he was a boy and he had no other close male relatives in the delta at that time, so far as I know. It is significant, however, that he did not make the gift himself. On the day that the horse was delivered, the father asked his daughter whether or not she wanted to marry Spa (he had seen her two or three times previously on visits to her camp), but she merely hung her head and refused to answer. Spa's friend returned on three successive days, meeting the same response each time, but was successful on the fourth day. When the girl agreed, arrangements were made for Spa to come to her bed that night.

It seems quite possible that Spa used this method of arranging for his marriage, in place of personal dealings with the girl, because of a wide disparity in their ages (he was about 22 or 23 years old) and the consequent lack of opportunity for him to make the usual advances. Also, the girl, being a virgin, would have had less freedom to talk with boys and make her own choice. This girl, like Spa's second and fourth wives, had not yet menstruated, but was otherwise mature.

The marriage occurred in early summer, and Spa slept with his wife without sexual intercourse until late in the fall, after he had made a trip to Yuma to work a few days and buy supplies. On the night of his return, he attempted coitus. The girl did not protest at first, but when Spa had inserted his penis only part way, the girl cried out, twisted away from him, and threw him off. The experience had been so painful that she would not let Spa try again. It was not until the following spring, after the girl had started menstruating, that Spa succeeded in having intercourse with her.

Three years later, when Spa arranged for his fourth wife, he not only went to considerable trouble to get a horse, but also gave the girl's father 25 Mexican pesos in cash. To earn this money, Spa spent much of the harvest season pulling and poling a small boat loaded with farm produce from Pokohap to Yuma, a distance of about 35 miles. It is not clear whether the corn, beans, and watermelons were his, or whether he was working in cooperation with other Indian farmers. In any event, after the harvest season, he walked to a place called La Huerta in the Baja California mountains, to get the horse. La Huerta was the home of his mother's Diegueño relatives, and it is quite possible that the horse was given to him, although I failed to inquire about this.

After securing the horse, Spa returned to the delta and arranged to open negotiations with the girl's father. This time he got one of the girl's male relatives to act as go-between, paying him a shirt, a pair of pants, a silk handkerchief, some tobacco, and a dollar and a half in cash.

The trend and details of the negotiations that followed were, for some reason, outstanding in Sam Spa's career, because my notes indicate that he needed little prompting to tell the story and told it with much animation and in some detail. On the first day, when the boy arrived in the girl's camp with the horse and cash, the whole evening and half the night were spent in discussion, both between the negotiator and the father, and between father and daughter. The latter conversation was one-sided, however, for it was reported that the girl refused to speak and merely hung her head when her father talked to her. On the next night, the boy tried again and with no better luck. On the third night, the girl's mother is reported to have talked at great length with the girl. She told her daughter that her father needed the horse so that when he went to Yuma he could ride and not walk; also, that he needed the money so that when he went to Yuma on the horse, he would have something with which to buy clothes and tobacco. The mother's words were apparently effective, for the girl finally agreed.

The marriage, however, did not take place for nearly a year; it was postponed until the girl had menstruated. During this period, Spa visited in her camp frequently, but never slept with her. The manner in which the girl made it known to Spa when he could come to her bed was, perhaps, typical. One night when Spa was visiting in the girl's camp, he heard some boys talking about him; one told the other that Spa would probably sleep with the girl that night. When Spa heard this, he knew that he would be welcome, and so after the people in camp had gone to sleep, he left his own bed and joined her. He slept with her for three nights, just making love, and on the fourth night she permitted intercourse.

Sam Spa's last three wives were mature women who had been married a number of times before. In each case he "just started living with them," initiating the marriage in the usual fashion by coming to their beds at night. He lived with the last two until their deaths.

DIVORCE

In the eyes of the Cocopa, "divorce" in the sense in which we use the word took place only when a functioning, independent family had been established and when the breakup of the family meant that obligations (to children, to other relatives, or to members of the camp) would not be met. If a couple quarreled and the wife left her husband, and he wanted her back, he went after her in a few days and attempted to bring her home. If the man left, his family tried to induce him to return. If this failed, his wife sent someone to get him, but she did not go herself. If the separation lasted, members of both families used their influence to try to patch up the trouble; however, if it finally appeared that nothing could be done, the younger children went to live with their mother in her family's camp, while the older children could elect either to stay with their father or to go with their mother.

The dissolution of a trial marriage (that is, any marriage of short duration) was not always traceable to any particular fault or to quarrels between the couple. Jim Short "liked" his first wife and they got along well together, but he decided he wanted another girl. Sam Spa's second wife just got tired of living with him. He was considerably put out, but there was no indication of serious incompatibility, or of any real fault on either side. In some cases, a breakup came when couples could not get along, or when one or the other was "lazy" or "cranky." When Spa's fourth marriage ended, he had no quarrel with his wife and was not concerned because she had left him, but he did quarrel with her father about the return of the horse and money he had paid for her.

Divorce was expected when a couple had been living together for two or more years without having children. It was recognized that such individuals would often produce children after a change of partners, since sterility was rated a natural biological fault that had no known cure but was not necessarily permanent.

A baby born into a short-term marriage was never, apparently, given to the deserting partner. Sam Spa and Alice Olds were questioned on this point and indicated that babies were considered an asset, and that their loss was the price for breaking up a family that had not yet become independent. A baby left with its father, in such a case, was cared for by his mother and sisters or other women in his camp. There could be no such thing as an orphan or a bastard in Cocopa society. Although in Sam Spa's case it was sometimes the wife who dissolved the marriage, the usual pattern, I am sure, was for the husband to leave the wife, so that babies were retained by her family. Jim Short did this, and the following statement probably describes a common occurrence: "Boys would move around and stay with a girl until she was pregnant and then they would leave."

The impression that might be gained from my notes is that a Cocopa marriage, once firmly established, was seldom disrupted by quarrels, fighting, and disagreements, and rarely ended in divorce. However, the first part of the statement is probably erroneous and the second nearer the truth. In this, and in other contexts, my notes lack the detail of comings, goings, fights, and gossip that surround family life in other societies. Cocopa families no doubt had their troubles, but there was nothing I could do to induce my informants to give me the details of family and group quarrels and fights. When I found that nothing of the kind would ever be volunteered, I fell back upon direct questioning, and the following result was typical:

Q. What did the captain do when there was trouble in camp?
A. There was no trouble.
Q. There never was any trouble while you were living at Pokohap?
A. No.
Q. Didn't the men ever fight?
A. Yes.
Q. What did they fight about?
A. A man lost some *čeł* in a gambling game and they fought.

The process was endless and answers were short and evasive. Even Sam Spa, who broke the taboo against naming dead relatives, could only rarely bring himself to give an account of fighting or quarreling.

Thanks to our bringing about an accidental meeting of two of our informants, however, we learned of an incident revealing the emotions and hard feelings that could erupt in a Cocopa camp. One afternoon in May of 1947 when we were living near Somerton, we had both Sam Spa and Alice Olds at our home the same day and took them home together when we had finished our interviews. The next morning Alice Olds complained to one of our interpreters, telling her that she would not again ride all the way home with "that old man" (Sam Spa). She did not like him and wanted nothing to do with him. It turned out that she was the mother of Spa's fourth wife, the one for whom he had paid the father a horse and 25 pesos about 1900. She had good reason to dislike Sam Spa, she said, because he divorced her daughter with no more reason than some gossip that she was running around with other men, and when he left he forced her husband to give him two horses as a return for the bride price. Furthermore, she said, Spa in those days was cranky and selfish and lazy. He always had money given to him by his sisters, who were Yuma prostitutes, and he "made fun of me when I tried to plant a big farm to feed my family."

The fighting, quarreling, and divorce must have been quite an event in all their lives. Spa some years before had told me of the breakup of his fourth marriage:

One time when I returned from a trip, after I had been living with my wife in her father's camp for about a year, I learned that she had been sleeping with another man and that her father and mother wanted me to move out of their camp. I complained to a leader in my camp and we went to my wife's camp and hid in the bushes to see whether or not some man was sleeping with her. Her father [who was Matokwam, the real leader of the Cocopa in that area] saw us and came out to see what we were doing hanging around his camp in the dark. My friend said that we wanted to know what "bad things" were going on, that I had paid for the girl and that it was not right for me to lose her. He told Matokwam that he had a gun, and knew that he might get hurt, but he demanded the return of the girl.

The arguing and quarreling apparently went on most of the night, with Spa's friend first asking for four horses in compensation and finally settling for two, one of which he took for his own trouble.

FAMILY LIFE

Families, singly and in groups, came and went in the delta as they saw fit, and made their own decisions as to the time and place for gathering wild rice in the estuary or pine nuts in the mountains. When I asked Sam Spa whether or not the heads of families were expected to consult with the band leader in matters of planting, land ownership, rabbit drives, or expeditions, he acted surprised. The captain or the band orator, he said, talked to the people regularly. He told them to plant big crops, gather plenty of mesquite, take care of their families and children, and stay out of trouble, but only by way of advice. He did not attempt to tell any family what to do. When families or individuals representing several families worked together, they did it voluntarily, and named a temporary "boss" who gave a minimum of direction and had no authority. In strictly group affairs such as a mourning ceremony, a harvest festival, and certainly warfare in the old days, the captain was given some degree of authority. He was often called upon to settle disputes between families or groups of kinsmen, but whether any official authority was involved is doubtful. Certainly there was no established mechanism for enforcing his decisions.

The Cocopa did not live in villages but maintained scattered houses, roughly and informally grouped into clusters of friends and kinsmen, and, secondarily, grouped around favored farming or gathering areas. If house sites were permanently located on high ground near the fields, they were strung along the main stream or sloughs; if farms were not near flood-free areas, the people maintained summer camps near their fields, and after the harvest was gathered, moved to winter sites along the mesas and sand hills. In Wi Ahwir territory these sand hills projected from the mesa in a series of fingers, upon the tips of which two or three families made their homes. In 1900, such camps extended for a distance of about seven miles north of Mayor. Mike Alvarez gave me a list of 41 camps that were located in this seven-mile strip about 1895.

It is important to note that there was no village "plaza" — no easily accessible meeting place for any of the

groups. Social contact was made by men and women visiting back and forth between each other's camps. If they happened to be within walking distance of the captain's camp, that was always the most popular place for informal gatherings, but for most Cocopa men and women, visits to this central meeting place were usually confined to ceremonies and celebrations. The following type of statement appears frequently in my notes: "In the evening I went to a neighboring camp to visit," or, "Some people would come over and visit in our camp."

Life around a camp of this kind was a complicated process, and much of the give and take of interaction is lost to the investigator who is forced to use informants. My observations do not fit the data secured from informants for this report since the whole mode of making a living has changed. In the old days, the women must have been exceedingly busy with their gathering and household duties, but by 1940 to 1950, the men were working for wages and most of their food was purchased in stores. On almost every visit that we made to a Cocopa camp we found the women with literally nothing to do.

My informants gave me a picture of a busy household with a high degree of mutual cooperation. Nothing in my notes indicates an interest in or a submission to unilateral authority. A chart of family structure made in terms of individual responsibilities would be more nearly true to actual conditions than a chart designed to show lines of authority.

In the winter when there was little to gather, men were kept busy hunting and fishing, while women had comparatively little to do. During the rest of the year, men and women were about equally occupied, so that circumstances often demanded that they help each other, and formal patterns of a division of labor did not stand in the way. A man carried wood and water if his wife was busy, and a woman helped in the fields, at house building, and with other tasks if her husband had other more pressing chores. Such behavior extended to children and other members of the household.

In spite of frequent patrilocal residence and the clustering of houses of kinsmen in a single camp, the Cocopa family was essentially of the conjugal type; that is, the functioning unit was a man and his wife and their children. If, as was frequently the case, one or more relatives joined this group, there were no formal modes of family extension. Loyalties and responsibilities were primarily between a man and his wife and their children, and were secondarily extended to other kinsmen.

The Cocopa recognized the separateness of the basic family unit by referring to *own* fathers, mothers, children, and siblings as *mayai ahan* (real relatives). When I asked, for example, who would be expected to give the greatest help in a mourning ceremony, the answer was: *mayai ahan*. The data in Table 6, taken from my census, show some of the variations in composition of the households.

TABLE 6
Composition of Cocopa Households

Camp A, Near San Luis, Sonora, 1940
House Aa:
1. male head of household
2. wife of 1
3. son of 2
4. daughter of 2
House Ab:
5. brother of 2
6. wife of 5

Camp B, Near San Luis, Sonora, 1940
House Ba:
1. male head of household
2. wife of 1
House Bb:
3. son of 1
4. wife of 3, daughter of 2
House Bc:
5. male head of household
6. wife of 5, relative of 2
7. child, son of 5 and 6
8. child, daughter of 5 and 6
9. sister of 6
House Bd:
10. brother of father of 2

Camp AA, South of La Grulla, Sonora, 1944
House AAa:
1. male head of household
2. wife of 1
3. male "uncle" of 1
4. female "cousin" of 1
House AAb:
5. male head of household
6. wife of 5
7. baby, daughter of 5 and 6
House AAc (brush shelter in corner of ramada):
8. old woman related to 1

Camp BB, South of La Grulla, Sonora, 1944
House BBa:
1. male head of household
2. wife of 1
3. child, son of 1 and 2
4. child, daughter of 1 and 2
5. baby, daughter of 1 and 2
6. old man, relative of 1

Camp CC, South of La Grulla, Sonora, 1944
House CCa:
1. male head of household
2. wife of 1
3. child, son of 1 and 2
4. child, son of 1 and 2
5. child, son of 1 and 2
6. mother of 1
House CCb:
7. male head of household
8. child, son of 7
9. child, daughter of 7

House CCc:
10. son of 1 and 2, head of household
11. wife of 10
12. child, daughter of 10
13. child, daughter of 10
House CCd:
14. adult male, relative of 1

Camp L, near Colonia Carranza, Baja California, 1940
House La:
1. adult Mexican
2. wife of 1
House Lb:
3. old man, relative of 2

Camp M, near Colonia Carranza, Baja California, 1940
House Ma:
1. male head of household
2. adult daughter of 1
3. adult daughter of 1
House Mb:
4. son of 1, head of household
5. wife of 4

Camp N, near Colonia Carranza, Baja California, 1940
House Na:
1. male head of household
2. daughter of 1
3. husband of 2

Camp O, near Colonia Carranza, Baja California, 1940
House Oa:
1. male head of household
2. wife of 1
3. child, son of 2
4. child, daughter of 2
5. child, daughter of 2
6. old woman, relative of 1

Camp P, near Colonia Carranza, Baja California, 1940
House Pa:
1. male head of household
2. wife of 1
3. baby, son of 1 and 2
4. baby, son of 1 and 2
5. old woman, mother of 2
6. old man, husband of 5

Camp R, near Mayor, Baja California, 1940
House Ra:
1. old woman head of household
2. American old man, husband of 1
House Rb:
3. male head of household, brother of 1
4. wife of 3
House Rc:
5. old woman head of household, sister of 1
6. adult woman, daughter of 3
7. adult woman, daughter of 3
8. adult woman, daughter of 3
9. adult woman, daughter of 3
10. adult woman, related to 1
11. child, son of 10
12. child, male relative of 1

BIRTH

Children were important to the Cocopa, and babies were welcome. At every celebration or group meeting, the captain urged the young people to get acquainted and get married, so that there would be "lots of Cocopa." Birth itself, however, was not a major interest, and little attention was paid to the event outside the immediate family.

Danger to the mother was clearly recognized, but was not one of the culturally defined "anxiety" situations. There were no rites or magical practices in anticipation of the birth, and few taboos. Most of the required behavior came after the birth of the child, and referred explicitly to a restoration of ritual purity, rather than to an avoidance of physical danger. I questioned three informants on this point, and the material from Tom Juarez is probably typical:

Q: When your wife was big were you afraid she might die?
A: Yes, I was worried, and a little bit afraid and so was my wife.
Q: What did you do?
A: People have to take care, day and night. When she started to hurt they put her on the ground and the mother helped to push down the baby.
Q: What do you mean take care?
A: I had some good leaves and boiled them to make a drink to bring the baby. The leaves come from Kamia country in the mountains.
Q: Who fixes the leaves?
A: Anyone.
Q: Did you carry something in your pocket, or around your neck, or did your wife do that, to prevent trouble?
A: Some do, but I didn't.
Q: Did you try to have the right kind of dreams so your wife would be all right?
A: I wanted to have a dream, but I couldn't.
Q: How about your wife?
A: She tried to have a dream but I never asked her if she did have one.

As soon as labor pains began, both the husband and wife were forbidden to eat salt, meat, or fats, and were required to use a scratching stick. This continued for a 12-day period after the birth of the child. For the first four days of this period, both plastered their hair at night with a mixture of mud and the juice from crushed arrowweed roots, and washed it out each morning. For the next four days the hair was covered with plain mud, and for the last four days it was treated with a mixture of boiled mesquite sap and water. There were no other taboos for the husband, who was expected to continue with his work without interruption, both before and after the birth of the child.

During pregnancy, according to Sam Spa, the mother could not eat a gopher, since the gopher digs holes and if she were to eat one the baby would "die and come out." She could not eat a pumpkin damaged by a raccoon, or a watermelon damaged by a coyote; if she did, her "ears would burst." She could not eat corn that rats had disturbed or anything touched by a kangaroo rat, as rats never cover anything, so this would make her heart flutter. If she happened to walk over a beaver track, the baby "would come right out."

At the beginning of labor, the mother retired to her house with a midwife, preferably her mother, and other women. Normal parturition was accomplished with the mother in a sitting position, with outstretched legs, and supported from behind by the midwife, who braced her knees against the woman's back and pressed down with her hands on the woman's stomach. Another woman took the baby. Only women were allowed in the house unless trouble developed or the birth was delayed, in which case a male or female shaman was called. The special treatment consisted in "smoking tobacco around to make the baby come out." The afterbirth was severed from the umbilical cord by the midwife with a clam shell or bamboo knife and was then "thrown on the trash pile" by anyone. Immediately after the birth, an arrowweed fire was built on the house floor. When the floor was heated, the ashes were scraped out and the mother placed over the heated area. The midwife then pressed down on her stomach "to expel the remaining blood." This treatment was continued for 12 or more hours.

The baby was washed, wrapped in soft cloth, and taken to a shaman for inspection and treatment. The doctor felt the new baby to discover its condition. Sam Spa, who told me of this practice, assured me that the baby was taken to the shaman, and that he (or she) was not called in for the purpose.

Shortly after birth (I did not learn exactly when), the women helpers spread a black mineral paint above and below the baby's eyelash roots. At the same time, they spread a black solution made from cooked pumpkin over the baby's body. The mother's face was painted with red ochre mixed with pumpkin-seed oil. No belt was put on the baby, and there was no final purification rite for the parents.

When the baby was two to four days old its ears were pierced, and the umbilical cord was buried after it dropped off. A few days after the birth, when it had been decided that the baby would live, it was placed in a cradle and its head was strapped to a warm, dirt-filled piece of cloth "to make the head flat."

So far as I know, there was no rite or symbolic behavior on the part of kinsmen or others to recognize the addition of a new member of the group. A baby did not receive a name for two or three years, and the naming was without ceremony. There were no gifts for a new baby or its parents, and no formal visits from relatives.

In the case of a first child, according to Sam Spa, the ideal pattern called for sexual restraint between the married couple for a period extending from a month before birth until the baby could walk a few steps. Spa said: "When the baby gets big enough to walk then have *opat* [intercourse]. When the baby is still small, if you rub that thing in, maybe make another baby and maybe lose it." During this period, the husband was also forbidden to eat fat or meat. I did not discover until later that my informant was talking about both sexual and food taboos specifically in terms of a first baby. The food taboo was lifted for subsequent children, but I failed to discover whether the sexual taboo was lifted as well. In the case of a baby's death, sexual intercourse could be resumed after the eighth day following the death.

The ideal time for conception was just before dawn on the day following the restoration of ritual purity after menstruation. Conception in the early evening was to be avoided, ideally, since it might produce an ugly or a "bad" (*hačak*) offspring. In order for conception to take place, it was necessary to "hit a girl right," and this was a matter of luck. Subsequent intercourse, if "right," would produce twins, but Sam Spa was not too sure on this point. The mother knew that she was pregnant when menstruation stopped, because the growing child had formed a "plug." Sam Spa believed that the baby ate and drank when the mother did, and had never heard that the mother's menstrual discharge had any connection with pregnancy. The male semen provided the amniotic fluid, thus excessive intercourse during pregnancy "made too much water around the baby."

Alice Olds, who was probably in her late seventies in 1947, gave us the following information on childbirth and her own experiences.

I was eleven years old [the interpreter doubts that she was quite so young] when I was first married and I had not yet menstruated. After I menstruated four times I became pregnant. In those days I wore nothing but a willow bark skirt and when I menstruated I tucked the strands of the skirt between my legs to catch the blood. I had only one skirt, so when it became soiled I washed it in arrowweed root to make it pure again. I wanted a baby and so I could not eat salt, meat, or fat while menstruating.

When I became pregnant my husband and I kept right on working as usual. We kept on having sexual intercourse until about a month before the baby was born. When I felt the first labor pains I became frightened and ran away. When the pain stopped I stopped running and when it started again I ran again. My mother and the midwife finally caught me and took me home and held me down. Then they worked on me a little while and the baby came. To help the baby come, my mother got behind me and pressed down on my stomach with her hands. I was sitting on the ground with my legs bent at the knees. The midwife was there to catch the baby but it hit the ground and was swollen up from the bump.

When a woman starts having labor pains a crowd of women usually gathers in the house to watch her, because it is a dangerous time. The mother may scream at them and throw dirt at them when she is in pain. They are there because if the mother should die they will be on the spot to start crying and so help the family.

When the baby is born it is washed in plain water, the cord is cut, and the baby is placed in its first cradle. It is given no food for four days and then it is taken to a medicine man who works on the baby. The baby may have swallowed some of the mother's blood so he has to tell the family whether it did or not. He works on the baby, pressing to make its bowels move and make it urinate. If the baby is ill the treatments go on for four days.

For the first two or three days after the baby is born it is given only drops of water dripping from the mother's finger. To get me ready to feed my baby my mother put my breasts in a bowl of hot water and squeezed them. I also started eating corn gruel so that I would have milk for the baby.

For the first four days after the baby was born my mother washed it with *mat moši* [a fine, white silt]. This cut the "grease" that he was born with, and made the first head hair fall off the baby faster.

During the first year, according to Alice Olds, the baby was treated with a salve or ointment containing red ochre. This prevented chapping and was also a protection against the cold. The ointment was made by mixing red ochre with deer lard and a paste derived from roasted pumpkin seeds.

The baby was kept in its cradle for about a year. When it woke from a sleep it was taken from the cradle and allowed to crawl. The baby was fed whenever it was hungry, and when it got sleepy it cried for the cradle and slept in it.

CHILD TRAINING

The Cocopa did not take the processes of child training for granted. They were highly verbal on the subject, and set certain explicit standards for training and for the behavior of "well-trained" individuals.

Greatest reliance was placed upon semiformal talks, which combined elements of explicit instruction and moral suasion. These talks began as soon as the children could understand and continued for as long as the children were a part of the family. In matters of discipline, moral behavior, and the creation of a "good heart" in the child, I could detect no important division by sex. Specific instruction in specialized tasks was between a father and his son, and a mother and her daughter.

I doubt very much if I could overstate this matter of constant verbal admonition and instruction. It was certainly given far greater emphasis than in our society. Parents' talks to their children were mentioned by all my informants, not only in responses to my questions on the subject of child training, but also in statements volunteered in many other contexts.

The same patterns of moral suasion and appeals to conscience are found at the group level. Such statements are found in the creation myth and in the messages of minor talkers, orators, and captains.

Semiformal talks, in which a father or a mother called the child to one side, seemed to be fairly standard in pattern; at least, the content of the talks repeated to me was quite similar. Sam Spa said:

My father told me what to do. He told me how to get along with people, not to talk back to older people and not to be cranky. If people came to visit, to feed them. If a boy is tall, it is not good. It is better to be short. My father told me to sit down, he wanted to talk to me, that I was small and didn't know much, and that he did. He told me to work hard and have plenty to eat, to "look up" when visitors came, and to feed them.

When he was a very little boy his mother told him "to stay in camp, not to run away or I might step on something sharp [rattlesnake?], not to go to another house or they might feed me something that would burn. She told me not to cry and not to fight."

Sam Spa thought of himself as a "good" man who had never been in serious trouble, either as a boy or in his adult years — a typical Cocopa response that may be quite apart from the actual record. However, it is significant that when I asked him why he had behaved himself, he said: "My heart is good. If it says no, I don't do it. My father didn't live very long but he told me not to steal, not to fight, and I have remembered what my father said." (At the time of the creation, some people were evil because they didn't "hear" or didn't "remember" what the creator told them.)

When a child persisted in misbehaving, he was punished by whipping, usually with light arrowweed branches. Both parents administered this punishment to both sexes, but only when the children were young. Irritation on the part of the parents or any older person resulted in a verbal rebuke, with the pitch of the voice lowered, rather than raised, if repeated rebukes became necessary. We first noticed this behavior when a child two or three years old persisted in chasing some hens who were confined in a pen. The repeated rebukes quieted the rumpus but in the end the parents had to remove the child from the pen. It was not uncommon for irritated older people to throw dirt or small sticks at a misbehaving child. Threats were common, and for small children they alluded to the visitation of a ghost or an evil fox.

Children were corrected in our presence; they usually obeyed if they were old enough to understand, but not always. Maria's son, two or three years old, persisted in his demand to nurse. He paid no attention to his mother's reprimands (she was busy painting pottery for us), and finally had his way by crying and beating on his mother's arm and shoulder.

When children were over 12 years old, corporal punishment ideally came to a stop, and absolute parental authority was relinquished. Sam Spa told me that in the case of unruly and cranky boys or girls who ran away from home (even if they were as young as 10 or 11), there was nothing that the parents could or would do to get them back. Runaway boys could go to relatives, and girls looked for boys and lived with them. The English word "cranky" was used very broadly to describe uncooperative, quarrelsome, or sullen individuals.

Babies and young children were fed whenever they were hungry, and, according to Alice Olds, they ate all the time. They were never neglected or left in the care of immature children while mothers went out to gather; if several neighboring women had small children, one of them always stayed in camp with the babies and small children while the others went to gather. Older girls, however, were expected to help their mothers by feeding and watching the younger children.

Boys were not trained to spartan behavior during the period of this report. None of the fathers of my informants ever urged them to rise early, to train themselves by racing, or to harden themselves by swimming in cold water or going without adequate clothing. In the days of warfare, however, there was probably some tendency in this direction. Sam Spa told me that the war leader selected likely boys of 10 or over for war training. He had them race, go without food and water for long periods, and run naked through the thickets of arrowweed and young willows. By the time my informants were born, no boys ever did this.

As in all societies, there were explicitly verbalized ideal patterns for sexual behavior among the Cocopa, and both the father and the mother instructed their children in these matters as soon as they were old enough to understand. Such instruction usually took the form of moral preachment having to do with the Cocopa definition of restraint in courtship and marriage, masturbation, incest taboos, taboos relating to sexual intercourse during menstruation, and the like. Training, however, was not all moral preachment. Childhood violation of taboos, such as that on masturbation, was quickly and severely punished, often by whipping.

The Cocopa were by no means prudish, however, in their treatment of the existence of male and female genitals and of coitus. Sex as a fact of life was freely discussed and often the subject of jokes. Personal names of males, for example, often had reference to genitals or the sex act. There was no attempt at privacy in micturition: men and boys simply turned their backs, while women were concealed by their skirts.

Toilet training was not considered a matter of importance. Pads of shredded willow bark were used in the baby cradle to collect the baby's urine and excrement. Babies who wet or fouled their mothers or other caretakers were not punished. Gradually as they grew older and were able to walk they were encouraged to go outside the house to urinate or defecate. Eventually, when they were old enough to understand, they learned proper toilet habits. A child who would not learn at the expected age was talked to and, eventually, punished.

TOYS, GAMES, AND GAMBLING

Children's play hours were spent in imitating the ways of their elders, for almost no games or toys are mentioned that do not reflect adult life.

Alice Olds said that when girls and boys around five to eight years of age played together they would "play house," building a tiny house with a shade where they played with dolls. They pretended that they were married and that the dolls were children; they even made little baby dolls. When girls played together a stick would represent a husband. Sam Spa was a little more explicit about "playing house." He said that when they played that they were married, they "did the way their parents did; the boy would get on top of the girl, but he couldn't do anything. Then they made babies of mud." Children also made dishes, pots, and other household equipment in miniature. During the time of our fieldwork Cocopa children were playing with homemade dolls and with fired and unfired clay dishes and pots. In addition the children, of course, had cheap tin and plastic toys, and it was not unusual to see the children pulling toy wagons and tricycles along the dusty roads near their camp. One traditional Cocopa toy was still popular — the ring and pin game. The toy itself consisted of a string about 8 to 10 inches long, knotted at one end so as to hold 15 to 20 doughnut-shaped rings of gourd, and attached at the other end to a slender 6-inch stick. The object was to toss the string in such a way as to impale the gourd rings, one after another, with the point of the stick (Spier 1933: 338, 344).

The most popular game for men was referred to in Spanish as *peon*, in Cocopa as *mičuuɬ*. The Cocopa thought of the game as one of skill, rather than chance. One side, consisting of four players, tried to read the movements, actions, and voices of their four opponents and so determine in which hands they held four white egret bones and, redundantly, in which hands they held four blackened sticks of arrowweed. Fifteen arrowweed sticks served as counters. Not only did the groups of four players bet against each other, but each group had its supporters among non-players who also bet on the outcome of the game. While the betting was taking place and the four men holding the peon sticks were passing sticks from hand to hand in an attempt to confuse their opponents, a singer and his chorus of men and women stood behind the peon holders and sang songs relating to the peon game. A referee was always present to settle possible arguments and, although my notes do not say so, the chances are very good that each side had the support of one or more shamans who could influence the outcome through magic.

I did not record the rules of the game itself and must therefore depend upon Gifford's description (1931: 47):

> The players on one side hid all eight black and white pieces in their hands, which were held behind their backs (nowadays under a blanket). One man on the opposing side guessed the location of the black pieces. If he made many bad guesses another then tried the guessing. In calling, the guesser used directional terms. Thus, he called east or west if the players were facing north or south. If they were facing north, the call "east" meant for them to expose their right hands, the call "west", their left hands. Each time he guessed the location of a black piece, it, and the companion white piece, were passed to his side. For the black sticks not exposed the guesser lost one counter each [i.e. the referee gave the stick holders one of the fifteen counters for each black stick missed]. When all of the black pieces had been guessed, the guessers became the hiders.
>
> The counters which the umpire handed out were all kept in the center first. Then, after they were distributed to the two teams as won, they were passed by the umpire from one side to the other as called for.

According to Sam Spa, a variation of this game was played before he was born. In this variation only egret bone pieces were used, and the four players whose turn it was to conceal the location of the egret bones buried their hands in soft dirt or sand. To conceal the location of the pieces, they could keep them in one hand or the other or leave them in the sand on one side or the other.

A women's dice game, called *taol sopas*, had two or four players (one or two on a side). The dice consisted of four pieces of split willow branch about five inches long, each with a round surface and a flat surface, the latter being decorated. The player whose turn it was to throw the dice held the sticks in one hand and bounced them from a flat, hard surface with sufficient force to scatter them. To start scoring, a player had to throw three with flat side down and one up. Subsequent throws were scored according to the number of dice with flat side up. The player lost the dice to the other side if two or three of the dice landed flat side up. As the dice changed hands, 15 tally sticks were used to keep score, and the side winning 13 or more of the tally sticks won the game.

Both men and women played the hoop and pole game (*a·čuR*). The hoop used by the Cocopa was relatively small, about 7 inches in diameter, and the pole was long and heavy — about 6 or 7 feet long. The object of the game was to hurl the pole at the rolling hoop in such a way as to stop its momentum and cause it to fall upon the pole. In Spier's description of the game among the Maricopa there was a contest in which two men each threw a pole at the hoop (Spier 1933: 336).

Many other games involving athletic prowess were enjoyed. Among the most popular of these was a kicking ball race in which each runner lifted and propelled a ball with his toes as he ran to a determined point and back. The Cocopa, according to our informants, used a ball shaped from wood. They also engaged in relay races and shinny (a form of hockey but much more informal).

Gambling was associated with all these games, and wagers were made with beads, hair belts, belts made from American cloth, and money (after the boats began running on the river, and Cocopa worked for wages). Sometimes there was betting on horses, but not many people had them. So far as Sam Spa was concerned, nothing could match the excitement of a horse race. Spa said that gambling made a family poor — not because of the losses, since food and supplies were never wagered, but because of the time spent away from work.

FAMILY RITES

The most important ritual value, from the point of view of the individual and the family, was the maintenance and restoration of ritual purity (*čosip*). This purity could be lost through contact with the dead and with enemy scalps, and in connection with childbirth and menstruation. A state of special ritual purity was required in warfare, in hunting some game animals, and for participation in the mourning ceremonies. This state required advance action in the form of smoking, bathing, and abstention from certain foods and sexual intercourse. However, failure to perform these rites or to observe the taboos did not produce impurity, but simply jeopardized the undertaking. Some acts (such as a boy's eating of his own game, improper sexual behavior, or visitation by a dead relative) brought about a state of impurity that could not be restored by the above means, but whose effect, when punishment in the form of illness resulted, could with luck be cured by a shaman.

Automatic losses of purity associated with menstruation and childbirth were strictly a family concern. The mother treated the menstruating girl, and a wife and husband together performed the rites associated with menstruation after marriage and with childbirth. Further evidence of family unity, in the matter of ritual values, was the rule forbidding not only the boy himself, but also his parents and other close kin as well, from eating the game and fish he caught.

At the onset of menstruation and for the succeeding three periods, each girl went through a rite of purification under the supervision of her mother or mother-substitute. The rite was repeated each day for four days. During this time the girl could not eat meat, fat, or salt; she was also forbidden to touch herself, and had to use a scratching stick instead. In addition, she was expected to maintain a serious attitude, lest she grow up frivolous, and to refrain from unnecessary talk, lest she develop into a garrulous woman.

Treatment started at about noon on each of the four days. The mother took the girl to a prepared and sheltered spot near the house where water, previously warmed, was poured over her. After this bath, the girl was permitted to eat a light vegetable dish, preferably a corn gruel. During the morning before this bath and the afternoon following it, the girl rested in camp: she was kept in semi-isolation and was not expected to do any work or join in the activities of the household. Toward evening of each day, the girl was given a second warm bath. She was then stretched out on a bed of arrowweed over heated sand, where for about an hour her mother pressed her body with one foot and then another, from head to toe. This treatment was to make the girl grow and give her a beautiful body. On the fourth night, following the heat treatment, the mother mixed the pounded skin of arrowweed roots with warm mud and plastered the girl's hair. This mixture was left on all night and washed off the next morning in the final warm water bath. Some mothers rubbed the warm mud all over the girl's body, but this practice was not common. The rite was strictly a family affair; no shaman was called in, and there was no singing or dancing. I do not know what the mother told her daughter at such a time, but, from other evidence, I suspect that the treatment was accompanied by a semiformal talk on ideal patterns of behavior.

The same concept of impurity was applied upon the occasion of a girl's first four menstrual periods after marriage. At that time, however, both the wife and her husband were equally unclean and underwent identical purification rites. Both were required to bathe in warm water each morning (one account noted that it was preferable to have the girl's mother pour water over them) and to pack their hair each evening with the arrowweed and mud mixture, removing it in the morning bath. During the four-day period both had to abstain from meat, fat, and salt, and to use a scratching stick. Sexual intercourse was forbidden during this time, but there was no restriction upon other activities. Once the restrictions associated with the first four menses were over, a menstruating woman could go about all her usual activities without restriction; however, she was supposed to be careful not to come near a sick person or to let a sick person touch anything that she had handled.

In the days of warfare, a scalp-taker underwent a 16-day period of purification, the last 12 days of which were spent at home, where his wife assisted him in the purification rites.

So far as I was able to learn, these were the only rituals held by and for the family. The initiation ceremony, the funeral, and the mourning ceremony were, of course, of great concern to the families involved, but they were conducted by the group and, from the anthropologist's point of view, were group ceremonials.

There was no family fetish, no altar, no family offering of food, and no ritual or magical practice associated with the family farm, with the minor exceptions noted in

Chapter 3. Religious rituals appeared to be as near a minimum in this group as in surrounding tribes, and they were much less important than among the Yuman tribes of southern California.

SICKNESS, SHAMANISM, AND WITCHCRAFT

My informants were uniformly reluctant to talk about sickness and death. They avoided my questions by a change of subject or silence, so I made no serious effort to gain information of this type until my third trip into the field. In 1944, when I persisted in my questions regarding cremations, Frank Blue, interpreting for Jim Short, became so emotional that his lips trembled and tears rolled down his cheek. He was not personally involved, but he must have let his thoughts wander to recent deaths in his own family. Alice Olds became so nervous when questions came too close to the death of her husband that she finally "froze" and refused to answer questions of any kind. Tom Juarez, even after I came to know him rather well, told me that he had never been ill in his life, knew nothing about curing, and hadn't the faintest notion of how a shaman worked. Sam Spa and Frank Gomez were the only two men who could, in the end, talk about the subject without visible sign of emotion.

A great deal more work will have to be done before any clear understanding of the Cocopa attitude toward sickness, death, shamanism, and sorcery will emerge. I consider this area of behavior, plus the dream beliefs, as one of the important keys to an understanding of the culture, but a serious analysis must await the time when contemporary behavior can be observed at length and in full living context. Present-day (1975) investigators need not be concerned that the Cocopa have become so modern as to have lost the practices and beliefs surrounding this area of their lives.

The material that follows is generally reliable, but probably represents a mere fraction of a wide and varied series of individual and local group idiosyncrasies (see Gifford 1933). The Cocopa were evidently not only interested in curing but were willing to experiment and change their practices. They were also highly ambivalent toward the practitioner who could help their sick relatives but who was, at the same time, a powerful witch. The dilemma was solved in the past by importing Pima shamans for important individuals who could afford the expense. In recent times, "Christianized" Indians from other tribes have introduced the concept of ceremonial therapy in the form of healing cults, in which the efficacy of the treatment lies in group participation in rites, rather than in the power of the practitioner.

Sickness was of vital concern to everyone in the family, and the invalid could depend upon his relatives for unlimited nursing, personal care, and material support for the employment of shamans. For minor illnesses, home remedies were known; these remedies were chiefly a series of decoctions prepared from wild plants. I made no special inquiries on this subject, but find voluntary reference to plants used as a cathartic, as a medication for pregnant women, and as a cure for snake bite. All such remedies reported to me grew in the territory of California mountain Indians to the west of the Cocopa, while all outside shamans (including the modern cult leaders) came from the Arizona desert tribes to the east. The sample of divergent origins is small but probably significant.

When Sam Spa was a baby, he was severely ill. His father called in a shaman (a "brother") for a curing rite, but at the same time traded with some mountain Indians for a plant known to be a violent purgative. The medicine was normally reserved for adults and was considered highly dangerous for children because of its strength. However, the father and mother gave the remedy in desperation but did not tell the shaman what they had done. Spa said: "After the shaman worked on me, my bowels ran off for a day and a night. Then I sat up but couldn't see and felt around and found corn and ate it. I had been sick for about two years. The shaman didn't know about the medicine and thought he did the curing."

The Shaman as Family Doctor

The Cocopa had no organized groups whose principal purpose was to deal with the supernatural. Shamans were not organized, and there were no "priests" except in so far as funeral orators and group leaders might be so classified in their capacity as directors of funerals and mourning ceremonies. Shamans, in the days of warfare, were responsible for predicting the course of events and used their "dream spirits" for this end. There is evidence that some men attempted weather control, but this was never an important Cocopa interest. During the latter part of the 19th century, Cocopa shamans confined themselves to the curing of individuals, and could very well be thought of as "family doctors."

Shamans were usually elderly men who had been dreaming, to prepare for their work, since they were young boys. The longer a man had been dreaming, the more powerful he was. The shamans were serious men who were recognized for their abilities in curing as well as in other cultural activities. A visiting Yavapai "Christian" who headed a healing cult bothered the Somerton Cocopa because he didn't "act like a shaman." He was always smiling and joking, even during a ceremony. Most of the shamans, according to Jim Short, "had it in their hearts to help people, and they would always do the best they could."

Shamanistic power could be derived only through dreaming, and the dreams were fairly stereotyped. Sam Spa said:

In a dream some bird or insect comes to get you and takes you [through the air] to *wi čawał* [Feather Mountain, a rock island at the head of the Gulf] or to *wi spa* [Mayor Peak in the Cocopa Mountains]. At Feather Mountain [also at Mayor Peak] there is a white buzzard, white eagle, white spider, white tarantula, white night hawk, and another white bird like a hawk. These animals are all in a circle around a hole where *kwıs hamo'h* [rat] is living. This is a small brown mouse or rat. The rat builds a little house while all are watching. All the white animals have clubs so they can protect the rat. If someone dreams of one of these animals, the bird will take the dreamer to the mountain — fly with dreamer.

On reaching the mountain the bird reports to the rat. The rat looks at the dreamer and returns to his hole. On this first visit the dreamer only stays a little while then comes home. The next time he goes by himself. After getting there they teach him how to cure. One night or two nights. The rat does the teaching. On one visit the dreamer is taught one thing, on another he is taught something else. If he goes often enough he can cure almost anything.

No two informants gave me the same account, but the essential elements did not vary. The dreamer was carried to some sacred mountain (the scene of some event, but not a place of curing, in Cocopa myths) and there received instruction in the treatment of a specific disease. The instruction was by "contemporary" animals, and there is no suggestion that the dreamer was returned to the period of the creation. Learning, apparently, was confined to imitation. One of my younger informants said: "It is just like watching a picture show." The dream is called *šemowòp spir* (dream hard). Sam Spa explained the power of the rat and birds by saying that they came up at (were born out of?) the place where Sipa (the creator twin) had been cremated (see Chapter 9). This gave them the power that Sipa possessed.

Shamans were ordinarily paid, but would work for nothing if the patient was really destitute. One shaman worked on Sam Spa all one night but was not paid because Spa had nothing to give him at the time. There was no way of estimating the amount usually paid: it undoubtedly depended upon the resources of the patient and his family. Thirty dollars in American money was the highest amount recorded for the period before 1905. About 1910, one shaman worked over Sam Spa's baby daughter for two nights and was paid five dollars in American money.

A shaman would not continue with a treatment if he thought it was useless or if he felt another man should be called in. Jim Short said: "After a shaman starts working he can tell whether things are going right. No one knows it but him, but if he doesn't have the power he has the family call another shaman."

The usual cure consisted in alternate singing and manipulation. The following methods were used by various shamans for various diseases: body pressing, rubbing, brushing with a feather, saliva blowing, sucking, sucking an incision to draw blood, blowing accompanied by a verbal *ah-h-h*, and blowing cigarette smoke.

The following was probably a typical performance:

The shaman built a fire and laid the patient near it. He then took a bath, painted one eye black, the other red, and white around his mouth. He had an eagle feather in his hair, wore a necklace and belt, and four pendants made of pieces of mirror around his neck. The shaman came in and put one mirror on the sick man's forehead, one on his chest and stomach, but kept one in his own hand [to see the witch?]. He sang and went around the sick man, then blew on him. He worked on him until daylight, blew on him, sucked, rubbed the sick man.

Q: Did he suck anything out?
A: No.
Q: Had the witch taken his soul away?
A: Yes. He used the mirror to get it back. He could look all over with it. The next night the shaman did the same thing: started singing the song that they sing when a man is going to get well. The people didn't believe this, said the patient looked too badly. He worked on the man for three nights; gave the man a bath again and some food. For two days the patient ate two times a day, after that he ate three times a day. Then the shaman put mud on his head on the fourth night and the next day gave the patient a complete bath and after that he was cured.

Many stories were told about the prowess of Mayor, the Wi Ahwir captain of the period before 1880. His cure from wounds sustained when he was a boy fighting the Yuma is worth repeating:

Mayor was fighting the Yuma and was killed. He got up at noon and was killed again the next noon and got up again at sundown. The next time he got up after four days. The worms ate one eye but he shook the others off.

When Mayor was dead there was a big, high ramada. Coyote started hollering [another version said a shaman threw a coyote skin down and it came alive], first from the south, then west. He hit his tail on the ground, got sand on his nose and leaned over Mayor, and the sand fell off his nose on to Mayor. Mayor got up alive. Coyote said: "That is the way to do it. It is also the way to cure killing by ghosts and from snake bite." He gave Mayor the power to do all this. Mayor didn't dream this, the coyote talked to him.

I heard two stories of the importance of Pima shamans. When Sam Spa was about 10 years old, a group of Maricopa and Pima men came to visit the local leader. One of the Pima men, a shaman, was asked to attempt the cure of a sick man:

The Pima shaman took the sick man outside to a prepared ground and all the people came around — men, women, and children. The shaman told the captain to have the people stand still, not to make any noise. The shaman started singing, four different songs, and started talking in Pima. The Pima chief then started to talk. The shaman said to the people that he knew what the trouble was, that something was lodged in the man's heart. He could take it out but if he did the man would die. If it wasn't taken out the man could live six days. He asked if he should take the chance and remove the object. The man's relatives said, yes, to take it out. The shaman sucked out the object and put it in his hand. It was yellow. He held it in his hand and everyone came to look. It moved as if alive. The doctor then asked if the people wanted to know who had inserted the object. Everyone kept quiet. They didn't want to know. The man died the way the doctor said he would.

When the band leader fell ill, about three or four years later, his family wanted to send for a Pima shaman, but he refused at first: "big men never had a shaman." Later he agreed, and his son went to the Maricopa villages to find a shaman. When he returned, according to Sam Spa, three Pima men and three Maricopa men came with him:

One was a Pima shaman, the others were his helpers. The shaman sat back in the house with two of his helpers. They had a rattle and a basket. The shaman used the rattle and the two men rubbed the basket with sticks. The sticks were decorated with buzzard feathers. The shaman started a song and started to use his rattle, then stopped because the rattle wouldn't work. It was "too heavy" to lift. The shaman and his helpers just sat there all night. They couldn't do anything because the rattle wouldn't work. They went home the next morning.

A short man, with his face painted black and feathers in his hair, had put *wi spa* [Mayor Peak] in the rattle and that was why it couldn't be lifted. The man who put the mountain in the rattle was Pete Dominguez, so the shaman said.

Causes of Illness

Certain "natural" causes for sickness were recognized, but in the majority of cases, illness supposedly resulted from the violation of some taboo, from a visitation by some dead relative, or (most usually) from witchcraft. Sam Spa's illness reported above was attributed to a stomach injury sustained when his cradle was knocked down and he was stepped on by some running boys. At another time in his life, he became ill because a horse had thrown him. A cold wind or a dust storm could cause certain types of chest trouble, he asserted, but just how clearly the natural and the supernatural were distinguished here, I do not know.

A very serious illness was frequently attributed to soul loss, brought about when a dead relative appeared in a person's dreams and persuaded him that the land of the dead was a much more desirable place than this world. This idea was bound up with a general fear of the dead and the belief that seeing (but not hearing) a dead person was a sure

omen of disaster. It was recognized that some of the older people had lost so many friends and relatives, and were so lonesome and often suffering in this world, that they welcomed the appearance of relatives and the resulting final illness.

Illness through witchraft (*pišnopɩs*) was dreaded, but there was no clear pattern either in the nature of the illness thus caused or in methods employed in witchcraft. My material shows quite clearly how beliefs, such as witchcraft, when of high cultural interest, are elaborated with every opportunity for borrowing. The following statement was accepted by the Cocopa even though they recognized its foreign origin. The informant was Frank Gomez:

The way to kill people is to get a frog, tie a black ribbon around its belly, and hang the frog up. Talk to the frog and give him the name of the victim. After three days take the frog down, turn him loose, and pin a safety pin in the ribbon in the shape of a cross, bury this, and the victim will die.

Another way is to make a doll of sticks, punch holes where you want the victim to have sores, and cut notches on the stick for the number of months the victim will live. There is no use to call a doctor if you are sick from this cause.

The foreign elements in the following story by Sam Spa have probably been added to an established Cocopa pattern:

The leader of the Mat Skrui Cocopa had been seriously ill before he died and the people knew that four or five witches were after him. He said they brought a net once to take him but he broke loose. Next time they brought an airplane but it wouldn't fly. Then they tried to run a stick through him but failed. Finally they brought an automobile, tied him hand and foot and took him away. That was when he died. [Note success on the fourth attempt.]

The witches also fixed it so he couldn't eat or drink. Everything was sour on his stomach. All he could do was to smoke.

His soul was tied up and taken away in an automobile. That was why he died.

His son knew who the witches were, but they were relatives, so they couldn't do anything. Both men and women were doing this. The leader was a witch too and these relatives decided to kill him. They changed into rats, birds, and cut the "wires" leading out of his house so he wouldn't be able to protect himself.

The use of feces to produce illness and death is recounted in the creation myth (see Chapter 9), but I found no evidence for a belief in the use of body products in witchcraft. Hair and nail clippings were left where they fell, and so far as I know, the disposal of feces was dictated only by modesty.

The violation of taboos was a common explanation for illness in former times. The best example of this came from

Sam Spa, who was sick for about a year after his first marriage (see above, *Sam Spa's Marital Experiences*).

Anyone could be a witch in Cocopa society, but the most powerful witches were the shamans. Witches typically gained their power by dreaming of "eagle brother" (a Cocopa boy turned cannibal in a myth; see Chapter 9), who would instruct them in the art and come to their aid in particular cases. A man working with "eagle brother" power painted his face black and wore eagle feathers in his hair. Witches also dreamed of another bird, which, in the creation myth, had the power to kill his enemies. A really powerful witch, according to one account, started having such dreams before he was born, while dreams for curing did not start until after birth. The pattern of this dream experience was the same as for shaman-dreams, discussed above.

That not all witches were shamans is indicated by the following exchange:

Q: Who was causing the leader's death?
A: The Pima shaman said that Pete Dominguez put Mayor Peak in his rattle so he couldn't cure the leader, and that Dominguez must have made him sick in the first place.
Q: When the people found that Dominguez put the mountain in the rattle what did they do to him?
A: Nothing. They just didn't do anything.
Q: Was he a shaman?
A: Before the Pima shaman told them he was a witch, the people had thought him a good man. He was not a shaman.
Q: Where did he get his power?
A: Those people never told how they got their power. Don't tell even their family their dreams.

This reference to the refusal of a witch to divulge the source of his power was explained to me by Sam Spa. Following is a summary of what he said: There is a society of witches who maintain their power by killing victims and eating them or eating a part, such as the victim's heart. Very often they kill their own closest relatives and this is why they never want to talk about their "dreams."

The Execution of Witches

When compared with other societies in the Southwest, such as the Navajo (Kluckhohn 1944), the Cocopa made relatively little use of the custom of accusing individuals of witchcraft as a method for controlling aberrant behavior, and relatively great use of the custom of executing declared or suspected witches. I have records of the killing of 14 witches for the time period 1880 through 1945. What percentage this is of the actual number of witches who were killed during that time I do not know. I am sure that one of my informants, who was born about 1875, told me all of the cases he knew about and remembered. He lived most of his life in Mexico, however, and so had little or no knowledge of the Cocopa around Yuma and Somerton after 1900. Prior to 1900 his knowledge was mostly confined to his own band. I think that it would be safe to say that during the 65 years up to 1945 a witch was killed at least every two years on the average, a very high rate for such a small society. A summary of the circumstances surrounding the killings that were reported to me is contained in Table 7.

Systems of behavior and beliefs concerning shamans and witches changed after about 1920. Before 1920, the killer or killers made no effort to hide their identity, most individuals accused of sorcery were shamans, and some made no effort to protect themselves against a threat of death.

In almost all cases where I have adequate information, the killing of an accused witch is fairly obviously traceable to scapegoating in conjunction with a higher than usual number of deaths. In the period of my fieldwork, at least, these deaths occurred in families where all or most of the members were suffering from what appeared to me to be tuberculosis. In all cases the Cocopa explained a witch killing by stating that he or she had brought about the death of one or more victims. In two cases, however, it is more than likely that witchcraft was a rationalization for executing a man whose physical violence was feared by others. In addition, in one of my recorded cases, the killer appears to have been a homicidal criminal and was later killed by his victim's relatives.

The following case (Table 7, No. 1) may be typical for the period 1880 to 1900. Sam Spa is the informant:

Some men who were attending a small mourning ceremony [chekap] were playing peon and one of the players was a man who had lost two fingers of one hand. After a while he pulled a knife and said that he was going to kill someone. Someone overheard him say that he was going to kill a man who was living near his own watermelon patch nearby. The eavesdropper ran and told the intended victim, but the man looked in a mirror and said: "I am dead already, I cannot hide." Then he went to sleep.

Later in the night three men went to kill him and found where he was sleeping. They cut his head with an ax and cut his throat and stomach with a knife. The dead man was a shaman who had tried to cure some people but they died. The man with the missing fingers believed that the shaman had killed some of his relatives. The shaman had said earlier that he would be alive again after four days. One lady wanted to delay the cremation to find out, but other people went ahead with the funeral the next day. After they put the dead man in the pyre and the fire was burning hot, he stood up and walked around and then fell back in the fire.

Some relatives wanted to kill the murderers but the captain persuaded them to forget about it.

TABLE 7
Circumstances of the Killing of 14 Cocopa Witches, 1880-1945
(– indicates no information obtained)

Case No.	Approx. Date	Victim a Shaman	Victim's Sex	Victim Bragged	Victim Warned	Victim Resisted	Death Avenged	Feud Started
1	1880	Yes	M	No	Yes	No	No	Threat only
2	1880	Yes	F	Yes	No	No chance	Yes	Yes
3	1890	Yes	M	Yes	No	Yes	No	Yes
4	1890	No	M	No	No	No chance	No	Threat only
5	1890	No	M	–	–	–	–	–
6	1890	Yes	M	–	–	–	No	Threat only
7	1915	Yes	M	Yes	Yes	No	No	No
8	1918	Yes	M	–	No	No chance	No	–
9	1920	Yes	M	–	–	–	Yes	No
10	1930	No	M	–	–	No chance	Attempt made	No
11	1930	No	M	–	–	No chance	No	No
12	1942	No	M	Yes	No	No chance	No	No
13	1942	No	M	Yes	No	No chance	No	No
14	1945	No	F	–	No	–	No	No

In another case from the same period (No. 6), some relatives of a murdered shaman started after the killers armed with bows and arrows. When they came near the killers, they found themselves opposed by a group of the killers' relatives, and a serious fight was threatened. In the end, and after some skirmishing in which no one was seriously injured, three captains were called in and succeeded in putting a stop to the fight.

In more modern times the men who were responsible for the killing of a witch were not always known to the Cocopa community and never known to the Mexican or American authorities. This fear of European criminal law no doubt was sufficient to prevent feuds or threats of feuds. The following are typical examples of the killing of witches in modern times. The informant was Frank Gomez.

The Cocopa do not like to live together in large groups because they might get in trouble with witches. One time [about 1942] a large group of Cocopa were living on an *ejido* on the Baja California side of the delta. One man had a camp nearby. He got drunk and bragged that he was a witch. When he went to bed some men wired the door of his house shut. He had a lamp with him and maybe the lamp fell over and maybe the men set fire to the house and burned him to death. [Table 7, No. 12]

A little later seven or eight men were drinking and one of them bragged of being a witch. Another man picked up a piece of iron and smashed his skull. No one did anything about it. [No. 13]

6. BAND ORGANIZATION AND LEADERSHIP

The Cocopa, at least during the latter part of the 19th century, did not constitute a "tribe" in the usual meaning of that word. There was a common name, a common language, some feeling of unity, but no common leadership or political machinery for centralized government. The people who called themselves Cocopa were divided into four separate groups or bands, each with an independent leader, each politically autonomous, and each occupying a particular section of the delta (see Fig. 6). In important matters, the four band leaders acted together. Leadership itself, however, was little stressed, and the heads of the various groups, as we shall see, had very little actual power. The general looseness of the Cocopa's sociopolitical organization appears to have been but another reflection of the lack of formal patterns in other departments of their culture.

In one respect, the Cocopa differed markedly from the other Yuman tribes of the Colorado River. The Mohave and Yuma, according to the published descriptions of those tribes (Kroeber 1902: 279; 1925: 727; Devereux 1939a: 100; Forde 1931: 140), had a highly developed feeling of nationalism, that is, a feeling of close tribal solidarity and an elaborated consciousness of group difference and group integrity. Kroeber (1902: 279) says of the Mohave:

> In spite of a loose internal social organization, the tribe seems to have regarded itself as very distinct from all others. The conscious feeling of the tribe as a unit or body, such as exists so strikingly among the Plains Indians, is however not so strong among the Mohave as a feeling that all members of the tribe are inherently and psychically different from all persons of other tribes. There is a sense of racial rather than of tribal separateness. Marriages with other tribes were few. Not only sexual connection but ordinary intercourse with other races were regarded with disfavor, as being a specific cause of sickness.

Forde (1931: 140) gives very nearly the same picture for the Yuma:

> Despite this segregation [into groups], tribal solidarity was strong and a tribal leader, probably head man of one of the more powerful groups, was recognized as leader of the people. . . . The Yuma is arrogantly conscious of his distinctness from the other surrounding peoples.

It is quite possible that, prior to the arrival of the U.S. Army in 1850, the Cocopa were organized under a single leader even though they lived in separate groups. It is clear, however, that their lack of a feeling for "tribal solidarity" cannot be a development that occurred only after intertribal warfare was ended. The most persistent questioning brought me no evidence whatever for a feeling of tribal separateness and exclusiveness, but rather pointed quite definitely to the opposite. Cross-tribal marriages were frequent, but even more interesting was the Cocopa's willingness to share their delta lands with outsiders — the outstanding example of this being the Paipai settlement sandwiched between two groups of Cocopa in the lower delta (see Fig. 6). Furthermore, all but one of the Cocopa groups were composed of a large percentage of "foreign" families: Diegueño, Paipai, Kiliwa, Kahwan, and Halyikwamai. I have no way of making an accurate estimate of the percentages of outsiders, but from some direct, and much indirect, evidence I would surmise that it was as high as 30 percent among the Kwakwarsh Cocopa, and as low as 10 percent among the Hwanyak Cocopa. The Mat Skrui, the one band that were supposedly unmixed (because their speech was unaffected by foreign elements), probably remained so because of their more isolated location in the northeastern part of the delta.

In attempting to discover the composition of the various bands and their speech differences, it developed in my interviews with Sam Spa that the extreme southwestern group, the Kwakwarsh, were Paipai-Diegueño-Cocopa, influenced in speech by the Diegueño element, which was composed mostly of Kwatl Diegueño speaking a slightly different southern dialect. The Wi Ahwir were Diegueño-Cocopa, heavily mixed with Diegueño-speaking people using a dialect spoken in the vicinity of the California-Mexico border. The Hwanyak were Kahwan-Halyikwamai-Cocopa, mostly Cocopa, but including in the community the descendants of many Kahwan and Halyikwamai families who remained in the delta after these two tribes had left the region. The Mat Skrui, with no such mixture attributed to them by my informants, were, interestingly enough, sometimes referred to as the *koapa' ahan* (real Cocopa).

The presence of outsiders in the delta not only influenced the speech of the various groups, but also brought about physical mixture. There was no indication of a feeling against intertribal marriage, and it was a frequent occurrence. In my 1944 census of living Cocopa, which included more than 220 individuals, 23 were known descendants of such marriages. Being highly incomplete, this record does not include the Cocopa men and women who sometimes went outside the delta to marry and make their homes. There was no chance for me to verify this practice, beyond recording the statement that it occurred. Sam Spa's sister left the delta to marry a Diegueño man in the Baja California mountains, and Diegueño men frequently came into the delta to get wives. Two children, then living with relatives near Mayor, had been brought back to the delta after their fathers, two brothers, had died in the mountains. These two men had gone to the mountains and married either Diegueño or Paipai girls. M. R. Harrington of the Southwest Museum told me that a number of years earlier he had met three Cocopa men living near the site of the old Santa Catarina mission in Baja California, where they were working on a ranch and had become permanent residents.

BAND SOLIDARITY

Just how solidly each of the Cocopa bands was knit together is extremely difficult to determine. Overtly, there was a clear awareness of the fact that different bands had different leaders, and I never had any difficulty in securing the names of these leaders and the order in which new leaders were named. In addition to separate leadership, there were certain activities that unified the bands and set them apart from each other. However, the most important bar to their consideration as "subtribes" was their lack of names or other symbolic devices for expressing their separateness. This is of such interest as to warrant giving my evidence in some detail.

About 1870, the earliest time for which I could secure reliable data from my informants, the four Cocopa bands were led by Mayor, Pete Rios, Laguna, and Montaña. Informants told me that Mayor was leader of the Wi Ahwir Cocopa, and that Laguna was leader of the Hwanyak Cocopa, but they did not refer to the other two bands by name, saying rather that Pete Rios lived at *čaman kwowao* and Montaña at *ha?a kɪlɪkel*. These are place names, and I assumed at first that the group had taken the name of the principal habitation site.

During my 1943 field trip, working with Sam Spa, I continued to use these place designations but discovered that he was using some other names. It developed that he spoke of the extreme southwestern band, with its principal site at *čaman kwawao*, as the *kwakwarš* (yellow people), and the northeastern band, with its principal site at *ha?a kɪlɪkel*, as the *mat skrui* (in-between-country people). I was naturally of the opinion that my earlier conclusion was wrong, that the bands were consciously set apart by name in the Cocopa mind, and that I had missed getting these names before because of the difficulty of working through

an interpreter. But when I later asked Jim Short the name of the band whose captain, when Short was a boy, was a man named Raft, Short's immediate answer was that they were Cocopa. I then explained that the people under other captains were also Cocopa and that what I wanted was the special designation for this particular band. Considerable repetition of the question and conversation between the interpreter and informant followed. Finally, Short began naming the lineages of the people who lived in the area, giving first the lineage affiliation of the captain. (The word for "tribe" and "lineage" is the same: *šɪmuɬ*.) I then explained that members of these lineages also lived in other bands and that what I wanted was the name of the whole band together. He repeated that they were Cocopa, and that was the only answer I could get no matter how I worded my questions. Finally, convinced that Short recognized the existence of the band, but did not identify it by name, I asked him if they were called the Mat Skrui Cocopa. The name apparently meant nothing to him as a band designation, nor did the name Kwakwarsh Cocopa. It can only be assumed, since Short grew to manhood in a group neighboring both the Mat Skrui and the Kwakwarsh, that the people thought of themselves as "Cocopa" and did not classify themselves by bands, even though there was considerable overt awareness of separate band leadership, territory, and activities, and even though there were some linguistic differences.

The origin of the name Wi Ahwir (water-against-the-mountain) was unknown to my informants, but the name Hwanyak, for the group around Colonia Lerdo, was of recent origin. *hwanyak* is the Diegueño word for "east." One day perhaps around 1890 a Diegueño, on his way to visit the Cocopa at Colonia Lerdo, said that he was on his way to see the eastern Cocopa, the *hwanyak*. He was among the Wi Ahwir Cocopa at the time, and my informants told me that from then on the Wi Ahwir began calling the group on the Colorado River the Hwanyak. The name became well recognized, and on occasion I tested this by asking any Cocopa I happened to meet whether or not he was a Hwanyak. The question always appeared to make sense and brought an immediate "yes" or "no."

The instability of band names, as recorded by visitors, is demonstrated by the fact that at the turn of the century the members of the band we call Hwanyak, who lived mostly on the west bank of the Colorado River, referred to themselves as *Xáwilkunyavœi* (river home people) (Lumholtz 1912: 251). Later, in the early 1930s, Gifford's informant referred to the band as *ah hwa·t nyamat* (water flowing red land) and at the same time reported that the Wi Ahwir Cocopa used the name "easterners" to refer to the band. Gifford (1933: 260) transcribed the word for easterners as *kwaenyak* (my *hwanyak*).

To sum up the matter of band organization and identification, it is my present opinion that I was trying to force my informants to give me a classification and identification of bands that would fit my preconceived notion of such things, and that in the process I failed to secure an understanding of the Cocopa view of this part of their political system.

CAPTAINS

Jim Short told me that the bands did not have "chiefs" before the coming of the Spaniards. He said that before that time there had been orators and war leaders and that the "chief" or "captain" was named by the Mexicans and Americans and given "papers" that designated his authority.

Sam Spa never generalized on the subject of captains. He knew who the captains were, he knew the succession of leadership in each group, and he could tell me at length what this or that captain did, but I doubt very much that he ever conceptualized an "office" apart from some concrete man. Perhaps because my interpreter could never focus our questions and answers in the same frame of reference, Spa could never define and distinguish the words he was using in speaking of captains, their helpers, and orators. I could pin him down: *Q*: The *kwɩnami* is a war leader? *A*: Yes. *Q*: The *komšiare* is a captain? *A*: Yes. *Q*: The *čapai ahan* is an orator? *A*: Yes. Then he would put me back where we started: *Q*: Then why did you speak of Montaña as *čapai ahan*? *A*: *čapai ahan, komšiare, pitan, čapai pɔhwe*, they are all the same. Similar responses were made by Mike Alvarez and Tom Juarez. These older men had experienced their culture as a going concern and had never stopped to question the organization. There was neither development of nor interest in formal symbols and no verbalized awareness of the structure of the political system.

My younger informants and interpreters, however, had become aware of the system of titles and offices in American culture; they could see what I was trying to get at and could give me the neat answers I seemed to want. Their statements will clarify the essential structure, but they must not be translated as a reflection of Cocopa attitudes, since this would read a formality into Cocopa society that did not exist. Frank Blue said:

> *mišhare* means mad-dog, crazy person, mean, ugly. But the old people used it to mean a leader. A *mišhare*, or captain, is *komšiare*, a man who takes charge of a whole group and gives orders. A *čapai ahan* [orator] just tells what they ought to do. He can give advice to a man on the street, to children, give food. A *mišhare* gives orders.
>
> Lucas is the reservation captain (*mišhare*) and he can order men to dig ditches, clear brush, and so on, but a *čapai ahan* only tells what he sees wrong.
> *Q*: Was the *mišhare* the war leader [*kwɩnami*]?
> *A*: Yes, he had to be.
> *Q*: What happened if he got too old for that?
> *A*: Someone would be named to take his place.

Jerry Greer explained to me that the captain was just like any other orator most of the time, but that he did have some authority. The orators, he said, were just like "vice-presidents," and a man had to be a good orator before he could be named captain (this was probably strictly true only for post-warfare days). The real difference, to him, however, was that a captain always had a helper while an orator did not. His father was an orator (*čapai ahan*) but he was also Lucas's helper (*popoke*). (Orators are discussed later in this chapter.)

The captain's duties, as might be guessed from this difficulty with terminology, were vaguely defined, and his actual authority, in spite of Blue's statement, was almost nonexistent. His influence depended upon his personality, the number of people under him, and his reputation, gained through length of time in office. He was in direct charge of certain band activities and ceremonies — the initiations, the large mourning ceremony (the kerauk), and the activities surrounding formal group visits. It was his principal duty to maintain order, to settle disputes, to urge cooperation in group activities such as dam building and rabbit drives, and to advise the people. He acted when there was something "important" to be done, or when there was "trouble." Sometimes, when it was necessary to organize a ceremony or gathering, or when something of importance needed clarifying, he talked to the people. When things were going well, and in the normal course of events, these talks were made by the band's orators.

That the captain took an active part in maintaining order among the people was indicated by a number of accounts given me. Frank Gomez had been told the following story about an event that occurred in 1870. One time a man stole another man's wife and, with the help of others, took her by force to his camp. The husband followed, and during his attempt to recover his wife, a fight started. People in the camp tried to settle the trouble but failed, so they sent for the captain. When he arrived he immediately sent for the wife and questioned her concerning her preference for either of the two men. She told him that she wanted to stay with her husband, but that this other man had taken her away by force. After further questioning of the two men, the captain ordered the husband to return home with his wife; he ordered the other man to leave the woman alone in the future, and in addition to give her husband a horse for the trouble he had caused.

When Sam Spa was a boy, a Cocopa shaman lost his patient and was accused of witchcraft. At the funeral, some of the relatives of the deceased began drinking and decided to kill the shaman. They talked it over with the captain of the Kwakwarsh band, who advised them against it and succeeded in stopping them from acting at that time, although later they did kill the man. In another fight involving the killing of a shaman, three band chiefs conferred and were able to avert what might otherwise have been a serious battle. These accounts were given to me by Sam Spa. Jim Short also mentioned the efforts of the captain to stop fights that followed the killing of a witch.

Marital difficulties (within an independent, well-established family) were also taken to the captain when they reached any degree of severity. Both Jim Short and Mike Alvarez told me that it was the duty of the captain to talk to the couple and attempt to adjust their difficulties. Alvarez said that if a wife cooked for her husband, took care of the children, and worked hard, the captain would insist on her husband's staying with her, but that if the wife was no good, didn't take care of her husband, and ran around all the time, the captain would not blame the man for leaving her. Jim Short gave me the attitude from the point of view of the husband, and said that the captain would protect a man who really wanted to keep his wife. If the husband had been good to her, had not beaten her, and had always brought food into camp for their children, the wife would be told that she should stay with him and not leave. If the trouble in such a case was in connection with adultery, the captain would bring pressure against the paramour; if this failed, he would, in the end, have the adulterer sent to Ensenada, in Baja California (Ensenada was at one time the capital of the Northern Territory, and therefore had a Mexican jail). Short did not know what punishment would have been given an adulterer in pre-Spanish days. These were ideal patterns for dealing with marital disputes, and I could seldom get stories of actual cases of the captain's intervention.

There is a possibility that in the days of active warfare between the Cocopa and the Yuma there was no band captain in the sense that this title is being used here. Political and social affairs may have been in the hands of the *čapai ahan* (orator), while the leader of the group was the war leader, the *kwɩnami* (see Chapter 10). In 1870, three of the four leaders were *kwɩnami* as well as *komšiare* (captain); the fourth had come into office after the wars had been stopped. I have no knowledge concerning their predecessors. Thus the matter of whether or not there were separate political and war leaders in the days of active warfare cannot be settled here.

That the Mexicans after 1880 exerted considerable influence upon the political structure of the society is quite evident. Band captains were given official "papers" and were instructed in their duties. They were to see to it that the people "behaved," did not injure any Mexican or American travelers, and did not fight among themselves. The Mexicans also named a "policeman" and a "judge" to assist the captain. According to Sam Spa, when Raft was named captain of the Mat Skrui Cocopa about 1887, he left immediately for Ensenada to get his "papers," and was accompanied by a number of his own people as well as by Jack Row, captain of the Wi Ahwir Cocopa. The Mexicans wanted to know where he lived, how many people were under him, and how he had come into office. When they were satisfied that he was a legitimate leader, they gave him a document showing that he had the authority of the Mexican administration to enforce order, and they asked that he name a policeman and a judge to back him up. These men were also given papers. Sam Spa said that former Cocopa leaders had Mexican "papers," but that they had not had assistants appointed by the Mexicans. Jack Row had similarly been given papers when he became the captain of the Wi Ahwir Cocopa about 1885 or 1886; he too had the help of a "policeman" but got rid of him when the man made several "arrests" of which he disapproved.

The issuing of these "papers," with the weight of Mexican authority behind them, undoubtedly gave the late-19th-century captain a formal sanction of authority that had not existed before. However, so far as I know, the man who was given authority by the Mexicans was already accepted as a leader by the people. There were no arbitrary appointments and no manufacturing of a chief out of whole cloth, as occurred elsewhere.

INHERITANCE OF LEADERSHIP

Both the ideal and actual patterns called for inheritance of the captain's office in the male line. This did not have to be a son, but could be some close relative of the same lineage. The rule was by no means inflexible, however, and if the presumed successor did not measure up to expectation, another man would be chosen. All my informants and all the actual data agree on this point.

Between 1870 and 1918, only three of the nine newly elected captains were unrelated to the old captain or were not members of his lineage. The new leaders and their relationship to the old were as follows:

Wi Ahwir: Mayor succeeded by Jack Row, no relation, about 1885. Row succeeded by Mike Alvarez, a relative of the same lineage, about 1918. Tom Juarez, who in an earlier day would probably have succeeded Alvarez, belonged to the same lineage as did Mayor.

Kwakwarsh: Pete Rios succeeded by Gonzalo, no relation, about 1877. Gonzalo succeeded by his son Pedro, about 1906.

Hwanyak: Laguna succeeded by his son Urias, about 1881; Urias succeeded by Felix, no relation, about 1905.

Mat Skrui: Montaña succeeded by his "brother" Negro, about 1881; Negro succeeded by Montaña's son Raft, about 1887; Raft succeeded by his son Lucas, about 1910.

When a captain died or decided to resign his office, the family heads of the band got together and discussed the selection of a new leader. These were highly informal affairs, according to Sam Spa, and it is my belief, from what he said, that informal discussions between the older men of the band settled the succession in anticipation of the actual election. After Montaña died, Spa said, the people had a meeting and wanted Negro to take over the leadership because they felt that Montaña's son Raft was not yet ready for the job. Negro was an "older brother" of Montaña and did not want to take the office on account of his age, but he finally consented. Spa said that he attended the meeting but was not old enough to have a voice in affairs (he was about 15). Six years later, Negro called a meeting of the group and said that he was old, tired, and too sick to visit around any more, and that they should name another man to take his place. He suggested his nephew Raft, Montaña's son. Raft had been acting as orator for the group and had been preparing himself for the office, so everyone agreed.

Jim Short said that a captain was chosen on the basis of his personal character, his ability as a speaker, and his popularity with the people. If possible, some relative of the former captain was chosen, but this could be disregarded. When Jim Short was about 16, Felix was elected to succeed Urias as captain of the Hwanyak. Short said that the people had a big meeting and celebration to which members of other bands were invited. The older men talked the matter over for several days, and finally "one of the men just pointed to Felix." This meant that he had been chosen and "everyone was satisfied." My notes on this interview show that I could get no clear statement from Short as to the exact procedure. I made the following summary statement at the time: "The selection seems to have been the result of previously formed informal opinion as to who would succeed."

No informant volunteered the information that a captain should have had the right kind of dreams, yet they all agreed, when asked, that the man doubtless had been given some power, in a dream, to lead the people. Mike Alvarez, holding a precarious position as "leader" under highly disrupting modern conditions, volunteered nothing about dreams for leadership, but when asked, told the following:

Before Jack Row [his predecessor] died I had a dream that I would be captain. I was in a big grove of trees, and there were a great many people there, Americans, Yuma, and Cocopa. I looked into a mirror that was on a table and saw Row. I looked again and he was gone. This meant that Row was going to die and that I would be captain. Someone, I don't know who, gave me papers in the dream to show that I would be the leader. The next day I told Jack Row about the dream and he said maybe that would happen and maybe it wouldn't; that maybe I would die first since I had not been so well lately. Sometime later, when Row did die, I had another dream. Row came and talked to me in the dream, and told me that I had better hurry up and take over the people or they would scatter. The next day I told this dream to two or three other people and they

agreed that I should take over right away and be captain and hold the people together.

Frank Gomez told me that a captain ordinarily dreamed of his predecessor, who instructed him in these dreams. The captain never talked about such dreams, however, probably because of a taboo against speaking about the dead. He also had dreams in which šakwɩla (one of the orator birds in the creation myth) gave him instruction; he could talk about these dreams if he wanted to.

ORATORS

Orators were not elected, and they had no authority whatever; they were simply "good" men who knew how to talk. The number of such men was not fixed. Since formal orations were included among the duties of the captain, a man who aspired to that office or who was in line for it by inheritance first became an orator.

There is nothing in my notes to indicate that the orator acted as the spokesman for the captain. Each captain had his helper (*popoke*), who was one of the leading orators of the band, but this title was a reference more to his position as one of the captain's friends and backers than to any official duties assigned to him. When the captain had any speaking to do, he did it himself. In fact, the helper could not ordinarily speak for him, since it was the distinguishing feature of the captain's behavior that he would tackle controversial subjects. An orator never did such a thing, confining his remarks to good news and the promotion of ideal patterns.

Sam Spa said that an orator normally talked in the morning, when he "felt it in his heart" that he should. Some orators stood on top of their houses "like a rooster" and gave a speech whether there was an audience or not. During the spring of 1947 when we were living in a Cocopa camp near Somerton, the head of a Cocopa group in Sonora came to visit us, and each morning during his three-day stay he delivered an oration in the style described by Sam Spa.

Whenever people came together for a visit, especially when members of another band were in camp, the orator was expected to add a formal speech to the captain's welcome, or to make the welcome himself if there was no captain present. All subgroups living apart from the main captain's camp had an orator who acted as an unofficial leader. When these various subgroups came together at a general band gathering, each of their orators would make a talk.

What was perhaps a typical example of the position of the orators was given to me by Mike Alvarez during discussion of an initiation ceremony. At the conclusion of the ceremony in which Alvarez had taken part, Jack Row, leader of the Wi Ahwir Cocopa, called all the people together and talked to them about the importance of initiating the young men, saying "that it was a good thing, that it was just what the people needed." When he had completed his talk, five or six orators from the various Wi Ahwir camps each made a speech. They talked about the good time the people could have at such gatherings, and then each related the news from his own camp: incidents of daily life, illnesses, recent visitors, and movements of families.

That oratory must have been an important part of all traditional group activities is indicated by the fact that it was one of the few elements surviving in modern Cocopa culture at the time of our fieldwork. I was able to observe the procedure on four occasions: once in Somerton when an orator visited us (as described above), another time in Somerton at a religious gathering, and twice in Sonora when I was entertained semiformally by one of the Sonora groups. At the Somerton gathering (a weekly semi-Christian "sing" introduced by an educated Yavapai), Jim Short opened the meeting with a talk that lasted about 20 minutes. On this occasion, as on the others, the speaker began his talk without preliminary warning, and the first few sentences could not possibly have been heard above the noise of the crowd. Gradually, however, the individual conversations died down, and the speaker was given the fairly complete attention of the adults present. Children continued to play and run through the crowd, but no attention was paid to them. While delivering his talk, Short stood quite erect, his left hand hanging loosely by his side and his right hand placed against his chest. My interpreter, a little later, gave me a summary of what Short had said. He first welcomed all the people to the meeting, and urged them to pay attention to the ceremony and take part in it. He then devoted the major portion of his talk to giving his people advice of a paternal nature. He told them to work hard, take care of their families, and stay out of trouble. The "trouble," occasioned by drinking, was given the greater share of attention. Short told the people that the American sheriff tried to be fair to them, but that he could do nothing with men who had been drinking; he was forced to arrest them, put them in jail, and make them pay a fine. He said that his people wanted to get along with the Americans and that the best way to do that was to remain sober.*

My reception in Sonora during the summer of 1943 was, perhaps, a fairly representative example of the behavior occasioned by the entertainment of visitors. I had sent word from Somerton, saying that I would visit a particular group in Sonora within a day or two, that I would bring my interpreter and two or three other Cocopa men from Somerton, and that we would have some food for a "celebration." We arrived in camp late in the evening, unloaded our supplies, and sat around talking as the women of the camp prepared a meal. While we visited, families from surrounding camps began to arrive, and within an hour or two 20 to 30 people had assembled.

After the meal had been served and visiting had resumed, the camp orator (there was no captain) stood up and began to talk. He assumed the same posture used by Jim Short, and his tone of voice and method of delivery seemed quite formal in comparison with that of ordinary Cocopa conversation. The orator was given the complete attention of his audience. Two or three times during the talk and at its close, perhaps at some cue from the speaker, the audience emitted rather loud grunts, quite evidently expressions of approval. When the orator had finished, my interpreter gave me a summary of what he had said: He and his people were glad to see us again, they had looked forward to this visit, and they were particularly glad that I had not turned back after discovering how bad the road was. He urged the people to show us that we were welcome and to stay late so that they could sing and talk.

Within a few minutes, one of the Somerton Cocopa who had come with us stood up and talked for about half an hour. He first told of our trouble in reaching the Sonora camp and then recounted all the news from Somerton. When he had finished, my interpreter made a talk. He reviewed, from beginning to end, the story of all the experiences he had had with me during my visits with the Cocopa. This talk was followed by two or three more, and then the singers produced their gourd rattles and the balance of the night was spent in singing.

---

*There was an inverse correlation between drunkenness and oratory at group gatherings. Cocopa drinking was no great problem in Arizona, was only slightly troublesome in Sonora, and was quite common and highly disruptive in Baja California, especially around 1940 when a number of Cocopa families were living on an *ejido* there. At the time of our fieldwork there had been no meetings with talks by orators in Baja California for many years.

Lon Ray, Constable in Somerton in 1944, had the following to say about Cocopa drinking: "There are only four men here who ever give me any trouble. When they get drunk I just lock them up and let them go in the morning. There are a couple of Cocopa prostitutes that get drunk once in a while, but most of the men and almost all of the women never take a drink and never start any trouble if they do drink. I have learned not to take a bottle away from them. If they don't have to empty a bottle before I catch them they will take it easy and stay sober. I think the Cocopa are better behaved than the Yuma. . . ."

7. MEETINGS AND CEREMONIES

THE IMPORTANCE OF STRUCTURE AND SYMBOLISM

So far in this report I have been describing the behavior of people who get married, have babies, build houses for shelter and privacy, grow crops for food, hunt, gather, go visiting, play games and gamble, seek relief from sickness, and manufacture tools, pots, and baskets. Through the descriptions of these customs the American reader can understand what went on, as a Cocopa would understand the same kinds of descriptions of American life. When the outsider notices a change in or an addition to Cocopa culture, it is at this level of description — and the Cocopa have, in fact, changed their tools, modes of transportation, ways of making a living, styles of houses, methods for curing a sick person, and the like. Knowing all this, the non-Cocopa reader might well wonder why it is that the Cocopa (along with most southern Arizona and southern California Indians) have had such great difficulty in adjusting to the American way of life and, especially, such great difficulty in raising their standard of living.

An ethnography is no place to present a full-scale discourse on theories of culture change and acculturation. However, as a step in this direction, I do want to use the device of separating the kinds of data presented in Chapters 3 through 6 from the kinds of data presented from Chapter 7 on. In general, Chapters 3 through 6 describe how the Cocopa met their ordinary living needs. Chapters 7 through 9 and Chapter 11, on the other hand, describe the meaning of life and the symbols and structures that fostered the Cocopa's desire to maintain their traditional beliefs and customs.

Americans who have been interested in persuading the Cocopa to change their way of life, and those Cocopa who actively have sought to raise their own standard of living, have fixed their attention on the kinds of activities described in the preceding four chapters. They saw real progress when uncertain and unprofitable subsistence farming gave way to wage work; they have agreed that steel tools are a blessing to a stone-age people; they have welcomed tar-paper roofs, grocery stores, needles and thread, and anything that rolls on wheels. What the Americans and "progressive" Cocopa did not see, and would rarely understand, was that additions and changes in Cocopa life never were, and never would be, accepted on

surface appearance alone but would always be subject to conscious or unconscious review by members of the society in terms of the structural and symbolic tenets and patterns of Cocopa culture as a whole. Every activity, in other words, is a unit combining both technology and symbolism; a unit with simultaneous qualities of form, structure, purpose, meaning, and value. More than this, cultural activities relate to each other and depend upon each other.

In barest outline, the processes of culture change may be stated as follows: the context (since culture is a social phenomenon) is one in which two or more individuals agree or fail to agree to a change in the behavior of one or more of the parties in interaction. Many factors, of course, are involved in reaching a consensus, not the least of which is immediate personal gain on the part of one or more participants. But the factor that is of importance in the Cocopa case is the system of agreements and constraints in the patterns of Cocopa culture. By agreements I mean changes that are congruent with the Cocopa view of life. By constraints I mean just the opposite — changes that a Cocopa might find discordant or distasteful. Cultural constraint, of course, is always conservative, always in favor of the status quo, and therefore gives way, however slowly, to other forces in the environment that demand a change.

Cultural conservatism or constraint operates at the level of overt behavior. For example, the Cocopa, when they came in contact with Americans, were very reluctant to give up the use of a baby cradle as an efficient instrument in child care. But the point that I want to emphasize is the element of cultural constraint in other aspects of culture. In Chapter 7, Cocopa meetings and ceremonies are viewed by me as being symbolic of important values in Cocopa life and of their view of the nature of the universe. In practical, unemotional terms it would make no difference to the Cocopa whether they cremated their dead or practiced inhumation. But they do not view a cremation in practical, unemotional terms. When and if the Cocopa accept inhumation it will destroy or require a "rewriting" of the entire fabric of their mythology, their religion, and the many social control functions inherent in their funeral and mourning practices and beliefs. In Chapter 8 I describe the Cocopa system for the division of labor and the assignment of rights, duties, and obligations to classes of individuals. Here we have the very heart of human social order when compared with organizations of subhuman animals. There are no laws of nature, theology, psychology, or any similar philosophy or science that say that a man must share his family's food with other families in his community if they are hungry. But the Cocopa believed this to be a natural law — a matter of human nature — and they have not changed or modified their behavior in this respect without great emotional stress and strain. It is a typical situation, among countless others, in which the Cocopa division of labor and their assignment of rights, duties, and obligations within the group have prevented or slowed their acceptance of changes that would have brought them closer to American and Mexican beliefs and practices.

In Chapter 11 I come perilously close to the limits of my knowledge. On the basis of my ethnographic data on Cocopa customs two or three generations back, and on the basis of my field experience with living members of the tribe, I have inferred and deduced that there are what I call "value themes" that function to influence the mode and meaning of many areas of Cocopa life. In this I have accepted the proposition set forth by sociologists that life in America has been, and to a large extent still is, dictated by what they describe as the "protestant ethic" (work as a value in itself, wealth as a symbol of virtue, thrift and saving as signs of the moral man, and so forth). If America has a protestant ethic, the Cocopa have a Cocopa ethic, and this fact becomes terribly important to the Cocopa because the two sets of value themes are almost diametrically opposed to each other. The result has been that it is very difficult for a Cocopa, or a small group of Cocopa, to accept more than the surface behavior of their American neighbors, and so in most cases they fail to develop the motivational structures that make for success in America or in modern Mexico.

* * * * *

During the last half of the 19th century there were four events for which a group larger than the family would gather as a unit: political meetings held at the captain's camp, fiestas, funeral ceremonies held at the time of death, and mourning ceremonies held a year or more after a death. The fiesta was a celebration sponsored by some local leader or band captain for the purpose of entertaining visitors, and usually came in the fall at harvest time. The mourning ceremony, equally important as an occasion for entertainment, was also held in the late fall.

LOCAL POLITICAL MEETINGS

At irregular intervals, the captain would hold a meeting of the band. There was no effort to bring all the people together for such an affair, and the meeting was usually attended only by the families living nearby. Such meetings were never formal and never had "business" to conduct,

except upon the occasion of the appointment of a new captain. They were held for the purpose of hearing a talk by the captain, and were only a little more elaborate than, but similar to, the frequent small local gatherings when the orators told the people "how to live."

It is worth noting that all group activities except the funeral ceremony provided the opportunity for a special plea that the people have a good time, play games, laugh, joke, sing, and be happy. This conscious effort to promote a display of carefree behavior was repeatedly recorded in my notes. The joking, laughing, happy, fun-loving nature of the lower Colorado tribes, as described by almost every author, thus appears to be a consciously cultivated pattern rather than a spontaneous and largely unconscious disposition or mood of the people. My own observations failed to settle the question. The Cocopa in Baja California were quiet, serious, and unfriendly on most occasions; they very seldom exhibited "mirth" or any behavior that would indicate joking or bantering. Around Somerton, and in most of the Sonora camps, however, the people were notably different in this respect. Men and women were constantly laughing and looked happy. It is, perhaps, significant that Cocopa society had disintegrated to the greatest extent in Baja California; families were badly scattered, and their poverty was extreme.

FIESTAS

The big celebrations and dances (*yamas patei*) were held by band captains for the entertainment of other bands and even other tribes, and they were fairly formal. An invitation was sent to another Cocopa captain, to the leader of the Imperial Valley Kamia, or to the Maricopa villages, asking them to come for a visit on a certain day. (The Yuma-Cocopa enmity continued throughout the 19th century, and no Yuma groups were ever entertained at these celebrations.) On one occasion, according to Sam Spa, the captain of the Mat Skrui Cocopa called the family heads together and suggested that they invite the people from another band to join them in a harvest celebration. At the end of two days, when all arrangements had been made, he sent a messenger to notify the other group that they would be expected to visit on a certain day. In preparation for the festivities, families in the host band moved to the captain's camp, bringing with them equipment and the food that would be prepared over communal fires for the visitors. The contributions of food, according to the stories I collected, were generous. Each family brought enough for themselves and to spare, with no thought to their own later needs but rather with an eye to the pleasure in abundance that marked these affairs. There was no conscious thought that the contributions were being made to the captain, who in turn, as a "big man," could give a fiesta and thus gain personal prestige or authority.

The women, Sam Spa said, had food cooking in pots all over the camp, and the hosts and visitors were urged to eat all they could. At the end of the celebration, guests were given surplus supplies to take home.

The visitors timed their arrival for the afternoon or early evening; they approached their host's camp in a group, led by their captain. The hosting captain went out to meet them, followed by his people, but the visiting captain spoke first. In a formal talk, he told the other captain and his people that things had been very quiet at home and that they welcomed this opportunity to come visiting and to have a good time. He then made a full report of all the news at his camp, the state of their harvest, any trouble that had occurred, and the amount of sickness. In reply, the host captain said that he had seen no one in a long time and his people were glad to have visitors. He urged everyone to be happy, to have a good time, to have all they wanted to eat, and to join in the games. He also encouraged the young people to get acquainted with each other so that they could get married. Finally he reported all the news of his own camp. After these talks were completed, the older men of the two groups mixed together and visited, but the younger people kept apart and maintained a shyness that was gradually broken down as the celebration continued.

If the celebration was a big one given by a captain, it lasted four days and four nights, during which time there was dancing and singing at night, and gambling games, horse races, and kicking ball contests in the daytime. The best runners in each group were chosen for the kicking ball contest, and it provided opportunity, as did horse racing, for much gambling. Fiestas were also occasions for the initiation of both boys and girls (discussed at the end of this chapter).

There was undoubtedly a pattern for these celebrations, but I could discover none. My informants simply told me that the people "felt good" and had plenty to eat, so they just decided to give a dance. There was almost certainly no even exchange of visits between groups, and the place and time, apparently, was simply a function of the state of the food supply. The gatherings provided a break in the routine of interaction at harvest time, especially for women, and there was an even more important change in food resources, so that the timing of these activities might be explained by the symbolic recognition of changes in the routine of life as well as by the more mundane fact that the required surplus food stores were available. On the other hand, when extra food was available during the spring and summer, celebrations and mourning ceremonies similar to those held at harvest time took place.

There was some indication that the greatest satisfaction went to the host group. On one occasion between about 1895 and 1900, the captain of the Mat Skrui Cocopa went to considerable pains to urge the building of dams and dykes that would give his people an early harvest and the resulting chance to invite neighboring groups to a celebration before their own crops had ripened.

The smaller celebrations (*yamas ɪlčes*), sponsored by local leaders and men with many relatives who were in a position to help out, were more informal and seemingly spontaneous. Orators who had the necessary kinship support were expected sooner or later to invite neighboring camps to a small celebration.

Here, as in the case of the big dances, there was no thought that surplus food was being channeled into any one man's camp to be used by him and as he saw fit. There was not the slightest indication of "wealth display," nor was there a direct attempt to gain prestige through a display of generosity as such. Every Cocopa depended upon his own labor for his food resources. A man's prestige was the result of his more or less accidental occupation of the senior position in a large group of close relatives, and of his possession of qualities of leadership and energy that would bring families and their food into his camp for the celebration.

FUNERAL CEREMONIES

Measured by elaboration of ceremony, by formalization of patterns, and by emotional content, the Cocopa of the late 19th century made death their greatest cultural interest (Kelly 1949a).

While Cocopa were reluctant to talk about illness and death with outsiders, these matters provided the real "news" of the society, and visitors going from one group to another were expected to give this type of information above any other. All this became quite apparent in the course of our fieldwork. The most interesting bit of evidence, however, came to me in a letter from Mr. Al Frauenfelder of Somerton, a local merchant whose store had come to be a sort of headquarters for the Cocopa. Frauenfelder had been writing letters for his Cocopa friends for a number of years and had the following to say:

Say, Bill, did it ever strike you that these Cocopa are unduly interested in death? Seems to me I have written several letters for about four different ones, to their sons in the army, and always the writer tells me to tell his son that so and so died and they burned him. Of course, so would I tell my boy about the deaths of acquaintances, but I would also tell him of the births and marriages. [These are] equally important and natural events, but the Cocopa think death has 'em all beat for importance. For example, several fellows told me to write about this man who died in the penitentiary, but nobody told me to write about the fine pretty twins that a Cocopa girl gave birth to. But the twins are splendid kids, and I wrote three letters for their grandfather to the twins' father and I'm damned if he didn't tell him about some fellow ... must have been eighty years old, dying but he never mentioned the twins.

The name of the dead is never spoken by relatives or spoken by others in the presence of a dead person's relatives. Even mention by circumlocution or by the use of a kin term is frowned upon, except under specified circumstances, such as at a funeral or mourning ceremony where reference by kin term is permitted.

The outstanding economic consequence of death was the practice of destroying all the property of the deceased. In former times, this included literally everything possessed by a person or shared by him with the family: the house, equipment, clothing, and food. Thus, no accumulation of capital could take place from one generation to the next.

The Cocopa had only a vague understanding of the cessation of life processes and instead centered their interest upon the separation of soul and body at the time of cremation. When I questioned Jim Short about the possibility of the departure of a soul at the time of death, it was obvious that he had never thought about the matter. The soul, on being released from the burning corpse, was thought to hover over the area for a greater or lesser time, depending upon its reluctance to leave this world, and was then carried by an invisible owl to a Cocopa paradise in the south where it lived for an indefinite period, but not without ultimate extinction. Only twins lived forever, in a special heaven, from which place they were periodically reborn as new sets of twins.

My Wi Ahwir informants told me that the land of the dead was on the western shores of the Gulf of California, at a place called *kerauk hap*; my Hwanyak informants said that it was near the head of the Gulf on the Sonora side, at a place called *ha ʌlʌl* (El Doctor). Both sites are located in the barren salt flats; however, they were pictured by the Cocopa as being, for the dead, a place of green fields with plenty of horses and food, where people were always holding big celebrations and had plenty of time for gambling and games.

In former times, a shaman could tell in advance when a person was going to die, and told the family. When Jack Row died, according to Tom Juarez, they knew two days ahead that he would die, and the captain of the Mat Skrui Cocopa, who had been called to help his fellow captain, told the men to cut wood and have the pyre ready.

Any person who stopped breathing, or whose breath became very light, was thought to be dead. Sam Spa "died" once when he was a boy — he stopped breathing. One day when we were passing a camp in Baja California, the women suddenly started screaming and wailing. We stopped the car to find out what was wrong and discovered that a young girl had just "died." Her mother and sisters were quite out of control in their wailing and the girl's father was so convinced of the girl's death that he asked me to take him to the camp of a Mexican official who could give him permission to burn the body. When we arrived back at camp, the girl had revived, and she was alive and well when we left the area a week or so later.

Grief, at the time of a relative's death, was expressed in violent public behavior that, from the point of view of an observer, seemed to reach the limit of physical endurance. Members of the family (father, mother, husband, wife, siblings, and offspring) began their crying, wailing, and screaming with the announcement of death (or upon the announcement by the shaman that death was close), and they continued with almost no relief until the body was cremated. Cremation, in most cases, took place the day after death, so that mourning frequently continued without interruption for more than 24 hours.

I had no way, at the time, to measure the "honesty" of these expressions of grief. Tears were real enough and much of the time gave the appearance of being uncontrollable. There were, however, many cultural devices clearly designed to stimulate the grief reaction. After the death, each arriving friend or kinsman was expected to approach the members of the bereaved family, hold them with an arm around the shoulder, and join in the crying, repeating this action several times during the period before cremation. Songs and dances at frequent intervals were a cue for the cessation of crying and wailing, but at the end of a song, grief broke out with renewed strength. Many reminders of the dead were introduced: the singing of his or her favorite songs, the playing of a favorite game, the frequent verbal accounts of life incidents by the orators. All such action ended in increased wailing. At one funeral that we attended, two teams of men played peon (the "hidden stick" game), a favorite with the deceased, across the bed upon which his body was lying.

Grief so expressed, and thus encouraged, mounted in intensity and died away in recurring periods. As the grief expression died away, the family members were left as the only persons crying or wailing, and at such times their emotions, in the funerals we witnessed, appeared to be drained away and their behavior continued by conscious forcing. An extreme form of grief expression that was reported to us was not exhibited at the funerals that we attended. According to American informants who had visited other funerals, Cocopa men and women, at the funeral of an important man, and at the crests of emotion, would shriek, tear their clothes, bound into the air, and roll on the ground.

The ceremony itself was rather a simple affair, so far as formal equipment and funeral behavior were concerned. The body was washed and dressed by relatives. (In the case of a 19th-century leader his relatives put on his nose pendant, painted his face black, put red in his hair, and dressed him in his best clothes, including pants he did not usually wear.) After being dressed the body was placed upon a rough ladder-shaped bier (described in Chapter 4), wrapped in blankets, and transported to the home of the band captain or of one of the lesser leaders. There the mourning took place, and the pyre was prepared nearby. The formal funeral ceremony was held under a ramada and began about two hours before the burning of the body. The nearest relatives gathered immediately around the bier, sitting or standing, and beyond these, but separated by an aisle to be used by singers, was the assembled crowd. The ceremony was opened by one of the group orators, who made a long and formal talk on the need for courage, the inevitability of death, and the friendship of those who would take part in the ceremony. At irregular intervals other orators spoke and the grief-provoking reminders of the man's life took place. Also irregularly, a singer with two helpers circled the bier singing Cocopa songs, particularly those favored by the deceased. During the songs, women relatives danced backward facing the singers and carrying bundles of clothes that would later be burned. Relatives and friends who chose to do so could dance facing these women.

In addition to the band orators, there was one man who acted as the official funeral orator. He spoke intermittently throughout the funeral, but assumed his official capacity only when the relatives were ready to transport the body to the crematory pyre. It was this march from the mourning shelter to the pyre that was intended to function as the mechanism for the removal of the dead person's spirit from earthly connections. The orator's talk was, in part, in the form of an argument to the spirit of the dead person. Successful enterprise, in Cocopa magic, involves three attempts, with success on the fourth try. The orator's speech, in keeping with this, was in four parts, each ending with a short pause and the setting down of the bier, the fourth stop being at the pyre, where the body was deposited on the crematory logs.

Six men carried the bier. When they reached the pyre, the two men in front walked in, the middle two stepped aside, and the rear two helped place the litter within the pyre. Then they unwrapped the deceased, rolled him in the "box" with the blankets off, lying on his right side with his head to the east, facing north.

Jim Short described a pyre as follows. The pyre was made to fit the dead person. Three dry logs were put on the bottom, and three on each side, one on top of the other (or two on each side for a baby). The side logs were held in place by posts driven upright into the ground on the outside, and the logs were tied to the uprights with willow bark. Dry arrowweed was put on the ground, and the sides of the pyre were lined with it. There were small split limbs at the head end, also upright, and fifteen logs held in reserve for a grown man: one placed under the left arm and leg, and the others piled on top. The bier was leaned against the south side of the pyre.

In the funerals described to us the intensity of wailing and crying was not markedly stepped up with the climax of burning. The greatest intensity of grief came, on the contrary, during the last minutes in the mourning shelter when close relatives kneeled at the bier and embraced the wrapped body of the corpse.

A Child's Cremation

Our attendance at the cremation of a child in 1944 provided the following details, particularly on the latter part of the ceremony, which we had neglected in our field interviews.

The pyre was about three feet high, and three by five feet across. Logs were laid horizontally on three sides, the fourth (west end) being left open. Surrounding these were upright bundles of arrowweed, held in place by being tied to five upright stakes, one on each of the long sides, and three at the enclosed end. The logs on the inside were three to four inches in diameter, and the upright stakes about two inches across. After the blankets and ties in which the body was wrapped were thrown out, to the south, short logs were placed horizontally inside, perpendicular to the long axis, from east to west. Then a pole was placed under the left arm and leg, the body being on its right side, facing north. When these preparations had been completed, members of the family and other relatives threw clothing, shoes, and blankets on the pyre as an offering to the dead child. In addition, special gifts of clothes, blankets, ornaments, and money were thrown on the pyre and dedicated to other dead relatives of the mourning family. This latter act is in keeping with the Cocopa belief that deceased relatives should be mourned long after their own funerals have taken place.

After the offerings had been placed on top of the logs that enclosed the child's body, the singers and the same women who had circled the bier in the ramada made four separate processions, going around the pyre twice each time in a counterclockwise direction. On each of the processions, they stopped at the northeast and southwest corners. There the head singer made a short talk, a repetition of the performance in the ramada. After the fourth circuit, the funeral orator made another speech. At its close the parents returned to the ramada and the cremator set fire to the arrowweed packed around the pyre. When the flames were well started, women relatives began stripping off dresses and throwing them on the flames. Some women removed as many as three dresses that they had put on over their regular clothes.

Some wailing continued as the fire burned, but individuals and groups soon started leaving for their homes. The father's brother, who had maintained a constant sing-song wailing throughout the ceremony, remained standing on the south side of the pyre until the flames were almost burned out. After about an hour, when the pyre was beginning to fall apart, the chief cremator picked up a long pole and pushed the logs around to start them burning again, and then placed them in such a way that they would complete the burning of the body.

In the meantime, five women sat near the pyre on the north side, with their backs to the pyre, while one of the women cut the hair of two of the five. When the cutting was finished, one of the other women gathered up the hair and the five returned in the direction of the ramada. The mother and father left the scene of the burning, and went to a nearby canal and bathed.

The next morning before daylight, the cremator returned to the pyre, dug a hole about four feet deep, and buried the ashes left from the burning. A small mound of earth was piled up over this grave. In former times the cremator would have dug four holes at the corners of the pyre, filled them with the ashes, and then obliterated all signs of the burning and burial.

Just at dawn, after the burying of the ashes, the father and mother returned to the cremation ground and underwent a short cleansing rite: they took a warm bath, washed their hair, and finally took a smoke bath, standing in the smoke from green arrowweed branches that had been thrown upon the fire used to heat the bath water. At the close of this rite the mother had her hair cut. Formerly parents and other very close relatives performed this ceremony for four mornings, during which time they were not permitted to eat meat, fat, or salt. This was also the occasion for a small "cry."

Under normal circumstances following a death, even that of a baby, possessions would have been burned either after the cremation or the next day. This particular couple was living in a rented house on an American farm, and so nothing was burned except at the pyre. The baby's cradle was broken into small pieces, tied in a bundle, and thrown into the river. It was not burned, since that would have prevented the birth of more children.

MOURNING CEREMONIES

The Cocopa interest in death and the dead is most clearly revealed in their mourning ceremonies, the kerauk and the chekap. Both were given to commemorate and honor a family's close relatives who had died during a span of years preceding the ceremony. More specifically, their purpose was to send to these same relatives the gifts and offerings that could not be assembled in the short time preceding their funerals, to make a final farewell to the dead so that they need never again be mentioned or mourned, and to avoid the illness or evil that a dead ancestor might visit upon the living. And the anthropologist might add that the kerauk and the chekap constituted the only Cocopa religious ceremonies and must therefore be assumed to have functioned as rites of intensification symbolic of the greatness and rightness of the Cocopa way of life.

From the point of view of an outsider, Cocopa death practices typify the way in which a society has hit upon some universal event that is then developed into an affair of great cultural interest. The choice, however, and the elaboration of destructive practices, have had far-reaching effects in the lives of these people. Among other things, because of the requirement that all family property be destroyed at the time of the death of any member and again at a mourning ceremony, there was no opportunity for the society to build its resources from one generation to the next.

Both the kerauk and the chekap stem from a basic mourning ceremony pattern which, in aboriginal times, had its locale in southern California, northern Baja California, and western Arizona. The mourning ceremony is identified with Yuman-speaking tribes but was also known to the Shoshonean tribes of southern California (Dubois 1908). It is more than possible that the chekap originated on the Colorado River and was in the process of being replaced by the Diegueño version of the kerauk during the last half of the 19th century. It is certain that the kerauk was given with greater frequency, and replaced the chekap at an earlier time, among the northern and western Cocopa than among the Hwanyak Cocopa in the southeastern corner of the delta. So far as I know, the full four-day chekap had not been given since about 1898 among the Hwanyak and not since about 1880 among the other bands. The kerauk was still spoken of as a living part of Cocopa culture during the period of our fieldwork, but it was obviously losing its place in Cocopa culture; the last one took place near Somerton about 1946. I was not present in Somerton at the time and I cannot now explain why I later failed to secure more than casual notes on the affair.

The Cocopa deny any hand in the origin of the kerauk and explicitly credit it to the Southern Diegueño. For evidence, they point out that the chekap had neither songs nor dances, and that many songs in the kerauk are in Diegueño words and are sung to the accompaniment of a Diegueño deer's-hoof rattle. A rough trait count verifies this opinion but also shows that important aspects of the Diegueño ceremony are lacking, and that in the Cocopa kerauk there are a number of Paipai, Yuma, and Mohave traits not found in the Diegueño ceremony (Drucker 1941: 148–50).

Other differences between the chekap and the kerauk lay almost entirely in their formal qualities. For example, the Cocopa kerauk lasted six (originally eight) days, while the chekap varied from one to four days. The chekap was under the direction of a religious leader, while the kerauk was under the direction of a political leader. In spite of these differences, the meaning and function were probably identical. Why one should have been held and not the other in any particular instance, I do not know. My informants said that it was simply a matter of preference.

During the 19th century mourning ceremonies were probably held almost every year in one section of the delta or another. There was no set time for them; they were held when any single group of kinsmen had sustained a series of losses and were sufficiently motivated to go to the very considerable trouble to prepare for one. There was probably a combination of circumstances that precipitated these affairs, not the least of which would have been pressure generated by the conscious or unconscious feelings of the members of the society, since it is certain that the mourning ceremonies functioned for the benefit of the group rather than just for that of the sponsoring kinsmen. The question raised here is an example of the inherent problems that arise when the ethnographer must work exclusively with informants and cannot reconstruct the full range of overt situations, let alone the subtleties of motivation.

The Kerauk

When a family head decided to give a kerauk for his deceased relatives, he talked the matter over with all his kinsmen, particularly those belonging to the lineage of the deceased person who was to be given central attention. If all agreed, they started at once to accumulate the necessary stores. Great quantities of clothes — as many as 50 complete outfits — were needed. They also had to have enough food on hand to help feed 300 to 500 visitors for six days, enough to give away in generous gifts to selected visitors, and enough to distribute, in fairly lavish fashion, over the dance area. Other requirements included supplies of eagle, owl, and other bird feathers, various headdresses, a "sacred" deer's-hoof rattle, a supply of wild tobacco, cane sections for cigarettes, and specially cut willow posts, rafters, poles, and arrowweed branches for the kerauk structures.

Materials were also required for the construction of an effigy of the sponsor's deceased father or other relative to be honored (a kerauk was almost always given explicitly in memory of the sponsor's father, even though other relatives, both male and female, were to be honored as well). If the Cocopa kerauk was to be patterned after the Paipai version, tanned deer hides would be needed for the effigy. If the Diegueño version was to be used, mishkwa "blankets" would be required. Mishkwa (*mɪškwɔ̃*) is the Diegueño word for a rush grass (*Juncus textilis*), a coarse, tough, reed-like plant that grows about 4 feet tall, in tussocks; its branches or stems were used as the warp of a mishkwa blanket. The plant was reported by Davis (1919: 27) as growing in the Jacumba Canyon in California near the Mexican border. The Cocopa, however, said that the only mishkwa suitable for the kerauk effigy had to be obtained from an area in Paipai country in the Baja California mountains; they identified this area as belonging to the *kwɪnyu* Indians, no doubt a Paipai lineage.

All these preparations required at least two years, and often took as long as four years. In the days before 1890, clothes could be made almost entirely of native products. After that time, however, clothes had to be bought or be made from store-bought cloth, because everyone had changed over to European clothing and the mourners had to use replicas of the clothing worn by their dead kinsmen.

The greatest difficulty under aboriginal conditions was the accumulation of adequate food resources. The problem was solved by planting additional acres of farm crops and harvesting surplus wild food plants for storage. The harvest of one year was stored, held over untouched, and added to the harvest of the following year when the ceremony was held. It is important to point out, however, in connection with an understanding of Cocopa subsistence activities, that this behavior indicates the true scope of their possible food resources. Working under the stimulus and within the pattern of this enterprise, the Cocopa could and did increase their production. However, the kerauk was undoubtedly dependent upon good harvest years and could be postponed if a given crop did not mature.

No publicity was given the family plans during the years of preparation. As Jim Short said: "We did not know what those people were doing until they made the [formal] announcement."

The last really elaborate kerauk was held about 1898 in Wi Ahwir territory, while Jack Row was captain. It was sponsored by a man who was very ill at the time, and who died a few days after the close of the ceremony. It is possible, although my informants would not say so, that he gave the kerauk in a final effort to pacify the ghosts of his relatives who were causing his sickness. His death was attributed to this cause, but it is also true that a kerauk site is itself a particularly dangerous place, because dreams about dead relatives who attempt soul-stealing are most common around a kerauk. There were three shamans in attendance at this kerauk, in readiness to treat just such sickness.

Although I have a record of, and some information on, at least 15 kerauk ceremonies given by the Cocopa between about 1890 and 1946, the following material is based principally on the 1898 kerauk mentioned above. The informant was Sam Spa. Notes were checked against an independent account given by Tom Juarez, who from early boyhood had been learning the kerauk songs and who provided me with a chronology of the kerauk ceremonies he attended between about 1887 and 1926. From his accounts it must be assumed that for the above years, at least, the three northern and western Cocopa bands were giving closely related ceremonies with some stability in form. It must also be assumed, since Gifford's account (1933: 295-8) differs from mine on some points, that the Hwanyak kerauk was, to some degree, another variation. This is not surprising, and in fact is to be expected, since this aspect of Cocopa culture was certainly in a state of flux.

Preliminaries

The 1898 kerauk was given by a man named Piedra principally for his father, but with ten deceased relatives "in mind." Six of these relatives were impersonated by living dancers and the father was represented by a life-size effigy.

When the crops were harvested, and the time came for the ceremony, Piedra called all his relatives together at his camp. For four nights they "cried" together in private ceremonies. I neglected to ask, but I suspect that this was a simple version of the Cocopa chekap (described in the next section), given as a preliminary to the "foreign" kerauk. On the fourth night, the band captain was called to join in the ceremony and to consult with the family head on plans for the kerauk. While the actual direction of the kerauk was in the hands of the captain, there was close cooperation throughout between these two men, who consulted with each other frequently. My account may overemphasize the position of the captain.

Throughout these first four days, for the following three "preparatory" days, for the six days of the kerauk proper, and for four days after, all of Piedra's close relatives, who would be the mourners, were under special restrictions and performed special rites to maintain their ritual purity: sexual intercourse was forbidden, and all meat, fat, and salt were taboo. The mourners were also required to take a warm bath each morning just before daylight. Except when taking part in the ceremony, they stayed inside their temporary shelter and later the kerauk house.

Before daylight on the first morning of the three preparatory days, three old men were sent, each to different sections of the valley, to tell the people that they would be expected at the kerauk site in about two days. On arrival at a camp, the messenger started crying and, on hearing this, the people assembled and cried just a little since they understood the meaning of this action. The messenger then sat down with the leaders of the camp, and they smoked cane cigarettes brought for the purpose. These people notified their neighbors, and the old man went on to another district.

In the meantime, the mourning relatives, led by the band captain, started clearing the area where the kerauk house was to be built. Willow poles and arrowweed for the structure had long since been cut and stacked nearby. When the work on the clearing was completed, they started building a U-shaped brush shelter (č?kowən oya'o) for the mourners about 50 feet to the north. This shelter, which was without a roof, was constructed of upright posts, horizontal poles, and perpendicular arrowweed branches. It was about 30 feet long and 20 feet wide, with walls as high

as a man could reach. The opening was to the east. This structure was built under the direction of the captain, with the mourners and friends supplying the labor. The mourning families moved into this shelter with their supplies and stayed there until the kerauk house was built. On the day after this shelter was built, visitors who lived nearby began to arrive and to establish their family camps.

By the third day most visitors had arrived, and during this third morning one of the visiting captains sent a boy to notify the host captain that the visitors were ready to come to the kerauk. They all then assembled behind this captain and approached the kerauk area, where they met the host captain, who was followed by members of his band and the mourning relatives. In an earlier day, the two captains would have come together and signaled their greeting by quick lifts of their heads, making their long nose pendants swing out and flash in the sun. In 1898 neither Jack Row nor the visiting captain wore such pendants (which were designed to be worn by war leaders), so they proceeded directly to an embrace (arms around each other) and a handshake. This was the signal for the mourners to stop crying and for the visitors to come forward to embrace them.

When the greetings had been made, the host captain gave a speech in which he welcomed the visitors and issued instructions to both visitors and hosts on arrangements for feeding the people, supplying firewood, and such matters. Young men of both groups spent the afternoon gathering a supply of wood for the camps and for the ceremony. (Sam Spa was one of the young men responsible for maintaining the wood supply.)

After the evening meal, the captain made another talk. He said that the mourners would spend the night in the mourning shelter, but that this need not distract the other members of his band or the visitors, who should spend the night in enjoying themselves: "The young men and girls should see each other and maybe some will want to get married. Those who play games must name a referee to take charge so there will be no trouble."

The Kerauk House

The following day, the first day of the kerauk ceremony, activities started before daylight when the man who had been selected to build the kerauk house (because of his experience with the job) started digging the post holes. When the holes had been dug, some of the women mourners came out of the shelter and threw corn and beans into them and over the surrounding ground. (In an earlier kerauk reported by Tom Juarez, which had been held in the month of May, pine nuts were used for this purpose, and they were quickly gathered up and eaten by visiting children.)

After breakfast the host captain called the people together for another talk in which he told them that the kerauk house would be built that morning, and that the helpers selected from among the non-mourners by the builder should carefully follow his instructions. The captain encouraged the helpers to hasten their work so that the mourners could stop their crying and feel better. Then at a signal from the chief mourner the builder and his helpers started for the place nearby where the poles had previously been stacked. Each man had been told what to bring so that all of the material, except the arrowweed bundles, could be carried in one trip. With the builder and his helpers went a group of women mourners carrying baskets and pottery jars full of corn and beans. Before anyone touched the stored poles, these women threw the food over them and the whole group stopped for a few minutes to "cry." At another signal from the chief mourner the poles were picked up and carried to the kerauk site, where they were first set on end and then lowered to the ground very gently. The poles were again sprinkled by the women, and there was a brief pause for "crying."

The kerauk builder then sent the same helpers to bring in the arrowweed that had previously been cut and tied in bundles, and the builder, assisted by another group, began working on the kerauk house. The work was rushed with all possible speed, with the mourners standing close by and continuing their crying until the house was completed.

The central part of the structure, measuring about 16 feet north to south and about 12 feet east to west, was built as follows. Six upright posts were buried about 8 inches in the ground, placed in pairs in such a way as to support three east-west beams. These beams were then covered by 50 to 60 cross-poles and the whole was covered by small bundles of arrowweed branches (Fig. 28). This central structure was then enlarged by about 6 feet on three sides (north, south, and west) and these three sides were enclosed with a framework of posts and horizontal poles that served to support a wall of arrowweed bundles. The roof extensions were built to slope away from the central structure and were constructed with a framework of rafters, which were covered by cross-poles and more bundles of arrowweed. The front (east side) of the kerauk house was left open and a courtyard was formed by extending the north and south house walls for about 25 feet. A small opening was left in the west wall through which the mourners could come and go. Before noon, when the house was finished, three additional posts were set up: one near the center of the courtyard opening and the other two just beyond the ends of the fences. Three flags were tied to these posts: a white one on the center post, a black one on the south post, and a red one on the north post. When the construction of the kerauk house was completed, the captain called all the workmen together and gave them special gifts of food to take to their camps.

During the afternoon, men and boys carried all the supplies from the mourners' temporary shelter to the

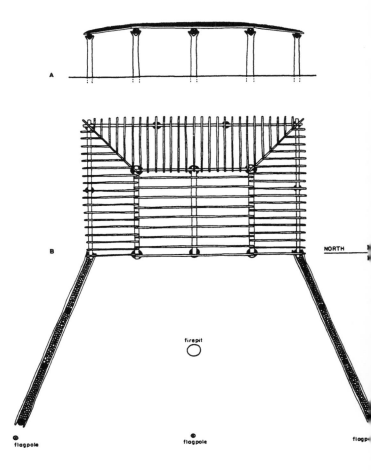

Fig. 28. *a.* Front or east elevation of kerauk house, showing three of the six main roof supports and two of the smaller outer posts supporting the roof extension. *b.* Plan of kerauk house and courtyard fences. (After Gifford 1933: 296.)

kerauk house. The supplies included all the food and a number of large pottery vessels filled with the clothes that were to be used in the ceremony. Special equipment, also brought into the kerauk house at this time, included the deer's-hoof rattle to be used by the singer, supplies of wild tobacco and cane cigarettes, woven mishkwa blankets containing clothes to be worn by the six impersonators, feathers to be used for decorating headdresses, and materials to be used in the construction of the effigy.

When the move was finished, about two or three o'clock, the captain assembled everyone again in order to tell them to spend the rest of the day in games. Hoop-and-pole games were organized, including one between champion women players of the visiting bands. There was also a horse race with much betting; gambling games, including peon (see Chapter 5), were played along the insides of the two fences of the court.

Formal ceremonies for the first night of the kerauk got started about sundown and were focused on six dancers, three men and three women, who were dressed and painted to impersonate deceased members of the mourning family. Since the 1898 kerauk was being held explicitly to honor the chief mourner's father, he would be represented on the last two days of the kerauk by a life-sized effigy. In addition to these seven identified individuals, 40 to 50 other unidentified deceased relatives were to be honored by visitors who would wear "mourning garments," which had been brought to the kerauk by members of the mourning family and would be "sent to dead relatives" by being burned at the end of the kerauk.

As soon as fires were started inside the kerauk house and in the courtyard between the kerauk fences, the captain selected the six impersonators. They were brought into the back of the kerauk house where the clothes were stored, and each was given a bundle containing clothes, headgear, ornaments, weapons or tools, and paint. These materials would permit each individual to dress and decorate himself or herself in a manner representing as closely as possible the deceased person being impersonated. When the impersonators finished dressing, the chief mourner then pointed to each and repeated the kin term he would actually have used to address the individual being represented.

When all was in readiness, the kerauk singer took up his rattle, and he and his two assistants, one on each side, went to the front of the kerauk house and sat in front of the southernmost of the front posts. The impersonators followed and sat behind them. After a brief wait, the singer and his helpers stood up and started their song, *wa čosi* (house purifying). This and other kerauk songs, along with kerauk instructions, had been given to two men (a Southern Diegueño and a Cocopa) by animal and human supernatural beings they met in a journey through Diegueño territory, according to Tom Juarez (see *The Origin of the Kerauk and Its Songs*, Juarez's account of this journey, in Chapter 9). While singing *wa čosi*, the singer and his helpers proceeded in a dancing step clockwise around the central court fire. On the second round, they were joined by some of the impersonators. Not all the impersonators went around the first time, because they had never done this before; they were "ashamed" and wanted to see how it was done. After several circuits, the singer stopped and took the lead in a "cry" that lasted for about 20 minutes. (In Tom Juarez's version, during the next song and dance around the fire, the singers and impersonators were joined by the mourners.) The visitors, with non-mourners from the local band, stood around the court and watched the dance.

At the close of this one song sequence, about an hour later, the first day and night of the kerauk came to an end. The impersonators removed their clothes and returned to their camps to take a "purifying" bath. The mourners retired to the back of the kerauk house for a night of sleep.

The pattern for the six days was to be one night of sleeping alternating with one night of dancing.

The following day was spent in games, gambling, and visiting, while the mourners remained in the kerauk house. At sundown, the captain called the people together for the first full night of dancing and mourning, and made a talk in which he told all those assembled "to do the best they could" to help the mourners.

In addition to the six impersonators, about 40 men, women, girls, and boys were assembled in the kerauk shelter to dress in the clothes that would later be burned. Other men were chosen to wear red cloths, slit to go on over their heads. One specially able dancer was selected to wear an elaborate headdress called *hoyɪr*, a red cloth decorated with small beads around the edges, and with feathers stuck in the back.

The singer and his two helpers took the same position as on the night before, and the group of impersonators and dancers assembled behind them. At a signal from the captain, they all sat down in unison, simultaneously making a soft sound: "oooh."

As the singer started singing, he rose slowly and walked to the court fire. When he had moved into position, the impersonators and dancers followed, forming a north-south line behind him, facing east. When they were all in position, the singer stopped his song and they all joined his lead in "crying." At the end of this "cry," the singer and his helpers began another song and made three clockwise circuits of the courtyard fire. While they did this, the mourners came out of the kerauk house and embraced the impersonators. When the impersonators were released, they joined the singer in another dance around the fire, and this time three additional helpers joined the singer and danced around the fire in front of him, moving backward. The song used to accompany this dance, called *saiyao patai*, was one of the Kamia (Diegueño) songs used in the kerauk. During the dance, the mourners stood in line in front of the kerauk house facing the court. At intervals during the night the singing and dancing stopped, the impersonators embraced the mourners, and they all "cried" together. Singing and dancing did not end until daylight. The physical contact between the mourners and the individuals who were impersonating the mourners' close relatives must have been a dramatic and shocking experience. It was a final farewell, since a Cocopa would never again mention or refer to these kinsmen. This is something difficult for Americans to understand (or to remember in their dealings with the Cocopa), since it is our custom to ease the pain of losing close relatives by frequently mentioning their names and by keeping various mementos.

The third day was devoted to gambling, visiting, and sleeping. The captain made his usual morning talk, but there was no ceremony either during the day or at night.

Some families from remote sections of the delta and from neighboring tribes were still arriving during these first few days. As soon as they made camp, they would come into the kerauk shelter where they "cried for a minute" with the mourners.

The ceremony on the fourth night was a repetition of that on the second night. My informants, however, added the detail that the singer's helpers yelled a good deal during the night, "to keep the people awake and to rouse their spirits." This behavior may have been more typical of this night than of the first night of dancing.

The Mishkwa Effigy

On the morning of the fifth day, about 10 men, under the direction of the captain, began the construction of the effigy to represent the chief mourner's deceased father. This effigy was called *mɩškwə čapai pasei* (man made of *mɩškwə*) and was life-size, or somewhat less. My notes on the form and method of construction of the mishkwa effigy are not as complete as I would like, and I have therefore added detail from Davis's (1919) description of the Diegueño effigies. The mishkwa blankets themselves, which had been made ahead of time, were constructed by placing the mishkwa stems side by side, like the warps on a loom, and then weaving across them with sinew or fiber strings at about 6-inch intervals (see Fig. 29). The head and the body of the effigy were made of two facing mishkwa blankets cut to shape, stuffed with straw, and sewn together around their perimeters. The head was made by cutting horizontal slits in the mishkwa blankets where the effigy neck would join the body, leaving an uncut area in the middle. By rolling the side sections toward the center, a cylindrically shaped head and neck was formed. This was covered by a white cloth, on which eyes, nose, and mouth were painted in black. The top of the head was covered by a scarf, the shoulders were decorated with two long tufts of eagle feathers, and other feathers were placed at intervals around

the rim of the body to form a fringe. The arms and legs were represented by sticks inserted into the body (Fig. 29).*

The making of the effigy, which occupied the morning hours and part of the afternoon, was accomplished in a rhythmic fashion accompanied by songs. For example, the front and back parts of the effigy, which had been cut and were ready to be put together, were held by two men who swung them back and forth, singing to a rattle accompaniment as they approached each other on their knees. When they met, a third man held a bundle of straw (like an automobile tire) between the two parts while other helpers sewed them together.

When the effigy was completed, about two or three o'clock in the afternoon, it was turned over to the same expert dancer who had worn the *hoyɩr* headdress in the earlier dances. He circled the court four times, dancing backward and counterclockwise in front of the singer, his two helpers, and the six impersonators, holding the effigy high over his head or resting it "piggy-back" upon his shoulders. At the close, the image was placed on top of the kerauk house. No other ceremony or dance was held on the fifth day.

Tom Juarez gave a different account. The image for the kerauk he described was called *čɩpučur* (not *mɩškwə*); it was made of two round pieces of buckskin held in shape by wooden frames and stuffed with grass straw (Fig. 30). Instead of a head, the *čɩpučur* image used a head ornament (*sukwily*) made of two crossed sticks wound with various colored yarns (obviously a copy of the Mexican "guardian eye" or "God's eye" fetish). One side of the buckskin body cover was painted to represent the chief mourner's father, and a necklace and ear and nose pendants were hung on this small painted figure.

On the morning of the sixth and last day, the captain, after his usual morning talk, directed the six impersonators to dress again in the clothes of those being mourned and to make every effort to duplicate their usual dress and idiosyncrasies. The impersonators were then lined up in the courtyard behind the captain; behind them came four of the women mourners carrying pottery jars full of food, and four more carrying money and clothes. Led by the captain, they proceeded to a point about 100 yards east of the kerauk shelter, and returned. In the course of this trip the women carrying food threw it on the ground and over the heads of the assembled crowd. The captain then dropped

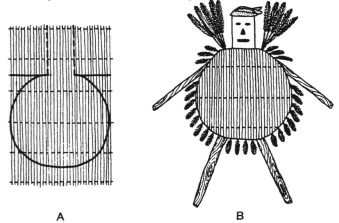

Fig. 29. Mishkwa effigy used in kerauk ceremony. *a.* Mishkwa blanket showing lines along which cuts were made to form the front and back pieces of the effigy (see Davis 1919: 28). *b.* The completed effigy.

*Rather than fill these descriptive statements with parentheses expressing doubt about the accuracy of my field notes, I have elected to use positive statements. Since I depended entirely upon information from interviews, it is inevitable that many mistakes have crept into my notes, and I am sure that this was particularly true when informants described impersonators and effigies. They discussed these subjects (relating to known dead) with great reluctance and were openly irritated when I responded to their statements with question after question in an attempt to clear up any possible misunderstandings.

Fig. 30. **Kerauk effigy made of buckskin, with painted representation of person being mourned.**

out, and the impersonators and mourners made three more trips over the same route, increasing their speed with each journey. After the second trip, the women carrying clothes and money began throwing it to the crowd. When food jars were emptied, they were broken and full ones secured. On the last trip back to the kerauk shelter, the women and impersonators ran full speed and all gave loud cries while beating their open hands against their mouths.

At the close of this race, the three male impersonators removed their costumes, but the women remained for a special women's ceremony that was led by a woman singer (selected by the captain) and two helpers. These three lined up in the kerauk shelter in front of the impersonators, facing east, and began a song to the accompaniment of two pottery paddles clapped together by the woman singer. While singing, the three women danced backward and forward a few steps each way. At the end of the first song, the singers and impersonators all went out the rear door of the kerauk shelter. Starting a new song, they danced four times around the outside of the kerauk house and court-yard fences, the impersonators going backward and the singers going forward, facing them. At the end of the last circuit they entered the kerauk shelter at the front, and the ceremonies ended for that morning. If there was to be an initiation ceremony (see the final section of this chapter), it too was held during this final morning.

During the afternoon, food, money, and other gifts were given to all those who had helped in the cer-

emony — including the impersonators and those who had dressed in the clothing to be burned — and several horses were given away.

The Final Night

After dark, some men went about 40 feet east of the kerauk fences and built a 3-foot-high arrowweed replica of a cremation pyre. After the pyre was built, the singing and dancing of the second and fourth nights was repeated, except that the group of 40 to 50 people dressed in the mourning clothes formed a circle, shoulder to shoulder, and danced around the court fire. The singer and his helpers circled the fire in front of them, and for the last part of the night they were joined by the man carrying the effigy, who danced backward in front of the singer. There was alternate singing and crying as on the other nights.

Just before daylight, at a signal from the captain, the impersonators retired and the singer, his helpers, and the dancer carrying the effigy began a dance that carried them four times around the kerauk house counterclockwise, and four times around the pyre, counterclockwise. At the close of this dance, the effigy was placed upon the pyre in the same position as for a human cremation: head to the east, face to the north. (This could be a misunderstanding, since all other accounts indicate that the effigy was placed upright in the pyre). All the clothes that had been worn by the impersonators were then placed on top of the image. When everything was in readiness, the pyre and the kerauk house were set on fire by non-mourners appointed for the job. The visitors and mourners stood well back from the fires; there was a general wailing and crying, as at a cremation.

Shortly after daylight, when each family had made sure that none of its members was sick, the visitors left for their homes. People who were ill stayed to be treated by the kerauk shamans. The chief mourner and some of his relatives stayed to sleep on the ashes of the kerauk house for four days. (The chief mourner at the 1898 ceremony, who had been ill throughout the kerauk, died on the third day of this period.) It is very probable that within a day or two after the close of the kerauk, the sponsor's house and property would be burned. This was the pattern for a chekap (to be described next), and there is a reference to this in my notes, but I may have misunderstood. As a regular practice some items used in the kerauk were not burned but were saved for the next kerauk; these included eagle feathers, the deer's-hoof rattle, the *hoyır*, and other headdresses worn by dancers.

"How a kerauk is to be performed" is described in the myth concerning the origin of kerauk songs given to me by Tom Juarez (see Chapter 9). This part of the account, however, is not a part of the song origin myth, and therefore it must be presumed that it is based upon Juarez's knowledge as a kerauk singer and knowledge gained by attending a large number of kerauks during his lifetime. I have already mentioned the use of an alternate effigy form as described by Juarez. Other differences between the account given by Sam Spa and the one given by Juarez refer to the eighth day (kerauks lasted six days but there was also a tradition of eight days), as follows.

In the afternoon 15 to 18 men and boys, and the same number of women and girls, were taken to the kerauk house, where they were dressed to impersonate dead relatives. Another two boys, who were to ride horses in a race, were dressed as impersonators and, in addition, had their hair dabbed with wet white earth, their faces painted, and a feather placed in their hair. When all were ready, the two boys were mounted on horses equipped with fancy saddle blankets and new bridles and took their position on the north and south sides of the men and women impersonators. At a signal from the captain they all ran slowly for a short distance to the east and then returned, repeating this race two times. Then for the fourth and final race, the women dropped out and the men and boys, flanked by the boys on horseback, raced over the same course but returned as fast as they could run. This last time an individual led the men for half the race (to the east only), hollering all the time with his hand beating against his mouth. During each of the four races women mourners threw corn, beans, clothes and money over the impersonators. When the race was finished the host captain gave the two horses to two visiting captains, who had them slaughtered immediately and the meat distributed to the camps of visitors.

At nightfall dances and songs started again and continued until midnight, when the effigy was taken from the kerauk roof and carried by a man who circled the kerauk house. Then the singer sang a song to "strengthen" the chief mourner. Another song described how the singer was going to dance to the "pyre" (a 3-foot-high pile of arrowweeds) and dance around this counterclockwise once, then return to the shelter to sing four more songs, and "that is all." He did this, and then said (in a song) that he would start the fire. He started for the arrowweed "pyre," singing four songs on the way. These were "fire" songs and included a song telling the story of the death of Eagle (*spa*, who was killed to provide the feathers for the kerauk), his cremation, and the kerauk given for him. Other songs told how the clothes used by impersonators and the effigy were to be burned.

When these songs were completed the host captain gave the signal for the end of the kerauk. The impersonators danced four times around the "pyre" and then took off their clothes and ornaments and placed them on the "pyre" with the clothes facing east. Then the man who had danced with the effigy placed it on the arrowweed in an upright position at the east end of the "pyre" and facing east. The arrowweed "pyre" and the kerauk house were then set on fire. If everything had been done correctly, and if all officials, and especially the kerauk singer, had the proper power, through dreams, to conduct the kerauk, the smoke from the fires would drift to the land of the dead (*kerauk hap*) carrying all of the mourners' gifts and all of the food to the impersonated relatives.

In his description of the kerauk Tom Juarez added this bit of information: On the last night (or perhaps even earlier), when the largest crowd was assembled and people were milling around and excited, some trouble was apt to start. To forestall this, the visiting captains met with the host captain in a formal and public conference in the courtyard. The visiting captains each appointed a "war leader" (*kwınami*) and in a speech told the people that if trouble started, if anyone threatened to use a gun or a knife, they would direct their "war leaders" to subdue the troublemaker, or tie him up, or kill him if necessary so as to insure peace and quiet during the kerauk.

The Chekap ("Cry")

In contrast to the lively interest and full knowledge my informants displayed when describing the kerauk, they were both vague and bored when it came to the chekap. I have separate accounts from Jim Short and Sam Spa but far from a complete picture of this event. Spa had not seen a full-scale chekap since he was seven or eight, and Short was not much older when he saw his last one.

The important thing that emerges, besides their historical independence, is the great contrast in formal quality between the two ceremonies. Even discounting the difference in interest and memory on the part of my informants, it is still quite evident that the precision of timing and organization that marked the kerauk was absent in the chekap. On the second day of the chekap, for example, the mourners were supposed to have the mourning clothes ready for the dance that night, but Short said, "If the clothes were not ready, then they gave the dance the next night." At the kerauk, food was thrown over the dance area and given to visitors according to a fixed schedule. In the chekap, the mourners distributed food at irregular intervals, except when the chekap house was built. The kerauk was a six-day ceremony, and there was no variation in the pattern. The chekap lasted four days, two days, or a single day.

The chekap, like the kerauk, was sponsored by a single family, with related families joining in. It was also an occasion for mourning all their relatives who had recently died. Since the disposal of food and other gifts was one of the central features of this ceremony, families planned well in advance of their announcement. For a really big affair, they stored food through two harvests so as to have adequate supplies on hand. Sam Spa said that it was a matter of personal choice whether the sponsor undertook the management of the ceremony or whether he turned his task over to the captain. In any event, in contrast to the kerauk, there was very little for the manager to do, since the ceremony itself was under the direction of the band's funeral orator. (The Cocopa funeral orator had no official place in the kerauk; there, a comparable but not so important position was held by the kerauk singer.) Both informants agreed that there were but two "officials" for a chekap — the funeral orator and the house builder. This last functionary was a man who "knew how" and who filled this post at all chekap (and kerauk?) ceremonies.

As in the kerauk, messengers were sent out three or four days in advance of the first, or house-building, day. During the interval, the mourning families assembled at the camp of the sponsor, but there was no "crying" and no ceremony until the night before the house was to be built.

Certain taboos were imposed upon all the members of the mourning family, starting with the ceremony the night before the building of the chekap house. The mourners were supposed to eat only a little gruel; they were forbidden fish, meat, fats, and salt; and they bathed and washed their hair each morning. These restrictions continued for four days after the chekap. According to Jim Short, the mourners were not supposed to sleep during any of the four nights of mourning.

On the morning of the first day of the ceremony, work was started on the construction of the chekap house. I did not learn the details, but in essentials the procedure was the same as for the kerauk house. The construction material had been prepared in advance. Men and boys were delegated to bring the poles, posts, and arrowweed to the building site; they were accompanied by women of the mourning families who threw food over the material, into the post holes, and over the courtyard. The structure was built according to the same plan as the kerauk house.

After the completion of the chekap house, the visitors walked away a distance of 500 to 600 yards and then approached the chekap shelter in a body, led by their funeral orator. The host band, including the mourners, also led by their funeral orator, walked a short distance to meet them. When the two groups came together, the orators began a formal talk, both speaking simultaneously. My informants did not know what was said. This talk was accompanied by crying, and at its close the mourners, still crying, backed up and retired into the chekap house. This part of the ceremony was in the late afternoon, but according to Jim Short, it might be delayed to early evening if the shelter were not finished in time. (The kerauk house, it will be recalled, was built according to a strict time schedule.) There were no further ceremonies that day.

Part of the first day and most of the second day were spent in gambling, horse racing, and visiting. Here, as at the kerauk, the young people were urged to get acquainted and to get married. In the chekap that Sam Spa remembered, the sponsor gave away two or three horses on the morning of the second day, with the provision that they could be kept by their new owners if they could ride them through the assembled crowd without having them seriously injured by knives in the hands of the men. Any horses that were injured or killed in this race were butchered and eaten by the visitors during the ceremony. In the meantime, the mourners spent the day in preparing the clothes to be worn by impersonators that night.

After dark, fires were built and impersonators were chosen and brought into the shelter to put on their costumes. Here, as in the kerauk, every effort was made to dress these people in the customary fashion of the dead relative being represented. Favored face painting was used, and replicas of necklaces, armbands, women's basketry hats, sandals, musical instruments, and the like were all supplied. During this night and succeeding nights the same costumes and impersonators were used.

The pattern was to spend the night alternately resting and crying. The crying was initiated when the funeral orator began to talk and halted when he stopped. During his talk, the impersonators of the deceased individuals circulated through the crowd in the courtyard and "greeted" one visitor after another by throwing their arms around them. Men embraced men, women embraced women. Additional talks by the captain and other orators were given during the night, but I do not know whether these talks were also accompanied by mourning.

The chekap house was burned on the final night, just before dawn. The impersonators removed their clothing and threw it on top of the chekap house, or in a pile in the center of the house. Nothing else was burned, and there was no image and no pyre. Whatever food was left over was divided among the visitors to take home.

A friend or distant relative set fire to the house, and visitors and mourners cried and wailed when it burned, as when the kerauk house was burned. This was the end of the ceremony, and visitors left for home at once. Within two or three days, the house and all the possessions of the chief mourner were burned.

The two-day chekap was simply a shortened version of this ceremony. The day of the house building was followed by two nights of "crying," and the shelter was burned at dawn on the final night.

The one-day chekap was a small affair in which the family invited relatives and friends to come to their camp for a "cry." It lasted for one day and one night, or just for a single night, and was marked by the burning of clothes on a specially built pyre of arrowweeds. There was no house and no impersonation, and nothing else was burned.

Another type of one-day chekap probably occurred with some frequency. It was held whenever a deceased relative died away from home and therefore could not be cremated with the usual ceremony, or when relatives who were unable to attend a cremation came to visit the family.

There was no special structure built and nothing was burned. The families involved simply came together during a single night for the purpose of mourning and crying.

INITIATION CEREMONIES

Boys and girls nearing the age of marriage were "initiated" in a combined ceremony as a part of the big harvest fiesta (*yamas*), or in connection with the kerauk. Initiation in connection with the chekap was explicitly denied by Sam Spa and Jim Short, but Mike Alvarez had his nose pierced on the second day of a small chekap ceremony. Since the initiation ceremony never occurred alone, and was open only to the relatives of the sponsors of a fiesta or mourning ceremony, some of these affairs may have been motivated by the initiation element.

Initiation was not a rite of passage in the usual sense. Age-sex roles were not altered, and there was no symbolism that could be interpreted as marking the transition from one social condition to another. Neither was it strictly a puberty rite, except that the ideal pattern called for its performance after the participants had attained sexual maturity and before marriage. Central attention was upon the boys rather than the girls: the main feature of the ceremony was the piercing of the boys' nasal septums by the war leader. This would indicate that the original purpose was an initiation of boys as warriors. The possibility of an association between warfare and nose piercing is also strengthened by the fact that the war leader was the only man who wore an elaborate nose pendant (see Chapter 10). Some older men wore a simple bead, but most males went through life without ever making use of the hole in their septum. Another "war" interpretation was given by Sam Spa, who explained that the races to the cardinal points during the initiation were intended to give the boys strength for fighting.

Gifford's account of the ceremony (1933: 291), from older informants, is more elaborate in certain parts than mine, and there is no doubt that initiation declined both in favor and in interest during the latter half of the 19th century. The last Wi Ahwir ceremony was held around 1895-1900, and the last ceremony at Somerton, according to Gifford, was in 1914. The Wi Ahwir ceremony was the one in which Mike Alvarez was initiated. Alvarez said: "At the close of the ceremony the people said they would never hold another one. Jack Row [the captain] tried to change their minds, but the people got mad and said 'no more.' Finally he said: 'All right. This will be the last time.' "

Taboos and cleansing rites for the initiates were rather strict. They were given nothing to eat for the first two days and were on a strict diet during the entire initiation period; they were expected to maintain a serious attitude and to talk as little as possible; scratching themselves with their fingers was taboo, and a scratching stick was provided for

this purpose; every morning and every evening, they were given a bath in warm water.

The initiation ceremony was a four-day affair followed by twelve days of restrictions and ceremonies to restore ritual purity to the initiates. Two days of the four-day initiation proper coincided with the last two days of a kerauk or of a fiesta.

Following is an account of the ceremony in which Sam Spa participated as an initiate at about 18 years of age (around 1890). Six boys, including Spa, and two girls, all related to the mourners, went through the ceremony, which was associated with a kerauk given by relatives of Spa's mother. The four-day ceremony was held under a specially built ramada near the kerauk house; it also served as the sleeping quarters for the initiates (the boys on one side, the girls on the other).

The initiation began before daylight on the fifth day of the kerauk (the day the effigy was made). All participants took a warm bath and then assembled in the initiation ramada, the boys in a line in front, the girls behind. The captain opened the proceedings with a speech in which he thanked the boys and girls for coming to the initiation, and thanked their relatives for giving the kerauk and so making it possible. He then went on to explain the necessity for tattooing the girls and piercing the noses of the boys: "When you die you can go right into that place and be with your people. If you didn't have this ceremony you would live with your head in a hole and everyone who comes by could kick you and make fun of you."

At the close of the speech, the boys were handed a pan of water with which to rinse their noses and were told to sit up straight with their heads held high. At this point four visiting women (the basis for whose selection I do not know) were given gifts of pine nuts by the wife of the chief mourner. When the last of these women retired, the nose piercer (*čapai nyiho*) approached the boy at the left side of the line, and with a slow but steady motion ran the point of a sharpened nail through his septum. He then inserted an arrowweed stem and broke it off so that it extended a short distance on either side of the nostril. While this was going on, a man standing nearby made a loud cry, punctuating it by stopping his mouth with the palm of his hand. The nose piercer then proceeded down the line of boys, with only a short pause between operations. During this time the girls' chins were being tattooed. This was done by an experienced woman, who broke the skin on the girls' chins in the desired line by punching it with a row of cactus thorns held between her fingers. When blood flowed from the punctures, a black mineral from the Baja California mountains was rubbed in, the spot washed off, and puncturing resumed. Spier (1933: 102) describes the same procedure for the Maricopa.

When the piercing and tattooing were completed, the boys and girls were dressed in new clothes and their faces were freshly painted. They also put on new necklaces of shells, and the boys were given new eagle feathers to put in their hair. All were supplied with scratching sticks, which were tied with a cord around their wrists. Then the captain turned them over to a proctor who directed their action for the remainder of the four days. He was a young man, a relative, who joined in all the action and taboos. In payment for his services, he had the right to take his choice of the boys' new belts, armbands, and necklaces.

After the proctor took charge, the boys and girls ran four times around the ramada and then to a point about a mile north, where they stayed quietly in a shady spot until evening. Then they ran back to the kerauk area and went around their ramada another four times. When they came to a halt in the ramada, four more gifts of pine nuts were made to four visiting women by the chief mourner's wife. After a warm bath, the initiates were stretched full length in a heated trench, where the girls were pressed by women, and the boys by men, for about an hour (the pressing treatment is described in Chapter 5, under *Family Rites*). At the end of this treatment, the initiates were sent to sleep in the ramada.

The next morning they had a warm bath and ran to a point a mile south, where they spent the day. On their return, they had another bath and went to sleep. This sequence was repeated on the third day, when they ran to the west.

On the fourth day the initiates had their faces completely covered with white paint. Then they raced to the east, but this time they stayed away only until noon. At this time the proctor was dismissed, and whatever ornaments he did not take were given to friends. That night, the second after the burning of the kerauk house, the captain and the chief mourner stayed with the initiates. The next morning the initiates were free to go to their homes, where they were required to undergo twelve days of purification. On the morning of the first of the twelve days they had their hair washed in a concoction of water and ground arrowweed roots. They were permitted to eat a small quantity of corn gruel, and this diet was gradually increased during the next eleven days. Hair washing went through a set pattern. It was washed in arrowweed juice for four days, plastered with plain mud for the next four days, and plastered with mud mixed with mesquite sap for the final four days. At the end of the twelfth day, when this final preparation was washed off, all taboos were lifted; the initiates could return to a normal diet and throw their scratching sticks away. These requirements were identical for both boys and girls.

8. DIVISION OF LABOR AND ASSIGNMENT OF RIGHTS AND DUTIES

Civil rights, women's rights, Chicano rights, gay rights, and others all point to the storms that brew when a society's attention is directed toward some changes in its system of rights and duties. But most of the time and in most areas of their lives, members of a society are unaware of the existence of the rules they use to decide who is to do what, and what rights, duties, and obligations accrue to those selected. We fix our minds on the purpose of an activity (Joe and Harry are hired to fix automobiles) and seldom question how certain individuals are selected or assigned to the activity in the first place, or how rights and duties are distributed among those individuals.

The above statements relate to the familiar sociological concept of "role." Role refers to the behavior of a class of individuals performing similar actions. Role behavior has two aspects: the actors possess certain attributes or qualities (*structuring principles*) in common (this defines the class), and there is a regularity in their behavior that may be described abstractly in terms of patterns of rights and duties. Structuring principles include such criteria as age, sex, kinship, residence, education, seniority, wealth, physical fitness, and so on. The criteria then become associated in the minds of the participants with rights and duties so that the behavior of individuals in a wide variety of concrete situations becomes formalized, and this behavior is then directed, to a greater or lesser extent, by what is expected of a young man, a grandmother, a wealthy woman, and by other similar structuring principles, rather than by the intrinsic nature of the activity. Knowing these principles, the ethnographer has made the first and basic step toward understanding the variations in behavior from one society to another, and the reader gains an understanding of some of the difficulties inherent in cross-cultural adjustment on the part of individuals. In American society marriage is the principal criterion that is used in assigning the tasks, and the rights and duties, necessary for the establishment and maintenance of a family. Young couples are expected to be independent and responsible for their own maintenance. This pattern, as we have seen, is quite foreign to the Cocopa pattern, in which young couples were encouraged to get married but were not expected to maintain themselves independently. The consequence has been that young Cocopa couples have had great difficulty understanding and accepting the American pattern, particularly the American demand that young people start early in life and work conscientiously and regularly to learn a profession or trade.

AGE AND SEX DISTINCTIONS

The Cocopa, like all other people in the world, made constant and well-recognized use of differences in age and sex as a guide to expected behavior. They differed from many other societies, however, in seldom demanding strict compliance with established patterns, and in the informality of the behavior. They were also unusual in that they did not define specific points in the life cycle where important behavioral changes were expected to take place.

The following age grades were recognized rather clearly in terminology, much less so as behavioral segments:

Baby	*hočał*
Child	*mıčuwił* *
Boy	*hyomik*
Girl	*nyɛsha* *
Man	*čapai* * (*apa'*)
Woman	*nyɛsak* *
Old man	*kurak*
Old woman	*kwaku* *

The starred terms were heard most frequently. *čapai* actually means "person," but has come to mean "Indian." It is often used as a synonym for the very rarely heard *apa'* (adult male).

A baby became a child when it was able to say a few words and walk without help. The male child became a "boy" when he attained full mastery of the language and was able to understand verbal instructions; Sam Spa suggested a chronological age of six or seven years. At that time, the boy experienced his first break with female society and entered upon his career of training for manhood. The female child, in sharp contrast, was not accorded a sex designation, in terminology, until her breasts began to develop, nor was there any important alteration in her training program. She continued to help her mother and other female relatives of the household, and, as from the beginning, assumed new responsibilities as her training advanced. The terminological recognition *nyɛsha* has reference to the development and maturation of her reproductive capacities, so that the period of "girlhood" ended, and she became a "woman" in Cocopa eyes, not with marriage or with sex experience, but with the birth of a child.

The boy became a "man" when his wife became a "woman," but that was a purely terminological shift. It would be impossible to show any radical change in behavior from the time that he began training under the men until the time when he finally established himself as the independent head of his own camp. The time for the latter event depended upon many circumstances.

The onset of old age, as in most societies, was without remark. There was a gradual recognition of the loss of physical capacity, and, in terminology, a double designation was frequently employed to mark this phase: *nyɛsak kwaku* for women, and *čapai kurak* or *apa' kurak* for men.

It will be seen from this summary that the grades overlapped somewhat for the two sexes, and that boys were pushed in the direction of responsibilities, while girls were treated as children for a rather prolonged period. Table 8

TABLE 8
Age Grades by Sex

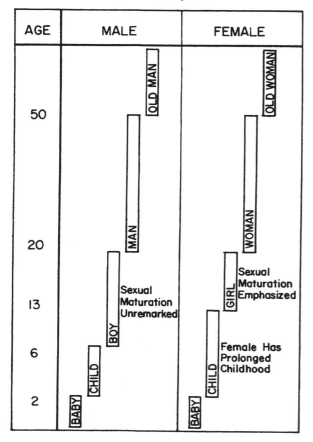

shows the grades translated roughly into our system of chronological age.

There was no discernible change in nonsexual behavior to signal the beginning of puberty in boys. The child was a "boy," gradually learning his tasks and assuming new responsibilities, from the time that he started his specialized training until he established a camp, when his manhood was generally recognized. The difference was notable only in the fact that, as he approached maturity, boyhood games were abandoned in favor of courting activities.

The first sign of puberty in girls, the appearance of breast development, was well noted in terminology and to an increasing extent in behavior. The girl's training process continued, but freedom of movement was gradually curtailed until, with the appearance of suitors, she lived and slept "behind her mother." Her marriage did not bring independence, and terminologically she was still a girl, and her mother's daughter or her mother-in-law's helper, until her babies were born.

Since none of the periods of a person's life called for any very apparent alteration in behavior, attitude, or interests, it is unlikely that any psychological tensions developed in this connection — and if they did, I was unable to detect them. Where tensions or frustrations might occur — in prolonged childhood for girls, or early boyhood for boys — the flexibility of actual behavior undoubtedly acted as sufficient release. Still more important, perhaps, was the recognition of gradual change within the grades. In fact, it is a largely arbitrary procedure to break the Cocopa life cycle into more than central phases separated by more or less extended periods of transition. The Cocopa never made age-behavior, and seldom made sex-behavior, an end in itself. There was a realistic recognition of biological and intellectual changes, and the assignment of rights and duties to fit the changes in the individual. This recognition is most strikingly shown by the fact that sexual maturity, and not chronological age, degree of training, or independence, marked the onset of sexual activity.

There was a special ceremony for girls at the first menstruation (see Chapter 5), and an "initiation" ceremony for both boys and girls (see Chapter 7). How these rituals functioned in the period preceding the time of this report can only be conjectured. During the lifetime of my informants, the rituals were not important and bore no relationship to a rite of passage. The marriage ceremony, usually important as a rite of passage when such a rite has been neglected at an earlier age, was entirely absent.

Men and boys were highly active in all affairs of the camp and group; women were also active, but much less aggressive. Information on earlier days and my own observations establish the fact that while men were the initiators and the principal agents in affairs, the orators, doctors, messengers, and leaders in all activities, the women were by no means submissive or submerged. Although less mobile than men, they were never isolated and always, if they were mature, took an active part in the discussion of affairs and were given full attention when they spoke.

Josepha, for instance, was the owner of land and cattle in Baja California, and lived with her brother in Camp R. When some Mexican farmers encroached upon her land, she sent her brother and a Mexican man (married to one of her nieces) to stop them. She could not, in Cocopa society, take an active part in visits to the Mexican camp or the settlement of the dispute..The men, however, followed her directions and arranged the settlement in accordance with her wishes.

Alice Olds illustrated the independence of women when she decided one day that she had had enough of interviewing; every man in camp, including those who were supporting her, was on our side, but nothing could change the old lady's mind.

When we hired our first interpreter, I had to accompany him to his home to get his wife's permission. He was chopping wood for a living, and she had control of the income. Before I could hire her husband, I had to agree to pay him only in her presence. He was a notorious drunkard and neither his wife nor I could keep him sober, but her position as a woman and a wife left her far from helpless in the situation.

When I look over my notes and think back over all the Cocopa women whom I saw, however, the general picture is of quiet, self-effacing persons, sitting in the background or busy around the fire. This was particularly true of the younger married women. We lived next door to Mike Alvarez's daughter and her Mexican husband for about six weeks, and never saw her do anything but attend to her household duties. She never visited our camp or any other, and left her own dooryard only when absolutely necessary. Frank Gomez's wife, Jim Short's wife, and the half-dozen other married women that we frequently saw were this way. They almost never left camp; they never made a visible show of authority; and they never played a leading part in action outside the management of their households.

The following is a fairly typical comparative example of the behavior of men and women. On an early trip into Sonora to learn the number and location of Cocopa living in that section, I visited one camp after another, interviewing the family heads. At the first camp, both the men and the women assembled to hear what I had to say and to discuss the business of recording their names and kinship connections. So far as I could determine, the women were as active and influential in this discussion as the men. However, when I left for the second camp, some of the older men, but none of the women, went along to talk over the matter with their neighbors. The women of the second camp again took part, but none of them left with the men when I went on.

Young people were shy and bashful with strangers, both Indian and non-Indian, and avoided aggressive behavior

with anyone. In the presence of strangers, the boys and young men would hang back, while the girls and young women would either stay out of the group or actually hide. The girls in Maria's camp always hid when we visited there, and when we spent as much as half a day in camp, it would take them an hour or more to come close enough to watch and listen. Such behavior was not entirely for our benefit. Two young Cocopa boys came into camp one day, and the girls immediately disappeared. This was purely age-sex behavior; there were no kinship or other avoidances in Cocopa culture.

When Sam Spa and Jim Short were boys, they visited nearby camps where there were girls, and, joining other boys, sang and shouted and said funny things so that the girls could hear them. The point was to try to make the girls laugh. Spa said: "Boys and girls, meeting in a camp, do not talk to each other. The boys talk together, and try to get the girls to laugh. If a boy has his eye on a particular girl, he will see her turn her head or hide her face, but he knows that she hears him."

This bashfulness, and the restriction upon the movements of girls, particularly those who had reached marriageable age, was abandoned at all group ceremonies and celebrations. Those occasions seem to be evidence of periodic license in a society where restrictions were normally imposed. In the eight or nine accounts that I have from various informants concerning harvest festivals, mourning ceremonies, and community celebrations, mention is always made of the opportunities that these occasions afforded for courting. Girls, who at all other times were seldom allowed to show themselves, were permitted to circulate freely in the crowd, and it was expected that the young people would get together. A favorite ploy, mentioned several times, was for the boy to play the game of chasing the girl to whom he wanted to talk.

Cocopa boys and young men, traveling with us from camp to camp, invariably stayed in the background when we stopped at a house. There was a gradual edging forward that consumed as much as 30 minutes before they became a part of the group. More frequently than not, greetings and introductions, when necessary, took place between these boys and the camp members when we were leaving rather than upon our arrival. When Sam Spa was packing his blankets to go with us from Sonora to Somerton, he said that he had not gone visiting for so long that he "would feel just like a boy" when he got to Somerton.

The above conduct was in marked contrast to the behavior of children. Boys and girls under 10 were disciplined, but not shy. They did not run from strangers, never hid as rural children are so apt to do, and were permitted unusual freedom of movement and action in camp. On the several occasions when I attended a more or less formal meeting, I was impressed by the fact that no one paid the least attention to the shouting and running children while speeches were in progress. On other occasions, when the children became too boisterous, someone would "shush" them, or, quite frequently, throw a small rock or a stick in their direction.

There was no childhood period of complete leisure and play for either boys or girls. From the earliest age, they were expected to help around camp, in gathering, and in farming. When I asked my informants what they did when they were children, they invariably responded with some account of carrying wood or water, gathering eggs, chasing birds and animals out of the fields, or helping with the planting. Even discounting this retrospective type of selection, there remains a reliable body of data showing that everyone in a Cocopa camp was expected to contribute some labor in accordance with his physical capacity.

Further questioning, of course, revealed that the maturation process for both sexes consisted in a gradual change from the age when most hours were spent in play, to adulthood when most hours were spent in work. At about 10 years of age, when the girls stopped playing with their brothers, there was a gradual shift from mixed play groups to groups organized by sex. This division for recreation continued through adult life, with athletic and gambling games usually being exclusive to men or to women.

Children, as might be expected, were explicitly treated as children in matters pertaining to the business of the camp, group affairs, and gossip. Young boys, in particular, were admonished to stay away from groups of women when they were talking, and all children were discouraged from "hanging around" an adult gathering, particularly an assembly of men at the captain's camp. Jim Short said that "there was always a big crowd around the captain's house, so boys didn't go there." I had great difficulty learning what took place at a group meeting because, at the time such meetings were being held under the old Cocopa system, all my informants were too young to take an active part. However, in contrast to our society, children and young adults had considerable autonomy in matters pertaining to their personal affairs.

In all roles for which dream power, ability, training, or rank served as structuring principles, the factors of age and sex also counted as important criteria. No role that rested upon abilities (whether achieved or ascribed), not even a role requiring physical endurance, was open to the young man or woman. The universal ranking of individuals was first upon the basis of age and sex, and secondarily upon other qualities, achieved or ascribed. Different roles fell to men and women of varying age categories, of course, with the more active roles (war leadership, hunting and fishing direction, and the like) going to the mature males, and the less active (shamanism, funeral direction, speech making, and group leadership) assigned to the older persons.

All such roles were gradually relinquished with old age. Old men and women were grouped with the physically incapacitated, losing all rank and the roles that depended upon rank as their physical powers diminished. There was no honoring of the aged, no leaning upon their accumulated wisdom, and, in fact, an explicit belief that their usefulness to the society had come to an end. This was in spite of the fact that one of the chief interests of Cocopa society was the honoring of the dead.

KINSHIP TERMINOLOGY

There is a considerable structural difference between the use of "kinship" as a structuring principle where kinsmen form a group, as in a family or a lineage, and the use of "kinship" as a structuring principle when kinsmen find themselves interacting in other institutions. When the term "daughter" is used, for example, it should be specified whether this term refers to a *role* in family organization, or whether it refers to a kinship criterion for behavior when father or mother and daughter interact in their capacity of playing roles in a religious, political, or other institution. Kinship terms in Chapter 5 usually referred to specific roles in the social structure of an organized group of kinsmen. Kinship terms in this chapter are diadic (person-to-person) terms that tend to signify certain rights and duties existing between two persons because of the degree of their kinship. It is the kinship that counts and not their membership, or lack of membership, in the same family, lineage, or clan.

Societies symbolize in terminology certain types of kinship relationships because those relationships call forth certain rights and duties. In Cocopa society any given person (ego) will call his father's older brother's son (as well as his own older brother) "older brother" (*kasa*), because this term symbolizes ego's rights and duties with respect to that person. In American society we would call that same person "cousin" because, in contrast with the Cocopa, our rights and duties in our relations with our own siblings are different from those in our relations with the children of our father's and mother's brothers and sisters. In brief, the same terms are used when the rights and duties are essentially the same, and different terms are used when rights and duties differ. The above is a statement of the principle, and the theory of origin, of kinship terms, but in real life the situation is not so neat. Kinship terms tend to remain fixed while rights and duties change. In the Cocopa case, where in earlier times kinship obligations were enormously important, the rather elaborate terminology given here was equally important. As the Cocopa become more "Europeanized," kinship obligations will relax, but among those who use the Cocopa language most of the older terminology will very likely persist.

The Cocopa used 44 terms of address (see Table 9) to make the following distinctions among selected consanguine kin: generation, lineal position, collateral position, and sibling birth order. In some instances distinctions also depended upon the sex of the speaker, sex of addressee, or sex of intermediate kin. In addition to the 44 terms for

TABLE 9
**Kinship Categories Classified by Generation
and by Term of Address**
(*m.s.* = male speaking; *f.s.* = female speaking)

Great-Grandparents' Generation

1. great-grandfather	*kɩyi*[1,3]
2. great-grandmother	*sɩyi*[1,3]

Grandparents' Generation

3. father's father	*nʸɩpa*
4. mother's father	*nʸɩkʷa'o*
5. father's mother	*nʸɩma*
6. mother's mother	*nʸɩka·*
7. grandparent's brother	*kʷɩnka·s*
8. grandparent's sister	*sɩnʸkəs*

Parents' Generation

9. father (*m.s.*)	*nʸɩku*
10. father (*f.s.*)	*nʸa?a*
11. mother	*niča*
12. father's older brother father's male relative in older sibling line[2]	} *kʷɩnui*
13. father's younger brother father's male relative in younger sibling line	} *kʷɩska'o*
14. father's sister father's female relative	} *nʸɩpi*
15. mother's older sister mother's female relative in older sibling line	} *nʸɩsi*
16. mother's younger sister mother's female relative in younger sibling line	} *nʸɩmu*
17. mother's brother mother's male relative	} *nʸɩkwa*

Speaker's Own Generation

18. older brother male parallel cousin in older sibling line son of mother's female relative in older sibling line son of father's male relative in older sibling line	} *kasa*
19. younger brother male parallel cousin in younger sibling line son of mother's female relative in younger sibling line son of father's male relative in younger sibling line	} *nʸɩhol*
20. older sister female parallel cousin in older sibling line daughter of mother's female relative in older sibling line daughter of father's male relative in older sibling line	} *haxčisa*
21. younger sister female parallel cousin in younger sibling line daughter of mother's female relative in younger sibling line daughter of father's male relative in younger sibling line	} *nʸɩsus*
22. male cross-cousin (*m.s.*) son of father's female relative (*m.s.*) son of mother's male relative (*m.s.*)	} *xɬa*
23. female cross-cousin male cross-cousin (*f.s.*) daughter of father's female relative daughter of mother's male relative son of father's female relative (*f.s.*) son of mother's male relative (*f.s.*)	} *ɬa*

consanguine kin there were at least 8 terms for individuals related by marriage (affinal kin; see Table 9, last section).

Kinship terms were first collected as a system from Jim Short, and the system was then checked against kinship data as they were disclosed in the course of fieldwork. Ordinarily a kinship system is collected through the use of genealogies — that is, the informant is asked to give the kin term he or she uses when addressing, or referring to, specific individuals who are related to him or her in a certain way (e.g. a woman's brother's daughter). But in Cocopa society there are almost always dead relatives involved in chains of relationships, and this, because of the taboo against referring to anyone who has died, made the use of the genealogy method painful if not impossible. To solve this problem, I bought a collection of toy soldiers (for men) and toy nurses (for women) and laid these out on the

24.	son (*m.s.*)	*homa*
25.	daughter (*m.s.*)	*apasa*
26.	issue (*f.s.*)	*s?a'·o*
27.	older brother's child (*m.s.*)	
	child of son of parent's relative in older sibling line (*m.s.*)	*ɩska'o*
28.	older sister's son (*f.s.*)	
	son of daughter of parent's relative in older sibling line (*f.s.*)	*hans?a*
29.	older sister's daughter (*f.s.*)	
	daughter of daughter of parent's relative in older sibling line (*f.s.*)	*sɩs?a*
30.	brother's son (*f.s.*)	
	son of son of parent's relative (*f.s.*)	*xenʸɩpi*
31.	brother's daughter (*f.s.*)	
	daughter of son of parent's relative (*f.s.*)	*sɩpi*
32.	sister's son (*m.s.*)	
	son of daughter of parent's relative (*m.s.*)	*wɛn*
33.	sister's daughter (*m.s.*)	
	daughter of daughter of parent's relative (*m.s.*)	*siwɛn*
34.	younger brother's son (*m.s.*)	
	son of son of parent's relative in younger sibling line (*m.s.*)	
	younger sister's son (*f.s.*)	*wič*
	son of daughter of parent's relative in younger sibling line (*f.s.*)	
35.	younger sister's daughter (*f.s.*)	
	daughter of daughter of parent's relative in younger sibling line (*f.s.*)	
	younger brother's daughter (*m.s.*)	*sɩwit*
	daughter of son of parent's relative in younger sibling line (*m.s.*)	

Grandchildren's Generation

36.	son's son	*a·a'o*
37.	daughter's son (*m.s.*)	*axka*
38.	daughter's son (*f.s.*)	*aka*
39.	son's daughter	*si·a'o*
40.	daughter's daughter	*sixka*
41.	sibling's grandson (*m.s.*)	*ka·s*
42.	sibling's grandson (*f.s.*)	*kə·s*
43.	sibling's granddaughter (*m.s.*)	*sikas*
44.	sibling's granddaughter (*f.s.*)	*sikəs*

Great-Grandchildren's Generation

(1.)	great-grandson	*kɩyi*[3]
(2.)	great-granddaughter	*sɩyi*[3]

Affines (incomplete list)

45.	wife	*waswei*
46.	wife's father	
	husband's lineal relative	*kunye*
47.	wife's mother	*srunye*
48.	wife's brother	*nyðwa·šu*
49.	wife's sister	
	sister's husband	*čpa?am*
50.	brother's wife	
	son's wife	*unya*
51.	daughter's husband	*kɛhka*
52.	husband	*kurak*

[1]Some informants said the use of *kɩyi* and *sɩyi* as terms for greeting friends was a Yuma practice and not Cocopa. The Cocopa term for greeting a friend was said to be *nʸeɬ*. I have heard both used at different times.

[2]"Older sibling line" means that the lineal ancestor of the person being addressed was an older sibling of the lineal ancestor of the speaker.

[3]Reciprocal terms.

table in patterns that would cue the informant to give me the kinship terms employed between any two persons. An example of my explanation might run as follows: This "soldier" (a hypothetical Cocopa) is married to this "nurse," and one of their younger sons has a son, and one of their older sons (the older figure indicated by a block of wood placed underneath) has a son. What do these sons call each·other? Answer: The son of the younger brother calls the son of the older brother "older brother" (*kasa*), and the son of the older brother calls the son of the younger brother "younger brother" (*nyɩhol*).

When the Cocopa system is compared with other systems in the world it is referred to as "collateral" in Lowie's classification (1932: 569) because it distinguishes lineal from collateral kin, and maternal from paternal kin in the parental generation. Within the "collateral" category, the

Cocopa system is further identified as "Yuman" according to Spier (1925: 75). In the "Yuman" system, father's older brothers and mother's older sisters are distinguished from their younger siblings (see Table 9, terms 12 and 13 and terms 15 and 16). Similarly, a man distinguishes between the children of his older brother and those of his younger brother (see terms 27, 34, and 35), and a woman distinguishes between the children of her older sister and those of her younger sister (see terms 28, 29, 34, and 35). There are four terms for sibling in the "Yuman" system: older brother, older sister, younger brother, younger sister. Parallel cousins are siblings; cross-cousins are called by special terms, or are less frequently styled siblings. Children of a man are son and daughter; a woman's children are more frequently called by one term. Four grandparental terms are used: father's father, father's mother, mother's father, mother's mother; conversely, four grandchild terms are used: man's son's child, man's daughter's child, woman's son's child, and woman's daughter's child. Tribes using this system are: Cocopa, Yuma, Mohave, Havasupai, Imperial Valley Kamia, Southern Diegueño, Northern Diegueño, Desert Cahuilla, Cupeño, Luiseño, Serrano, Kitanemuk, Kawaiisu, Tübatulabel, Southwestern Pomo, Wind River Shoshoni, Uintah Ute, Southern Ute, Papago, Northern Tepehuane; possibly Biloxi, Wappo, Southern Pomo, and even Northern Wintun.

The Cocopa system itself may be summarized as follows: mother's older sister is distinguished from mother's younger sister, but her brothers are given a single term. Father's older brother is distinguished from father's younger brother, but his sisters are given a single term. The recognition of the birth order of father's brothers and mother's sisters is reflected in the terminology for their children and children's children, but, on the latter two levels, the speaker's lineal and collateral kin are merged. For example, the same term applies to older brother, son of father's older brother, and son of mother's older sister. Since birth order is not noted for mother's brothers or for father's sisters, it is not reflected in the terminology for their children or their children's children; that is, the same term applies to son of father's sister and son of mother's brother, regardless of the relatives ages of the siblings in question.

Sex of addressee is noted, except in three instances: a woman uses a single term for all her own children; a woman also groups all of her cross-cousins under a single term; and a man uses a single term for his older brother's children and the children of his parent's older sibling's sons.

Sex of speaker is always indicated in addressing a person of one's children's generation, and almost always in addressing a person of one's children's children's generation. In one's own generation, it is required only in the case of addressing one's male cross-cousin. In the parental generation it is remarked solely in addressing one's own father.

KINSHIP BEHAVIOR BY CATEGORIES

The following information on kinship behavior is far from complete by categories and lacks the volume of data required for valid generalization. Emphasis is on cross-family relationships and special types of behavior within the family, as distinct from the day-by-day family behavior treated in Chapter 5.

The mother and her husband, or the individuals assuming this relationship, held themselves responsible for directing and teaching the children of the household. In return, they expected the children to learn the tasks assigned to them, and to obey their orders. A grown boy (allowing for the Cocopa viewpoint that everyone, including children, should handle his own affairs) owed a certain allegiance to his father, even after marriage, and was expected to follow his direction. A father was supposed to teach his son his own specialized skills and "to bring him help in his dreams." Jim Short said: "Family position was maintained by a father talking to his sons. He could tell them how to live, how to do things, if he were an important man. Men of little importance had nothing to tell their sons."

A father did not enter directly into the marriage plans for either sons or daughters, but in those cases where a groom was expected to make a present to his wife's family, his father helped him. The father's responsibilities to his daughters outside the routine of camp life seem to have been very few, beyond joining his wife in "talking" to them and providing the necessary supplies for an initiation ceremony.

The mother's first responsibility, in addition to the teaching process, was to see that her daughter was kept away from boys until she reached marriageable age. This guarding, constantly referred to as "keeping the girl behind her," was probably quite strict in a normal household of good reputation. The mother also had charge of the girl's menstrual ceremony and her initiation ceremony, and was the preferred person to assist at childbirth. By extension, the mother also assumed responsibility for the direction and further training of her daughters-in-law. If the boy planned to bring his bride home, it was the ideal pattern for the mother to go to the girl's camp to get her. If the marriage took place at a celebration or ceremony, it was the boy's mother's duty to invite the girl to accompany her home.

Individual responsibility was emphasized, even for children, and if a situation were defined as being a person's own business, the parents did not interfere. The outstanding case in my own experience involved an interview with Tom Juarez, who was giving me some information concerning his son. The son, married and with two babies, heard his name mentioned and came over to question the purpose. He was prejudiced against Americans, who had recently deported him, and was angry at his father for helping me.

In the conversation that followed, my interpreter and Sam Spa tried to make the son change his mind, but his father, although clearly willing to cooperate with me, said not a word.

While the majority of Cocopa respected and helped their parents, there were, of course, exceptions. The most notable was Sam Spa's son (his only child). It was something of a scandal that he spent all his money drinking, lost his wife through failure to support her, and did not help his father, who was forced to live with more distant kin.

The prescribed behavior toward parents did not extend to relatives of the parental generation except as the relationship was altered by the assumption of parental roles. Uncles, aunts, grandfathers, and grandmothers were in most instances treated merely as relatives. In the sibling class, however, parallel cousins, particularly those related through brothers, tended to be equated with siblings. Just how strong this feeling was, and how it worked in actual behavior, would require more detailed study than I was able to devote to it in the field.

My notes contain fairly frequent reference to "brothers" but almost none to "cousins" (see Table 9, terms 18, 19, and 22). For example, I wanted a list of Mike Alvarez's relatives around Somerton. His response was to give me a list of his male kin and their "brothers," that is, members of the same lineages. In recording statements about former captains, I learned who their "brothers" were.

While parallel cousins and first cross-cousins were forbidden to marry, the taboo did not extend to more distant cross-cousins. There was a mild respect relationship between classificatory siblings of opposite sex. They played together when they were children, but tended to stay apart as they grew older. A boy never became familiar with or touched a girl whom he called *haxčisa* or *nyɨsus* (younger or older sister). They could not joke with each other, and their behavior was one of respect. For example: *hałpua* is the general term for female urination, but in reference to older women the term *smałmuwa* was used; a boy also used the latter in speaking of his "sister," no matter what her age.

In connection with a girl's marriage, there was fairly frequent reference to "brothers" but almost none to fathers. The brother was expected to "talk" to his sister if the family wanted her to marry a particular boy. If she gave her consent, it was the brother who notified the successful suitor, took care of him in camp, and advised him when the girl and her mother were ready for him to start sleeping with the girl. However, in most cases, these things were arranged directly between the girl and her lover. When Sam Spa wanted to marry his fourth wife, he felt the need of some help, and so called upon her brothers. These boys, real brothers and parallel cousins, agreed to talk to the girl.

In later life, siblings were expected to help each other, but at the same time they were permitted to protest each other's behavior to a certain extent: a man or a woman could appeal to a spouse's siblings if a separation were threatened in the family.

Grandparents were parent-substitutes, both in the matter of helping their grandchildren and in their expectation of help from them, but the chief responsibility of a grandfather was to pass on his special knowledge, especially as an orator or shaman, to his grandson. Grandparents were always called upon to help at the birth of their grandchild; a woman's mother was preferred as the midwife, but if she were not available, and the couple were living with the husband's parents, his mother would take over. A grandfather was expected to make the baby's cradle, or at least to gather the materials for it.

I have almost no reference to the uncle class. In specific cases, the father's brother was mentioned, but I could not be sure that the behavior pertained to this particular relationship. Mike Alvarez's uncle gave him his name and held a naming ceremony for him; Sam Spa's uncle attempted to train him to be a doctor; the uncle of Spa's third wife helped him in his courtship; Spa asked help from his mother's brothers in buying a horse to pay for one of his wives. There is nothing in these statements, however, to indicate patterns of relationship, and my informants did not give me accounts of general patterns that I could trust.

KINSHIP BEHAVIOR IN GENERAL

While the elaboration of Cocopa kinship terminology was no doubt correlated with certain aspects of behavior in an earlier day, nothing in my notes indicates that an equivalent degree of formalization of kinship behavior prevailed in the late 19th century. It was an event in my interviews when informants singled out particular kinsmen (by kin term) for certain tasks or responsibilities. When the relationship (using the same kin term) was removed by more than one degree, the designation, upon further inquiry, almost always dissolved to a mere sense of preference. Other kinsmen or even neighbors, it turned out, could serve equally well if circumstances intervened to prevent the fulfillment of the ideal pattern. My informants told me, for instance, that one of the grandfathers was expected to make a baby's cradle. However, many babies in any society may not have a grandfather, or the grandfather may be in such a situation that he cannot do the work. Under such circumstances, a substitution is necessary and expected. In Cocopa society such a substitution was made at the least provocation (a feature of their culture that runs through this entire report), so that I was almost always at a loss to decide whether or not a regularity existed. Kinsmen were separated from non-kinsmen in the assignment of rights and duties, and close relatives were separated from distant relatives, but reducing these separations to precise pattern formulation would certainly do violence to the Cocopa view of their social relationships.

While kinship formed a separate category in the minds of the Cocopa, it was always modified by the principle of residence. Relatives living together in a multi-family Cocopa camp tended to feel a greater obligation toward each other than toward relatives living in different camps. In brief, the kinship factor was modified according to where the relatives in question lived. During the many years that Sam Spa lived with a much older "cousin," they treated each other as father and son; the relationship was clearly a function of residence, with the added factor of a difference in age.

This same tendency to take residence into account, along with kinship, extended to the local group. Near neighbors, by the very fact of proximity, were pulled into the inner orbit of interpersonal obligations, and the informality of the kinship system permitted a smooth meshing of these two concepts. This is simply another case, among the many well verified throughout my notes, in which the Cocopa view of human behavior did not permit formality of pattern to interfere with a direct solution in terms of total circumstances.

All things being equal, however, the first line of obligation was to one's own parents, and from them to relatives in the patriline. This is a generalization from actual behavior, but it is confirmed by other factors. There was a tendency toward patrilocal residence in Cocopa society, so that kinship behavior was a reflection of the composition of a camp, which consisted of the camp leader, his sons, and their wives and families. (Patrilocality may have been more formally developed in an earlier day, or, more likely, was a tendency among the Cocopa that was reinforced by their close historical association with California groups, in which localized patrilineages were highly developed [Kelly 1942].) The lineage system, which will be discussed below, was another element in establishing close ties between patrilineal kinsmen.

A second line of obligation, and a highly interesting one, was to patrilineal kinsmen's wives and *their* immediate kin. A man's wife, brought to live in the camp of his kinsmen, became their responsibility: she could call upon them for help at any time. In case she were widowed, the responsibility became doubly effective; it was considered proper, but not obligatory, for the woman to marry one of her husband's brothers. Frank Blue, one of our interpreters, volunteered: "Even if my brother were married to a Yuma girl, and she wanted something, I would have to go there to help her."

This line of obligation through the wife was further reinforced by the alternate system of matrilocal residence. While a boy's first duty, after marriage, was to his own kinsmen, he was, nevertheless, expected to live with and work for his wife's family, if their need were greater. In later years, when he had established his own camp, members of his wife's family, left destitute by death or illness, could make their home with him. In fact, in this situation people seemed to prefer going to a daughter or

other female relative rather than seeking help from kinsmen in the male line.

The following specific examples of in-law obligations are of interest:

> Sam Spa lived in a certain man's camp because the man's *wife* was a distant relative of Spa's.
> Jim Short explained the presence of Bill Ortega at a man's camp by saying that the father of the man's *wife* was Ortega's "brother."
> When a certain leader died, he had a small son who went to live with his *sister's husband*.
> Manuel Leon, blind and about 70, lived with his *daughter* and her Mexican husband.
> Mike Alvarez lived with his *daughter* and her Mexican husband.
> Sam Spa and his mother lived with a male "cousin" for many years because his *wife* was Spa's father's sister, and because Spa called him "x⁺a" (see Table 9, term 22).
> Spa's second *wife's* grandmother lived with them.

I am quite unable to make a general statement with respect to kinsmen in the matrilineal line. Mother's siblings and parents were separated, terminologically, from father's siblings and parents, but beyond this separation there was no recognition of the separate lines of descent. The general preference toward patriliny defined the position of these kinsmen, except for cousins, uncles, nephews, and nieces (as defined by the Cocopa), which were equated on both sides of the family.

THE LINEAGE SYSTEM

The weighting of the patrilineal line, however slight it may have been, was in keeping with the system of lineages. Lineages in Cocopa society were unorganized and unlocalized, and so did little to reinforce or formalize the wider patrilineal system. This statement, like so many others, could be reversed with almost equal validity; our knowledge of the force of symbols, however, would tend to justify the cause-and-effect relationship that I have suggested. A symbol denoting some common quality is of little importance unless the symbol also stands for an organized group. The totem, for example, is a powerful symbol for the regulation of behavior when it also stands for an organized and closely interacting group; it loses force when either or both of these factors are missing.

Ordinarily, lineages would be treated as cooperative groups and discussed under the type of activities pursued by such a group. The late-19th-century Cocopa, however, were not organized by lineages, and lineage membership was no more than an additional principle in the kinship system. In other words, it was a cross-cutting system, not a unit for behavior in itself.

Lineages (šumu⁺) were patrilineal, exogamous, nonlocalized, and nonautonomous. They possessed certain animals, plants, or natural phenomena that may loosely be termed

TABLE 10
Cocopa Lineages, Totems, and Women's Names

Lineage (šɪmuł)	Totem (sohwe)[1]	Women's Name (pðčɪðmip)	Lineage (šɪmuł)	Totem (sohwe)[1]	Women's Name (pðčɪðmip)
hač?am	crow; wildcat	katmuš	homos[2]	dust	hɛlðput
hač?am hɛlka	" "	"	nʸa'o	deer	łɪmuš
hač?am ramðs	" "	"	?ðmawi	rattlesnake	sumawi
hač?am pate'yi	" "	"	čɛmowar	horny toad	kʷaxɪya·s
mɪškwi·š	wildcat; screwbean	"	kʷ?ał	buckskin	hamasu'łyð
kʷɪnʸe·łʸ	wildcat	"	keopas[2]	?	keopas
yɛsčðkʷinʸ	dove; crabs; wild rice	sðkuma	kðpðkʷi·š	conch shell	kðpðkʷis
sxu·ł	?	"	sampu·k	black snake	sampu·k
xsa'·i	dove; crabs; wild rice	"	ha·r	insect secretion	xatspa·s
pɪł·pa·ł	" " " "	"	sxu·ł yɪkɪču·rp	wildcat	nʸɛmi
kʷɪxa·s	coyote	škuš			
s?i·ł	coyote; salt	"	*Paipai Lineages*		
kʷðrup	coyote	"	kʷɪłʸxʷat	buckskin	škuš
yɪpsał	"	"	xama'o	coyote	kw?ał
ixaʰ	?	"	heyi·s	?	kopa?il
salo·x	?	"	xʷa·t	?	ułʸu
xʷanʸɛk	frog	hupsa·s	čɪkowe'nʸð	black bug	čɪkowa·n
čuyi·ł	"	"			
xɪłšðwa	night hawk	ułʸu	*Diegueño Lineages*		
nʸɛmðwɪʰ	" "	"	kʷ?ał kamʸa[2]	coyote	škuš
ɪspin	" "	uru	hełmiyap	"	"
pače'·yð	frog	hipa	sil·pa·	mescal plant	sil·pa·
komalʸkwilʸ	?	"	kʷ?ałwa	?	?
mahok	pack rat	kʷɪsčar			
mɪtʸðspaʰ	eagle; mescal fiber	kʷɐxčal	*Imperial Valley Kamia Lineage*		
?ɛr·maš	cloud; wind	kʷiya	nʸełʸ	?	hupasi·n
čɪlače'i	coyote	kʷɪčua·l			
xɛłkaʰ	wildcat	sðkami			
nʸɪhi	eagle	hamaso·l			
hawiłapa	river	kʷas			

[1]Cocopa words for the totems are as follows: crow, ka·k; wildcat, nʸɪme; screwbean, iš; dove, ɪleku; small crab, ɪpi; large crab, yawɪr; coyote, xa'tspa; salt, s?ir; buckskin, kʷ?ał; frog, hanʸah; pack rat, amɪl; eagle, spa; mescal fiber, spa maał; cloud, kʷłi; wind, mitsha; wild rice, nʸepa yekalyek; dust, moput; mescal plant, maał; night hawk, karu; deer, kʷak šmałayak; conch shell, helkʷiš; black bug, araslawan; river, hawɪł; rattlesnake, awi; insect secretion, nʸɪhar; horny toad, kʷičɪyes; black snake with white spots, henyðmpok.

[2]No known members.

"totems" (sohwe). Another feature of this system was that all the women of each lineage possessed a common personal name (Kelly 1942). Table 10 lists the 50 lineages, with their totems and women's names (pðčɪðmip), recorded as having been in existence before 1900.

Membership in a lineage was theoretically by descent through one's own male ancestors from a mythical original member; one Cocopa male for each lineage was created and given his lineage by the creator.

All informants agreed that members of the same patrilineage could not marry, even if the pair concerned were members of different tribes. Nor should anyone marry a person who belonged to the mother's lineage. In the 112 marriages of which I have record, there is no single case of violation of the patrilineage exogamy rule. However, a man's marriage to a woman belonging to his mother's lineage did not create an adverse reaction because, as some informants said, "There are so few people now, it cannot be helped." (Other marriage restrictions are discussed in Chapter 5.) Where lineages carried the same name (e.g., *hač?am*, *hač?am hɛlka*, *hač?am ramðs*, and *hač?am pate'yi*), they were considered a unit under the exogamy rule. However, exogamy did not extend to lineages having only the same totem or the same woman's name (see Table 10).

Because of the tendency toward patrilocal residence, there was a certain grouping by lineages within the delta, but this grouping was by no means more than a tendency, and there was no feeling that any particular section of the delta belonged to any specific lineage.

The totemic feature was no more than the belief that certain animals, plants, and natural phenomena "belonged" to the various groups. The totems, together with the lineage name, were assigned by the creator. It was intended, according to one informant, that the totems would express the character of the lineage members. All lineages were assumed to have had at least one such totem, even if my informants could not remember it. My attempts to learn current attitudes toward these totems met with complete failure. Informants were consistently indifferent, and there was frequent uncertainty in naming totems belonging to particular lineages. Although a few women's lineage names were the same, or similar to, the everyday name for the totem, I did not find among the Cocopa the intimate association of the women's names with the totem noted for the Mohave (Kroeber 1902: 278) and Maricopa (Spier 1933: 186, 192).

Although it is more than likely that many of the lineages listed in Table 10 were introduced from the outside, I can be reasonably sure of only ten that were imported: five from the Paipai, four from the Diegueño, and one from the Kamia. The *kwɨɬ^yxwat, xama'o, heyi·s*, and *x^wa·t* lineages (listed as Paipai) were said to have been brought in by Paipai men who married into the Cocopa tribe. These men were members of the Paipai camp located on the Colorado River. The origin of the *čɨkowe'n^yð* lineage, also attributed to the Paipai, was not known. A Hwanyak Cocopa chief who died about 1885 belonged to this lineage, so it cannot be a recent Cocopa acquisition. The four lineages attributed to the Diegueño were recently introduced by men from that group who married into the Cocopa community. The Kamia lineage (*n^yɛɬ^y*) is represented by only one family (living near Somerton), whose ancestry is definitely Kamia. It is of considerable significance that when these non-Cocopa families were absorbed into the Cocopa community, their lineages were added to the Cocopa system.

I have record of 13 adult Cocopa who had no lineage affiliation. Eleven of these traced their paternal descent through some non-Indian. I do not know the genealogies for the other two, but Jim Short explained the situation by saying that when the creator was giving out the lineage names, the ancestors of these two became tired of waiting their turn, and so left without a lineage.

At the present time, the Cocopa tend to equate their lineage names with Spanish and American surnames. The equation, however, is not complete, since families with only Spanish or American surnames are thought of as not having a lineage. The Spanish name recorded for men of the *hac?am* lineage was consistently "Tambo." Meigs (1939: 87) reports that "Tampo" is the Mexicanized name for members of the Diegueño *Jat'am* lineage. "Pesada" (Spanish for "heavy") has been adopted as a surname by members of the Cocopa *k^wɨn^ye·ɬ^y* lineage. A number of such "translations" were obtained, but they represent only folk etymology. Not more than three or four of the lineage names were translated for me, and the attempt to secure more met with disagreement between my interpreter and the informant, or failure. The lineage name *mɨt^yðspa^h*, for example, was translated first as meaning "throw-away cornhusks"; my interpreter raised some question, and the meaning was changed to "eagle."

When the Cocopa visited abroad, or acted as hosts to foreigners, members of lineages of the same name would ordinarily seek each other out. Both Sam Spa and Mike Alvarez told me that Cocopa and Diegueño families of the same lineage name camped together in the mountain areas where pine nuts were gathered. One Cocopa man who had not been in the United States since 1928 rode from Sonora to Somerton with me; he planned to stay with a family that he did not know and had never visited because the head of the family was a member of his lineage. My contact with one Baja California group that had been reported as unfriendly to Americans became quite amicable because my interpreter belonged to the same lineage as the leader of the group.

In the mourning ceremony, the man who was to be the leader informed the members of the lineages to which the people to be mourned had belonged, and these members were expected to furnish an important share of the supplies.

I asked Jim Short why one old woman was being cared for by a family to which she was not related; he replied that he did not know, but that her mother must have been a member of the family's lineage.

Specific religious duties that could be performed only by members of certain lineages were denied by the Cocopa, but were recognized as a Diegueño trait. A certain mourning ceremony song was said to belong to the *k^wɨxa·s* lineage of the Baja California Diegueño; only members of that lineage would "dream" and subsequently use that song.

The Naming System

All of the women of a Cocopa lineage were given a single name, the women's name (*pǝčiǝmip*) for that lineage. For example, all of the women who belonged to the *hačʔam* lineage were called *kałmuš*, all those belonging to the *sʔi-ł* lineage were called *škuš*, all those belonging to the *nʸemǝwɩʰ* lineage were called *utʸu*, and so on (Kelly 1942: chart 3, p. 686). In some instances the same women's name was used by more than one lineage. The women's name *kałmuš*, for example, was used by women who belonged to six different lineages.

The use of the women's name was totally automatic — if a woman belonged to a certain lineage she was referred to by the women's name for that lineage. However, in addition to the women's name, a baby girl might at any time be given a personal name by her parents; she frequently continued to be known by this name until she married and had a baby of her own, at which time her own "baby name" would be dropped. Another alternative to the employment of the women's name was the custom of addressing or referring to a woman by her age term plus the name of her lineage. For example, a woman ordinarily referred to as *škuš*, her women's name, might be called *kwaku sʔi-ł*, or "old woman *sʔi-ł*." Other age terms were: grown girl, *nyesha*; woman, *nyɛsak*. Gifford (1918: Table 4) was the first to report this Cocopa practice, but his informant apparently did not tell him that the second element was a lineage name. At the time of our studies all of the very old women were referred to by their age term (*kwaku*) plus the name of their lineage. Sam Spa said that in those cases where an old woman might not have a lineage she would be referred to by her age term plus her personal name, which, in recent years, would be a Spanish or American family name.

I am of the opinion that the lineage system and the system of naming women, while connected (since women's names were inherited through the lineage), were essentially unrelated (Kelly 1942). Informants and others, for example, always knew a particular woman's "women's name," but they did not always know her lineage affiliation, especially when some unrelated lineages had the same women's name. Thus, the women's name functioned as a device for personal identification independently of the lineage system. Since, under this system, many Cocopa women carried the same women's name, I raised the question of positive identification. It was not a problem my informants took seriously (since, in their type of society, the thrust of a chin to the east could serve to identify a particular woman 15 miles away). In answer to my questions, however, my informants suggested that the women's name could be used in connection with a lineage name (where the same women's name was used by more than one lineage) or a woman could be identified by the

location of her camp, or by connecting her with her husband or some other relative.

Whatever may be the history or the function of this system of naming women, in actual practice it eliminated the need for women to be concerned about using a personal name that might have been used by someone now deceased. This was a problem for men, whose personal names were subjected to community review before adoption in order to make doubly sure that it had not been used before by a known person. Pre-adolescent boys, when they got their "real" name, and all men later in life who desired to change their name, invited relatives, friends, and as many old men as possible to a social gathering where the proposed new name was reviewed.

ABILITIES: ACHIEVED AND ASCRIBED

In addition to using age, sex, kinship, and residence as criteria for placement in roles, the Cocopa assigned certain tasks, with their rights and duties, on the basis of ascribed and achieved abilities — such as supernatural power, training, experience, intelligence, and personality.

All Cocopa of a given age and sex were assumed to be proficient in the day-by-day demands of their culture. All women were expected to know how to prepare and cook food, how and where to gather wild products, and how to manufacture the tools of their work. All men were farmers, hunters, and fishers; all knew how to build houses and rafts and how to make the weapons and tools required in these activities. Some were more skilled than others, but there were no specialists in the ordinary tasks of living. When a man or woman was selected for some work or office based upon his or her ability, it was for an unusual activity that required only one or a few persons, or for a position of leadership.

Ability, in the sense of having the necessary intelligence, energy, and supernatural power, rested ultimately upon having had the requisite dream or dreams for any and all tasks and roles throughout a person's life. If a man was energetic, intelligent, and experienced, it was assumed that he also possessed the necessary "power." If a man claimed the dreams but lacked the other qualities, he was not taken seriously. Mike Alvarez was a perfect case in point: he claimed the dreams that were required for an orator and leader, but because he lacked the experience and personal force necessary for leadership, he was never generally accepted. Even such specialized tasks as shamanism, which rested primarily upon supernatural power, were recognized as depending upon experience — long experience in dreaming itself, and long experience as a practitioner.

Although fighting skill and war honors may once have given a man high prestige and positions of leadership, the Cocopa since the days of warfare have placed an ability to speak above all other accomplishments. (Almost every informant sooner or later made this point; my notes from

Jim Short, Sam Spa, and Mike Alvarez are full of references to this talent.) There was a large element of training, experience, and sheer oratorical power involved, but the definition of a good speaker was, perhaps unconsciously, wider than that.

A Cocopa "speaker" was a mature man who had high standing in the community, cultural "know-how," and capacity for leadership. No man could attain high rank who was not a speaker, and proficiency in speaking was prerequisite to becoming a captain, group leader, captain's orator, or funeral orator. Each of these roles had its own specialized oratory, however; a man who could "speak for the captain" did not necessarily have the knowledge to give a funeral oration, for there were many archaic phrases (and perhaps some invented phrases) used that were passed on from one funeral orator to another. Jim Short was a captain's orator, but could not be a funeral orator: "I am not a funeral orator or captain. I don't know how to talk that way. I am *čapai ahan*, just an orator and leader. . . . I am also *popoke*, a captain's helper, because I can talk at meetings." Ability acquired through dreams was assumed for all these men, but it was especially important for the funeral orator: Bill Smith "dreamed about speaking at funerals," according to Short, "and dreamed with the help of both his grandfather and father."

Every band had men that were called *čapai ahan*. These were the lesser leaders and orators, from among whose ranks the captain was chosen. The selection rested heavily upon a man's proficiency in the art of oratory. I asked Sam Spa whether or not Fred Ringo was captain of the Sonora Cocopa, and Sam replied, "He has never talked yet [in this way]; maybe in a year or two he will get started and be captain; he has a good heart, good mind, needs only to talk more, to be a captain."

Next after oratorical skills, attributed or actual knowledge was the basis for assignment to specialized tasks. With the possible exception of shamanism, specialized tasks were within the reach of almost any mature man; however, certain men were somehow selected, and their right to do the job was then explained in terms of special knowledge. The man who cut the poles for a mourning ceremony (kerauk) house, for example, did it for all the ceremonies within his band. The same was true for the man who cut the poles for a cremation, and for the man (often the same man) who built the frame upon which the body was transported. There was a "ditch boss," a man who took charge when a group worked together on an irrigation system. The "nose piercer" at an initiation ceremony served at all such rites; he, however, was a man with a reputation for having steady nerves, and in the days of warfare, he was the war leader. Some men were noted as singers and always led the songs at celebrations. In the planting of wild grass seeds, the planter was required not only to be in a state of

ritual purity, but also to have specialized knowledge for the task (see Chapter 3).

Shamanism was open to both men and women, but few women among the Cocopa attempted cures, and these were only for minor ailments. Emphasis was upon specialized knowledge and experience, but "dream power" was the ultimate authority. (The abilities required of shamans are treated in detail in Chapter 5.)

Outside the areas of religion and group leadership, most tasks were assigned in accordance with circumstances. Even in certain instances where a formal pattern might be expected, it was absent: there was no special "hunt boss" on a rabbit drive, no organization of the parties going to get wild rice or pine nuts, no assignment of relatives outside the immediate family to special duties at a burial or mourning ceremony. When I asked who carried the body to the pyre, I was told that any group of men could do it, provided they were strong enough.

RANK

Rank, of course, depended to a greater or lesser extent upon all the criteria already discussed. It may be treated as a separate category, however, since it also rested upon a definition of social conduct which, among the Cocopa, undoubtedly assumed a position of unusual importance. By rank, I mean the general assessment of a person's worth by his neighbors and kinsmen. In operation, it is that quality which influences others. People work with great energy at a task promoted by a popular man; there is extra interest at a party attended by "important" people.

Rank among the Cocopa rested upon the factors of age, sex, abilities, social conduct, and, to a minor extent, the standing of the individual's family. The absent criteria are most significant: wealth, lineage, class, caste, race, religion, residence priority, and membership in a secret society or association.

Rank in an ultimate sense was determined by a man's everyday behavior, by what he did rather than by who he was. Frank Blue explained:

> We know each other because we are close together; we know each other like a book. If a man or woman is always trying to give, and not take; gives food to a poor family, more than half of what he has. If a young man sees an old woman, he gives her money or clothes if he is working. Talk to people, be nice to people. A lot of people can stand a lot of gossip, others can't. We like people who laugh at gossip and we laugh at people who get mad; but some people get mad, too. We like people who talk nice and who always smile. Some groups meet in sorrow, someone is ill or someone has died, then a man comes from a long way to be there, no matter what it costs him in time and effort.

Sam Spa said much the same thing: "A man becomes unpopular by the way he talks, always grouchy, mean, doesn't talk right. A popular man is one who jokes, speaks nicely, always feeds visitors, will go with other men to help in work."

The Cocopa divided their neighbors and kinsmen into three unofficial and personally assessed classes: (1) those who fell below the standard of conduct for many reasons, such as stinginess, bad temper, laziness, or violation of taboos, were called *čapai hačak*; (2) those who conformed in minimum fashion to the standards of conduct, who took no part in community affairs, and who lacked the personality traits required for distinction in the society were described as *čapai yowaiyɛk*; (3) those who had special talents, took an active part in community affairs, and gave more than their share of celebrations were known as *čapai pɔ́hwe*. These descriptive terms were widely used, seemed to have been earned by long-term behavior, and were not easily subject to reversal. A more complete study of personality and ranking would soon discard these descriptive terms, however, since personal assessment among the Cocopa was far too subtle for such general treatment. Beyond the matter of personal opinion involved, "good" men had their faults, "average" men had their special virtues, and "bad" men could be counted upon for noble behavior under certain circumstances.

Jim Short referred to an old man in Mexico as being *hačak* (bad) because he drank, stole, and gambled. When I pointed out that drinking and gambling were fairly common in Mexico, Short said, "He drank all the time, but he wouldn't work, either. He wouldn't help others, never did anything good. He never gave, and he didn't have anything to give, he always took." (The man's name, *tuk*, coincidentally sounded like "took," but the pun was lost upon my informant.) This old man was a River Paipai who had joined the Wi Ahwir Cocopa, and he was without relatives in the valley, so far as I knew. He traveled back and forth along the delta road in Baja California, stopping in camps where the people would feed him. We met him on the road almost as frequently as in camp, and he always begged me for money when we picked him up. One of the Mexican husbands in a Cocopa camp could not understand how the Indians put up with him. He told me that the old man never pretended to earn his way; instead he sat around camp all the time, never even offering to bring in wood. (Only two Cocopa ever begged me for money. One was my first interpreter; the second was the son of a former captain in Sonora, and, so far as I know, he was recognized as a sober, industrious man. Children never solicited me for anything, even on our return trips, after we had given them candy and fruit.)

My first interpreter was another *čapai hačak*; however, he was not merely lazy. He worked now and then, usually chopping wood, but he could be counted upon to get drunk on the proceeds. When drinking, he had the reputation for

being unmanageable, and he was a mean fighter when provoked. There was little question that most of the men, certainly including Mike Alvarez, were frankly afraid of him when he was drinking. He was married, but he and his wife lived with her daughter's husband, who had a regular job on a Japanese farm when we were in Mexico in 1940.

No one to my knowledge ever accused either of these men of witchcraft, although to be *čapai hačak* was to run this risk. A third man who had an evil disposition, drunk or sober, and who lived on his neighbors while spending whatever money he earned on liquor, was definitely classed as a witch. I could never learn the basis for the accusation in his case, but I learned from Frank Gomez in the fall of 1944 that he had been killed the year before for being a witch.

Women as well as men were *hačak*. The term was applied to women who neglected their children, who drank and gambled with the men, and who were continually accused of adultery. Violators of sexual taboos were referred to as *hačak*. Only a *čapai hačak*, for instance, would have sexual intercourse with a virgin wife on the first night of their marriage. The term, however, was not ordinarily used in connection with premarital sexual experimentation on the part of girls. Such a girl simply had poor judgment, and she was called *nɨwe apit* (crazy heart).

The origin of evil behavior was explained in the creation myth as follows: Sipa [the creator twin] returned and told the people again about the seasons and that they should have a captain and what he was to do, and how he should talk to the people. Some of the people did not listen to Sipa; they did not hear, and so they are the *hačak*. The others listened and they live right.

The difference between a "good" man and an "ordinary" man was far more difficult to determine. Younger men, women, and older people who had no outstanding qualities were all "ordinary" (*yowaiyɛk*). The following concrete case, with Sam Spa as informant, is revealing:

Q. Did your cousin [the head of the camp where Spa lived as a boy] go to the meeting at the captain's camp?

A. No, he was *yowaiyɛk*.

Q. Did all the people around there speak of him as being *yowaiyɛk*?

A. Yes, to each other, but not to him.

Q. What did he do?

A. He never said anything; couldn't talk; he didn't stay around the fire, he just stayed home; didn't go visiting. He played with a long pole and the ball game and gambled. He lost horses, beads, belts, and shirt.

Q. Is that why they didn't think much of him?

A. He won sometimes, too.

Q. Did he work pretty hard?

A. Yes, he worked hard and always tried to have enough for the family to eat.

Other information on this man reveals that he was a steady worker, a good farmer, and a dependable family man. It is quite clear that industry, as such, was not an important ingredient in the ranking system.

While the semiformal characterization of "good" was reserved for mature men, with the implication that training and experience as well as good intentions were involved, some women were recognized as rising above the ordinary. The same types of criteria applied as in the case of men: they were steady mothers and wives, kept a clean camp, always had food ready for visitors, and did their share of the cooking at celebrations and ceremonies. In addition, they were leaders among the women, and exerted no little influence upon the men of their household.

The term *čapai pǝhwe* was also something of a title accorded the sons and grandsons of captains and leading orators. Sam Spa referred to a number of men by this term. In each case, the individual was the direct descendant of some famous man, but I was never sure that this was the only consideration. It was true that, if a boy was otherwise acceptable, he was given preference for an office held by his father or a close relative in the paternal line. The term may have been used in anticipation of the place that such a young man would earn for himself.

I doubt very much if this ranking system was ever consciously an element of motivation in the sense that a boy might be told: "If you do so and so, you will some day become *čapai pǝhwe*" (or "*čapai ahan*"). In 1943, I wrote the following comment in my notes:

All this is difficult to get at in an interview. Neither Frank Gomez nor Sam Spa can understand the idea of becoming an important, respected man. Such recognition seems wholly in the course of events and not consciously aimed at beyond the simple desire to live by the rules of good behavior for this society.

A week or so later, while interviewing Jim Short, with his son (who had graduated from high school) as an interpreter, I noted the following:

Line of questioning in an attempt to discover what an ambitious man could do to gain a higher position in the tribe. Questions directed at the interpreter in the hope that he could compare American and Cocopa attitudes. The general trend of his answers indicates that no one would entertain the thought of consciously trying to get ahead.
Q. How does a man get to be a leader?
A. A man's position depends upon dreams. If he has the right dreams, he will be powerful; if not, there is nothing he can do.
Q. Is your position a better one because your father is an orator?
A. Yes. His powers [dreams] can be transferred to his children.

9. MYTHOLOGY

THE CREATION MYTH

[The story of creation was given to me by Sam Spa. Once launched on the narrative, he gave the account with great animation and interest, frequently standing to act out the dramatic incidents. The interpreter was Frank Gomez, whose command of English was so slight that I habitually edited his statements in note-taking. Terms and phrases have been retained wherever I thought there was a chance that the peculiarity stemmed from the Cocopa way of thinking rather than from Gomez's difficulty with English. Perhaps not all the incidents that will be recounted below belong to the creation story, but I am sure that Sam Spa considered his account to be a single unit in Cocopa mythology.]

The Creation of Man

Sipa and Komat, the creator gods, were under water and in the ground, living the way a child lives in its mother. All the earth was covered with water. They began talking about coming out. Komat smoked a cigarette to get extra strength and, because he was the older, he pushed Sipa out ahead of him. When they reached the outside Komat became the younger and Sipa the older, because Sipa came out first. These two creators were twins (ha·wƏk). On their way up through the water, Komat asked his brother how he did it, and Sipa replied that he opened his eyes. When the older brother opened his eyes in the water he was blinded.

There was no ground, so they had the ants — flying ants (mat kau·R), little red ants (heɫmišu·R), and big red ants (šmoyu·ɫ) — dig out hills of earth to make the ocean go down and to supply the land.

After the ground became dry in spots, Sipa and Komat started making men. Both made all kinds: Indians, Mexicans, Chinese, Americans, and so on. While they were working, they asked each other what kind they were making; if it happened to be a Cocopa, the reply would be Cocopa plus the name of his lineage.

Komat, the blind twin, after a while had to urinate, so he got up and walked into the bushes. While he was gone, Sipa changed the people he had made for the ones Komat had made, because they were better. When Komat returned, he felt of the men and knew he had not made them, because they were deformed and badly made. He said nothing and went ahead making some more. Then he went to the bushes to urinate again and while he was gone Sipa changed his fox (pereha'u, a cross fox) for Komat's fox (matkawa, a kit fox). When Komat came back, he knew that the animals had been changed because he could hear his fox beating his tail against the ground. He could also tell the difference in the fur of the animal he had. Komat then called his fox by name: "čemwa mesir." When his fox heard this (although Komat called very quietly), he scratched and tried to get away. Komat kept on working on his men all this time.

After all the men were made, they were ready for eyes. Sipa suggested that they be put in each of the ten toes. Komat said that this would not do because they would get hurt, and that the men would be unable to see when they walked in water or in mud or dust. He said that the best place for the eyes was in the head. Sipa finally agreed, so now all men have two eyes in their heads, well above the ground, and if one gets hurt the other can be used.

Sipa made a bow and arrow, and when this was finished, he shot the arrow into the air and it came down and hit Komat. Komat asked him why he shot the arrow that way, and explained to him that he should only use the bow and arrow to kill animals. Komat was sitting down at the time and the arrow came from behind and hit him in the back. The wound was not serious.

Everything was dark, so Sipa attempted to make a sun. He made a very small one, and the light was no better than the moon. Komat did not like it, so he started making a sun by easy stages. When he had finished, he threw the sun into the east and after that it traveled east to west so that the people could know when to get up, when to work, and when to go to sleep. Sipa was going to throw his sun away, but Komat said: "No, let it stay, it will be the moon." The people can then tell the seasons, the months, and the days by the moon.

When these things were finished, Sipa again changed his people for the ones made by Komat. When Komat discovered this substitution, he was very mad this time. He reached up and broke the skies and then went down into the earth, leaving a hole. Sipa reached up and held the skies

---

NOTE: The main text of this chapter consists of translations of informants' stories. My comments and interpolations are enclosed in brackets.

and jumped over the hole with his feet because smoke, air, electricity, and other things that cause death were coming up. Some of this escaped onto the earth through Sipa's toes.

The following sicknesses were introduced at this time:

im kƏnu·i — bones hurt and swell.
čƏmamuwa·r — an incurable running sore on torso.
koRƏp pouša — a pain in the side caused by an intrusive object.
ao·ax or *ao si·rk* — children's croup.
koRƏp xwƏt — pain all over; cured by drawing blood.
hi·akwir — stomach trouble; feces are white with streaks of blood, or may be green; patient cannot eat.
šmalus ptei — skin disease with sores; a "big" smallpox.
šmalus ramƏs — smallpox.
mɩšpauk — like smallpox but patient recovers quickly.
ninyel sakwas — mumps.

[The informant became thoroughly tired of this business and finally said "that is all." Urging resulted in only one more: *kapɩuhał* — sore eyes.]

After the sky was fixed and the ground covered, Sipa sat down and made some more people. Then he started sorting them. He put them down in a row and repeated the name of the tribe for each: *koapa', kwa?ał, kwa?ałwa, yɩkwele'o, hamasuł, kakwał, kwinyahes, kamya', hkwas, kƏwi, kahwe, hłikhłak, li'pa, kw?ał·mɩtsha, kwɩsan, humha·p, yaupai hwa·t, semowau, htpanyia', khwan, hatpas·ma', hatpas.*

The place where these twins came out of the sea, and the place where these people were made and where Komat went back into the ground is called *wa kunyuR* (striped house).

After Komat went back into the earth, Sipa made more people and wanted to tell them how to talk and live, so he built a house to put them in. This house was made of adobe bricks and was later turned to stone so that it is now striped. It is on a mountain about 30 miles east of Tucson [this seems too far from Cocopa territory]. The Maricopa know where this place is.

Near the house, at *wa kunyuR*, there were two horses and riders: a Cocopa man on a white horse and a Yuma man on a black horse. The Yuma horse fought off the Cocopa horse, and the tracks can still be seen.

While in this house, the children learned how to play. One game was called *skoƏk*. This is a game of pushing with feet. The Yuma and Cocopa children play this; they do not get mad, just play. All the tribes played this game together. The Yuma boy pushed over the Cocopa boy and he started to cry. The Maricopa boy (*htpanyia*) came over and went against the Yuma boy. The Yuma boy whipped the Maricopa too.

Outside the house was a forked post with a single cross-pole. On this pole were hanging sixteen chickens, eight at each end. Sipa asked a boy from each tribe to turn the pole. None could do it. Then he asked the Cocopa boy and he turned the pole. This was a sign that he would always be strong and a good worker.

Another game that they played was *yo hwap*. This is a game in which boys divide up and throw clods at each other. On one side were the Cocopa, Pima, and Maricopa. On the other side were the Yuma, Mohave, Yavapai, Diegueño, and Kamia. The Paipai and the Kiliwa were too young for this game. The Yuma started throwing and made the Cocopa run and cry. Then the Maricopa jumped forward and chased the Yuma.

Another game was *keleho mɩčučɩm*. The game was to shoot at each other with arrows that were blunt on the end. There were four or five boys on each side, but this time the Yuma and the Mohave were against the Cocopa, who stood alone. The Cocopa boys started running and crying; then the Maricopa came to their aid, and they whipped the Yuma and Mohave.

They also learned games for adults but did not play them.

[There was a break of several days in the interview at this point, and when I saw Sam Spa again I asked him several questions before he went on with the story.

Q. "Did Sipa make women as well as men?"
A. "When Sipa and Komat were making men they also made women."
Q. "When did these figures come to life?"
A. "When an object was finished it was laid on the ground and then came to life when Sipa or Komat said what it would be."
Q. "Did they give the people their lineage name at the same time?"
A. "No, Sipa did that later."
Q. "Did Sipa give them their different languages when they were created?"
A. "No, the people did not eat or talk at *wa kunuR*. They were just like new babies."
Then Spa went on with the story:]

While the people were still at *wa kunuR*, Sipa brought money, gold, horses, cows, and other things and divided them among all the people. The Mexican and the American were the youngest and they cried so much, asking for everything, that the Cocopa boy finally said: "Give it all to them and shut them up."

Sipa then handed out the lineages. He kept this up for several days until some of the people got tired of waiting, finally got mad, and said they could get along without a lineage. A man who lives in Baja California has no lineage and no name for his daughters on this account. At Yuma there is another man without a lineage. The women of his family are called *škuš*, but this name doesn't belong because they have no lineage.

Sipa then started giving other things to the Indians. He gave the Cocopa bows and arrows, two kinds of fishing nets, pottery jars, clothes, and all the things they used in the old days. He gave the Diegueño these things, but also gave them some things the Cocopa didn't have: the *mıškwə'* image for the kerauk (mourning ceremony), the deer's-hoof rattle, boiled honey to be used by the women when they paint streaks on their face in a mourning ceremony, tobacco, cane cigarettes, a rabbit net, and a throwing stick.

When all this was finished, Sipa took the people to the sacred mountain in Mohave territory called *wi kami*. At *wi kami*, Sipa built a big house (*wa čawip*). Everybody went into this house and began playing games, singing, and having a good time. They were old enough now to talk. Sipa stretched out at the door to watch them.

Coyote Dies and Is Cremated

Every day Coyote took his little sister Snake in his mouth and threw her around. Finally Snake complained to Sipa, and asked him to do something for her. Sipa took whiskers from his chin and thorns from the mountain bush *kwaak* and put them in her mouth for teeth. Sipa also smoked a cigarette and blew the smoke into Snake's mouth and then took ashes and rubbed them on Snake's face. He then told the little girl that if Coyote threw her around again to bite him.

That night everyone was in the house when Coyote came in and asked for his sister. He finally found her coiled on a post. He picked her up and threw her against the post. Then the little snake girl began to cry and Coyote, laughing, picked her up again and threw her against another post. Then, still laughing, he went to pick her up again. When he did this, Snake bit him on the right paw. [The informant had been working up to this climax and stood up to tell this part of the story. He was evidently pleased at the turn of events and was laughing when he told how Coyote got what was coming to him.]

Coyote didn't pay any attention to the first bite and started to pick up Snake again. This time Snake bit him on the other hand. Then Coyote began to feel the pain and stopped. He sat down, then went outside a while, then came in, then went out. His paws began hurting bad (*pəmlal*) and he was writhing with pain. In an hour or so he died.

No one knew what to do or how to cry. After a while the locust (*hanyou*) began to cry [sound of locust imitated by informant]. Sipa did not like this, and came around and shut his mouth. When Sipa did that, Locust could not hold the crying that was inside so he split open and it spilled all over. This caused everyone to start crying.

In a little while, three birds (these are the orators) began to talk. The first bird was *šakwila'*, the second was

hanmıšip, the third *kup·sma'nya*. They also built a funeral pyre and a platform to hold Coyote. When everything was ready they put Coyote on the pyre, piled logs on top of him and set it on fire. All the people watched to see how it was done. It was summertime and midday, so the people had to retreat to the ramada, but they kept on crying.

Two frog girls, *hipa* and *səkami*, sisters of Coyote, stayed near the fire and cried until it was burned out. The people in the ramada stopped crying, but these two girls stayed at the pyre and cried from one noon to the next. *səkami*, the older, decided to have her hair cut short just like a man. *hipa* did the cutting with a knife given her by Sipa, and then *səkami* cut her hair. *hipa* asked her sister if she knew why her brother Coyote had died. They talked with each other about revenge for his death and they thought so much about it that it made them kind of crazy. They finally decided to get revenge on Sipa for giving Snake the teeth, and causing Coyote to die.

Sipa is a Victim of Witchcraft

They went underground to a place called *mokwin təuR*. This is a Yuma word, and it is a place in the first range of mountains north of Yuma. At this place, Sipa was in the habit of defecating at midday. There was a rumbling noise when his feces hit the ground. One frog girl got underneath and caught the excrement in her mouth and ate it. There was no noise. Sipa wondered at this, and so defecated again to see what would happen. There was still no noise because the other frog girl took the excrement this time. The ocean at that time reached this place and the frog girls were under water.

Sipa walked away and soon began to feel bad. By the time he reached home, he was writhing with pain. At home, the three birds were still talking. Sipa vomited white, then red, then yellow, then black. These were wild food plants and the people learned later how to eat them. At the same time, a song came out of Sipa, called *hspeləp*. He told the people that when he died they should not put his face to the east on the pyre, but to turn it a little north, otherwise much sickness would result.

Coyote Steals the Creator's Heart

In the meantime, Coyote had another brother. This Coyote, people knew, wanted to eat Sipa when he died.

The three birds took the last ember of fire from the first Coyote's pyre, hid it in the ground, and put Quail over it to hide it. This is what made the spots on a quail's breast.

Then Sipa died. Coyote was told that there was no fire and that he must go to the sun to get some. As soon as he was out of sight, the people started to burn Sipa.

Before he was quite dead, a long series of songs came out of Sipa. As these emerged, Sipa's wife stood by, crying, and gave names to the songs: *wa lho*, empty house; *čuman kwakoł*, raised end, long; *čuman wak wak*, raised end, [?];

čuman kwθ⁺ kwθ⁺, raised end, fast beat with rattle; *t⁺ša hain*, loud, good; *t⁺ša haleu·t*, loud, short; *ša' lιmθš*, name of a small bird; *ka·k*, crow; *šayi*, buzzard; *hatspa*, coyote; *sohwθs*, the sound of a basket being rubbed and beaten alternately; *auhwar*, a musical sound [?]; *h⁺a*, moon; *hanya*, frog; *sιxapιlap*, mescal ash used for face streaks: a crying song; *čuman kwιnymih*, wildcat, a Mohave-Yuma word; *sθir*, salt; *kerauk*, a mourning song; *owikp*, [?]; *mičapai*, people; *akwak hantι⁺*, wild deer; *kapιt*, turtle; *hama ornes*, quail [note use of Spanish words]; *hu⁺ lui*, smells bad — people say it is a Shoshonean song.

After Sipa's death, the two frog girls came back, made other frogs from dirt, and distributed these around. The people killed these frogs, scattered them, but the frog girls got away.

šakwila, one of the orator birds, told the other animals — Wildcat, Fox, and others — that they could not run very fast, that Coyote could beat them. Coyote agreed, so *šakwila* told Coyote he would have to run fast (to get fire) and not to look back. When Coyote was gone, Quail got up and they started a fire with the red hot coal that Quail had been hiding.

Sipa had a stick in the ground that reached to the sky. *čιmkwιra*, another bird, climbed this stick to watch Coyote and to see how far he went. At first he reported that Coyote was half way, then he saw Coyote coming back; he could see his dust. Coyote had brushed the sun with his tail and set it on fire. His first jump was two or three miles long and so violent that the fire went out. When he went back to light it again, the old lady who was taking care of the sun asked him what he wanted fire for. He told her that the man who had been taking care of all the people had died, and that they wanted fire to cremate him. Then she said: "I can see the fire now, they are almost through." Coyote turned and saw the smoke. When he saw that, he ran back as fast as possible.

This was when the bird lookout said that he was halfway back. The people were amazed at this and wanted to know how he could come so far so fast. The bird said that he didn't know, but that he could see his dust. Then the bird reported him only two or three miles away. When they heard this, the three orator birds advised the people to get sticks and stand close together around the pyre.

When Coyote reached the group, he wanted to know why the people tried to fool him. The orators told the people to pay no attention to what he was saying, but to watch him closely. Coyote begged for a place in the circle so that he could mourn, but all the time he was just looking for a place to get through. He kept on crying and begging to be allowed to jump right in the fire and die with Sipa. Then he came to the place where Badger and Skunk had been placed. It was a low spot in the circle so Coyote jumped over. Sipa's heart had not yet burned, so Coyote grabbed it and started to run. The people all went after him with their sticks, but he dodged and the people hit each other. Night

Hawk (*sθur*) went to the outside of the crowd and waited for Coyote. When he came by, Night Hawk almost caught him, but not quite.

Coyote ran first to *wi kwιse* (greasy mountain), and after turning around to make sure no one was following, he ate a piece of the heart, leaving a grease spot. Then he went to the Yavapai country and ate some more. At this place, some blood was spilled, turning into *kwιnyι⁺* (black mineral paint). Then he started back this way. He stopped again and more blood was spilled, forming the red rock *kwa'R*. At each stop, he ate a little. At his next stop, the blood turned white and formed *mat hapa* (white mineral paint). At the next place, *mιčkwas* (yellow ?) was formed. Then he turned east toward Maricopa country and went on beyond and stopped at some water. He stopped here to take a drink and to bathe. When he came out of the water, he was cold and shivering, so he picked up the rest of the heart and went to a big grove of cottonwood trees to take a nap. The nearness of the heart and Coyote caused all the birds in the trees to die, and they fell down, but the trees were always green after this. When Coyote woke up, he came on to *keyamačus*. This is in Cocopa country, in the first pass in the Cocopa Mountains north of Mayor, where water stands after a rain. From this place, Coyote turned north and wherever he stopped, he spilled blood and formed the rocks that are now used to make paint. By this time, Coyote was a little crazy, so he ran west and then back and forth at the edge of the ocean.

Sipa Returns as a Culture Hero

After Sipa's death the three orator birds (*šakwila, han mιši·p*, and *škwmanya*) started talking about how the people were forgetting how to live and how they wanted Sipa to come back. They talked day and night. *škwmanya* finally said that they would have to send *če⁺pu hθma⁺* (white roadrunner) after Sipa, who was still walking toward heaven, and so Roadrunner tried to catch him before he got there. Roadrunner called to Sipa and told him that the people had forgotten everything: when it was summer, when it was winter, when to gather their crops, and everything. Sipa told them that he could not go back, that they couldn't have forgotten because he had told the people how to live just a short time ago.

Roadrunner came back and reported his failure, so they sent Badger after Sipa. Sipa was close to heaven, but Badger caught up with him and told the same story Roadrunner had brought. This time, Sipa sent word to get all the people together. There was a big house with a fire in the center. The orator birds were there. Sipa came with a big noise, like an airplane. There was a cloud of dust and everything shook. When there is an earthquake now, it is Sipa moving around, because his back gets tired. Some people were asleep and woke up with a loud holler and all were afraid of the noise.

When Sipa started talking, the people couldn't see him so they were afraid, but the orator birds knew what it was and told the people to be still. Sipa told them again all about the seasons, how to tell summer from winter, that the mesquite gets green in the spring, and many other things. He showed them how to store food in order to have something to eat in the winter when things were frozen, how to build houses, how to hunt, how to take care of babies, how to gather, and all the things of that kind. He told them that they were to have a *mıšiare'* (captain) and what he was to do, and how he should talk to the people. Some of the people didn't hear, and they are the *hačak* (evil persons). Others listened and they live right. Some people don't hear and so they steal and kill people. It is the same now when the captain talks and some people don't listen.

After Sipa had finished talking, he went back. Then the ones who hadn't listened sat up and asked what he had said, so the three orator birds repeated Sipa's speech. The people were young and didn't have much sense so they still didn't understand very well.

When Sipa was still alive, he built a big steam boat and the ocean covered everything. He put a lot of people in the boat, but a lot stayed on land and they were drowned. The boat stopped on top of *wi kami* when the water went down, and the people came off the mountain on a big wide road. A man who had been living there showed them the way. On the way a snake with a great big head and big rattles tried to stop them. The man put up his hand and the snake settled down. Then a scorpion appeared; he was as big as a horse. Then they met soldiers with rifles, and then another group of soldiers, but nothing stopped them.

On the boat there had been one house on top of another with a hole in each for an entrance. Any man who could go there and stay would have many dreams and lots of power. In the hole you can hear the noises of people talking: Cocopa, Diegueño, Yavapai, Yuma, American, and Mexican. Any one who stays there four days and fasts and purifies himself could learn to speak American and Mexican and have power to cure.

One man went there by himself and got lost and ran out of water. The people found him and brought him back and cured him, but he lost his hearing. This man went to *wi kami* to get more power to talk. He also wanted to be a doctor. He was still alive when I was a boy.

Coyote and the Frog Girls

After Sipa's death the two frog girls had lived long enough for their hair to grow and now it was nice and long. They dressed their hair, put beads on their wrists and around their necks, and went walking along the ocean. They also had their faces painted: their eyelids were blackened, their tattoo lines were emphasized with additional black paint, and they had vertical red lines on their cheeks with a cross line under each eye. They were talking about getting married.

Coyote, by this time, had recovered his senses and was returning home. He was also all dressed and ready to get married. His face was painted; he had beads around his neck and wore a raw-hide wrist band decorated with fringe and white painted circles. His hair was fixed and he had two eagle feathers stuck in the back.

When the girls saw him, they both wanted him. They began quarreling about which one would have him and finally decided that both would marry him and he could sleep in the middle. But first, before they let Coyote see them, they decided to see whether or not he was any good. One took off her willow bark skirt and threw it in the road and then they both hid. They thought to themselves that if Coyote only smelled the skirt, he would be all right, but if he raised his leg and began pawing the ground this would show that he was *hačak* (an evil person).

When Coyote came up, he smelled the skirt, walked around and smelled again, then raised his leg and pawed all around the skirt. The girls left without letting him know that they had been near.

Then the girls went along the beach and finally sat down and started making beads. The girls spent all their time at this work and the beads piled high all around them. Then the girls died and both turned to stone with the beads. One of the mountains is called *wi hipa*, the other *wi sɔkami*. These are on the ocean, far away in the west where the land ends.

Coyote Sponsors a Kerauk for Sipa

By this time, Coyote had "learned something" so he went back to where the people were to find the orator birds. Five years had gone by since Sipa's death. Coyote told these birds that he wanted the people to feel better and so he would give a big kerauk (mourning ceremony). He wanted to build a big house so that people from everywhere could come. The birds agreed to help him.

Coyote said that the poles had to be cut, and told the orator birds to attend to this. Finally the poles were ready and the people brought them and built the kerauk house. When it was finished, they all went inside to start crying.

Coyote told them that *sɔur* and *sɔur howɔk* (Night Hawk and Second Night Hawk) were war leaders, and he wanted them to fight to see which one would be killed. *sɔur* was in the east and *sɔur howɔk* was in the west. They came together and met over the door of the kerauk house, fighting with clubs. *sɔur* broke his club in this encounter and so *sɔur howɔk* won the fight. Some *šyeya hačak* (witches) were present so after that witches were always present at a kerauk.

This was at *wi kami*. Coyote sent to get more people and then set out for the ocean to get *mahiawi*, a big snake. Coyote brought the snake to the kerauk house and started coiling him inside. But there wasn't enough room, so Coyote told the people to build a bigger house; the snake still wouldn't go in. They rebuilt the house four times.

After the fourth time, when the snake still wouldn't go in, Coyote got a sharp knife and cut the snake in half. [This was a big joke and the informant had a good laugh when he demonstrated how Coyote cut the snake in half.] The tail half of the snake rolled around on the ground inside the house and the head half went back to the ocean. Then Coyote set fire to the house and burned the snake. This was the first kerauk. But in the meantime another coyote decided to have a kerauk just south of *wi nyai* (Cerro Prieto) in Cocopa territory. He burned the snake there just the same way.

After the house was burned, there was a black spot. Coyote said this was the mark of the tail of the snake and that it would always show in the charcoal when anyone died. He told the people to cover this over, to let water run over it so there would be no trace. He picked up his *saur* (the "spirit" and cane of Sipa) and punched a hole in a big mountain so the river would start running. The river washed past the place where the kerauk house had been and took half of it away. The other half is still there and is called *wi kami*. After that the river went by that place and never stopped and is still running so the people can drink. The river runs red and muddy out into the ocean as far as Feather Mountain, then it spreads out.

The Cannibal Brothers and Hal Kwichat

Coyote then stuck his spear (*šaur*) into the ground and made a mountain: *wi keruačač* [also recorded as *wi kerutata*]. This mountain is on the California side of the border. Near the mountain where the *halk kw?čat* (snake-fish) people lived, there was a good-looking young man named Spat Kwamai. This was his name in Mohave. The young man took a bath in the lake early every morning and fixed his long hair. There were many good-looking girls there: Cocopa, Diegueño, Yuma, Mohave, and others. These girls liked the young man so that they came to sleep with him, a different girl every night, but the boy paid little attention to them. One morning, when the moon was still up, a young girl came down from the moon to the lake where the boy was washing his hair. The girl asked the boy into her house and when he was combing his hair and couldn't see what she was doing, she grabbed him and forced him to have sexual intercourse. He went home after that and began to feel ill. He kept getting worse and worse and finally went to bed. After a while he started growing feathers, then wings, then he got feet like an eagle, then an eagle's nose, and, with everyone watching him, he flew away. He had turned into an eagle. He flew north, west, south, and east, and then he came back. He grabbed his father and took him to the mountain (*wi keruačač*) and started to eat him. After that, this boy (Spat Kwamai) continued to fly down from his mountain to pick up good-looking Cocopa boys and girls. He would take them to the mountain to eat them.

There was another young man, named Koma Sumhot Malei. He had a dog and was always taking his dog around to fight other dogs. His sister, *česi kurθpai*, told him to stop these dog fights but he wouldn't pay any attention to her. One day his dog *hat mɪšowak* (hairy dog) lost a fight and the young man stopped eating. Then he hit someone with a spear.

One morning he got up and told his sister that he was going to see his brother Spat Kwamai, the cannibal [now an eagle]. She tried to stop him, but he started out anyway, leaving his dog behind. While he was traveling toward the mountain, Spat Kwamai was out looking for more people to eat and found two to bring back to the mountain. As he approached he saw his brother Koma trying, without success, to climb the mountain, which was always inaccessible when Spat Kwamai was gone, but could be climbed easily when he was home. After Spat Kwamai landed on the mountain with his two victims, Koma came up to him and Spat Kwamai offered him some of the human flesh. At first Koma refused, but finally he accepted and so became a cannibal like his brother. Spat Kwamai was elated over this because now he would have someone to help him take people, even though his brother couldn't fly and would have to walk off the mountain.

Finally only one human being was left, a man by the name of Hal Kwichat [Whale]. When he saw that he was alone he went out into the ocean and called all the ocean people together for a meeting. He told them that if the cannibal finally succeeded in eating him, the world would return to darkness. It was up to him to put a stop to the cannibal's activities and he intended to kill him. He told the ocean people that if he were successful, there would be a cloud of red dust and they could start singing, but if it got dark they would know that he had been killed, and they would have to start crying.

In the morning, there was a fog of different colors and the people swam through the water. Hal Kwichat sent a rock whistle and Night Owl ahead of him to spy on the cannibal and to give the warning. When Koma got up that morning he decided to leave, but Spat Kwamai stayed on the mountain. Night Owl was on a rock nearby watching and the rock whistled. Spat Kwamai heard the whistle but could see nothing, so he flew up and looked at the river. All he saw was a fin sticking out of the water, so he dove and started to pick up the fish with one finger, but it was too big so he used two fingers, then three, then his whole hand. This was still not enough. Then he flew up and came down with both hands. This was just at daylight. Hal Kwichat was the fish [i.e., a whale], and when Spat Kwamai came down the second time he grabbed him and pulled him under water. They fought until noon and finally the fish drowned the eagle cannibal. Then he made a ramada from the eagle's feathers and rested. A cloud of red dust rose in the air and the ocean people had a big dance.

When Koma returned to the mountain, he found that his brother had gone and he started to look for him. He asked a bird, čelkɪlkɛl, but he just shook his head. He asked Night Hawk, but got no answer. He asked the mountain and it cried so he went to the river and saw where the fight had been. He knew what had happened then and started crying. First, he went to Eagle Mountain (*wi spa*, Mayor Peak), where he sharpened his spear (*šaur*), then he went to his sister's home. He put feathers in his hair, a necklace around his neck, a bow guard on his arm, and a belt around his waist.

His sister asked him where he was going and he told her that he was going back to his brother. When he left this time, he took his dog. He really intended to find Hal Kwichat, who had killed his brother. He started before sunup and soon came to the place where Hal Kwichat was stretched out naked and asleep. In one of his testicles was good river water and in the other was salt water. Koma used his spear on the testicle with fresh water but nothing happened. Then he hit the other and salt water gushed forth. It was really the ocean and it started rising. Koma started running and the water followed him so he put down his loincloth to stop it. This did no good so he put his belt down. Still nothing happened so he planted an arrow in the ground, then his wrist band. Nothing could help him.

The arrow became Feather Mountain and can still be seen out in the Gulf. The wrist band became *kerauk hap* [a rock formation near the Gulf believed to be the land of the dead; there is a large split in the rock which, from a distance, looks like a hole]. The spear became *wi hmokah* [a rock formation near Mayor]; the necklace became *nemisap* [a rock south of the Laguna Salada where white sand has climbed high up the slope in long streaks]; and the head feather became *wi shapɪł* [foothills at the southern end of Mayor Peak].

Finally, Koma came to his sister's house where she was making some pots. He asked her to help him, but she refused and said that she had told him not to go. He was tired, out of breath, and crying. Still she wouldn't help him. Hal Kwichat was almost on him now and making loud noises. Koma took some wax out of his right ear and flipped it at Hal Kwichat, and it hurt when it hit him on the head. Koma took some more wax from his left ear and this time he killed Hal Kwichat. This was at *nɪpanyak spu kwɪnyɪr*, at the southern end of the Cocopa Mountains. The body floated with the water all the way up to Cerro Prieto (*wi nyai*). *spu kwɪnyɪr* [black mountain] is the wax from the right ear, *spu kwakwas* [brown mountain] is the wax from the left ear. *nɪpanyak* is the evidence of blood from the fatal blow. There is a hole in the rock at *smal uyao* where the sister was making pottery and this is the hole that was left when Koma took the wax from his ear.

When the water receded from Cerro Prieto, Hal Kwichat's body was left stranded. It became rotten and boiled up and is now the place where the mud volcanoes are located. Cerro Prieto is Hal Kwichat's head. If you climb to the top, you either die in two or three days or you live forever. Right on top is a sand dune, and if you dig in this and get water you will die. If you don't find water you will live. A spot of white sand shows the place where Hal Kwichat was hit. You can't fly over this mountain in an airplane because it is too hot.

THE ORIGIN OF THE KERAUK AND ITS SONGS

[The following account of the kerauk was given to me by Tom Juarez, who was probably the only remaining kerauk singer among the Cocopa at the time of our field-work.]

I learned the songs and the kerauk ceremony in two dreams. In the first I dreamed of a blond woman who took me to the "cremation kerauk" and gave me the power to learn the songs. In my dream I was standing close to a white pole that reached into the sky. There was a kerauk house nearby with lots of people around and as the singer sang the kerauk songs they hit the pole, bounced from the pole to *wi spa* (Mayor Peak), then to *kerauk hap* (the land of the dead). At daylight it was time to burn the house but everyone was waiting for one man to appear. Then the man arrived, and when they burned the house half of him went into the house and the other half stayed outside [see above, *Coyote Sponsors a Kerauk for Sipa*, for the cremation of the giant snake (*mahiawi*)]. In my second dream the blond woman sent a young girl to teach me the kerauk songs. This girl said that the woman had died and had asked her to continue my lessons. She came to me dressed in silk robes, had her hair tied on top of her head, and had wings so that she could fly anywhere.

This was the way I learned the songs, but I am going to tell you the story of the two travelers and the way they discovered and learned the kerauk and its songs in their travels. One of the travelers was a Kamia [the Cocopa name for the Southern Diegueño living north of Santa Catarina in the Baja California mountains, who had a different version of the kerauk from the one given by the Southern Diegueño near the international border to the north]. The other traveler was a Hwanyak Cocopa [from the band in the southeastern corner of the delta]. These two men were at the "cremation kerauk" mentioned in my dream. This was in Cocopa territory so the two travelers were in an area where the Hwanyak knew the country and the Kamia was a stranger.

The first songs came to the two travelers at some water holes. When they reached the first water hole, the water was black. The next water hole was a *tinaja* [a rock formation holding water] and so they stopped to drink. The Cocopa said: "This water is yellow, it is not clear." By drinking this they learned something. They kept on traveling to another *tinaja* where the water was white. The

Kamia said this is *ha kiai* (white water). The word in Cocopa is *ha homał*. In the song the Kamia word was to be used. Later they came to another water hole where the water was red. The name of this song, red water (*ha hwat*), is the same in both Kamia and Cocopa.

They went on and came to a sand hill, a high red one. They went to the top and the Kamia said: "We have gone too far, we are at the end of the earth." The Cocopa said: "No, we are not half way yet." They were singing these words and the Kamia said: "We cannot sing all the way, we must finish before that." But the Cocopa disagreed: "We have enough songs for the whole distance."

Then they came to the edge of a desert where there was a lot of water and some tules. The tule had ripe pollen and the Kamia did not know what it was so the Cocopa had to tell him. He said (in a song): "Someone will come here later and eat this."

Then they traveled west into the desert and finally saw some bushes. From a distance the bushes looked like people and the Cocopa was afraid because he had never seen such bushes before. The Kamia said: "These bushes grow in the mountains and are called *hosił*; they must have been washed down here." Then they came to a palo fiero tree where a wildcat was lying in the branches. The Kamia was afraid of him so the Cocopa said: "He won't hurt us, but will run away from us. We need these animals and they will not bother us."

Then they went on and came to a shallow lake with many birds around it. The Kamia was afraid again but the Cocopa said: "There is no danger. These birds are called *homomuł* and were sent here for the Cocopa because they are good to eat. When they see us come near they will fly away." This song is in Cocopa.

After leaving the lake they came to the edge of some mountains (*wi opit*). They started to climb over the mountains but they were very high and so it was dark before they reached the top. Then they turned east and saw a big star on the horizon. This was just at daylight so they had a song about the star.

Next they saw a hummingbird sucking honey from some flowers in a bush. The bird was singing a song about how people used to get honey from flowers. The Cocopa and the Kamia had different words for this bird.

Then they came to a clear place where there were no trees and where it was very hot and dry. Coyote, who lived nearby in a mountain, came near the travelers and started singing: "We live here, the heat does not hurt me and I do not need water. I am used to this because I live here." Then Coyote sang another song: "I am thirsty so you must need water too and so I am going to show you where to get water." Then the Kamia said: "We will use this song but it is not easy — it is not the way we talk."

Then they went on through the desert and came to a cottonwood tree and the Kamia wanted to stay there in the shade. But the Cocopa disagreed, saying: "This tree stays green all the time, it is *pohao* [endowed with "creation power"], so we might die if we stay here. I can do something. I can make rain or I can make the wind blow to cool this country." He blew some smoke and kicked up some dust to start a whirlwind and in a little while it started raining. The travelers kept moving in the rain and the Kamia got wet and cold but the Cocopa stayed dry. The Kamia said: "I am cold and we need a fire." But the Cocopa would not stop and so he agreed to stop the rain. He held up his hands, smoked a cigarette, and the rain stopped. "The clouds and the wind," he said "belong to the Cocopa and I can make them come and go." He sang this in a song. [Tom Juarez interrupted himself here to recall that he had known some Cocopa men who could control the weather.]

The two travelers then went on to reach some water where they heard a noise like a bird. The Kamia was afraid of this, but the Cocopa knew that it was a *hamkwail* bird and he was not afraid, so they put this in a song. Next came a sand hill where there were many small pebbles. There they met an animal called *helkwao* [an all-white animal with a short tail] who was blocking the road. The animal started to talk [sing] to them and said: "I am leaving here; I live under a rock nearby and all I have to eat is rocks. I heard a long time ago that you were coming and I want to warn you not to stop because there is nothing to eat here." The Kamia was afraid but the Cocopa said: "He won't hurt us." They put this in a song and had to use the Cocopa word because the Kamia did not know this animal. The Cocopa said: "From now on these animals will get smaller because this one was born at the time of creation."

A little later they came to another water hole. A *ha kwis* bird was running around there and making a noise. The bird said: "You are here, I see you now. I have nothing to eat except some fish in the water. You can take them out with your hands and cook them here." The Cocopa said: "The song this bird is singing will be used." After a while they looked north and saw a black dust cloud. The Kamia said: "There is nothing here that we can use to build a house to get out of this dust." The Cocopa said: "*mahł kwayuk* does this — he will not hurt us." [*mahł kwayuk* is perhaps the God introduced by early Spanish missionaries, since it translates "one who lies down in the sky."] When the dust came up to them they kept on traveling. After a while it started to thunder and lightning and to rain. When the rain started, a lightning bolt hit a rock and broke it. This frightened the Kamia, who said: "This is the way the lightning is going to kill us." But the Cocopa reassured him saying: "No, the rain will just settle the dust and everything will be fresh." Then they saw an oak tree with dry leaves. A bird a little larger than a hummingbird was sitting on one of the branches and said to them: "I made all this dust and then the rain. Now I am going away and everything will be clear, no more dust or rain." This was a song.

After they left the oak tree they traveled a long way and finally saw an animal like a coyote, only smaller (*mat kawa*). He said: "I live here and have a lot of children. When they saw you they ran to hide, but I called them back and told them that you were good people — that you talk all right. If I had something to eat I would give it to you, but I have nothing." This was *mat kawa*'s song. The Kamia said: "We will use this song and call the animal by his Kamia name, *perðha'o*."

The travelers started out again and came to a soft, muddy place where they found nests full of eggs. All the birds flew away, but one stayed behind and said: "I saw you when you were at the colored waters. I hid then, but now I know that you will not hurt anyone. The others flew because they were afraid but I am not." This was his song. The Cocopa said: "We will use this song and call the bird *kwɪčum* in Cocopa."

[At this point there is a break in the story of the two travelers indicating an intermission in the songs being sung at a kerauk. The intermission (in the story or the kerauk songs?) is called *kwɪnyma·m*.]

When the travelers started out again they saw some white birds. Once again all but one of the birds (who was just like a person) flew away. The bird that remained said: "I have traveled all over the ocean looking for something to eat and I saw you coming from far off. I know you have come a long way and I know that I can talk to you." The Cocopa said: "This bird knows when it is nearly daylight. He gets up early and starts flying around; I have seen him do it. This bird is to be called *kwɪnðu'i* (pelican) in Cocopa and we will use this song."

Then the travelers went a long way to a slough where they saw a man and a young girl on a hill beyond the slough. The girl saw them and was afraid, but the man said: "These are the first people and I knew they were coming. They won't hurt us." The girl said: "There are no people around here." Then the man said: "It is all right, we can talk to them. Do not run away." The Cocopa and the Kamia heard this song and agreed to use it. The people are *šekwak* birds.

[At this point Tom Juarez had been telling the story of the two travelers for two days. He was ready to continue on the third morning when he said he had something on his mind that he wanted to say. He then spoke for ten minutes or so with my interpreter, who summarized as follows: Many Cocopa would not want me to tell this story because it might bring sickness. These songs are dangerous when they are sung at a kerauk, but they have doctors there to look after the people. They are just as dangerous when they are sung or translated outside the kerauk and we have no doctors to watch out for us. It is for this reason that I am glad we are working alone here and that no one can hear us.

I have no record of any other part of the conversation or of my reply, but I am sure that Juarez was merely making an observation and was not indicating an unwillingness to continue. In any event, the story picks up again as follows:]

Later on the travelers encountered a bunch of turkeys — this was about daylight and so the turkeys were up and looking for food. One of them said: "I have nothing to eat but I am looking for something now." The song is about *oRuč* (turkey) in Cocopa. A little farther along they met a *šemkwɪyul* (like a chicken hawk) who was sitting in a mesquite tree. He said: "I have nothing for you to eat. You will have to keep on your journey." This was put in a song. [At this point the interpreter explained to me that this happens in real life. When a traveler comes to an Indian camp the head of the camp is expected to prepare a meal for him. But sometimes, as in the above case, there is nothing, so the traveler must go on.]

The travelers then climbed a sand hill and from there they could see, in the distance, clumps of grass (*ma hose*). The Kamia was afraid they could not go through because of its thickness. The Cocopa said: "There must be a trail through and so we need not be afraid. God (*mahł kwayuk*) put this grass here and so it has to be here. There is nothing to fear." They put this in a song. Then they found a trail and traveled through the grass to a slough where there was some water. There they saw a *nyɪkwa?a* (a long-legged water bird) looking for some fish to eat. The bird said: "I have nothing to give you to eat. I start before daylight and sometimes catch only a small fish." They put this in a song. [The interpreter explained: "At a kerauk all these songs are sung four times, each time a little bit differently."]

After the travelers started out again they met a boy and a girl each carrying a white sack. When they came close the girl said: "I am afraid. These people might kill us." The boy said: "No these are our people too and that is why we meet them here." They had been gathering tule powder and that was what they had in the sacks. The Cocopa said: "When we started traveling we saw some tule, but it was larger and better because it was the first tule started by *mahł kwayuk*. The tule we saw had *pohao* (power) from this god. The tule you saw started later and so is not so large or so good."

When the travelers started again they reached some green mesquite trees. This made a good shade so they lay down. Coyote met them there, coming at a run from the opposite direction. When he saw them he stopped and said: "It is getting to be daylight. You had better get up and start again." The Kamia then asked: "Are there some coyotes here too?" The Cocopa said: "Yes. The first one we saw was big (*mahł kwayuk pohao*). They will be smaller from now on."

When they went on they saw a deer, heading south and away from them, who was being chased by two people. One of them was old and short, the other young and small, and they had a dog with them. The boy shot the deer and he fell. Then the dog ran up and bit him in the breast in such a way as to tickle him (*pelyoka't*). The deer then jumped up and started running again, and this was repeated several times. The Kamia and the Cocopa stood watching this until at the place where the sky and the earth meet (*mat kwim* [the horizon]) they disappeared. The Cocopa said: "Deer in the south are brown; east, they are black; north, red; west, white. Dreaming about a red deer from the north gives power and a doctor's knowledge. If a man has such a dream he will live a long time. If, however, he dreams of the other three directions he will not live long. It is the same with coyotes. Dreams about red coyote from the north give extra power to cure and a long life."

Then they went on and saw snow falling in the mountains. The Cocopa saw this and said: "What is this white we see — I am afraid of this." The Kamia said: "We are just starting into the cold country, do not be afraid." They kept traveling toward the snow until they saw some people. The Cocopa said: "I don't know these people. We had better go around them." They continued to walk until they saw a rock piled high with snow, and this frightened the Cocopa. He was afraid that the snow would fall and bury them. But the Kamia said: "If it falls it won't hurt us, we can brush it off. The rock will not move and that is why the snow piles on top of it. We will keep moving, but turn north here so we can find a pass through this snow and ice. There will be a way to go." As they turned north they saw a deer. He was standing still like the rock and snow was piled high on him, but he was throwing his front feet the way a fighting bull does. This made the Kamia afraid because he couldn't see how they could get past this animal. The Cocopa said: "This deer is mad because he hears deer fighting in the sky, but we will get through." Then he told the Kamia that this was a new kind of deer, a *kwak šahat*, and they would use this name in the song. When they went on past they turned to look at the deer and the Kamia said: "He is not going to do anything to us. Let's go back and find a better place to watch him." The Cocopa said: "If we do he will hurt one of us. Let's not do it. It is better to keep going."

The travelers then went on until they could see a snow-covered mountain. The snow where they were traveling was knee deep. The Cocopa said: "What shall we call this? Let's call it *sakupai* (something carried on top). When we first saw this mountain it looked close, but we have a long way to go and then we still have to climb to the top." They kept on traveling and the snow reached to their waists. The Cocopa said: "We started this so we have to keep on climbing. When we reach the top we will be able to see where we came from and where we are going." When they finally reached the top, the Cocopa said: "I don't know which way is farthest, the route we traveled or the one ahead of us." The Kamia was looking ahead where he saw a high hill and beyond that some low ground. When the Kamia saw this he turned south and saw a big, clear valley. Then he turned north and saw, in the distance, a body of water that was moving toward them. Then he saw a blackbird (*sokhwe*) flying close to the water. The Cocopa said: "The moving water sets the spiders, grasshoppers, and other bugs to jumping and so the bird is eating the bugs." After seeing this, the Kamia said: "We have stayed here too long; we had better go now." And so they started west.

After walking for a while the travelers came to an area strewn with rocks and pebbles, and the Cocopa, not being used to walking in the mountains, developed sore feet. Little by little the Cocopa dropped behind until the Kamia was about a hundred yards ahead of him. The Kamia saw a *mohwa* (a small animal living in a hole). The Kamia spoke to him and said: "We have come a long way and my friend has sore feet, so he falls behind and I have to wait for him." The *mohwa* said: "Why don't you fix some shoes like the Kamia use [sandals of mescal fiber]? There are a lot of mescal bushes here and it won't take long." So the Kamia said: "You know where these bushes are so you had better go get them and I will make the sandals." When the *mohwa* returned with the mescal leaves, the Kamia asked him what size the shoes should be, and he said any size would do. Then the Kamia made the shoes and the Cocopa put them on, but when they started walking he kicked the toes into the ground because he had never worn sandals before.

After a long walk the travelers saw a whirlwind. The dust was red and frightened the Cocopa. The Kamia said: "It will not hurt us. It is called *mat heyakwɪr*. It is found everywhere and does no harm to anyone." This [like all other incidents, the interpreter reminds me] was put into a song.

Then they traveled a long way and finally came to some piñon trees. The seeds were ripe and falling so the Kamia picked some and ate them. The Cocopa did not want to stop but the Kamia said: "I want to fill my stomach, these are good. The Kamia have this fruit and it belongs to them." The Cocopa said: "I don't know these things. The Cocopa have never eaten this and it might make me sick." This is the pine nut (*ɛhwi*) song. Then the Kamia suggested that the Cocopa take some nuts with him by tying them in the cloth of his breechclout. He said: "Then you can eat when you are hungry. Also, there are other types of food here, wild dates and acorns and *hosiɫ* (a red fruit on a bush) — all good Kamia fruit." But the Cocopa said: "We had better not take anything. You had better not eat anything either. I am going to travel on an empty stomach and you had better do the same." The Kamia thought to himself: "Perhaps I had better not eat. I'll go hungry like the Cocopa (except for the nuts I have eaten)."

They started out again and went through the area where they could see and smell the wild fruit until they reached the desert beyond. Then they stopped again and the Kamia said: "We have passed through the area of wild food and I don't know what we will find up ahead." They went a long way and finally found a damp, level place where a weed (*kɛmu'm*), something like a tule, grows. Nearby there was a single willow tree and there they saw a bird called *ša čɛlapu* (something like a *kwıcɔm*, only longer). It was coming toward them and then rested in the willow tree. The bird said: "I saw you coming from afar." The Kamia said to the Cocopa: "This bird saw us way back." The Cocopa said: "There are many of these back where we came from." The bird said: "I have been here a long time. When I first came there was water here. Then I left. When I came back this time I found the place dry."

The travelers moved on and finally saw a bird walking back and forth. The bird is called *mas* and has a curled blue tail and a crest. The Cocopa was afraid of this bird and stopped. He said: "I can't go through there, I am afraid of that bird going back and forth." He was afraid the bird would bite or scratch. The Kamia said: "He won't hurt us. He will run away when we get close. I know these birds." When they started on, the bird stepped to one side and when the men looked back at him he said: "I heard you speak my name. *mahɬ kwayuk* made me at the time of creation and so I am large. At the time of creation I was one of the 'people' (*čapai*)."

Then the travelers went on and finally came to a mesquite thicket where they found mesquite pods. The Kamia said: "I don't know what this is." And the Cocopa replied: "This is good fruit. All you have to do is smash it and mix it with water, or just chew the pod and swallow the juice. It is a good fruit for us and we can live on it. These pods here will fill our stomachs, but I am not going to eat. I said before that I would travel on an empty stomach and so we will go along through these mesquite trees without stopping."

After they had gone a long way to get beyond the mesquite trees, they heard a noise like a rattlesnake up in the mesquite branches. The Kamia asked: "What is that?" The Cocopa said: "That is the thing that makes the mesquite pods ripe. It is called *hanyao* (a cricket-like insect)." The Kamia said his word for the insect was *sıkusi*, and they gave that name to the song. They still had not eaten when they were ready to start again. The Cocopa said: "If we had eaten we would be full now, but we are not and there is no more mesquite the way we are going."

After traveling some more they came to a low place. Beyond was a high mesa, which they climbed. On the mesa were two houses, one the home of "old lady rabbit" (*hɬa kwaku*), the other the home of a young male coyote. Coyote was watching them and he said: "You have been coming from far away. My father saw you way back and he has told us every day that you are coming. I am a Hwanyak Cocopa and old lady rabbit is a Kamia. You can see that my house is a Hwanyak house and you can see that hers is Kamia style. It will not leak even if it rains a whole lot. When it rains for two or three days I have to go stay with old lady rabbit." This song was called *hatspa* and *hɬa kwaku*.

[There is an intermission in the songs at a kerauk at this point.]

After the travelers resumed their journey they saw some long, low rocky mountains. When they got close they saw a lot of buzzards (*šayi*) who started flying. The Cocopa said: "I know what these are, they are always looking for some dead animal. They are rotten, they eat maggots, and they stink badly. In the daytime they always fly looking for dead animals. At night they come down and sleep here. There are four kinds of these birds: *šayi*, regular buzzard; *šayi ha?a*, spotted buzzard; *šayi kwɔs*, brown buzzard; and *šayi ramas*, small buzzard." In each of these four buzzard songs the singer refers to the actions of the buzzard and his nesting place.

When the travelers went on, a high mountain came into sight. This was very high, and as they approached the Cocopa said: "How are we going to get through? We are going to have to turn back, or maybe we can turn south." The Kamia said: "If we turn back, the song will be too short. We will have to keep on going and go straight through because we cannot turn." After a while as they traveled [they are traveling west], they saw the mountain open, then close. The Kamia pointed this out to the Cocopa. He said: "We can run through when it opens. We can go one at a time and get through." The Cocopa said: "I am afraid. If you go first and get through, the mountain might not open again." The Kamia said: "It will not stop opening." The Kamia went through first, and when it opened again the Cocopa went through. The Cocopa said: "You were right about the mountain, we got through all right." The song made from this adventure is called *wi ahomi*. This means "created by the god," the same as *pohao*.

After they started traveling again the Cocopa saw the ocean. He didn't know what it was. The sun was setting over the water and blinded him. He said: "What is this that shines?" The Kamia said: "That is the ocean (*ha kusiɬ*). It never moves and will not come this way so we are going over there." When they started to move they were slowed down because they were walking in sand. The Cocopa said: "The water looks close but it isn't. I had better make the wind blow and bring rain to harden this ground." The Kamia said: "All right, that would be better." Then the Cocopa blew some smoke, kicked up some dust with his feet, and started a dust whirl, wind, and clouds. Then it began to rain. When they got near the ocean the Cocopa thought it looked like a high "mountain" of water and he was afraid. He thought that if he went close it would fall over on him. The Kamia said: "No, when we get close we will find a way to get through." This was his song and in Kamia it was called *ha kwi sipu*. When they came closer, near the edge of the water, they saw many fish jumping out of the water. They saw a *hal kwičat* [whale?] coming toward the water's edge. The Kamia was afraid of this and of the other large sea animals. The Cocopa said: "We can get a pole to support us and swim out into the ocean. We can use the log the way the Cocopa cross the river by putting it under one arm." The Kamia said: "This water is too wide. We won't reach any houses or people or land and these animals will swallow us. The ocean is as wide as the sky. If we die this way, the song will be too short. We had better turn south here." This song was given the Kamia name *hal kwitah*.

The travelers then started south along the ocean. The road was very rough and full of weeds and rocks. After moving for quite a distance they stopped and the Kamia said: "We knew this road before. It was a good road then, but now the trip is very hard." The Cocopa said: "Yes, this is a hard road, it is called *mat kusapu*." This is the road to the land of the dead. They went on, and after a time came to a small rock in the water. Two boys were on this rock, stretched out on their stomachs, and the ocean waves covered them as they rolled by. Seeing this, the Kamia said: "These two people are alive but I do not see how they can stay alive in the water." The Cocopa said: "They can do this because they are not like us [not people]. They knew we were coming, they saw us way back. We are nearing the land of the dead and we are getting near dead people (*lo hačak*). These boys are waiting for us here and they are dead people; that is why they can stay under water." This song is called *ha skrui soam* (face down in the middle of water). The Kamia said: "The two boys have been watching us. They walked toward us and then came back and got in the water. The Cocopa said: "These are a different kind of people. They do not walk the way we do but turn to dust or something and travel so quickly no one can see them. That is how they saw us coming." [My interpreter explains: When a person dies his spirit becomes invisible after the burning and no one ever sees it again. But it travels around and can see people.] The Cocopa continued: "These two boys are spirits. We can see them now because *mahɬ kwayuk* (God) wants to show us. But it is just for this one time and no one will ever see a spirit again." The travelers stood and looked at the boys and the Cocopa started a song, all about the water and the dead people. Then the Cocopa said: "We must go on now."

They walked along and finally saw a rock with someone sitting on top. When they came closer this person began to speak: "Come a little closer. I was a person before. Now I look different, but I have power yet. I know how to talk to you because I can speak Cocopa. I live here and have been here a long time. At night I travel the whole earth and that is how I knew you were coming. I go out every night and I saw you every night, but in the day I am here. You are just like I am — strong, not hungry, not tired, nothing hurts you — just like I am. You know me, I live here and see you

every day." The Kamia said: "Who is this person speaking Cocopa?" The Cocopa said: "He is *čopit* (horned owl), he is *pohao* (has creation power). When the people were created he was a person. When *mahɬ kwayuk* [now equated with Sipa?] died, all the people were turned into animals. This one was turned into a *čopit*. Now he has the power to kill [sorcerize] people." The Kamia said: "People die, but how can they be changed into birds? I thought when they died that was the end. How can he be a bird now, sitting here?" The Cocopa explained: "When *mahɬ kwayuk* made people, he made them of dust and wind. When they are burned they turn into ashes and then into a bird. When an animal dies, the flesh is consumed by worms. When everything is gone these worms are transformed into flies and fly away. The same when a person is cremated. The body is consumed by flames and the ashes are then transformed into a bird. The bird created is an owl." They were back in Hwanyak territory now, so it was up to the Cocopa to explain all this. But the Kamia kept asking: "How can ashes, coals, and wind be turned into a bird?" The Cocopa explained: "Fire, water, air, all are used to cook food. This gives a man strength. We also consume air when we breathe, and all this makes us grow and makes us strong. We need water to drink, and we need air to breathe. If there is no wind we have trouble breathing and if there is no air we die." This was called the *čopit* song. As with the others it has four parts. Each question is a part and each answer is a part. Fire, water, ashes, coals, wind are all special subjects for the song — all are important to man's life and so figure in his death and his transformation into a spirit owl.

The two started traveling again and after a long way they came to a mountain and a range of hills. They thought this might be *kerauk hap* (land of the dead), but they saw nothing so they went on. After more traveling they came to another mountain and they thought this might be it, but again they saw nothing. They started again and came to another mountain and saw what looked like a house (*kerauk hap* is shaped like a house). The land was level in front of them and they could see a great distance, and so they thought the "house" was close, but they walked a great distance getting to it. For a while the Cocopa thought the "mountain" was retreating in front of them but the Kamia could see that it had not moved. After they started traveling again they saw someone coming on the run. When they met, the "man" stopped and asked them: "Are you just going by?" It was a white coyote (*hatspa hamaɬ*). Coyote then continued: "I have been sick. I wanted to go meet you at the kerauk [where the journey had started] and show you the way here, but I was sick and couldn't get there in time." He pointed to the "house" and said: "That is *kerauk hap*. I know the kerauk too because I have given a kerauk myself. This was three years ago at *wi nyai* (Cerro Prieto) just east of there [where the journey had started]. It was a six-day kerauk. When I gave that kerauk, we threw all kinds of food around — beans, corn, black-eyed peas, and so on. The seed can still be seen there. I have everything here that was used [burned] in all the kerauks and chekaps that have been given until now. I have traveled the same route you did and I know everything you learned. That is how I could give a kerauk myself."

When the travelers reached *kerauk hap* they stood in front of the door. They saw only the rock with some marks pecked on it. Nothing else was on the outside because everything was inside the rock. They went inside and walked a little way back into the rock. There, against the wall, was a mark, one for each kerauk, including the one given by Coyote. Coyote said: "Do you see this? Now you know how things happen." The Cocopa said: "We were sent on this trip to see all these things. I can see the marks here of the kerauks that have been given." [My interpreter explains: The "marks" are the remains on the ground immediately after a kerauk has been given — burned remains of the kerauk house and fence, and the beans, corn, pine nuts, and other food strewn around the kerauk area.] Then the Cocopa said: "We can leave now, we have seen what is here."

As they moved on they came to some high land, then into a low place beyond. There they saw a watermelon patch full of big ripe watermelons. They also saw other kinds of fruit and grain found on an Indian farm. When the Kamia saw all this he said: "What is all this? I never saw anything like this before." He didn't know about farms because they were in Cocopa country again. Then they went on through the fields and started south toward a house they saw in the distance. This was a small, poorly built house and it looked empty. The Kamia said: "I don't think anyone lives here." The Cocopa said: "Maybe they are sleeping, taking a nap." They went up to the house and inside was a very old lady. She said: "I can't move." She had on a willow bark skirt and her hair came just to her shoulders. There was an old man there too. He was so old that his long hair had fallen off, leaving only some short hair. All he had on was a loin cloth. There was something between the two old people and they were drinking out of it and the old man was singing a song. It was a kerauk song, *wa katun, wa katun.* This was the last song given before the burning of the kerauk house. The old lady asked: "Do you still remember that song?" The travelers continued to watch. The old people were nearly blind and did not see or hear them. The Cocopa said: "You know this song very well." When they heard this, the old couple jumped up, afraid. They said: "What are you doing here?" The old man said: "I still remember the kerauk I saw. I was just singing and talking about it." The Cocopa said: "Are there more people here, or just you two?" The old man said: "There are others and you can see their fields and houses on all sides around here. You came through the center of the fields and the houses are on both sides." The Cocopa said:

"We are going on." And the old man replied: "*phwei* (Good)."

They took a trail from there going north and after a while they saw a very poor house. Someone was sitting on a bench in the door and he called: "Come closer." When the travelers came up to the house the man said: "I heard you coming, I have been waiting for you. Now you are here. I know everything you have done. Where you are going is not far, but you missed one part of your journey. You must have this to use in your song. I believe in you." The travelers replied: "If you know, you had better tell us. We can get it and take it with us. The people at home can see it then." The man at the house said: "What you need is the name for a song. The Kamia should call it *šeyota'i* and the Cocopa should call it *kerauk sayao.* And you need something else: a mishkwa [*meškwa*, a type of reed or a mat made of such reeds]." The travelers said: "*phwei* (All right)." Then the man left and brought back a bunch of mishkwa. When he brought this he showed them how to fix an image and how to sing and dance while it is being made. Then he said: "Another thing you need is eagle feathers to go with the mishkwa [the image]. Take these things to your home and you can make a mishkwa. When the two halves are ready you need a song to be used when the men bring the two parts together and tie it. Now you need another kind of feather. Turkey feathers or any long feathers will do. This is all I have to tell you, so now you can continue your journey."

The travelers turned south and finally came to a low canyon along the edge of the ocean. This was *wi čap* and there was water in the canyon where they saw something. An animal came out of the water and sat on the shore. Then he called to the travelers and asked them to come closer. He said: "I was made at the creation and came from the same place you did at the start of your travels. I came here through the ocean. I went west into the ocean and stayed there until I knew you were coming. I came to this hole of water to wait for you. I know the songs you have learned so now you need a rattle to go with them. If you had a rattle your songs would sound better. This is a *kwak ničersil* (deer's-hoof rattle). When you sing kerauk songs the young people will learn them. That is the way this will keep going. I am no account (*čapai nyayump*) so I can tell you very little. Maybe you should go on and you will meet someone who can tell you more." The water animal is called *ha šı?atš* (porpoise). This is a song.

The travelers continued their journey and came to a dry oak tree. There was an animal in the top of the tree but he was too small to be seen. The animal whistled and the men stopped to see what made the noise. Then when the animal held up his hand they saw him. He said: "I knew you were coming so I waited for you here. I heard what you have been saying — that you need one more thing. But in the kerauk you also need *hɔpšu anip* (a green belt) and *sakwil* (shells for a necklace). Another thing you need is *suwi* (a sea shell, green on one side and white inside, drilled and worn as a necklace with colored beads). You also need a *sokuly* (a "god's eye" head ornament for men). That is all. You can go on and probably meet someone else, I am of little account (*nyap čapai nyayump*)." His name was *han suiɬ* (lizard).

The travelers went on for a long way and then stopped to look around. They saw the ocean, which had turned east and blocked their southern route. The Kamia said: "I don't see how we can get by." The Cocopa said: "The first time we saw the ocean, we knew it was too wide and we turned then, so now we should turn east. This will be toward my country. If we tried to cross this ocean there would be no more songs." This was his song. So they started east over rough, hard ground, tearing their shoes to pieces. When their feet began to hurt, the Kamia said: "We must find something to make new shoes." The name of his song was *ɪmi salyal* (my feet). The Cocopa said: "In Kamia country we needed shoes but when we get to Cocopa country we can walk better."

So they went on, and finally came to a house. As they approached they saw a lot of people. The Cocopa asked: "What are we going to do?" The Kamia replied: "We will have to see what they are doing. Maybe somebody has died." When they came closer they could see that preparations had been made for a kerauk. A *čapai ahan* (leader) was standing in the east, facing west, and was talking about the two travelers. He said: "We do not know what to do with the mourning clothes, and we need an eagle. Perhaps you [the Cocopa] can tell us something." The Cocopa said: "I know what to do but the Kamia will have to say something. Your people are Kamia. When I get to Cocopa country I will talk." The Kamia said: "All you can do is kill the eagle for his feathers, then a lot of people can cry just as if the eagle were a person. You have to build a pile of wood to burn the eagle and if you have horses you should give them to some visitors. If someone dies, you have to cry and then burn everything he has, give other things away, and then later get some clothes and other supplies for a mourning ceremony. That is the way the creator did this, it is the law, *nesa·as sayuhat* (what has to be done)." Then the Kamia explained how a mishkwa image is made, how the kerauk house is built, and how to proceed with a kerauk ceremony. With these instructions, an eight-day kerauk was held. Then the Kamia said: "We are finished now and can go on. Maybe we will see some other people on our journey."

They traveled east from the ocean and mountains and when they came out of the mountains, the Cocopa said:

"We have traveled so far I doubt if we will see anything more. We are in Cocopa country now." They went on and shortly saw a man coming toward them. He had long hair and it was tied up so that he could run. When they met, the Kamia said: "What is wrong?" The man said: "I knew you were coming and I would meet you here." The Kamia said: "We have been to a kerauk for eight days and have just finished it." The man said: "Go ahead, continue your trip. You will soon see a *čapai ahan* (leader). I am *suuR* (hawk) and I am going to see another *čapai ahan*." After they took a few steps they turned to see where Hawk had gone, but he had already disappeared. The two men went on and the Cocopa said to the Kamia: "I know where Hawk was going. He is going after the deer's-hoof rattle and the eagle feathers. He is probably already home by now." After quite a while they saw a house and the Cocopa said: "We will go to that house and stop there." It took them a long while to get there. The house looked very little at first, and then as they approached they saw that it was a very big house with a big ramada. The Cocopa said: "This house is *pohao* (has creation power) and grows larger the closer we come. It will be very, very big when we get inside." As they approached the leader saw them and sent Hawk to meet them. Hawk told them that he had brought the rattle and the eagle feathers and that the people were waiting. When they approached the house all the people came out to meet them and started crying. After crying a while they stopped and the leader said: "You have come a long way. You must eat all you want and then have some watermelons." The Cocopa said: "We have eaten nothing on our trip. We were young men when we started and we have been traveling a long time. We are old now. Someone here tell us what is happening." The leader said: "We want to give a kerauk here the way you gave the other. All we needed was the rattle and the feathers. We have everything else. Another man here, *čapai seya patei* (shaman), will talk to us. He has to tell everything that has happened, then we can start." Then they built the kerauk house and the ceremony was ready to begin. But first the shaman spoke to the Kamia: "You know everything here. You are going to do the singing. I want you to start a song about the house." The Kamia said [addressing another Kamia]: "This is the kerauk house and this is the way you should sing. You now have a song for every part of the ceremony." Then they held the kerauk. When it was finished the Kamia said: "We can go on now. You know how to do this, so do not forget it. Do all your kerauks the same way I have shown you. Both the Kamia and the Cocopa can do this." The two travelers were standing together, facing the sunrise. Then they disappeared and no one saw what happened.

10. WARFARE

None of our Cocopa informants ever took part in warfare or in raiding. Some of the older people, however, when they were young, had listened to the stories told by participants, and there was still considerable interest in this activity. Sam Spa in particular was well informed on the patterns of warfare, the equipment used, and the personages involved. Thus, although the data in this chapter derive from an earlier time period than most of the other descriptive material in this study, warfare was of such importance to the total society that it must be taken into account as one of the determining factors in framing the culture as it existed during the latter part of the 19th century.

Comparing my material with the accounts of warfare as given for other river Yumans, I am of the opinion that the Cocopa were by no means as warlike as their northern neighbors, the Yuma and the Mohave. On the contrary, in this respect they seem more comparable with the Maricopa, as described by Spier (1933: 160):

Warfare occupied an unusually large place in the minds of the Maricopa for a people who by temperament were essentially mild-tempered and sedentary. They maintain that it was forced on them by raids of Yuma and Yavapai which had to be met or anticipated. While this seems much like the usual disavowal of aggression that can be heard from any of our western Indians, in this case I believe it to be true. No great premium attached to the man with a war record: the war leader was held in high regard, but the ordinary man who took a scalp or captive was not socially exceptional. . . . Nevertheless they talked a good deal of war, took pleasure in planning it, and brought up their sons to look forward to it.

This picture is in rather sharp contrast to that of the Yuma, about whom Forde (1931: 161) states:

. . . fighting was not justified merely as a virile pursuit, nor was economic need adduced as a factor; warfare to the Yuma possessed a strong mystical value as the means whereby the spiritual power of the entire tribe was enhanced and at the same time demonstrated.

It is of interest to note that in their creation myth the Cocopa have pictured themselves as having lost most of their battles, and give credit to the Maricopa for having pulled them out of many a scrape. Cocopa boys, in mythology, more frequently "run" and "cry" than stand up to "fight to the end."

HISTORY

Warfare among the river tribes was remarked by the earliest Spanish explorers and continued without cessation until the establishment of a permanent American army post at the mouth of the Gila River in the 1850s. That it was highly destructive of both human life and tribal existence seems indicated in part by the heavy reduction in estimated population and by the dissolution or merging of certain tribal groups before the period of direct European influence.

Alarcón (1904: 292) in 1540 spoke of "warre and that very great, and upon exceedingly small occasions." Oñate, in 1605, gave no account of actual fighting, but said that the people on the east side of the river "although of the same nation" were enemies of the people on the other side (Zárate Salmerón 1916: 277).

Between the time of Oñate's visit and the arrival of Kino in 1701, the Halchidhoma had moved from their position south of the Gila River to a strip of land between the Yuma and the Mohave. It must be assumed that they made the move to escape their enemies among the delta tribes. That this was not a successful attempt is shown by subsequent events as reported by Spier (1933: 160): ". . . while they were still on the Colorado, they were caught between Yuma and Mohave, who hammered away at them with repeated attacks. . . . In the end, they lost their foothold on the river and fled into Mexico."

Kino did not provide much other information concerning intertribal affairs in that area. A number of Pima accompanied him to the river — something they would not have done at a later time — and there is some evidence that visiting back and forth among delta tribes was taking place. However, that all was not quiet on the Colorado is indicated by the fact that Kino reported his success as a peacemaker, having left peace agreements among the Yuma, Pima, Halyikwamai, and other nations (Bolton 1919: 318). It would appear from his account, as was noted earlier, that the most important delta tribe at that time was the Halyikwamai.

If conditions were relatively peaceful at the time of Kino's visit, the same was certainly not true on various occasions when Garcés was on the Colorado between 1771 and 1776. From Garcés we get the first report on Cocopa, and also the first statement on their participation in intertribal warfare.

The dominant warlike tribes, according to Garcés (Coues 1900: Vol. 2, 446), were the Pima, Yuma, Halchidhoma (Jalchedunes), and Mohave (Jamajabs) (see Fig. 3). The Cocopa, he said,

. . . have always been friends of the Cuñeiles . . . and enemies of the Papagos who live on the coast of the [Gulf], as also of the Jalliquamais and Cajuenches [Kahwan]. The Jalliquamais and Cajuenches have always preserved friendship with the Quemayá of the sierra who extend to the rancherias of San Diego, as also with the Jalchedunes; and have been enemies of the Yumas and Papagos of the seacoast. The Yumas have always been on good terms with the Jamajabs, Yabipais Tejua, and Papagos of Sonoitac and of the seacoast; and have waged open war with the Jalchedunes, Cocomaricopas, Pimas Gileños, with all the nations down the river, and with the Jequiches [unidentified] of the sierra. The Jalchedunes have always been well disposed toward the Cocomaricopas, the Pimas Gileños, and all the nations that there are from the Yumas downward, as also toward the Papagos of the north, toward all the Yabipais excepting the Yabipais Tejua . . .; being unable ever to reconcile themselves with their enemies the Jamajabs, the Yabipais Tejua, the Chemeguet, and the Yumas. [Coues 1900: Vol. 2, 450-1]

When Garcés reached Cocopa territory in December of 1775, he discovered that the tribe had retreated from the northern and eastern sections of their land, as he had known it in 1771, and that they had only recently suffered a decisive defeat at the hands of their northern neighbors:

Dec. 12. . . . My next project was to cross the Rio Colorado [from Halyikwamai territory on the west side] and thus go to visit the Cucapa nation; and for this destination I departed the following day, as I will relate.

Dec. 13. I departed for the east, but could not follow that route, for all told me that neither to the east, nor to the south [on the east side of the river] were there any people; for, though it was true that I had seen many on the other occasion when I went alone through these parts, yet all had retired to that side of the river through fear of the enemy. [Coues 1900: Vol. 1, 181-2]

After spending several more days visiting in Halyikwamai and Kahwan camps, Garcés finally turned southwest to visit the Cocopa, who had previously concentrated themselves in the southwestern section of the delta:

Dec. 16 [17?]. Having gone 3 leagues southsoutheast I arrived at the Laguna de San Mateo. The Cajuenches who accompanied me took me over in their arms, and leaving me on the other side departed; for here ends their land and commences that of the Cucapá nation to whom they are hostile. I pursued my route, and traveling 4 leagues in the same direction arrived at (a rancheria of) the Cucapa nation; this was abandoned and destroyed, for here was the place where recently had fought the Yumas, Cajuenches, and Jalliquamais with the Cucapá. [Coues 1900: Vol. 1, 183-4]

It seems very likely that Garcés visited the river at a time of increasing intensity of warfare, which began, perhaps, with the withdrawal of the Halchidhoma to the north sometime between 1605 and 1701 and ended with the final expulsion of the Halchidhoma, Halyikwamai, and Kahwan from the Colorado early in the 19th century. Tribal alliances were being formed and broken and, at least in the case of the Halyikwamai and Kahwan, people were concentrating in larger settlements: "[I] halted at a rancheria of Jalliquamais of 200 souls, in form of a pueblo, such as the Cajuenches also build, the one and the other the better to defend themselves thus from their enemies" (Coues 1900: Vol. 1, 182).

Whipple, quoting a manuscript written by Don Jose Cortes in 1799, states that "They [the Kahwan], as well as the Talliguamays, erect their huts in the order of an encampment, enclosing them with stockades to shelter them in the event of attack" (Whipple, Ewbank, and Turner 1855: 123). There is strong suspicion either that Cortes amplified the statement by Garcés quoted above, or that his statement comes from some part of Garcés' diary unknown to me. Since none of the other river tribes are credited with stockades, the chances are good that the report by Cortes is not reliable.

The serious nature of these wars and the shifting of alliances are indicated further in Garcés' diary (Coues 1900: Vol. 1, 173-4):

Dec. 9. . . . It was really wonderful to see this land so abounding in crops, for the other time I was here [in Kahwan territory on the west side of the delta?], in the year 1771 [September and October], it was very barren; and on my asking the reason why, they told me that they had also planted much then, but could gather no crops, because the Yumas were their enemies, who descended upon them in harvest time, killed them, and laid waste their milpas; but now that they are friends they have plenty to eat.

It will be recalled that in the attack upon the Cocopa described by Garcés in his entry for Dec. 16, 1775 (quoted above), the Kahwan and Yuma were allies; it is also worth noting that Kahwan crops remained intact during the year that they were fighting the Cocopa.

Although I cannot definitely identify the tribes of the lower delta from Hardy's account in 1826, the chances are extremely good that they were River Paipai and Cocopa.

Pattie, a year later, identified these two tribes and no others; the Halyikwamai and Kahwan, according to Spier, had already moved north of the Gila. In any event, the lower delta was still being invaded by the Yuma, and the tribes of that region seem to have come off second best: one afternoon the Axua chief told Hardy that a neighboring tribe had attacked the Axua the night before, killing a number of men and capturing women and children. The attackers were said to be Yumas (Hardy 1829: 352-4).

Whether the delta tribes retaliated is not clear, but Hardy reported that on September 8 (ten days later) he purchased a five- or six-year-old child from a lone Indian who was said to have captured it from the Yuma the day before.

During the next 25 years, it must be presumed that raids and formal battles continued between the Yuma and the Cocopa, but that the more important battles were taking place between the Mohave-Yuma on one side and the Maricopa-Pima on the other. Yuma and Mohave accounts of warfare, gathered while some of the informants who had personal knowledge were still alive, speak mostly of the upriver battles, with Cocopa participating only in a minor role (Forde 1931: 160-4; Spier 1933: 160-76). During the decade 1848-57, the friends of the Cocopa were the Paipai, Southern Diegueño, Maricopa (including the tribes that had taken refuge with the Maricopa), and Pima. Their enemies were the Yuma, Imperial Valley Kamia, and Mohave.

The following account of Cocopa warfare comes entirely from Sam Spa. His information is secondhand, and although I have reason to believe that most of what he says pertains to the Cocopa, there is considerable chance that he has mixed Cocopa and Yuma accounts of war customs. He told me that his information came to him from two principal sources: his father, who was still too young to fight when war with the Yuma ended; and a Cocopa who took part in some of the battles and was still living "and strong" when Sam Spa was a young man. Spa's grandfather was a war leader, which may account for his interest in this aspect of Cocopa history.

WEAPONS AND FIGHTING FORMATION

Cocopa weapons in the period of tribal warfare up to the middle of the 19th century were the same as those found among other river tribes: bows, arrows, quivers, clubs, shields, lances, scalp knives, spears, and daggers.

Bows and arrows have been described in Chapter 4. Arrows were carried in quivers made of wildcat or coyote skin, or buckskin.

Clubs were called i·š and were made of ironwood. There were two types of clubs. One was a simple cudgel-shaped weapon (which could also be made of mesquite wood); this was the kind carried by boys who followed in the rear of the army before they became fighters. The other type of club was the famous Yuman "potato masher" (Fig. 31),

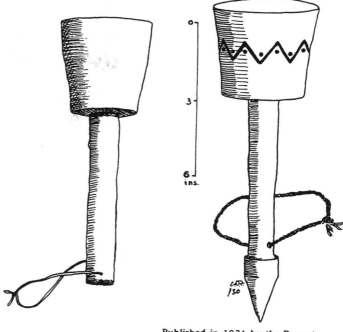

Published in 1931 by the Regents of the University of California; reprinted by permission of the University of California Press.
Fig. 31. Yuman "potato masher" clubs (Forde 1931: 161).

which was shaped with a sharp edge or rim around the forward surface. This club was typically used with an upward thrust so as to strike the enemy under the chin or in any area where the neck joins the head. Club size was determined by the strength of the owner, who, in the eyes of the Cocopa, belonged to an elite group noted not only for strength but also for bravery and endurance. The "potato masher" clubs were painted in red and black and the handles were perforated for the attachment of a carrying strap, which was wrapped around the fighter's wrist.

Club carriers also had a shield, iš čikðuð, made of buckskin or leather and equipped with a centrally located handle on the reverse side (Spier 1933: 136). The outer faces of shields were usually decorated in designs that used different colors in the four quarters of the surface.

Feathered lances or pikes were carried by selected warriors who advanced toward the enemy on the two sides of the war leader. They were about four feet in length, sharpened at both ends, and heavily decorated with feathers and strips of colored cloth (Fig. 32). Sam Spa said that they could also be wrapped in strips of coyote fur.

Scalp knives, as well as all other knives, arrowheads, and similar weapons and tools, were of course originally made of flint or other hard stone. None of my informants, however, had ever seen or heard of stone knives, since steel knives were in common use after earliest contact with Spanish priests and explorers. Spears and daggers were made of wood.

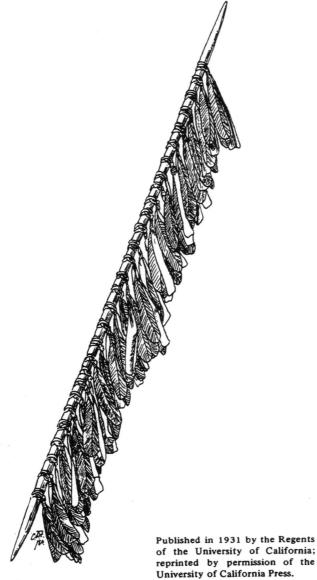

Fig. 32. Yuman feathered lance, similar to that used by Cocopa warriors (Forde 1931: 233).

In a formal war party, three men advanced in front of the army. The center man, who was the war leader, carried a war club and shield, and the men on either side of him carried the decorated lances described above. Following these three were men carrying clubs and shields; in the rear were the bowmen. Some distance behind this party came a group of young boys training as warriors, who carried short clubs made of tree branches for the purpose of dispatching any of the enemy who were wounded and left behind by the advancing army.

THE WAR LEADER

It is very difficult, at this late date, to discover the true relationship between the war leader and the political leader of each band. Jim Short, in one interview, said that the band leader was always the war leader and that when he became too old to fight he was replaced. On the other hand, Sam Spa's grandfather was very definitely a *kwɩnami* (war leader), but I could never get Spa to say whether he was a band leader or not.*

It is not clear whether the war leader took the initiative in organizing a war party, or whether this was in the hands of the band leader and shamans. My notes on this point refer to an actual case, at which time the band leader was also the war leader. There may have been no set procedure in this regard, but chances are that in times of warfare a war leader took charge of two or three bands acting as a tribe. As soon as the war party was organized, however, the war leader took charge and was given full authority. He told everyone what to do, and selected the men who would serve as bowmen and those who would serve as club men. On four separate occasions, during his account of war practices, Sam Spa said in effect: "The war leader has great power, he knows just what to do, people listen to him." It is highly probable that he was repeating the legendary fame of some particular war leader, but the statement is significant in indicating the strength of leadership possible under war conditions.

However this may be, the war leader was a man of great "power" in the eyes of his followers. This "power," together with his strength, speed, alertness, and cleverness in actual combat, came to him exclusively by means of dreams that began in earliest infancy, or even before birth, and continued throughout the period of his active participation in battle.

The war leader, besides directing the party in the field, also superintended the taking of scalps and the order in which men returned from the field. He may have been the man who later took charge of the scalps; at least, the scalp-keeper known to Sam Spa was a war leader.

With the exception of the two lance carriers, the war leader was the only man distinguishable from the ordinary warrior. The insignia that set him apart was a large and characteristic nose pendant (*meho sawin*, nose hanging), made of two pieces of sea shell (Fig. 33). This type of pendant was worn only by the war leader. According to

*My line of questions about war leaders led to my incarceration in the Mexicali jail during the last week of May in 1940. We had broken camp in Baja California, my wife had gone on to California, and I stayed behind for a few days to get better information on warfare. To do this, I rented a room in a Mexicali hotel where I met my informant and interpreter. Someone's suspicion was aroused by this unusual meeting between an American and two Indians, not to mention an eavesdropper's shock at hearing what appeared to be an American or German war spy gathering information on possible Indian fighters. One morning there was a knock on the door and when I opened it, two police officers put me under arrest. After several hours in jail I was able to convince the city magistrate that I was an anthropologist and that my conversation with the two Indians involved events that had occurred a hundred years earlier. No one bothered my informant and interpreter, who spent the day waiting for me at the hotel.

he would not last long. The war leader also dreamed of one other flying insect (*homkwinyawi*), described as being gray-yellow in color and 1 to 1½ inches long, with a split tail. This insect catches flies, spiders, and other insects.

These dreams also came to ordinary warriors, whose standing depended upon the number of such dreams they had. The war leader dreamed most frequently, however. In addition, just prior to going into battle, he had to have a special dream telling him what to do. This dream was called *šɩmow∂p pasa* (dream direction) and provided a plan of campaign, plus extra power, including the power to control natural forces — rain and dust storms.

WAR SHAMANS

The dream power held by the war leader was not considered a sufficient guarantee of victory or protection against enemy raids. Each Cocopa band had one or more shamans (*skwiᵞa' patai*) whose special duty it was to set the exact time for a raid or war party, to indicate the strength and disposition of the enemy, and also to warn of attack.

In one instance, as described by Sam Spa, the band leader (who was also the war leader) and the shaman met and decided to call all the men of the band to a conference to discuss the possibility of a war expedition against the Yuma. Two or three men were sent to all the Cocopa camps to call the men together. At this meeting, one of the few occasions where women were excluded, the men were asked to tell the shaman what dreams they had had concerning the enemy, and what other information they might have. After the conference, the shaman got up from the meeting and walked a mile or so away from camp. No one knew where a shaman went or what he did while he was away. When he returned, he told the war leader where the Yuma were located, what they were doing, and what the result of the battle planned against them would be. The shaman never talked directly to the assembled men, but told the group leader or war leader what he knew, and this message was then repeated to the gathering. There was much speech-making at such a meeting, but no singing or dancing.

The war shaman accompanied the war party and was the leading curing shaman among the six or seven who always went along with the warriors. To be a war shaman a man must have had the proper dreams: mostly he dreamed of Coyote in order to get the power to "see everything" and to cure people.

TRAINING OF WARRIORS

Training for warfare began when boys were between 10 and 12 and continued until they entered battle. As in all other departments of their lives, the boys were first made ready for their training as warriors by having had the proper sort of dreams in infancy and childhood.

The earliest training consisted of bathing in cold water, running long distances, walking on hot sand, and other such

Fig. 33. Nose pendant worn by Cocopa war leaders. The rounded (upper) piece was clam shell, the lower (flat) piece abalone shell.

Sam Spa, the Yuma war leader also wore a pendant of this kind, and in formal battles the two leaders, approaching each other at the head of their warriors, continually thrust their chins forward so as to make the pendants swing and flash in the sun.

A variety of animals and stereotyped situations were repeatedly dreamed about by the war leader. The outstanding dream involved the activities of a hawk (*su?ur*; Spanish: *gabilan paiero*). The hawk talked to the warrior and told him how he darted into a flock of ducks or blackbirds and took the fattest and best. He also frequently told how he broke his wing against a tree while diving, or was stuck in soft mud. This was a prediction of the expected fate of a fighter, although not an immediate expectation. The war leader also dreamed of the mountain lion and how this animal took his prey, or of the eagle and his power over all other birds.

If the war leader dreamed of a horsefly or of a mosquito it meant that he would be a great fighter, but that practices. Boys who became good at these things were noticed by the war leader and taken in hand for special training. They were shown how to fight and their endurance was given further tests. One such ordeal was a race through willow undergrowth during the winter when the branches were bare, or a whipping with bundles of the same wood. Cuts from the willow branches caused the legs to swell and become very painful.

Before going into actual battle, the boys were taken along on war parties; they followed in the rear of the fighters and killed the enemy wounded who were left behind. Boys as young as 10 years old went on these expeditions, and some became warriors when they were 15 or 16.

SCALPING

Sam Spa could give me no information on the conduct of men in battle, the average number killed, or details concerning the fighting. His interest — and it must be assumed that it was a reflection of the interest of the men from whom he heard the stories — was in the scalping of the enemy, the subsequent treatment of the scalp, and its use in a scalp dance (see Kelly 1949b).

When the Cocopa won a battle, Spa said, or when they could otherwise reach the bodies of slain enemy warriors, one or more scalps were always taken. The actual scalping and the subsequent care of the scalp was always done by a man who had not yet killed an enemy, who had had the proper dream for scalping, and who desired, through this activity, to gain prestige and power to kill an enemy in some future battle.

After a battle, the men were scattered; some were wounded and some were dead. The battlefield was "dangerous," and most of the men left for home as soon as possible. The war leader, warriors who had slain an enemy, and prospective scalpers, however, remained behind to take scalps. The one to be scalped, if there were a choice, would be a great warrior, or a man with extra long, fine hair. Sam Spa seemed to place most emphasis upon the quality of the hair, but pointed out that any man, to be a great warrior, had to take pains to grow a long head of hair. When the warriors had assembled around the dead man, they made a loud cry while rapidly beating their open palms against their mouths. While the crying was going on, the scalper took up large handfuls of dirt and rubbed them over his own face, neck, shoulders, and breast. He next started to remove the scalp, cutting the flesh with a stone knife.

Contrary to the Yuma practice, as described by Forde (1931: 165), Spa insisted that all the flesh of the face and head, as well as a strip of flesh on the breast as far down as the nipples, was taken. The scalp was torn off from the rear. Immediately after it was removed, the scalp was held in both hands by the hair close to the scalp, rubbed in the dirt, and then lifted high in the air and shaken violently. This performance was repeated four times while the assembled warriors continued their howling.

After rubbing the scalp in dirt and raising and shaking it four times, the scalper divided the hair into two strands, and placing the scalp against his pelvis, face out, tied the strands behind his back. When this was done, the warriors and war leader left and in a short time were followed by the scalper (or scalpers, if more than one scalp had been taken). The scalp was not kicked, and there was no dancing or singing.

Sometimes before a scalp was taken, the dead warrior was subjected to insulting treatment at the hands of a Cocopa woman who had lost a number of close relatives in battle and had accompanied the war party, seeking revenge. Sam Spa said that Cocopa women did not ordinarily accompany men to battle, or take part in the fighting, but that the Yuma and Mohave women did. I could wish for independent verification of the following account, which appears to me as being either an isolated incident, or possibly an account of someone's dream. Spa told it in response to my question as to whether Cocopa women danced naked in the scalp dance, as reported by Gifford (1933: 300). It was the only instance Spa knew of where a Cocopa woman performed some public act with her skirt removed.

The woman, in Spa's account, approached the dead man and stripped off her skirt. While she and the warriors cried and wailed, thinking of their dead relatives, the woman squatted directly on the dead man's face so that her external genitals came in contact with the flesh of his eyes, nose, and mouth. When she did this she cried and wailed, and dared the dead man to get up and do something to her.

Curing the Scalp

After the scalp had been taken, successful warriors, followed at some distance by the scalper, went directly to a place called *nʸɩwa čumawaš* (scalp soften) at the foot of the Cocopa Mountains, about four miles north of Mayor (see Fig. 34). For the next four days, killers and scalper, keeping out of sight of each other, were busy with purification rites. The killers observed strict food taboos, used a scratching stick, bathed each morning, and washed and treated their hair in the same manner as the scalper was required to do (see below).

The scalper, meanwhile, on the trip south, and always while at *nʸɩwa čumawaš*, was required to work the scalp constantly with dry earth, chew the ears and fleshy parts to release blood and fluid, and never let the scalp out of his hands — sleeping on his back with the scalp resting upon his chest at night.

At *nʸɩwa čumawaš* there is a small outcropping of white decomposed volcanic rock, which is easily scooped out with

Fig. 34. *Above*: Cocopa informants stand on outcropping of white earth that was used in "curing" enemy scalps. *Below*: Hillside area north of Mayor where the outcropping occurs.

Anita Williams

the hands. It was believed that this rock was an especially powerful material for scalp curing, and for four days the scalper spent a great deal of time rubbing the scalp with this material. This was the period when the scalp was most dangerous (and putrid?), and no one but the scalper dared stay in the vicinity. It was believed that he was in direct communication with the scalp, and that the scalp talked to him, especially at night, and told him how to go about the process of curing. The situation was filled with danger for the scalper; Sam Spa said that on many occasions, if the scalper was alone (as was often the case), he became so frightened, usually at night, that he could not last out the required four days and so threw the scalp away and left the area. No one else dared to get the scalp when this happened, and Spa suggested that "perhaps coyote got it."

Each morning during the four days, the scalper bathed in the nearby Hardy River, then washed his hair and the hair of the scalp in a mixture of arrowweed root and mud. (Although my notes state that the scalp was *washed* in this mixture, it is quite likely that this was a misunderstanding, and that during the four nights the hair of the scalp and of the scalper were kept in a *plaster* of that material, as was done during the next four days.) During this time, the scalper ate and drank nothing, not even water, according to Spa. He also could not sleep, because at night, when the scalp was resting upon his breast, it talked to him. Besides giving instructions concerning the curing process, the scalp told him that he would some day be a great warrior (*kwɩnami*) and that he would have good luck all his life.

On the morning of the fifth day, the scalper went to his own camp, where the curing and purification process continued for another twelve days. Immediately upon his arrival in his own camp, he washed his own hair and that of the scalp, and combed out the scalp hair to make it look as nice as possible. After the scalp was washed and combed, the scalper painted his face and body with red ochre and a paste made from pumpkin seeds, then took the scalp to a secluded spot in the brush and remained secluded for the balance of the morning. At noon, he returned to his house and was given a bowl of unsalted mush, his first food since the scalping. With this meal, his food taboos were gradually relaxed until by the end of the twelfth day he had returned to a normal diet. However, use of the scratching stick was required and sexual intercourse remained taboo throughout the curing process.

On the evening of the fifth day, the scalper plastered his own hair and that of the scalp with a mixture of mud and arrowweed root. This was washed off the next morning, the scalp was dried in the sun, and the hair combed to "make it look nice." During the night, throughout the twelve-day period, the scalp was hung in a tree close enough to be watched. Its power to harm was, by then, greatly diminished, and it continued to diminish as the twelve-day period progressed and the scalp was finally made "clean" (*čosi·p*).

The mixture of mud and arrowweed root was used on the fifth, sixth, seventh, and eighth nights. On the ninth to twelfth nights, plain mud was applied. On the thirteenth to sixteenth nights, mud mixed with boiled mesquite-wood sap was applied. After the final washing and combing on the morning of the seventeenth day (from the beginning of the curing process at *nʸɩwa čumawaš*), the scalp was entirely purified and the scalper could resume his normal life.

On the day that the scalp was finally cured, the scalper took it to the camp of his band leader, where preparations for a scalp dance had been made. Everyone was present on that occasion and they all had to "be happy," join in the dance, and have a good time. The scalper apparently took no special part in the ceremony, which was probably directed by the war leader.

Part of the preparation for the ceremony included the manufacture of a special pot to hold the scalp and the construction of a scalp house. The pot was about the size and shape of an old-style commercial Papago water container, 18 inches high and with a rounded, expanded body and wide mouth. It was sealed with a lid made of mud and straw. The scalp house (*wa čawip*) could not be described in detail, but was evidently a reduced form of dwelling house, supported by four posts, overlaid with branches, and the whole, except the entrance, covered with sand. During the following year, while the scalp was kept inside, the door was braced shut with poles.

According to Sam Spa, the scalp was not removed from the scalp house until a year had passed, when it was again used in a four-day scalp dance. At the close of this second ceremony, the mouth of the scalp was sewn shut (further evidence that the entire face skin was removed), and the scalp returned to the pot for three days, when the scalper came to get it. It had by then become nothing more than a bit of private property, and the scalper usually took it to a place called Real, in the Baja California mountains, where it could be traded to the Mexicans for a horse. I was unable to learn why the Mexicans were willing to pay so much for a scalp, or what disposition was made of the scalp before the arrival of Mexicans in the area.

The Scalp Dance

The scalp dance described by Sam Spa was held at the camp of his grandfather, who was a war leader and may also have been the band leader. The camp was at *si kwakuš*, near Chaman Kwawao, south of Mayor (see Fig. 6).

The scalp dance lasted four days and was held under a large ramada. During the first day, the people ate, visited, played games, and gambled. When the sun had nearly set, the people assembled for the first dance, which continued, with relays of dancers and singers, throughout the first night. After the dance had been in progress for some time, the scalp-keeper brought the scalp out of its house, put it on the end of an arm-length willow pole, and danced with it, holding it high over the heads of the people. He did this intermittently during the first night and at times during the dances that were held on the following nights. When not being danced with, the scalp was kept in a special place in the ceiling of the ramada. At the end of the final night of dancing, the scalp was sealed in the jar and placed in the scalp house, where it remained for the next year.

In the scalp dance, the singer stood in the center of the ramada facing east. Two helpers with rattles stood on either side of him; next to the men with rattles were some young men who were learning to be singers. The dancers faced west opposite the singer and used a dance step that carried them forward and backward in line. Men and women were mixed in the line, and some held each other's arms. During the daylight periods, when there was no dancing at the ceremony, the people spent their time gambling and playing games. Spa mentioned two games, the hoop and pole game and peon. The scalp dance was an occasion for lovemaking, as was true of almost all Cocopa gatherings:

> Boys and girls would go off into the brush together. The next day if a boy were questioned about going with a certain girl, he would say "yes." The girl would then be brought forward and asked about it. She would also say "yes." The people would then say that they should live together and the boy's mother would go up to the girl and arrange to take her home. This way the girl would go to live with the boy's family.

11. THEMES

Because Cocopa themes are so widely divergent from the themes of European-American culture, it is my opinion that they have been the most influential barrier to some possible changes in behavior that would have permitted the Cocopa a smoother and more satisfactory adjustment to the non-Indian world around them. This has been particularly true for the Cocopa living in the Yuma Valley, where the "protestant ethic," as discussed below, is pronounced.

The idea of cultural themes is not a new one, nor is the use of the idea confined to scientists. When we say that Jews are shrewd traders, Spaniards romantic, Englishmen reserved, and Americans arrogant, we are talking, however crudely, about the kinds of things I call themes. The scientific use of the concept of theme is not in the direction of describing the psychology of a race or group but is no more than an effort to reduce masses of detailed information to more general and more significant statements. The suggestion is that when a bit of behavior — for example, a man's ordering the meal in a restaurant — is repeated over and over so that it is typical for men to give orders in many situations, the repetition — the pattern — is more significant than the isolated instances of behavior. Some cultural themes are explicit in the thinking of the participants and are readily verbalized in explanation of this or that bit of behavior. Others are covert and can only be deduced by the observer or the sophisticated participant. What may be covert at one time may later become explicit. Most American men, for example, were surprised recently to learn that they were "male chauvinists." The important point is that there is an underlying form or idea in cultural patterns that is independent of the intrinsic aspects of a task and its immediate purpose.

Perhaps the most interesting aspect of Cocopa themes for a European or American reader is that they consistently reveal a way of life that is diametrically contrary to the "protestant ethic." A tabulation of differences (Table 11, adapted from Goldschmidt 1951) illustrates the point.

TABLE 11
Comparison of Cocopa and American Cultures

Cocopa	European-American
Socio-Economic Structure	
1. Family production	Industrial production
2. Traditional production techniques	Rational production techniques
3. Barter and gift exchange	Money as a medium of exchange
4. Capital resources unknown	Interest as a source of power and wealth
5. Labor exploitation unknown	Labor exploitation basic to economic organization
6. Indifference to wealth	Wealth status as a determinant of power, and wealth as an indication of status
7. Scattered family dwellings	Urbanized communities
Ethico-Religious System	
1. Work as a necessity	Work as a moral act
2. Indulgence in appetites (food and sex)	Asceticism in appetites (food and sex)
3. Notions of sin and guilt all but absent	Concepts of sin and guilt important
4. Supernatural beings and spirits	God as a stern father
5. Fatalistic attitudes toward success and failure	Concept of predestination

Some Cocopa themes that could be added or stated somewhat differently are the following:

1. Success in life depends upon supernatural instruction and aid, not on training, ability, or experience.
2. Life is to be lived directly, with the least possible preparation and formality.
3. It is human nature to be generous.
4. Each day takes care of itself.
5. The good life is indulgence for self and others.
6. No man (or group) can control, for his own purposes, more than his own labor and the natural resources he himself can use.
7. No one has the right to force another to do anything.
8. Social obligations are more important than economic obligations.
9. Technical tasks are means to ends and never ends in themselves.

Approaching the problem from another direction, the situation is perhaps best understood in terms of a series of concepts familiar to European-American society: independence, directness, informality, sobriety, and generosity.

INDEPENDENCE

For a Cocopa, the basic conception of his place in the social order rested upon the premise that each individual or, at most, each family, was essentially an independent unit with a minimum of rights and duties running between the individual and the larger society. This attitude is typical among many western tribes, but it is of particular interest here because it is not so clearly the function of environmental pressures.

In the political system, leaders were without formal authority, and the maintenance of order rested squarely with the individual citizen, who acted within a minimum framework of mores and in an all but formless structure. It was government by public opinion rather than by established laws, but this is not the vital test of independence. The patterns of public opinion were such as to permit each man almost complete freedom in choosing the place that he would assume in the society. Public opinion, for example, did not permit the definition of an office in terms of superordination. Prestige positions, when they did occur, took their prestige from the facts of personal accomplishment and never from the subordination of either individuals or classes. The captain, orator, shaman, and ceremonial leader held offices that were actually open to anyone, and were not dependent upon initial differences in social position.

Cocopa leadership was nearly independent of formal procedure; it would almost be proper to say that a Cocopa leader was an official but did not occupy an office. As Spier (1928: 235) expressed it for the Havasupai, a man was a captain because he took the lead in certain matters, rather than took the lead because he was captain.

If there is some question as to this interpretation of the official position of the captain, there is almost none in the case of orators who served, in certain respects, as subleaders. There was no set number of orators in any band, and anyone who felt so inclined (with the necessary but stereotyped provision that he had had the proper dreams) could become an orator simply by talking at every opportunity until, by practice and ability, he became good enough to be recognized as an orator.

There is a relationship between this lack of a tight political organization and the absence of economic and religious patterns requiring large-scale cooperation. Where subsistence and religious activities did include more than a single family, they were still interpreted as family enterprises, and it is clear that family members thought of themselves as politically autonomous and independent. Each family planted, gathered, hunted, and made seasonal expeditions with no reference whatever to direct band authority, and with minimum reference to the society as a whole.

It is in Cocopa religious life, however, that we get the clearest picture of this individual and family self-sufficiency and independence. Negatively, there is the absence of a priesthood and socially acquired supernatural power. Positively, the view of man's independent position with respect to the supernatural is clearly expressed in the dream beliefs.

The sole means of contact with the supernatural, the only means by which an individual could acquire supernatural power, was through a highly conventionalized fiction that was given verbal expression in terms of a dream. It must be emphasized that this experience was cast in a completely involuntary and spontaneous setting, as opposed to the usual form of the vision experience elsewhere in the west, which depended to some extent upon personal psychological qualities, so that it was not in fact open to all people.

Some investigators, searching for the distinctive nature of River Yuman cultures, have set them apart almost entirely on the basis of the all-pervasive nature of their dream beliefs. There is much justification for this, but it must not be over-emphasized. The Cocopa were not dream-ridden any more than highly animistic societies are spirit-ridden. It is true that Cocopa religion was built around the dream concept, and it is also true that a dream experience was required as validation in all manner of contexts: personal authority, technological knowledge, bravery, personal attractiveness, and good and bad luck. A Cocopa, however, did not use his dream power as a substitute for knowledge and personal effort; this power was a functional substitute for the magical concept in other societies.

There is no reason to doubt the occurrence of "power" elements in actual dreaming. Shamanistic and oratorical "dream knowledge" was based upon experiences that were told and retold in myths and tales. In any event, bona fide dreaming was unnecessary. Dreams were sometimes attributed to a period before birth, and authority for positions held late in life was traced to childhood dreams.

The effect of Cocopa dream beliefs was probably most important in matters of personal adjustment. A study along these lines would be most interesting, as the following case suggests. When Sam Spa was about six years old, an uncle started to train him to be a shaman. To promote the proper dreams, this man worked over Spa by blowing cigarette smoke into his mouth and by swinging him bodily in the four directions. A few days later Spa "woke" from a sound sleep and found himself alone in the house with dragonflies buzzing around a light near the roof. Some flew so close to his head that he had to dodge them. The next day he walked a short distance from his camp and saw some "stars" fall:

> I was afraid to be a doctor after that. I was even afraid to leave the house and for a long time I wouldn't go to the toilet alone. We were living near *uš škokwəs* at that time and I was afraid of everything for about six years until my uncle died. I never tried to be a doctor after that.

Sam Spa unquestionably experienced, perhaps in a nightmare, at least part of the stereotyped shamanistic dream, and for some reason reacted violently to the experience.

Not all dreaming, of course, was of the same quality. There were countless "dream interpretations," some taken seriously and some not. Spa, for example, was much amused one day when he told me about losing everything he had in a gambling game: "I had dreamed of picking up money so I thought sure I would win."

The factor of personal independence appears in many other contexts. The unformalized nature of the lineage system, the failure to develop a feeling of nationalism, and the inclination to live in scattered camps rather than in village communities are all cases in point.

One of the typical functions of a kinship organization is to give a person membership in an extended group that will protect him from certain hardships and provide him with help in time of trouble. The patterns required for this, however, necessarily make demands upon the individual and rob him of a certain amount of personal freedom (Linton 1936: 203). The Cocopa lineages functioned only tentatively in this direction, and it can be assumed that the strength of individualism was in part responsible. The almost complete lack of lineage functions, in fact, corresponds to the general absence of societies, associations, and larger cooperative groups.

It is significant that Cocopa houses were scattered. Burning of the house and selection of a new residence site took place after a death in the family, and there was a certain amount of moving brought about by the shifting of the river, but neither of these conditions seems adequate to account for the absence of villages. Cocopa families lived in scattered camps partly because they enjoyed the freedom of action and the freedom from community responsibilities that this afforded them.

It should be remembered, however, that premises never stand alone and that they do not provide all-or-none answers. Cocopa society was a going concern and, as such, depended upon the effort and cooperation of its component members. The kerauk ceremony, for instance, was based upon a system of balancing premises. It is only when the Cocopa are compared to such a people as the Hopi that the tendency under discussion is placed in proper perspective. Also, an active interest in the maintenance of individual action does not mean that private motivation and idiosyncratic behavior were more typical of Cocopa culture than of some other. Independence, in fact, is in itself a cultural choice and was conceivably as irksome to some people as regimentation would be to others. That Cocopa individualism was determined by some accidents of cultural choice is suggested by the fact that, from an outsider's point of view, certain social and environmental factors in the Cocopa situation should have produced a more complex social organization. Cooperative effort and the submergence of the individual — for example, in the building of dams, ditches, and dykes, and in the transportation and storage of farm products — would, if my analysis of the physical conditions is correct, have removed much of the uncertainty in their subsistence activities. In the social field, the density of population and relative stability of living conditions would not only have made a more formal type of organization possible, but, from our point of view, would almost have demanded this type of adjustment.

Quite the opposite environmental and social conditions prevailed in the case of the surrounding desert tribes. The severity of conditions in the physical environment, given the technological equipment of these people, greatly reduced the range of cultural choices open to them. This was perhaps most clearly reflected in the lack of complexity of social structure and in the virtual nonexistence of social stratification.

Environmental and social determinants were, in fact, so powerful in various sections of the western desert that such anthropologists as Julian Steward have made a good case for a functional relationship between certain types of sociopolitical patterns and certain types of physical environment. (The theory has been developed in a number of his publications, the most complete of which is his final report [1938] on the Great Basin.)

The rather surprising fact is that most of the Cocopa's desert neighbors had a more formal group organization, and consequently less personal independence, than the Cocopa. This was not so true of subsistence activities, but more formal organization did appear, in the west, in the lineage organizations, which were both social and religious in function. An individual in one of the California groups, such as the Diegueño, was tied to his lineage both in order to retain his position in society and in order to gain contact with the supernatural. The lineage leader, while he had no political authority as such, was definitely a priest and in a superordinate position relative to other members of the lineage.

DIRECTNESS

Associated with this quality of independence was the Cocopa tendency to short-cut the formal elements of behavior. The Cocopa were essentially "realists" in their day-to-day view of the world, and they preferred simple adjustments to their physiological drives and simple ways of meeting their social needs. The distinctiveness of Cocopa behavior in this regard became recognizable to me when I noticed, time after time, that the circumstances of a situation outweighed the formal elements of the social structure.

In the division of labor by sex and age, for example, there were few instances when the formal rule was not violated. Both men and women brought in wood, gathered mesquite beans, helped on the farm, carried water, and did many other things that in other societies are usually strictly confined to one sex or the other. Most of these tasks were the "usual" responsibility of one sex or the other, but the point is that there was no hesitancy on the part of men and women to do whatever job the occasion demanded. Within the sex categories it was typical for certain people to do certain types of work or to take charge of cooperative enterprises on the basis of "knowing how," rather than as a result of their holding some office or occupying a particular status in the society.

The method of attainment of supernatural sanction was itself an example of the "direct" methods of the Cocopa. The dream experience made a contact with the supernatural possible without the necessity for any activity on the part of the individual, without the use of any paraphernalia, and without the help of any other person. It was a purely personal, spontaneous, and involuntary experience providing a sure and direct contact whenever needed.

The very weak development of religious taboos generally, and the complete absence of taboos in agricultural practices, permitted the Cocopa a much more direct approach to ordinary tasks than is usually found. There were few food taboos pertaining either to kinds of food eaten or to the time and place for gathering and preparing food. Young men were forbidden to eat their own fish and game, and there were food taboos in connection with crises, but I could learn of no food that was not eaten on account of supernatural restriction, with the single exception of the dove — and there was some question about this.

Even in matters of sex behavior, courtship, and marriage, where cultures typically dictate an indirect rather than a direct procedure, the Cocopa boy and girl were minimally restricted. (The cultural situation noted here has been most fully analyzed by Benedict [1932: 13].) Marriage in most instances was a matter of individual preference, and except for incest restrictions, there were no formal barriers to the free choice of a mate. The direct method of mating was matched by an equally direct method of divorce. It was not until after a functioning family had been established and the society had some stake in the union that cultural restrictions to free movement were introduced.

This freedom is not to be understood as individual license; culture patterns always intervened between the individual and the solution of his problems. The point is simply that these patterns were seldom hedged by indirection or an elaboration of symbolism. The difference is made clear by reference to other patterns of Cocopa culture in which directness was the exception.

The curing shaman was subject to rules involving much indirect action, the principal one being the requirement that not just a single dream or series of dreams qualified a man to cure others. He must have had a long series of dreams, starting in childhood and continuing on into middle life. The insistence upon oratorical ability as a prerequisite to group leadership is another case in point.

INFORMALITY

It is well recognized that in all societies there are behavioral patterns that vary from high regularity in actual form (cultural clichés or rote behavior) to high variability around largely unconscious rules and codes. In some activities there are concrete patterns that are consciously adhered to by participants and that must be executed with rigid adherence to certain body movements and their sequence. In some magical practices, for example, the very power of the magic itself rests in a "law of exactness" that demands strict adherence to an unvarying execution of overt acts. On the other hand, there are patterns that are based upon unconscious adherence to general rules and standards, but that allow considerable leeway in the form of the act itself.

The great majority of Cocopa cultural patterns were loosely formed. There were habitual and customary ways of doing things, as in every culture, but variations of greater or lesser degree were permitted at a surprisingly large number of points that are usually held close to an established and verbalized norm by other societies. My attempts to obtain statements of habitual procedure from Cocopa informants made this quite clear. They were aware of form at certain points in an activity — as, for example, in the spacing of agricultural plants, or in the restrictions imposed upon a father at the birth of a child — but most of the attendant behavior was viewed by them as individual, and underlying patterns could be brought to mind only after reviewing a series of concrete instances. The reason for this, apparently, was that the society permitted just enough variation around a norm to prevent a clear formulation of that norm in the minds of my informants.

My material on Cocopa expeditions to gather wild rice is a case in point. There were, no doubt, repeated patterns in this matter since it was a difficult undertaking and required some planning. I could not learn, however, how the parties were formed, or what were the deciding factors in the selection and organization of the particular individuals who made the trip together. My informants told me that people went on this expedition when they felt like it, and went with any party they wanted to join. One informant remembered that they prepared living quarters on raised platforms in the mud; another was equally sure that the "usual" practice was to live on rafts.

Failure to settle upon a precise pattern in the methods of food storage and variability of procedure from one year to another or between families were also noted. The Cocopa used three types of storage baskets as well as large ollas for the storage of food. From the information given me, there was considerable individual variation in the use to which these storage facilities were put. Beans, grass seeds, hulled corn, and other such items were stored in a variety of containers, with no apparent interest in establishing precise procedure or careful measurement.

The material that I have already presented on subsistence contains a host of similar examples. One that was most typical, perhaps, had to do with the distribution of food. In most societies, considerable form is introduced into the matter of food sharing, so that status becomes important. Among the Cocopa, however, when a young man was forbidden to eat his own fish or game and was required to give it away, there were no particular persons sanctioned to receive it. He simply gave this food to people in a nearby camp who "needed it." It must be assumed that there was more to the pattern than this, but it would probably require direct observation of behavior to arrive at a satisfactory general statement.

Behavior patterns in the field of courtship and marriage were equally variable. There was a tendency to verbalize an ideal pattern, but the corresponding behavioral pattern, unless the experiences of my informants were quite atypical, touched upon precision of form at very few points. Such matters as length of courtship, kind and amount of gifts, set speeches, preparation of equipment and clothing, and a host of other things that are usually dictated by form in other societies were left to a range of individual choice by the Cocopa.

The Cocopa failure to form a tribal political system may be traced in part to this reluctance to introduce precise and rigid form into patterns, and there can be no doubt that the extreme looseness of their bands was a direct result of this and related attitudes. None of my informants could tell me, for example, the duties of a Cocopa band leader, and the information I have on the actual behavior of particular men indicates that there was considerable variability. There were limits, however, to what a leader could do and to the amount of authority that he could use. All band leaders, for example, were expected to visit with local groups with some regularity and were expected to take an active part in settling disputes, especially when violence was threatened. Some older leaders, in fact, resigned when these duties became too arduous. At certain points very definite behavior was prescribed: for example, the leader's formal greeting to a visiting band leader, the set manner of his orations, and the exact nature of his duties at a boy's initiation and at a mourning ceremony. But the time and place of meetings, the exact nature of punishment prescribed for certain offenses, the status of subofficials, seating arrangements at meetings, and a host of other, usually formalized, behaviors were not set in a rigid pattern.

One instance that impressed me most was Sam Spa's inability to state precisely the nature of invitations and acceptances for a harvest festival. It cannot be assumed that these matters were left to chance, but lack of rigid adherence to a set form prevented Spa from verbalizing either the ideal or the behavioral pattern.

SOBRIETY

Sobriety, mildness, and good humor, important in many patterns, are offset by hysteria, boisterousness, and suspicion in other patterns. The Cocopa culture promoted self-restraint in certain contexts but had developed well-recognized outlets in others. The close guarding of marriageable girls, which was so completely relaxed at group gatherings, is a case in point.

The usual tendency, however, was for patterns to be framed in accordance with a "sober" attitude. The acquisition of supernatural power was so devoid of personal manipulation that it approached simple fatalism. From the variety of ways in which this acquisition was accomplished in the surrounding areas, the Cocopa and other River Yumans selected the simple dream experience. Its use specifically excludes the necessity for putting oneself in a particular psychological state; the frenzy associated with a vision quest was definitely excluded.

So far as I know, there was no purely religious experience in Cocopa life, with the exception of funerals and mourning ceremonies, that called for a display of feeling or emotion. Even the frenzy experience that was associated with the use of jimsonweed in southern California was definitely played down by the Cocopa in favor of using the drug to induce lucky dreams (Gifford 1933: 305). In fact, the use of jimsonweed itself never was an important pattern among the Cocopa of the 19th century. Neither Jim Short nor Sam Spa had ever taken it or seen anyone else use it.

Cocopa social gatherings served as occasions for dancing, games, oratory, gossip, and gambling. There was nothing in the people's behavior, except possibly in the gambling games, that would elicit overt rivalry, violence, or great excitement. The social gatherings that I attended were characterized by expressions of good humor, mildness of conversation, and sobriety.

Individuals seeking psychological relief from fears or frustrations took advantage of culturally patterned forms of witchcraft accusations. This nonviolent response, however, became violent and lethal in extreme situations when the accused witch was killed for his supposed crimes.

Travelers and explorers in this region described the Cocopa as being pleasant to deal with, and this is in accord with my own experiences in the field. There was frequent verbal reference among the Cocopa to the need for maintaining good humor, as has been noted, and definite patterns of joking were built up around the interest. I have previously referred to the Cocopa as masters in social relationships. There is no doubt in my mind that the art of "getting along with other people" was a conscious interest in Cocopa society and that they trained themselves to become proficient in the art.

The exceptions to this general mode of patterning in Cocopa behavior occurred most frequently in connection with warfare and in the death and mourning ceremonies. There is not too much information available on the exact emotional nature of the scalp dance and victory celebration, but an interest in warfare as such, even though the Cocopa were definitely not as warlike as their neighbors, would presuppose some cultural encouragement of aggressive behavior.

Certainly the Cocopa were not "sober" in their attitude toward death, although the wailing that accompanied the burning of the body and the performance of a mourning ceremony were not completely uncontrolled. Wailing and crying, while very real, were also a formal part of the ceremony, and began and ended in a patterned relationship with the other aspects of the ceremony.

GENEROSITY

One of the most interesting aspects of Cocopa culture was the combination of highly developed patterns of generosity with an absence of any interest in wealth. These characteristics are at such variance with our own ideas of human motivation that they are difficult to conceptualize. There is no possibility, however, of mistaking the result of such an interest: Cocopa households were impoverished, and the cultural patterns operated in such a way as to preserve that impoverishment.

Gifts of food and cooperative work enterprises among the Cocopa operated on the rather widespread principle that relatives and neighbors should help each other, and that in the field of subsistence, at least, no one family

should have a surplus while their neighbors remained without food. The unusual character of the situation lay in the fact that patterns of reciprocity and formal social reward found elsewhere were absent. A Cocopa was expected to be generous, and he was rewarded for such action by the approval of his fellow tribesmen, but this was the generalized reward accorded normal human behavior, not a reward for distinguishing and personally meritorious self-sacrifice.

There was apparently no incentive whatever for the accumulation of property in order that rank, social position, or power could be gained in giving it away. The lack of such incentives works toward the inhibition of a wealth concept, and it is certainly true that there was not a rich class as opposed to a poor class in this society. No family made any effort to farm more land or store more food than they themselves could use or be expected to contribute as their share at celebrations. This was as true of the group leaders, orators, shamans, and other leading men as it was of the ordinary family head.

It must be emphasized again that such attitudes are indicative of tendencies, not fixed rules for all behavior. The Cocopa did not share all their possessions to the point that there was no private property. Such articles as weapons, armbands, feather ornaments, shell necklaces and earrings, and similar items were private property, and there was some prestige attached to owning and keeping such things. If this had not been so, there would have been little point to the gambling games, in which every effort was made to strip a fellow player of just such articles.

The Cocopa concern with generosity took its most elaborate form in connection with death. Patterns defining property rights in the possessions of deceased relatives are all but universal in society. Inheritance patterns constitute one of the means of building family capital, with each generation benefiting from the surplus accumulations of the preceding generation. The Cocopa practice, however, was diametrically opposed to such patterns. Every item of a person's material goods was destroyed at the time of his death; every man's death left his community as poor in private goods as it was at his birth. In the Cocopa funeral ceremony, interest also centered upon disposal of property belonging to living individuals, as well as that of the deceased. Later, at the big mourning ceremony, relatives completely impoverished themselves by destroying every item of material property and food that they could bring together. Large families worked for two growing seasons to accumulate the food required for such a ceremony. There was prestige to be gained by such action, of course, but it was not built into a system of prestige values. The emphasis was on disposal, in keeping with the Cocopa's total disregard for property accumulation.

REFERENCES

Alarcón, Fernando de
1904   The relation . . . . In *The Principal Navigations . . . of the English Nation*, by Richard Hakluyt, Vol. 9, pp. 279–318. Glasgow.

American Anthropological Association, Committee of
1916   Phonetic Transcription of Indian Languages. *Smithsonian Miscellaneous Collections* 66(6). Washington, D.C.

Barrows, D. P.
1900   *The Ethno-Botany of the Coahuilla Indians of Southern California.* Univ. of Chicago Press.

Bell, Willis H., and Edward F. Castetter
1937   The Utilization of Mesquite and Screwbean by the Aborigines in the American Southwest. *Univ. of New Mexico Bulletin, Biological Series* 5(2). Albuquerque.

1941   The Utilization of Yucca, Sotol, and Beargrass by the Aborigines in the American Southwest. *Univ. of New Mexico Bulletin, Biological Series* 5(5). Albuquerque.

Benedict, Ruth
1932   Configurations of Culture in North America. *American Anthropologist* 34(1):1–27.

Bolton, Herbert Eugene
1919   *Kino's Historical Memoir of Pimería Alta*, Vol. 1. Cleveland. (Reprinted 1948, Univ. of California Press, Berkeley and Los Angeles.)

Castetter, Edward F., and Willis H. Bell
1937   The Aboriginal Utilization of the Tall Cacti in the American Southwest. *Univ. of New Mexico Bulletin, Biological Series* 5(1). Albuquerque.

1942   Pima and Papago Indian Agriculture. *Inter-Americana Studies* I. Univ. of New Mexico Press, Albuquerque.

1951   *Yuman Indian Agriculture.* Univ. of New Mexico Press, Albuquerque.

Castetter, Edward F., Willis H. Bell, and A. B. Grove
1938   The Early Utilization and the Distribution of Agave in the American Southwest. *Univ. of New Mexico Bulletin, Biological Series* 5(4). Albuquerque.

Chittenden, Capt. Newton H.
1901   Among the Cocopahs. *Land of Sunshine* 14(3):196–204.

Coues, Elliott
1900   *On the Trail of a Spanish Pioneer: The Diary and Itinerary of Francisco Garcés.* 2 Vols. F. P. Harper, New York.

Davis, E. H.
1919   The Diegueño Ceremony of the Death Images. *Museum of the American Indian, Heye Foundation Contributions* 5(2). New York.

Derby, George H.
1852   Report of the Expedition of the U.S. Transport *Invincible* . . . to the Gulf of California and river Colorado . . . 1850 and 1851. 32nd Congress, First Session, *Senate Executive Document* No. 81. Washington, D.C.

Devereux, George
1935   Sexual Life of the Mohave Indians. Ph.D. dissertation. University of California, Berkeley.

1937a   Institutionalized Homosexuality of the Mohave Indians. *Human Biology* 9:498–527.

1937b   L'envoûtement chez les Indiens Mohave. *Journal de la Société des Américanistes* 29:405–12.

1939a   Mohave Culture and Personality. *Character and Personality* 8(2):91–109.

1939b   The Social and Cultural Implications of Incest Among the Mohave Indians. *Psychoanalytic Quarterly* 8(4):510–33.

1940   Primitive Psychiatry. *Bulletin of History of Medicine* 8(8).

Dixon, R. B., and A. L. Kroeber
1919   Linguistic Families of California. *Univ. of California Publications in American Archaeology and Ethnology* 16(3). Berkeley.

Drucker, Philip
1941   Culture Element Distributions: XVII Yuman-Piman. *Univ. of California Anthropological Records* 6(3). Berkeley.

DuBois, Constance Goddard
1908   The Religion of the Luiseño Indians of Southern California. *Univ. of California Publications in American Archaeology and Ethnology* 8(3). Berkeley.

Forde, C. Daryll
1931   Ethnography of the Yuma Indians. *Univ. of California Publications in American Archaeology and Ethnology* 28(4). Berkeley.

Freeman, Lewis R.
1923   *The Colorado River: Yesterday, To-day and To-morrow.* Dodd, Mead, New York.

Gabel, Norman E.
1949   A Comparative Racial Study of the Papago. *Univ. of New Mexico Publications in Anthropology*, No. 4. Albuquerque.

[143]

Gifford, E. W.
1918   Clans and Moieties in Southern California. *Univ. of California Publications in American Archaeology and Ethnology* 14(2). Berkeley.

1926   California Anthropometry. *Univ. of California Publications in American Archaeology and Ethnology* 22(2). Berkeley.

1931   The Kamia of Imperial Valley. *Bureau of American Ethnology Bulletin*, No. 97. Smithsonian Institution, Washington, D.C.

1933   The Cocopa. *Univ. of California Publications in American Archaeology and Ethnology* 31(5). Berkeley.

Goldschmidt, Walter
1951   Ethics and the Structure of Society: An Ethnological Contribution to the Sociology of Knowledge. *American Anthropologist* 53(4):Part I, 506-24.

Haeberlin, H. K.
1916   The Idea of Fertilization in the Culture of the Pueblo Indians. *Memoirs of the American Anthropological Association* 3(1). Menasha, Wisconsin.

Hardy, R. W. H.
1829   *Travels in the Interior of Mexico in 1825, 1826, 1827, and 1828.* Henry Colburn and Richard Bentley, London.

Haury, Emil W.
1976   *The Hohokam: Desert Farmers and Craftsmen.* Univ. of Arizona Press, Tucson.

Heintzelman, S. P.
1856-   Indian Affairs on the Pacific. 34th Congress,
1857   3rd Session, *House Executive Documents*, Vol. 9, No. 76, pp. 34-58. Washington, D.C.

Herzog, George, and others
1934   Some Orthographic Recommendations. *American Anthropologist* 36(4):629-31.

Hrdlička, A.
1935   The Pueblos. *American Journal of Physical Anthropology* 20(3):235-460.

Kate, H. F. C. ten
1892   Somatological Observations on Indians of the Southwest. *Journal of American Ethnology and Archaeology* 3:119-44.

Kelly, William H.
1942   Cocopa Gentes. *American Anthropologist* 44(4):675-91.

1944   A Preliminary Study of the Cocopa Indians of Mexico. Ph.D. dissertation. Harvard University, Cambridge, Mass.

1949a   Cocopa Attitudes and Practices with Respect to Death and Mourning. *Southwestern Journal of Anthropology* 5(2):151-64.

1949b   The Place of Scalps in Cocopa Warfare. *El Palacio* 56:85-91. Santa Fe.

Kluckhohn, Clyde
1944   Navaho Witchcraft. *Papers of the Peabody Museum of American Archaeology and Ethnology* 22(2). Cambridge, Mass.

Kniffen, Fred. B.
1931   Lower California Studies III. The Primitive Cultural Landscape of the Colorado Delta. *Univ. of California Publications in Geography* 5(2). Berkeley.

1932   Lower California Studies IV. The Natural Landscape of the Colorado Delta. *Univ. of California Publications in Geography* 5(4). Berkeley.

Kroeber, A. L.
1902   Preliminary Sketch of the Mohave Indians. *American Anthropologist* 4:276-85.

1925   Handbook of the Indians of California. *Bureau of American Ethnology Bulletin*, No. 78. Smithsonian Institution, Washington, D.C.

1928   Native Culture of the Southwest. *Univ. of California Publications in American Archaeology and Ethnology* 23(9). Berkeley.

1943   Classification of the Yuman Languages. *Univ. of California Publications in Linguistics* 1(3). Berkeley.

Linton, Ralph
1936   *The Study of Man.* D. Appleton-Century Company, New York.

Lowie, R. H.
1932   Kinship. *Encyclopedia of the Social Sciences*, Vol. 8. New York.

Lumholtz, Carl
1912   *New Trails in Mexico.* Charles Scribner's Sons, New York.

MacDougal, D. T.
1906   The Delta of the Rio Colorado. *Geographical Society Bulletin* 38(1):1-.

1907   The Desert Basins of the Colorado Delta. *American Geographical Society Bulletin* 39(12):705-29.

1908   Botanical Features of North American Deserts. *Carnegie Inst. of Washington, Pub.* 99.

Meigs, Peveril
1939   The Kiliwa Indians of Lower California. *Ibero-Americana*, No. 15. Berkeley.

Nichol, A. A.
1937   The Natural Vegetation of Arizona. *Univ. of Arizona College of Agriculture, Agricultural Experiment Station, Technical Bulletin* 68.

Parsons, Elsie Clews
1939   *Pueblo Indian Religion.* 2 Vols. Univ. of Chicago Press.

Pattie, James O.
1905   Pattie's Personal Narrative, 1824-1830. In *Early Western Travels, 1748-1846*, ed. Reuben G. Thwaites, Vol. 18. Arthur H. Clark, Cleveland.

Rogers, Malcolm
1929 Report of an Archaeological Reconnaissance in the Mohave Sink Region. *San Diego Museum Publications in Archaeology* 1(1).

1936 Yuman Pottery Making. *San Diego Museum Papers*, No. 2.

1945 An Outline of Yuman Prehistory. *Southwestern Journal of Anthropology* 1(2):167-98.

Russell, R. J.
1926 Climates of California. *Univ. of California Publications in Geography* 2(4) (reprinted in 1938). Berkeley.

1931 Dry Climates of the United States, I, Climatic Map. *Univ. of California Publications in Geography* 5(1). Berkeley.

Sapir, Edward
1929 Central and North American Languages. *Encyclopedia Britannica*, 14th ed., Vol. 5. New York.

Seltzer, Carl
1936 Physical Characteristics of the Yaqui Indians. In *Studies of the Yaqui Indians of Sonora, Mexico*, by W. C. Holden and others. *Texas Technological College Bulletin* 12(1):91-113. Lubbock.

Shreve, Forrest
1936 The Plant Life of the Sonoran Desert. *Carnegie Institution of Washington Supplementary Publications*, No. 22.

Smith, H. V.
1930 The Climate of Arizona. *Univ. of Arizona Agricultural Experiment Station Bulletin*, No. 130. Tucson.

1956 The Climate of Arizona. *Univ. of Arizona Agricultural Experiment Station Bulletin*, No. 279. Tucson.

Spier, Leslie
1925 The Distribution of Kinship Systems in North America. *Univ. of Washington Publications in Anthropology* 1(2). Seattle.

1928 Havasupai Ethnography. *American Museum of Natural History Anthropological Papers* 29, Part III. New York.

1933 *Yuman Tribes of the Gila River*. Univ. of Chicago Press.

Steward, J. H.
1938 Basin-Plateau Aboriginal Sociopolitical Groups. *Bureau of American Ethnology Bulletin*, No. 120. Smithsonian Institution, Washington, D.C.

Strong, W. D.
1927 An Analysis of Southwestern Society. *American Anthropologist* 29(1):1-61.

Sykes, Godfrey
1937 The Colorado Delta. *American Geographical Society Special Publications*, No. 19. New York.

Vasey, George
1889 New or Little Known Plants — *Uniola Palmeri*. *Garden and Forest* 2:401-2. New York.

Whipple, A. W., T. Ewbank, and W. M. Turner
1855 Report upon the Indian Tribes. *United States War Department Reports of Explorations and Surveys for a Railroad Route from the Mississippi River to the Pacific Ocean*, Part 3. Washington, D.C.

Williams, Anita Alvarez de
1974 *The Cocopah People*. Indian Tribal Series. Phoenix.

1975 *Travelers Among the Cucapa*. Dawson's Book Shop, Los Angeles.

Zárate Salmerón, Father Gerónimo
1916 Journey of Oñate to California by Land. In *Spanish Exploration in the Southwest, 1542-1706*, ed. H. E. Bolton, pp. 268-80. New York.

INDEX